Politicizing Sex in Contemporary Africa

Although sexual minorities in Africa continue to face harsh penalties for same-sex relationships, strong antihomophobic resistance exists across the continent. This book systematically charts the emergence and effects of politicized homophobia in Malawi and shows how it has been used as a strategy by political elites to consolidate their moral and political authority, through punishing LGBT people and dividing social movements. Here, Ashley Currier pays particular attention to the impact of politicized homophobia on different social movements, specifically HIV/AIDS, human rights, LGBT rights, and women's rights movements. Her timely account intervenes in Afro-pessimist portrayals of the African continent as a hotbed of homophobia and unravels the tensions and contradictions underlying Western perceptions of Malawi. It shows that, in reality, many lesbian, gay, bisexual, and transgender people happily call Malawi home, in spite of heightened antigay vitriol that has generated unwanted visibility for them.

ASHLEY CURRIER is Professor of Women's, Gender, and Sexuality Studies at the University of Cincinnati. Her first book, *Out in Africa: LGBT Organizing in Namibia and South Africa* (2012), was a finalist for a 2013 Lambda Literary Book Award. Her research on gender and sexual diversity organizing in Africa has been published in *Critical African Studies, Feminist Formations, Gender & Society, GLQ, Mobilization, Politique Africaine, Signs,* and *Women's Studies Quarterly.*

Politicizing Sex in Contemporary Africa

Homophobia in Malawi

ASHLEY CURRIER
University of Cincinnati

CAMBRIDGE
UNIVERSITY PRESS

CAMBRIDGE
UNIVERSITY PRESS

University Printing House, Cambridge CB2 8BS, United Kingdom

One Liberty Plaza, 20th Floor, New York, NY 10006, USA

477 Williamstown Road, Port Melbourne, VIC 3207, Australia

314-321, 3rd Floor, Plot 3, Splendor Forum, Jasola District Centre, New Delhi - 110025, India

79 Anson Road, #06-04/06, Singapore 079906

Cambridge University Press is part of the University of Cambridge.

It furthers the University's mission by disseminating knowledge in the pursuit of education, learning and research at the highest international levels of excellence.

www.cambridge.org
Information on this title: www.cambridge.org/9781108448376
DOI: 10.1017/9781108551984

First published 2019
First paperback edition 2020

A catalogue record for this publication is available from the British Library

Library of Congress Cataloging in Publication data
Names: Currier, Ashley, author.
Title: Politicizing sex in contemporary Africa : homophobia in Malawi / Ashley Currier.
Description: New York : Cambridge University Press, 2018. | Includes bibliographical references.
Identifiers: LCCN 2018026581 | ISBN 9781108427890 (hardback : alk. paper) | ISBN 9781108448376 (pbk. : alk. paper)
Subjects: LCSH: Homophobia–Political aspects–Malawi. | Homosexuality–Malawi–Public opinion. | Sexual minorities–Malawi–Public opinion. | Public opinion–Malawi. | Sexual minorities–Civil rights–Malawi. | Malawi–Politics and government–1994- | Malawi–Social conditions–21st century.
Classification: LCC HQ76.45.M3 C87 2018 | DDC 323.3264096897–dc23
LC record available at https://lccn.loc.gov/2018026581

ISBN 978-1-108-42789-0 Hardback
ISBN 978-1-108-44837-6 Paperback

Contents

Figures

Acknowledgments

Many people and institutions allowed me to complete the research for this book. First, Kim Yi Dionne, and Tara McKay introduced me to Malawi, an introduction I will always cherish. A collaborative grant that Kim Yi Dionne and I received from Texas A&M University allowed me to conduct my first round of fieldwork in 2012 in Malawi with Tara McKay. While Tara led a survey research team into Malawi towns and villages, I conducted interviews with more than fifty HIV/AIDS, human rights, LGBT rights, and women's rights activists; I had the opportunity to participate in my first round of survey research in Malawi. I am grateful to have had the chance to learn from these experienced activists. Funding from the University of Cincinnati's University Research Council and Charles Phelps Taft Research Center and an American Association for University Women Postdoctoral Research Leave Fellowship supported my 2014 fieldwork in Malawi. A Taft Center Fellowship gave me the time and space to complete most of the book and enabled me to bring Ebenezer Obadare to the University of Cincinnati as an expert reader on this manuscript.

Staff at Invest in Knowledge Initiative provided valuable research support during my 2012 and 2014 fieldwork trips in Malawi. In particular, Augustine Harawa, Davie Chitenje, Richard Kusseni, and James Mkandawire offered expert advice. Augustine's counsel and generosity buoyed my spirits while I was doing research. Charles Sisya drove me around Malawi in 2012 and 2014, and he worked as a driver and interviewer in 2014. Wezi Mzembe also worked as an interviewer in 2014. Both Charles and Wezi helped me interview lesbian, gay, and bisexual (LGB) Malawians; they conducted interviews in Chichewa and English. I learned a lot from Charles and Wezi during our time traveling throughout Malawi together.

This project would not have been possible without the staff, volunteers, and members of the Centre for the Development of People (CEDEP) welcoming me into their space and routines. Gift Trapence,

CEDEP's brilliant leader, graciously granted me access to CEDEP office space throughout the country and gave me permission to recruit CEDEP staff, volunteers, and members for interviews. Thanks to hardworking CEDEP staff and volunteers who communicated with gender and sexual minorities about the research project, research assistants and I were sometimes able to interview several people in one day during my 2014 trip. I cannot thank CEDEP staff and volunteers and staff at other nongovernmental organizations in Malawi enough for sharing their experiences and expertise.

Colleagues at the University of Cincinnati and beyond as well as members of my writing groups read and provided helpful feedback on multiple chapters. I would like to thank Michelle McGowan, Deb Meem, Tara McKay, Thérèse Migraine-George, Ghassan Moussawi, Furaha Norton, Carolette Norwood, Ebenezer Obadare, Michal Raucher, Sunnie Rucker-Chang, and Valerie Weinstein for reading and commenting on chapter drafts. I am very grateful to Valerie Weinstein for talking through and reading multiple versions of chapter drafts; I am very fortunate to call her a colleague and friend. Conversations with Nada Mustafa Ali, Gabeba Baderoon, Crystal Biruk, Alicia Decker, Kim Yi Dionne, Harri Englund, Amy Lind, Selina Makana, Anna-Maria Marshall, Sarudzayi Matambanadzo, Tara McKay, Liz McMahon, Deb Meem, Thérèse Migraine-George, Ghassan Moussawi, Alan Msosa, Chantal Nadeau, and Ebenezer Obadare greatly improved this book. I presented selections from this book at American University, Tulane University, University of Illinois–Urbana/Champaign, University of North Carolina, Chapel Hill, and University of Virginia. I also presented work from the book at the 2013 African Studies Association annual meeting, the 2013 National Women's Studies Association annual meeting, the 2014 African Studies Association in Germany Conference at Bayreuth University, the 2014 Causes Sexuelles: Sexualités et Mobilisations Collectives conference at the University of Lausanne, the 2014 American Sociological Association annual meeting, the 2016 *International Feminist Journal of Politics* conference at the University of Cincinnati, and at the 2016 African Feminist Initiative conference at Pennsylvania State University. I am incredibly grateful for Sarah Watkins' keen editorial eye, the guidance offered by Maria Marsh and Abigail Walkington at Cambridge University Press, and the scholars who reviewed an earlier draft of the manuscript.

The friendship and support offered by Furaha Norton, Bennett Kottler, and Valerie Weinstein nourished me as I completed this book. Dean Gerber provided loving companionship and occasional cheerleading along the way; I'm a better person for having him in my life.

Part of Chapter 3 originally appeared in a different form as Ashley Currier, "Arrested Solidarity: Obstacles to Intermovement Support for LGBT Rights in Malawi" in *WSQ: Women's Studies Quarterly* 42, Nos. 3/4 (Fall/Winter 2014): 142–159. Copyright © 2014 by the Feminist Press at The City University of New York. Used with permission of The Permissions Company, Inc., on behalf of the publishers, www.feministpress.org. All rights reserved.

Abbreviations

AHB	Anti-Homosexuality Bill (Uganda)
AI	Amnesty International
BBC	British Broadcasting Corporation
BGR	barometer for gay rights
CABS	Common Approach to Budgetary Support
CARER	Malawi Centre for Advice, Research, and Education on Rights
CEDEP	Centre for the Development of People
CHRR	Centre for Human Rights and Rehabilitation
CILIC	Civil Liberties Committee
COMESA	Common Market for Southern and Eastern Africa
CONGOMA	Council for Non-Governmental Organisations
CSO	civil society organization
DPP	Democratic People's Party
GALZ	Gays and Lesbians of Zimbabwe
GBV	gender-based violence
GTZ	German Technical Cooperation
HRCC	Human Rights Consultative Committee
ICCPR	International Covenant on Civil and Political Rights
IDAHOT	International Day Against Homophobia and Transphobia
IGLHRC	International Gay and Lesbian Human Rights Commission
IPI	Institute for Policy Interaction
KAP	knowledge, attitudes, and practices

LEGABIBO	Lesbians, Gays, and Bisexuals of Botswana
LEGATRA	Lesbian, Gay, Bisexual, and Transgender Association
LGB	lesbian, gay, and bisexual
LGBT	lesbian, gay, bisexual, and transgender
LGMM	Lesbian and Gay Movement of Malawi
MAM	Muslim Association of Malawi
MANERELA+	Malawi Network of Religious Leaders Living or Personally Affected by HIV and AIDS
MANET+	Malawi Network of People Living with HIV/AIDS
MBC	Malawi Broadcasting Corporation
MCC	Malawi Council of Churches
MCP	Malawi Congress Party
MHRC	Malawi Human Rights Commission
MHRRC	Malawi Human Rights and Resource Centre
MIDEA	Malawi Institute for Democratic and Economic Affairs
MLC	Malawi Law Commission
MLS	Malawi Law Society
MODEGAL	Movement for the Defense of Gay and Lesbian Rights in Liberia
MSM	men who have sex with men
NAC	National AIDS Commission
NCM	New Citizens Movement
NGO	nongovernmental organization
PETRA	People's Transformation Party
PP	People's Party
SMO	social movement organization
STI	sexually transmitted infection
STEKA	Step Kids Awareness
TRP	The Rainbow Project
UDF	United Democratic Front
UK	United Kingdom
UN	United Nations

UNDP	United Nations Development Programme
UNESCO	United Nations Educational, Scientific, and Cultural Organization
VOA	Voice of America
WSW	women who have sex with women

Introduction
Politicized Homophobia in Malawi

In *Politicizing Sex in Contemporary Africa: Homophobia in Malawi*, I analyze politicized homophobia and its material consequences on different Malawian constituencies, namely gender and sexual minorities and HIV/AIDS, human rights, lesbian, gay, bisexual, and transgender (LGBT) rights, and women's rights organizations. Two arguments motivate this book. First, I argue that politicized homophobia is a strategy used by African political elites interested in consolidating their moral and political authority.[1] This strategy necessitates that elites activate and politicize homophobia; the act of politicization turns homophobia from an interpersonal phenomenon into a wider set of antihomosexual discourses and practices that saturate political rhetoric. Theorizing how politicized homophobia operates as a strategy challenges Afro-pessimist[2] assumptions that homophobia is spreading unchecked like a virus throughout Africa, infecting politicians and African populations with rampant homophobia. Political elites in several African countries have used politicized homophobia to punish gender and sexual minorities while claiming to defend their country

---

[1] Political elites encompass elected state officials, high-ranking state appointees, traditional leaders, religious clerics, and media. For a discussion of elite actors involved in the politics of homosexuality in sub-Saharan Africa, see Joanna Sadgrove, Robert M. Vanderbeck, Johan Andersson, Gill Valentine, and Kevin Ward, "Morality Plays and Money Matters: Towards a Situated Understanding of the Politics of Homosexuality in Uganda," *Journal of Modern African Studies*, 50, no. 1 (2012): 106, 109.

[2] Afro-pessimism refers to perspectives that treat many African countries as having failed or failing states and emphasizes Africans' lack of agency and vulnerability to war, poverty, illness, and other social inequalities. Western perceptions of African governments and societies drive many Afro-pessimist assessments. John W. de Gruchy asserts, "'Afro-pessimism' provides a rationale for the West to forget the role which European powers played in the subjugation of the continent and the destruction of [African] econom[ies]." John W. de Gruchy, "Christian Witness at a Time of African Renaissance," *The Ecumenical Review*, 49, no. 4 (1997): 476.

against foreign and domestic critics.[3] Malawi constitutes an excellent country in which to study the contours and effects of politicized homophobia because it is not an exceptional case.[4] If scholars select cases in which homophobia is perceived to take a violent form, such a selection can distort explanations of politicized homophobia, as they will associate homophobia with violence. Although politicized homophobia remains an active strategy in Malawi, it has not inspired widespread antigay vigilantism that has unfolded elsewhere.[5]

Second, I contend that politicized homophobia in Malawi ensnares not only gender and sexual dissidents but also different social movements, such as HIV/AIDS, human rights, LGBT rights, and women's rights movements. As vocal critics of state corruption and financial mismanagement, these social movements became cast as dangerous opponents of President Bingu wa Mutharika's leadership. State, religious, and traditional leaders seized politicized homophobia as a strategy to besmirch activists' credibility, alleging that social movement leaders were secretly trying to legalize same-sex marriage and to upend

---

[3] Patrick Awondo, Peter Geschiere, and Graeme Reid, "Homophobic Africa? Toward a More Nuanced View," *African Studies Review*, 55, no. 3 (2012): 145–168; Ashley Currier, "Political Homophobia in Postcolonial Namibia," *Gender & Society*, 24, no. 1 (2010): 110–129; Marc Epprecht, *Sexuality and Social Justice in Africa: Rethinking Homophobia and Forging Resistance* (New York: Zed, 2013); Neville Hoad, *African Intimacies: Race, Homosexuality, and Globalization* (Minneapolis: University of Minnesota Press, 2007); Thabo Msibi, "The Lies We Have Been Told: On (Homo)Sexuality in Africa," *Africa Today*, 58, no. 1 (2001): 56–67; Stella Nyanzi, "Rhetorical Analysis of President Jammeh's Threats to Behead Homosexuals in the Gambia," in *Sexual Diversity in Africa: Politics, Theory, Citizenship*, edited by S. N. Nyeck and Marc Epprecht (Montreal: McGill-Queen's University Press, 2013), 67–87; Sylvia Tamale, "Confronting the Politics of Nonconforming Sexualities in Africa," *African Studies Review*, 56, no. 1 (2013): 31–45.

[4] Crystal Biruk, "'Aid for Gays': The Moral and the Material in 'African Homophobia' in Post-2009 Malawi," *Journal of Modern African Studies*, 52, no. 3 (2014): 447–473; Tara McKay and Nicole Angotti, "Ready Rhetorics: Political Homophobia and Activist Discourses in Malawi, Nigeria, and Uganda," *Qualitative Sociology*, 39, no. 4 (2016): 397–420.

[5] Ashley Currier and Joëlle M. Cruz, "The Politics of Pre-Emption: Mobilisation against LGBT Rights in Liberia," *Social Movement Studies* 2018: www.tandfonline.com/doi/abs/10.1080/14742837.2017.1319265; Human Rights Watch, *The Issue Is Violence: Attacks on LGBT People on Kenya's Coast* (New York: Human Rights Watch, 2015), www.hrw.org/sites/default/files/report_pdf/kenya0915_4upr.pdf; Human Rights Watch, "Uganda: Anti-Homosexuality Act's Heavy Toll," May 14, 2014, www.hrw.org/news/2014/05/14/uganda-anti-homosexuality-acts-heavy-toll.

the government. In addition, elites used politicized homophobia to divide social movements, fomenting discord among nongovernmental organizations (NGOs). Politicized homophobia constrained social movement campaigns and strategies, undermining solidarity partnerships between NGOs. In other words, politicized homophobia turned activists against one another. Portraying politicized homophobia as a phenomenon that only affects gender and sexual dissidents underestimates how government leaders, political parties, and other elites politicize sexualities to control postcolonial African politics.

To trace the rise and effects of politicized homophobia in Malawi, I draw on fifty-one interviews that I conducted in the summer of 2012 with HIV/AIDS, human rights, LGBT rights, and women's rights activists in Malawi about how politicized homophobia affected their organizing. Activist interviews highlighted how politicized homophobia interrupted social movement campaigns and sowed conflict among activist organizations.[6] I returned to Malawi in 2014 to interview eighty lesbian, gay, and bisexual (LGB) people about how politicized, social, and religious homophobias affect their lives, if at all.[7] These interviews allowed me to track the reach of politicized homophobia. I also gathered 1,921 articles from Malawian

---

[6] I developed a list of possible activists to interview from my review of Malawian newspaper coverage. I initially approached activists affiliated with the Centre for the Development of People (CEDEP) and Centre for Human Rights and Rehabilitation (CHRR) for interviews in 2012; these activists put me in contact with leaders of human rights, HIV/AIDS, and women's rights NGOs in Blantyre, Lilongwe, and Zomba. CEDEP staff also referred me to LGBT activists and volunteers who were willing to speak with me about their perceptions of how politicized homophobia influenced their organizing. I conducted all interviews in English.

[7] With assistance from CEDEP staff and volunteers, two Malawian research assistants and I interviewed eighty LGB people in Blantyre, Lilongwe, Mangochi, Mzuzu, and Nkhata Bay. CEDEP staff and volunteers helped circulate information among local LGB constituents about my interest in conducting interviews with interested LGBT people. I conducted interviews in English, and research assistants interviewed research participants in Chichewa and English. I provided food and nonalcoholic drinks for research participants, roundtrip fare for their trips on public transportation, and mobile telephone airtime vouchers to thank them for their time participating in interviews. Multiple efforts to recruit transgender-identified research participants were unsuccessful. My position as a white, US middle-class, cisgender bisexual woman researcher may have discouraged potential research participants from responding to interview invitations; in addition, they may have been uncomfortable with the prospect of being interviewed by cisgender Malawians.

newspapers from 1995 to the present that mention homosexuality and homophobia.[8] I analyze newspaper articles to identify how, when, and why homosexuality entered political discourse in Malawi and to classify and analyze different meanings that became associated with homosexuality.

Next, I describe gender and sexual diversity politics in postcolonial Malawi before explaining my approach to the politicization of homosexuality. Then, I theorize politicized homophobia as a strategy that political elites use. In justifying my preference for "politicized homophobia," I review different arguments for using "homophobia" as a concept. I also distinguish politicized homophobia from social homophobia before defining reactive, proactive, and preemptive politicized homophobias. After distinguishing my approach to politicized homophobia from the sex-panic framework, I introduce readers to what I call the "architecture of politicized homophobia," different tropes that combine to make it a malleable discourse and practice. At the end of the chapter, I present an overview of the book's chapters.

---

[8] My data collection goes back to 1995 for two reasons. Malawi transitioned away from a dictatorship to a democracy in 1994. John McCracken, *A History of Malawi, 1859–1966* (Rochester, NY: Boydell & Brewer, 2012). I anticipated that it would take some time for civil society actors to exploit the political opening that democratization represented before they addressed same-sex sexualities. Because Zimbabwean President Robert Mugabe began making antigay threats in 1995, I did not expect to find evidence of politicized homophobia in Malawi before this year. See Margrete Aarmo, "How Homosexuality Became 'Un-African': The Case of Zimbabwe," in *Female Desires: Same-Sex Relations and Transgender Practices across Cultures*, edited by Evelyn Blackwood and Saskia E. Wieringa (New York: Columbia University Press, 1999), 255–280.

To map the contours of politicized homophobia in Malawi, I gathered 1,921 articles from Malawian print and online newspapers published between 1995 and 2016 that mention gender variance, sexual diversity, and/or politicized homophobia. I collected articles from print newspapers on fieldwork trips to Malawi in 2012 and 2014, from Malawian online newspapers, from Malawian print newspapers' online repositories, and from Malawian newspapers on microfilm at my university's library and during two trips to the United States Library of Congress in Washington, DC, in 2012 and 2015. I gathered articles from four major Malawian news publications: the *Daily Times*, a daily print publication; the *Malawi News*, a weekly print publication; the *Nation*, a daily print publication; and the *Nyasa Times*, a daily, online publication. I developed a coding template so that I could identify tropes of politicized homophobia, which included assertions that homosexuality was un-African, concerns about sexual minorities recruiting heterosexual youth into same-sex sex acts, and worries that same-sex sexualities would lead to ethnic extinction.

The Malawian Context

Malawi has a "long precolonial history" of same-sex sexual practices.[9] However, British colonialism and President Hastings Kamuzu Banda's "brutal dictatorship"[10] installed heteronormativity, a system that rewards heterosexuality and gender conformity and punishes nonheterosexualities and gender nonconformity, as a cultural and political priority.[11] Whereas the transition away from colonial rule constituted an opportunity for state leaders to revise laws governing gender and sexual norms, this did not happen in Malawi.[12] Instead of enjoying the "rights and freedoms previously denied" to them under colonialism, Malawians suffered under thirty years of President Hastings Kamuzu Banda's authoritarian rule "remembered as much for widespread human rights violations as for strictly enforcing its 'four cornerstones,' namely unity, loyalty, obedience, and discipline."[13] In addition to quashing political dissent, Banda legislated morality to homogenize social norms, particularly those governing gender and sexuality. Under Banda's leadership, the government adopted antisodomy laws from British colonialists. His government also introduced the "Decency in Dress Act" in 1971, which proscribed women from donning trousers, miniskirts, or "skirts with slits"; the legislation tried to guarantee gender conformity and "control eroticized behavior and displays, especially those of women."[14] In this repressive environment, most gender and sexual dissidents "went underground" to avoid state-sponsored harassment and violence.[15]

---

[9] Msibi, "The Lies We Have Been Told," 67. See also, Marc Epprecht, *Hungochani: The History of a Dissident Sexuality in Southern Africa*, 2nd edn (Montreal, Canada: McGill-Queen's University Press, 2013), 114–115, 121–123.

[10] Undule Mwakasungula, "The LGBT Situation in Malawi: An Activist Perspective," in *Human Rights, Sexual Orientation, and Gender Identity in The Commonwealth: Struggles for Decriminalisation and Change*, edited by Corinne Lennox and Matthew Waites (London: Institute of Commonwealth Studies, 2013), 359. http://sas-space.sas.ac.uk/4824/9/13Mwakasungula_LGBTMalawi Activist.pdf.

[11] Rahul Rao, "The Locations of Homophobia," *London Review of International Law*, 2, no. 2 (2014): 169–199.

[12] Mwakasungula, "The LGBT Situation in Malawi."   [13] Ibid., 359.

[14] Lisa Gilman, *The Dance of Politics: Gender, Performance, and Democratization in Malawi* (Philadelphia: Temple University Press, 2009), 66.

[15] Mwakasungula, "The LGBT Situation in Malawi," 360.

In the early 1990s, foreign donor representatives began voicing concern about repression and human rights violations perpetrated by Banda's government. When donors withheld development aid to protest human rights abuses, Banda held national elections in 1994, which he lost; these elections inaugurated the transition away from authoritarian rule to multiparty democracy in Malawi.[16] Multiparty democracy under President Bakili Muluzi ushered in many changes. Under Muluzi's leadership, lawmakers redrafted the constitution in 1994 and negotiated new diplomatic ties with different countries, yet allegations of corruption and abuse of power marred his ten years in office.[17] After an unsuccessful attempt to amend the constitution to allow Muluzi to run for a third term as president, Mutharika was elected as president in 2004.

Malawian politicians began denouncing homosexuality in 2005 when human rights activists advocated for decriminalizing same-sex sex, which political, religious, and traditional leaders rejected. Politicized homophobia became a staple of political discourses after the 2010 prosecution of Tiwonge Chimbalanga and Steven Monjeza for violating the antisodomy law.[18] This case elicited outrage from Western diplomats, donors, and activists and motivated political elites' reactive politicized homophobia. As activists demanded that he fight politicians' corruption, improve the economy, and respect all human rights, in his second term as president, Mutharika turned to politicized homophobia deliberately and proactively to bolster his claim to authority. In a speech broadcast on radio in 2011 that echoed Zimbabwean President Robert Mugabe's antigay comments from 1995,[19] Mutharika alleged that

---

[16] Danielle Resnick, "Two Steps Forward, One Step Back: The Limits of Foreign Aid on Malawi's Democratic Consolidation," in *Democratic Trajectories in Africa: Unravelling the Impact of Foreign Aid*, edited by Danielle Resnick and Nicholas van de Walle (New York: Oxford University Press, 2013), 110–138.

[17] Diana Cammack and Tim Kelsall, "Neo-Patrimonialism, Institutions, and Economic Growth: The Case of Malawi, 1964–2009," *IDS Bulletin*, 42, no. 2 (2011): 88–96.

[18] Some news reports spelled Chimbalanga's first name as "Tionge." I opt for the spelling that appeared in most news accounts. For a discussion of activists' debates about how to spell Chimbalanga's first name, see Ryan R. Thoreson, *Transnational LGBT Activism: Working for Sexual Rights* (Minneapolis: University of Minnesota Press, 2014), 169–170.

[19] Aarmo, "How Homosexuality Became 'Un-African'"; Matthew Engelke, "'We Wondered What Human Rights He Was Talking About': Human Rights, Homosexuality, and the Zimbabwe International Book Fair," *Critique of Anthropology*, 19, no. 3 (1999): 289–314.

lesbians and gay men were "worse than dogs ... You'll never see dogs marry each other ... These people want us to behave worse than dogs. I cannot allow it."[20] Mutharika warned sexual minorities that publicizing their gender and sexual dissidence would provoke punishment. His comment also revealed the insecurity attached to politically and culturally sanctioned heteronormativity. His statement that sexual minorities "want us to behave worse than dogs" suggested that heterosexuals may not be so certain about their sexual orientation. Intimating that sexual minorities entice heterosexuals into same-sex sex, Mutharika promoted the notion that sexual dissidents corrupt heterosexuals culturally, morally, and sexually.

The strategic value of politicized homophobia to Malawian political elites is apparent in Mutharika's 2011 speech to a gathering of chiefs who opposed decriminalizing same-sex sex. Mutharika justified his expulsion of Fergus Cochrane-Dyet, the British high commissioner to Malawi, claiming that foreign diplomats and donors were trying to blackmail him into decriminalizing same-sex sex. In a display of defiance, Mutharika refused to "bow down to get the aid," which he claimed would have required him to decriminalize same-sex sex.[21] Politicized homophobia persisted after Mutharika's sudden death in April 2012. Within weeks of becoming president, Joyce Banda endorsed decriminalizing same-sex sex, but she and her administration withdrew their support for decriminalization when political opponents and religious leaders criticized the announcement, which I discuss in Chapter 4. Banda lost the 2014 presidential election to Peter Mutharika, Bingu wa Mutharika's brother. In 2016, in a meeting with Randy Berry, the United States special envoy for the human rights of LGBTI persons, Peter Mutharika's administration affirmed the government's antihomosexuality position.[22] Thus, political elites remain invested in politicized homophobia.

---

[20] Judith Moyo, "Malawi Leader Says Homosexuals 'Worse than Dogs,'" May 16, 2011, www.southernafricalitigationcentre.org/2011/05/16/malawi-malawi-leader-says-homosexuals-worse-than-dogs/.

[21] Agnes Mizere and Temwani Mgunda, "Don't Bring Foreign Cultures to MW: Bingu," *Daily Times*, May 11, 2011.

[22] Jacob Nankhonya, "Government Says Won't Change Policy on Gays," *Nation*, January 21, 2016, http://mwnation.com/government-says-wont-change-policy-on-gays/.

The Politicization of Sexuality

I treat the "politicization of sexuality" as a constellation of social, cultural, and political processes that police sexual practices, identities, and communities.[23] The politicization of sexuality involves media, political elites, and social movements inaugurating or intervening in debates about sexual communities, identities, and practices, demarcating boundaries between socially (and legally) acceptable and forbidden sexual practices, generating knowledge about little-understood sexual practices, and recommending collective action to promote, sequester, or repress certain sexual communities, identities, and practices. The politicization of sexuality often begins as a discursive process that generates legal, material, and policy consequences.[24] Although politicization can generate positive outcomes, such as introducing individuals to welcoming, supportive sexual minority communities, negative effects tend to outnumber the positive consequences of politicization.[25] Such negative outcomes include the stigmatization, persecution, and criminalization of sexual dissidence.[26] Historical research on the politicization of sexuality shows how state actors viewed the policing of sexual behavior as a means to instill moral and social values in citizens, thereby stabilizing state institutions and cementing their grip on power.[27]

Politicization often begins with groups subjecting an issue to public debate and "making previously unpolitical matters political."[28] At a minimum, politicization involves political elites transforming an issue into a social problem. Social problems theory tends to view the identification of a social problem as resulting from collective

---

[23] Deborah Posel, "Sex, Death, and the Fate of the Nation: Reflections on the Politicization of Sexuality in Post-Apartheid South Africa," *Africa: Journal of the International Africa Institute*, 75, no. 2 (2005): 129; Anne Marie Smith, *New Rights Discourse on Race and Sexuality: Britain, 1968–1990* (New York: Cambridge University Press, 1994).

[24] Michel Foucault charts how discourses produce sexual subjects. See his *The History of Sexuality, Volume 1: An Introduction* (New York: Vintage, 1978).

[25] Foucault, *The History of Sexuality*.

[26] Roger N. Lancaster, *Sex Panic and the Punitive State* (Berkeley: University of California Press, 2011).

[27] Michael Rocke, *Forbidden Friendships: Homosexuality and Male Culture in Renaissance Florence* (New York: Oxford University Press, 1998).

[28] Michael Zürn, "The Politicization of World Politics and Its Effects: Eight Propositions," *European Political Science Review*, 6, no. 1 (2014): 50.

consensus that a form of social "deviance" constitutes a social problem. Premised on social constructionism, social problems theory affirms that social problems only exist if members of that society believe that these problems are troubling.[29] In other words, an issue only blossoms into a "problem" in need of immediate containment, correction, or eradication if society legitimates it as such.[30] Whereas any collective can become involved in labeling an issue as a social problem, I emphasize political elites as actors who politicize sexuality. When social and political groups believe that sexual communities, identities, and practices are on the verge of overwhelming social and political structures, these beliefs can agglomerate into the perception that states and societies must contain social problems at any cost, even if these social problems do not really exist.[31] In other words, the collective construction of same-sex sexualities as a social problem politicizes them.

Politicization is an ongoing process that goes beyond initial pronouncements of a social problem. Other groups besides political elites can become involved in politicization. Past research attributes the politicization of sexuality to the actions of sexual rights movements, such as feminist, LGBT, reproductive justice, and sex workers' rights movements.[32] Such movements advance new or revised understandings of social concepts, such as bodily integrity, reproductive justice, and sexual identities. These movements also seek legal and social reform that will permit people to explore and act on sexual desires without fearing ostracism, job loss, or arrest. In this sense, sexual rights movements help politicize sexuality from the ground up. As politicization becomes more punitive, social movements associated with despised sexualities may become targets for vilification and isolation. When potentially negative consequences for defending reviled sexualities become too great, social movement leaders may distance

---

[29] Herbert Blumer, "Social Problems as Collective Behavior," *Social Problems*, 18, no. 3 (1971): 298–306.

[30] Blumer, "Social Problems," 302–303.

[31] Peter Meylakhs, "Drugs and Symbolic Pollution: The Work of Cultural Logic in the Russian Press," *Cultural Sociology*, vol. 3, no. 3 (2009): 378.

[32] Dennis Altman, *The Homosexualization of America* (Boston: Beacon, 1983); Mark Blasius, *Gay and Lesbian Politics: Sexuality and the Emergence of a New Ethic* (Philadelphia: Temple University Press, 1994), 15; Chi Adanna Mgbako, *To Live Freely in This World: Sex Worker Activism in Africa* (New York: New York University Press, 2016).

their organizations from these sexualities. Conversely, social and state repression of sexual minority communities can harden the resolve of movement leaders willing to challenge repressive action when defending their communities. Politicization centers media, social, and political attention on an issue or social group; this attention can metamorphose into unavoidable hypervisibility and susceptibility to surveillance.

Defining Politicized Homophobia

Politicized homophobia is one type of politicized sexuality. As a concept, politicized homophobia has value for scholars who document organized opposition to gender and sexual diversity and LGBT organizing, the scapegoating of sexual dissidents, mounting legislation curtailing same-sex relationships and visible gender transgression, and state-sponsored violence against gender and sexual dissidents.[33] Nevertheless, ongoing debates raise questions about the utility of the term "homophobia."[34] In this section, I theorize politicized homophobia as a concept and as a strategy available to political elites.

Homophobia. For some scholars, homophobia's origin as a term describing a pathological fear and hatred of homosexuals and same-sex sexualities makes it unsuitable for understanding social and political disdain for sexual diversity.[35] In their view, homophobia refers

---

[33] Tom Boellstorff, "The Emergence of Political Homophobia in Indonesia: Masculinity and National Belonging," *Ethnos*, 69, no. 4 (2004): 465–486; Rudolf Pell Gaudio, *Allah Made Us: Sexual Outlaws in an Islamic African City* (Malden, MA: Blackwell, 2009); Agnieska Graff, "Looking at Pictures of Gay Men: Political Uses of Homophobia in Contemporary Poland," *Public Culture*, 22, no. 3 (2010): 583–603; Kapya J. Kaoma, "The Marriage of Convenience: The US Christian Right, African Christianity, and Postcolonial Politics of Sexual Identity," in *Global Homophobia: States, Movements, and the Politics of Oppression*, edited by Meredith L. Weiss and Michael J. Bosia (Urbana: University of Illinois Press, 2013), 75–102.

[34] Karl Bryant and Salvador Vidal-Ortiz, "Introduction to Retheorizing Homophobias," *Sexualities* 11, no. 4 (2008): 387–396; David A. B. Murray, ed. *Homophobias: Lust and Loathing across Time and Space* (Durham, NC: Duke University Press, 2009).

[35] For discussions of the limitations and merits of homophobia as a concept, see Barry D. Adam, "Theorizing Homophobia," *Sexualities*, 1, no. 4 (1998): 387–404; Bryant and Vidal Ortiz, "Introduction to Retheorizing Homophobias"; Gregory M. Herek, "Beyond 'Homophobia': Thinking about Sexual Prejudice," *Sexuality Research & Social Policy*, 1, no. 2 (2004): 6–24;

to an individual-level prejudice, not to institutional- or structural-level oppression, making it less useful than other concepts. Some scholars offer concepts that could replace "homophobia" in scholarly analyses; these include "anti-LGBT hate,"[36] "anti-queer animus,"[37] and "queer-phobia."[38] Such terminological debates provide conceptual alternatives to "homophobia." Other scholars prefer "heterosexism" or "heteronormativity" to capture the cultural, social, and political structures that elevate heterosexuality and disparage nonheterosexual sexual formations.[39] Like Tom Boellstorff, I use "homophobia" instead of "heterosexism" or "heteronormativity" to refer to political elites' antihomosexual discourses and practices.[40] I view homophobia as a tool through which heterosexism and heteronormativity are achieved and sustained in discourse and social practice.[41] Heterosexism and heteronormativity reproduce the structural and social privileges afforded to masculinity and gender and sexual conformity and marginalize femininity and gender and sexual nonconformity.[42] Social and political institutions and cultural imaginaries are key locations for defending heterosexism and heteronormativity.[43]

Don Kulick, "Can There Be an Anthropology of Homophobia?" in *Homophobias: Lust and Loathing across Time and Space*, edited by David A. B. Murray (Durham, NC: Duke University Press, 2009), 19–33.

[36] Suzanne LaFont, "Not Quite Redemption Song: LGBT-Hate in Jamaica," in *Homophobias: Lust and Loathing across Time and Space*, edited by David A. B. Murray (Durham, NC: Duke University Press, 2009), 107.

[37] Ryan Richard Thoreson, "Troubling the Waters of a 'Wave of Homophobia': Political Economies of Anti-Queer Animus in Sub-Saharan Africa," *Sexualities*, 17, nos. 1–2 (2014): 25.

[38] Paola Bacchetta, "When the (Hindu) Nation Exiles Its Queers," *Social Text*, 61 (1999): 162; Daniel Heath Justice, "Notes toward a Theory of Anomaly," *GLQ*, 16, no. 1–2 (2010): 208; Kenne Mwikya, "Unnatural and Un-African: Contesting Queer-Phobia by Africa's Political Leadership," *Feminist Africa*, 19 (2014): 98.

[39] Mary Bernstein, Constance Kostelac, and Emily Gaarder, "Understanding 'Heterosexism': Applying Theories of Racial Prejudice to Homophobia Using Data from a Southwestern Police Department," *Race, Gender, & Class*, 10, no. 4 (2003): 54–74; Kristen Schilt and Laurel Westbrook, "Doing Gender, Doing Heteronormativity: 'Gender Normals,' Transgender People, and the Social Maintenance of Heterosexuality," *Gender & Society*, 23, no. 4 (2009): 440–464.

[40] Boellstorff, "The Emergence of Political Homophobia in Indonesia."

[41] Adam, "Theorizing Homophobia."

[42] Schilt and Westbrook, "Doing Gender, Doing Heteronormativity."

[43] Bacchetta, "When the (Hindu) Nation Exiles Its Queers."

Like other scholars,[44] I prefer politicized "homophobia" for its ability to illuminate how political elites attach negative meanings to same-sex sexualities, imbue this discourse with a policing function, and contest African nations' perceived cultural and political "backwardness,"[45] a hallmark of Afro-pessimism that originates in Western societies. The modifier "politicized" reminds observers that people must activate this form of mobilizable sentiment and discourse, whereas "political" risks locking the concept into an assumed, unchanging set of discourses. I also distinguish politicized homophobia from "state homophobia"[46] and "state-sponsored homophobia."[47] Although state actors play a significant role in creating and deploying politicized homophobia, other political elites, specifically religious and traditional leaders, participate in formulating politicized-homophobic rhetoric, practices, and policies. For instance, in 2010, the Malawi Council of Churches (MCC) rejected calls from Northern donors to cajole the Malawian government into recognizing and respecting gay rights. Flexing the MCC's moral and political muscle in the country, Bishop Joseph Bvumbwe, the MCC chairperson, upheld the government's antihomosexuality position and stated, "When a right threatens the right of the majority, that right is misplaced . . . It is a threat to the majority's right when our children see two men walking in the street saying they are lovers."[48] Bvumbwe joined the chorus of elites alleging that homosexuality threatened the nation's children.

---

[44] Michael J. Bosia and Meredith L. Weiss, "Political Homophobia in Comparative Perspective," in *Global Homophobia: States, Movements, and the Politics of Oppression*, edited by Meredith L. Weiss and Michael J. Bosia (Urbana: University of Illinois Press, 2013), 1–29.

[45] For a discussion of the harmful conflation of African societies with homophobia, see Epprecht, *Hungochani*, 14–16.

[46] Michael J. Bosia defines "state homophobia" as the "set of practices and rhetorics about homosexuality used by state actors to defend, to solidify, or to contest state authority." See Michael J. Bosia, "Strange Fruit: Homophobia, the State and the Politics of LGBT Rights and Capabilities," *Journal of Human Rights*, 13, no. 3 (2014): 261.

[47] Human Rights Watch (HRW) and The International Gay and Lesbian Rights Commission (IGLHRC), *More Than a Name: State-Sponsored Homophobia and Its Consequences in Southern Africa* (New York: HRW and IGLHRC, 2003). www.iglhrc.org/binary-data/ATTACHMENT/file/000/000/160-1.pdf.

[48] Bright Sonani, "Churches Condemn Donors on Gay Rights," *Nation*, March 19, 2010, 2.

I also distinguish between social homophobia and politicized homophobia. Although social homophobia can reinforce politicized homophobia, it is important to differentiate between the two. First, social homophobia may predate and outlast politicized homophobia.[49] However, the absence of politicized homophobia does not "necessarily signal the end of … social homophobia."[50] To understand how politicized homophobia dovetails with other oppressions, it is useful to imagine homophobia, like racism, as a "scavenger ideology" that becomes attached to other ideologies of vilification.[51] When crafting homophobia as a "scavenger ideology," agents of politicized homophobia borrow imagery from other oppressions to achieve desired outcomes, such as marginalizing political opponents and sexual dissidents. Thus, politicized homophobia can amplify and intersect with other structural oppressions, such as xenophobia and racism.[52] As a scavenger strategy, politicized homophobia acquires strategic utility for political elites; this utility emerges not from its coherence but rather through its ad hoc quality.

Second, social homophobia often depends on naming and recognizing individuals as queers, as in the case of family members who expel a child on suspicion of being lesbian, gay, or bisexual. In contrast, politicized homophobia does not require identifying gender and sexual dissidents before its deployment, although it often performs this disciplinary function. In other words, agents can target non-queers, such as political opponents, with politicized-homophobic rhetoric or action, marginalizing and queering them in the process. In 2004, Namibian President Sam Nujoma sought to discredit Ben Ulenga, a political opponent who was critical of Nujoma's interest in seeking a fourth term in office, by contending that he was gay. Nujoma alleged that while Ulenga represented the country on a diplomatic assignment to Great Britain, he "started drinking and to be useless, a gay (*eshenge*).

---

[49] Bacchetta, "When the (Hindu) Nation Exiles Its Queers"; Cathy J. Cohen, "Punks, Bulldaggers, and Welfare Queens: The Radical Potential of Queer Politics?" *GLQ*, 3, no. 4 (1997): 437–465.

[50] Patrick R. Ireland, "A Macro-Level Analysis of the Scope, Causes, and Consequences of Homophobia in Africa," *African Studies Review*, 56, no. 2 (2013): 52.

[51] George L. Mosse, "Racism and Nationalism," *Nations & Nationalism*, 1, no. 2 (1995): 164.

[52] Smith, *New Right Discourse on Race and Sexuality*.

He went to the white people to *yi ke mu ende komatako* [be taken from behind]."[53] Nujoma portrayed Ulenga as an emasculated pawn who betrayed Namibian interests.

Third, whereas social homophobia saturates interpersonal interactions, often playing out in intimate, familial spaces, politicized homophobia depends on the activation of political spectacle that enlivens public discourse with rumors and suspicions about sexual dissidents.[54] Heterosexist ideologies allow heteronormativity and politicized homophobia to flourish in Malawi. These ideologies include the perception that same-sex-loving people are subhuman, demonic, or psychologically stunted.[55] Although these antihomosexuality ideologies suffuse many societies, not just Malawian society, such isolated ideologies do not amount to politicized homophobia. Instead, those who politicize homophobia must activate antihomosexuality discourses and direct them at concrete targets. Politicized homophobia derives its potency from public drama. In contrast, social homophobia may remain dormant in families and communities and gain sporadic expression in religious congregations or over family meals. Simply put, social homophobia is ordinary, while politicized homophobia thrives in the exaggeration of the extraordinary.

The term "homophobia" also helps explain the mobilization of disgust and other emotions that political elites associate with homosexuality.[56] Martha C. Nussbaum treats disgust as concerned with the "borders of the body ... [T]he disgusted person feels defiled by the object, thinking that it has somehow entered the self."[57] The disgust that underlies politicized homophobia is "projective" in that the feared commingling with reviled sexualities is not "literal and

[53] Currier, "Political Homophobia in Postcolonial Namibia," 121.

[54] S. N. Nyeck, "Mobilizing against the Invisible: Erotic Nationalism, Mass Media, and the 'Paranoid Style' in Cameroon," in *Sexual Diversity in Africa: Politics, Theory, Citizenship*, edited by S. N. Nyeck and Marc Epprecht (Montreal, Canada: McGill-Queen's University Press, 2013), 151–169.

[55] Chimaroke O. Izugbara and Jerry Okal, "Performing Heterosexuality: Male Youth, Vulnerability, and HIV in Malawi," in *Men and Development: Politicising Masculinities*, edited by Andrea Cornwall, Jerker Edström, and Alan Greig (New York: Zed, 2011), 21–32.

[56] Such scholarship builds on the foundational work of Mary Douglas' *Purity and Danger: An Analysis of Concepts of Pollution and Taboo* (New York: Praeger, 1966).

[57] Martha C. Nussbaum, *From Disgust to Humanity: Sexual Orientation and Constitutional Law* (New York: Oxford University Press, 2010), 14.

physical, but imaginary; ... the projection of disgust properties onto subordinate groups is a common way of stigmatizing them as sick and inferior."[58] Politicized homophobia creates subordinated minorities, who may become enemies of the state, culture, and the family in hyperbolic twists. In this way, politicized homophobia acts as a political "form of expenditure" in which political elites eject the "enemy" through "excremental impulse ... like some despicable thing from which it is necessary to brutally break off."[59] In other words, politicized homophobia ejects unwanted elements from the national body.

In one sense, the "phobia" in "homophobia" is "metaphoric," as it refers not to fear so much as to hatred and disgust.[60] While "irrational passion" motivates much homophobia,[61] its lack of "fixed propositional content" makes homophobia a particularly malleable ideology and strategy.[62] In other words, politicized homophobia is "chameleonic."[63] For this reason, politicized homophobia can be unpredictable and accommodate contradictory homophobic threats and messages. According to David M. Halperin, the "discourses of homophobia ... cannot be refuted by means of rational argument (although many of the individual propositions that constitute them are easily falsifiable); they can only be resisted."[64] Understandable, testable logics do not motivate homophobic discourses; instead, these discourses are often contradictory and messy.[65] Illogical discourses are frustrating to encounter, as they operate as "systematic strategies of delegitimation. If they are to be resisted, then, they will have to be resisted strategically–that is, by

---

[58] Ibid., 20.
[59] Achille Mbembe, "On Politics as a Form of Expenditure," in *Law and Disorder in the Postcolony*, edited by Jean Comaroff and John L. Comaroff (Chicago: University of Chicago Press, 2006), 306. Judith Butler also uses the metaphor of excremental expulsion in *Gender Trouble* in theorizing the processes of subject-formation through exclusion. According to Butler, "[t]he boundary of the body as well as the distinction between internal and external is established through the ejection and transvaluation of something originally part of identity into a defiling otherness." Judith Butler, *Gender Trouble: Feminism and the Subversion of Identity* (New York: Routledge, 1990), 133.
[60] Janice Irvine, "Transient Feelings: Sex Panics and the Politics of Emotions," *GLQ*, 14, no. 1 (2008), 9.
[61] Altman, *The Homosexualization of America*, 64.
[62] David M. Halperin, *Saint Foucault: Towards a Gay Hagiography* (New York: Oxford University Press, 1995), 33.
[63] Biruk, "Aid for Gays," 469.   [64] Halperin, *Saint Foucault*, 32.
[65] Altman, *The Homosexualization of America*, 99.

fighting strategy with strategy."[66] I acknowledge homophobia's internal incoherence and do not reduce it to only an individualized or interpersonal phenomenon.[67] On a "structural level, … even the most irrational homophobic discourse can take the form of a coherent and authoritarian strategy."[68] However, the "repetition" of homophobic claims and discourses, no matter how preposterous they might be, can naturalize them, imbuing them with staying power.[69] I also recognize the material, social, and political effects that homophobia can have on people's lives, while resisting the temptation to diagnose and dismiss the "stupidity of queerphobia," which, as Daniel Heath Justice explains, confirms the sociopolitical privileges of those who engage in this "easy" critique.[70]

Although it is important neither to trivialize nor to exaggerate politicized homophobia as a phenomenon, locating homophobia exclusively in the global South raises important ethical questions. These ethical considerations include associating homophobia exclusively with populations of color and portraying the global South as mired in an ahistorical homophobia, a trademark of homonationalism, which is a form of "sexual exceptionalism" that rewards states with gay-affirmative positions and punishes those with antigay laws and policies.[71] In other words, it is incumbent on observers not to label homophobia as a problem only of postcolonial countries in the global South. Conflating homophobia with Southern postcolonial countries creates what Amar Wahab calls "categorical homophobia," produces "postcolonial nation-states … as self-evidently and exceptionally homophobic as a way of making them globally domesticable and therefore governable through western intervention," and renders countries in the global North as "gay-inclusive and post-homophobic" exceptions.[72] This is patently not the case, as

---

[66] Halperin, *Saint Foucault*, 32–33.
[67] For a discussion of contradictory logics of homophobia used by political elites in Great Britain in the 1980s, see Smith, *New Right Discourse on Race and Sexuality*, 17–18.
[68] Smith, *New Right Discourse on Race and Sexuality*, 189.   [69] Ibid., 193.
[70] Justice, "Notes toward a Theory of Anomaly," 208.
[71] Jasbir Puar, *Terrorist Assemblages: Homonationalism in Queer Times* (Durham: Duke University Press, 2007), 39.
[72] Amar Wahab, "Calling 'Homophobia' into Place (Jamaica): Homo/Trans/Nationalism in the Stop Murder Music (Canada) Campaign," *Interventions: International Journal of Postcolonial Studies*, 18, no. 6 (2016): 910.

elites in the United States, for example, continue to issue homophobic and transphobic threats.[73]

In addition, a particular racialization of homophobia treats it as a property of blackness, an example of the continuing racist demonization of black sexualities transnationally.[74] In the United States context, the association of homophobia with blackness has resulted in accusations that African Americans vote against LGBT communities and insistence from some white lesbians and gay men that African American LGBT people should address homophobia among African Americans.[75] Activists with the transnational Stop Murder Music campaign have identified Jamaica as an exporter of homophobia in dancehall music circulated throughout the Western hemisphere; in turn, this classification "Jamaicanized" homophobia.[76] Similarly, transnational fascination with anti-queer violence in South Africa conflates homophobia with Africanness, resulting in the "blackwashing" of homophobia.[77] This formulation positions African populations as inherently opposed to gender and sexual diversity and treats blackness as the "primary source of homophobia-related violence."[78] To contest racist assumptions about

[73] In July 2017, US President Donald J. Trump announced that the US military would no longer allow transgender people to enlist or serve. In his social media announcement, Trump stated, "Our military must be focused on decisive and overwhelming victory and cannot be burdened with the tremendous medical costs and disruption that transgender in the military would entail." Jonah Engel Bromwich, "How US Military Policy on Transgender Personnel Changed under Obama," *New York Times*, July 26, 2017, www.nytimes.com/2017/07/26/us/politics/trans-military-trump-timeline.html. By announcing the ban on transgender military personnel over social media, Trump may have intended it both to undo the LGBT rights gains made under the leadership of his predecessor, President Barack Obama, and to galvanize support among his socially and politically conservative supporters. In March 2018, Trump announced a policy that prohibits transgender people who "require or have undergone" gender-affirmation surgery from serving in the military.

[74] Anna M. Agathangelou, "Neoliberal Geopolitical Order and Value: Queerness as a Speculative Economy and Anti-Blackness as Terror," *International Feminist Journal of Politics*, 15, no. 4 (2013): 453–476; Greg Thomas, *The Sexual Demon of Colonial Power: Pan-African Embodiment and Erotic Schemes of Empire* (Bloomington: Indiana University Press, 2007).

[75] Amy L. Stone and Jane Ward, "From 'Black People Are Not a Homosexual Act' to 'Gay Is the New Black': Mapping White Uses of Blackness in Modern Gay Rights Campaigns in the United States," *Social Identities*, 17, no. 5 (2011): 606.

[76] Wahab, "Calling 'Homophobia' into Place," 916.

[77] Melanie Judge, *Blackwashing Homophobia: Violence and the Politics of Sexuality, Gender, and Race* (New York: Routledge, 2018), 2.

[78] Ibid.

the locations of homophobia, in this book, I theorize it as a strategy available to political elites interested in disciplining dissidents, defending the nation's reputation at home and internationally, and redirecting attention away from potential scandals.[79]

Politicized homophobia as a strategy available to political elites. Understanding politicized homophobia as a strategy reflects feminist theoretical developments that document how masculinist political elites use political and media apparatuses to police sexuality in the state and in society.[80] Feminist research, in particular, has identified masculinist,[81] "phallic"[82] discourses and structures that elites use to corral sexuality socially and politically. Such scholarship has notably explored the intimate ties between race, gender, sexuality, and nationalism, particularly as elites promote narrow visions of national heteronormativity.[83] Theorizing politicized homophobia's

---

[79] Categorical discourses that racialize homophobia resemble racist narratives about "African AIDS" that circulated in the 1980s and 1990s. See Cindy Patton, "Inventing 'African AIDS,'" in *Culture, Society, and Sexuality: A Reader*, edited by Richard G. Parker and Peter Aggleton (New York: Routledge, 2007), 387–404.

[80] M. Jacqui Alexander, *Pedagogies of Crossing: Meditations on Feminism, Sexual Politics, Memory, and the Sacred* (Durham, NC: Duke University Press, 2005); V. Spike Peterson, "Sexing Political Identities/Nationalism as Heterosexism," *International Feminist Journal of Politics*, 1, no. 1 (1999): 34–65. Tamale, "Confronting the Politics of Nonconforming Sexualities in Africa."

[81] Cynthia Enloe, *Globalization and Militarism: Feminists Make the Link*, 2nd edn (Lanham, MD: Rowman and Littlefield, 2016); Charlotte Hooper, *Manly States: Masculinities, International Relations, and Gender Politics* (New York: Columbia University Press, 2001); Amina Mama, "Khaki in the Family: Gender Discourses and Militarism in Nigeria," *African Studies Review*, 41, no. 2 (1998): 1–17.

[82] Shane Phelan, *Sexual Strangers: Gays, Lesbians, and the Dilemmas of Citizenship* (Philadelphia: Temple University Press, 2001), 54.

[83] Geraldine Heng, "'A Great Way to Fly': Nationalism, the State, and the Varieties of Third-World Feminism," in *Feminist Genealogies, Colonial Legacies, Democratic Futures*, edited by M. Jacqui Alexander and Chandra Talpade Mohanty (New York: Routledge, 1997), 30–45; Anne McClintock, *Imperial Leather: Race, Gender, and Sexuality in the Colonial Contest* (New York: Routledge, 1995); Cindy Patton, "Stealth Bombers of Desire: The Globalization of 'Alterity' in Emerging Democracies," in *Queer Globalizations: Citizenship and the Afterlife of Colonialism*, edited by Arnaldo Cruz-Malavé and Martin F. Manalansan IV (New York: New York University Press, 2002), 195–218; Jyoti Puri, "Nationalism Has a Lot to Do with It! Unraveling Questions of Nationalism and Transnationalism in Lesbian/Gay Studies," in *Handbook of Lesbian and Gay Studies*, edited by Steven Seidman and Diane Richardson (Thousand Oaks, CA: Sage, 2002), 427–442.

strategic utility in particular scenarios also thwarts attempts to classify a region as the world's "most homophobic" by focusing attention on how and why political elites implement it, thus demystifying this phenomenon. As a dynamic strategy, politicized homophobia both facilitates and constrains political elites. On the one hand, it enables political elites to consolidate their moral authority, control over the state, and influence over the nation's global reputation. On the other hand, it confines them to one limited register in engaging with gender and sexual minorities, social movements, and political opponents. Although political elites can target different groups with this malleable strategy, it still locks them into predictable, albeit contradictory, homophobic logics and threats. Yet politicized homophobia still has the power to frighten gender and sexual minorities and political opponents.

Elites in civil society, religious institutions, and media can activate and mobilize politicized homophobia; it does not belong exclusively to state leaders. Similarly, elites in different social and political institutions may deploy homophobia with divergent interests in mind. Mass media may publish homophobic articles to keep people buying newspapers, listening to the radio, and watching television.[84] Elites who make homophobic threats or use homophobic rhetoric may intend it to marginalize upstarts within a particular part of the political sphere but find that homophobia spirals into an uncontainable episode that inspires other media houses to join the fray, as S. N. Nyeck's research on homophobia in Cameroon demonstrates.[85] Episodes of politicized homophobia may also instigate state and nonstate repression. For instance, politicized homophobia in northern Nigeria, Senegal, and Liberia has emboldened local groups to engage in antigay vigilante action, such as physical violence directed against those perceived to be sexual minorities.[86] As homophobic state and nonstate repression

---

[84] Kenne Mwikya, "The Media, the Tabloid, and the Uganda Homophobia Spectacle," in *Queer African Reader*, edited by Sokari Ekine and Hakima Abbas (Dakar, Senegal: Pambazuka, 2013), 141–154; Cecilia Strand, "Homophobia as a Barrier to Comprehensive Media Coverage of the Ugandan Anti-Homosexual Bill," *Journal of Homosexuality*, 59, no. 4 (2012): 564–579.

[85] Nyeck, "Mobilizing against the Invisible."

[86] Currier and Cruz, "The Politics of Pre-Emption"; Human Rights Watch, "'Tell Me Where I Can Be Safe': The Impact of Nigeria's Same Sex Marriage (Prohibition) Act," May 14, 2016. www.hrw.org/sites/default/files/report_pdf/nigeria1016_web.pdf; Mouhamadou Tidiane Kassé, "Mounting Homophobic

varies across countries and regions, it is important to work with these variations carefully. Due to politicized homophobia's flexibility and "modularity," as theorized by Michael J. Bosia and Meredith L. Weiss, it becomes difficult to create an exhaustive typology for when, how, and why political elites turn to this strategy.[87]

I assert that politicized homophobia can serve as an expedient strategy for political elites seeking to punish gender and sexual dissidents, to bolster their moral and political authority, to weaken political opponents, to buttress narratives of national sovereignty, and/ or to deflect attention from sociopolitical controversies.[88] Conceptualizing politicized homophobia as a strategy available to political elites draws on scholarship that theorizes the state as an assemblage of actors that constantly make and remake the state.[89] An advantage to this framework is that it prevents treating the state as an unchanging, monolithic actor, when, in reality, it is a composite of contradictory actors. When sexuality is involved, the state is "fragmented, messy, contingent, and inconsistent."[90] As a form of "repression" in which political elites use discursive threats to marginalize and neutralize perceived opponents, politicized homophobia is not confined to state repression; it also encompasses nonstate, social repression.[91] Thus, I distinguish the deployment of politicized homophobia from the state's regulation of sexuality. The state regulates sexuality in many

Violence in Senegal," in *Queer African Reader*, edited by Sokari Ekine and Hakima Abbas (Dakar, Senegal: Pambazuka, 2013), 262–272; Babacar M'Baye, "The Origins of Senegalese Homophobia: Discourses on Homosexuals and Transgender People in Colonial and Postcolonial Senegal," *African Studies Review*, 56, no. 2 (2013), 109–128. For research on the political deployment of homophobic violence in countries undergoing political transition, see José Fernando Serrano-Amaya, *Homophobic Violence in Armed Conflict and Political Transition* (New York: Palgrave Macmillan, 2018).

[87] Bosia and Weiss, "Political Homophobia in Comparative Perspective," 5–7.

[88] Currier, "Political Homophobia in Postcolonial Namibia."

[89] Timothy Mitchell, "Society, Economy, and the State Effect," in *The Anthropology of the State: A Reader*, edited by Aradhana Sharma and Akhil Gupta (Malden, MA: Blackwell, 2006), 169–186; Jyoti Puri, *Sexual States: Governance and the Struggle over the Antisodomy Law in India* (Durham, NC: Duke University Press, 2016).

[90] Puri, *Sexual States*, 10.

[91] Myra Marx Ferree, "Soft Repression: Ridicule, Stigma, and Silencing in Gender-Based Movements," *Research in Social Movements, Conflict, and Change*, 25 (2004): 88.

ways. Jyoti Puri states, "States' preoccupations with sexuality are everywhere in evidence,"[92] particularly in the legal regulation of sexuality. The state's regulation of sexuality in different societies has entailed enacting laws criminalizing sexual practices, such as public sex[93] and same-sex sex, forcibly sterilizing women of color or restricting their reproductive capacity,[94] limiting pregnant people's access to safe abortion,[95] and adjudicating whether foreigners' sexualities make them suitable for entry into the country.[96] States are unlikely to abdicate their roles in regulating sexualities in the near future, given how many laws deal with sexuality. Although state regulation of sexuality can validate political elites' positions, such as by criminalizing sexual practices, politicized homophobia can operate independently of state regulation by turning minoritized sexualities into a public social problem or mobilizing nonstate repression against sexual minorities. When state leaders use politicized homophobia as a strategy of deflection, it can reassert the state's presence and consolidate a weakened state; in other words, the state appears to project a powerful image by deploying homophobia.

---

[92] Puri, *Sexual States*, 24.

[93] Lauren Berlant and Michael Warner, "Sex in Public," *Critical Inquiry*, 24, no. 2 (1998): 547–566.

[94] Amy Kaler, *Running after Pills: Politics, Gender, and Contraception in Colonial Zimbabwe* (Portsmouth, NH: Heinemann, 2003); Rebecca M. Kluchin, *Fit to Be Tied: Sterilization and Reproductive Rights in America, 1950–1980* (New Brunswick, NJ: Rutgers University Press, 2011); Jennie Lindsay, "The Politics of Population Control in Namibia," *Review of African Political Economy*, 13, no. 36 (1986): 58–62; Iris López, *Matters of Choice: Puerto Rican Women's Struggle for Reproductive Freedom* (New Brunswick, NJ: Rutgers University Press, 2008).

[95] Mala Htun, *Sex and the State: Abortion, Divorce, and the Family under Latin American Dictatorships and Democracies* (New York: Cambridge University Press, 2003); Susanne M. Klausen, *Abortion under Apartheid: Nationalism, Sexuality, and Women's Reproductive Rights in South Africa* (New York: Oxford University Press, 2015); Dorothy McBride Stetson, ed., *Abortion Politics, Women's Movements, and the Democratic State: A Comparative Study of State Feminism* (New York: Oxford University Press, 2002); Barbara Sutton, *Bodies in Crisis: Culture, Violence, and Women's Resistance in Neoliberal Argentina* (New Brunswick, NJ: Rutgers University Press, 2010), Lynn M. Thomas, *Politics of the Womb: Women, Reproduction, and the State in Kenya* (Berkeley: University of California Press, 2003).

[96] Eithne Luibhéid, *Entry Denied: Controlling Sexuality at the Border* (Minneapolis: University of Minnesota Press, 2002).

The presence of certain events, groups, or figures can instigate politicized homophobia. First, the perceived involvement of Western donors and diplomats in African political affairs can arouse suspicions about unfurling discourses about LGBT rights, leading to "homosexuality-is-un-African" rhetoric, a staple of nationalist politicized homophobia.[97] Second, the emergence of NGOs that endorse gender and sexual minority rights can rankle political elites who direct their anger at LGBT rights defenders. Even NGOs not directly involved with LGBT rights can become targets of politicized homophobia. Third, political spectacles like protests, trials, or scandals that concentrate public attention on same-sex sexualities for a sustained period of time constitute opportunities for political elites to deploy politicized homophobia.[98] Political spectacles can both act as initiating events for or consequences of politicized homophobia, which illuminate its strategic and opportunistic malleability.

Reactive, proactive, and preemptive politicized homophobias. Political elites can deploy politicized homophobia in a reactive, proactive, or preemptive manner or in a combination of these modes. Whether political elites use politicized homophobia in a reactive, proactive, or preemptive way hinges on the national sociopolitical environment and the country's position in a transnational political hierarchy. Thus, it is important to remember that elites in one national context may wield politicized homophobia quite differently from those in other places.

First, politicized homophobia may operate as a reactive strategy for political elites facing pressure from inside or outside the nation. In some contexts, the reactive use of politicized homophobia may signal the beginning of a cycle of an extended antihomosexuality campaign, sustained by the eventual proactive deployment of homophobic threats, discourses, and practices. Certain economic, social, and political scenarios can presage elites' use of politicized homophobia. Shifts in transnational economic and political priorities can produce a siege mentality in some political elites, leading to identification of convenient scapegoats to blame for economic, political, and social predicaments.

---

[97] Ashley Currier, *Out in Africa: LGBT Organizing in Namibia and South Africa* (Minneapolis: University of Minnesota, 2012), 121–123.

[98] Michael J. Bosia, "Why States Act: Homophobia and Crisis," in *Global Homophobia: States, Movements, and the Politics of Oppression*, edited by Meredith L. Weiss and Michael J. Bosia (Urbana: University of Illinois Press, 2013), 30–54.

Similarly, domestic political opposition and foreign criticism can drive cultivation of politicized homophobia. For instance, when the postcolonial nation-state is "under siege," nationalist politicized homophobia can ensue. In this scenario, as the state "moves to reconfigure the nation it simultaneously resuscitates the nation as hetero*sexual*."[99] Political elites work to preserve a national heteronormativity they characterize as under siege by external and internal forces. For some postcolonial governments invested in retaining power, "the habit of generating narratives of crisis at intervals becomes an entrenched dependable practice."[100] In the "context of crisis," politicized homophobia can become a strategy of convenience, allowing political elites to divert national attention toward gender and sexual dissidence and away from manufactured crises and orchestrated deceit.[101] Believing that most citizens harbor antihomosexual sentiments, elites may seize this reactive strategy to "win the support of the masses."[102] Thus, politicized homophobia functions as a "tool" political elites can use to shore up their weakening grip on power.[103] To be clear, reactive politicized homophobia is not a tool only available to embattled postcolonial state leaders; it can also unfold in democratic or authoritarian contexts.[104]

Events that surprise political elites can trigger reactive politicized homophobia. When local activists begin demanding LGBT rights in countries with little visible LGBT organizing, these demands can produce reactive politicized homophobia. For instance, some scholars

---

[99] M. Jacqui Alexander, "Not Just (Any) Body Can Be a Citizen: The Politics of Law, Sexuality, and Postcoloniality in Trinidad and Tobago and the Bahamas," *Feminist Review*, 48 (1994): 6; emphasis original.

[100] Geraldine Heng and Janadas Devan, "State Fatherhood: The Politics of Nationalism, Sexuality, and Race in Singapore," in *Nationalisms and Sexualities*, edited by Andrew Parker, Mary Russo, Doris Sommer, and Patricia Yaeger (New York: Routledge, 1992), 343–344.

[101] Bosia, "Strange Fruit," 259.

[102] Nyeck, "Mobilizing against the Invisible," 168.

[103] Katarzyna Korycki and Abouzar Nasirzadeh, "Homophobia as a Tool of Statecraft: Iran and Its Queers," in *Global Homophobia: States, Movements, and the Politics of Oppression*, edited by Meredith L. Weiss and Michael J. Bosia (Urbana: University of Illinois Press, 2013), 174; Tamale, "Confronting the Politics of Nonconforming Sexualities in Africa," 39.

[104] Michael J. Bosia's chapter in *Global Homophobia* enumerates several scenarios of state-sponsored homophobia that could be reactive in the typology I propose, although he does not use this term. See Bosia, "Why States Act."

view Zimbabwean President Robert Mugabe's reactive "diatribe" against lesbian and gay rights activists at the 1995 opening of the Zimbabwe International Book Fair as a response to the effort of Gays and Lesbians of Zimbabwe to secure a booth at the fair; when Mugabe and other ruling party loyalists witnessed how effective homophobic rhetoric was in galvanizing anticolonial nationalist support, they incorporated politicized homophobia into their political tool kit.[105] In Malawi, the arrest and prosecution of Chimbalanga and Monjeza, which I discuss in Chapter 2, elicited reactive politicized homophobia. As the trial attracted significant attention from international diplomats, human rights activists, and media outside of Malawi, local political elites gravitated to the reactive use of politicized homophobia to defend national sovereignty and (assumed) attendant heteronormativity.

Second, politicized homophobia may function as a proactive strategy, allowing elites to use it to consolidate their political authority over the state or other social institutions or to control transnational narratives about the nation. Proactive politicized homophobia can proceed sequentially from reactive uses of this strategy, particularly when political elites recognize its value in redirecting nationalist narratives or citizens' attitudes.[106] Anna Marie Smith's research shows how British Prime Minister Margaret Thatcher's administration in the late 1980s exploited homophobic claims to pass Section 28, legislation that barred local governments from "promoting homosexuality."[107] Thatcher supporters circulated claims that local governments were cultivating homosexual youth through "brainwash[ing]" methods that included normalizing same-sex sexualities and creating "lesbian and gay youth groups"; elites who used these homophobic claims intended to incite homophobia in local voters and garner support for Section 28, an example of the proactive use of politicized homophobia.[108]

---

[105] Jeremy Youde, "Patriotic History and Anti-LGBT Rhetoric in Zimbabwean Politics," *Canadian Journal of African Studies*, 51, no. 1 (2017): 67. Molly Manyonganise argues that Mugabe's statements coincided with electoral campaigns or "when the economic situation [in Zimbabwe] has seriously deteriorated." Molly Manyonganise, "'We Will Chop Their Heads Off': Homosexuality versus Religio-Political Grandstanding in Zimbabwe," in *Public Religion and the Politics of Homosexuality in Africa*, edited by Adriaan van Klinken and Ezra Chitando (New York: Routledge, 2016), 69.

[106] See Youde, "Patriotic History."

[107] Smith, *New Right Discourse on Race and Sexuality*, 184.   [108] Ibid., 193.

Proactive politicized homophobia can be particularly effective in defending postcolonial countries in the global South from accusations of "backwardness," upholding national heteronormative virtues, and condemning the hypocrisy of governments like that of the United States for maintaining contradictory stances on LGBT rights. Indeed, the development of proactive politicized homophobia can act as a counter discourse to "civilizational" discourses of progress promoted by countries in the global North.[109]

Proactive politicized homophobia can also be an effective tool of repressing and discrediting elites' enemies. In February 2012, an episode of proactive politicized homophobia in Malawi targeted no sexual minorities but rather involved discrediting and shaming Ralph Kasambara, a lawyer, human rights activist, and former attorney general who criticized President Mutharika's leadership. In 2012, three men approached Kasambara at his office, and he claimed that these men were trying to "assassinate" him and "petrol-bomb his offices and residence in Blantyre."[110] After trying to defend himself against their assault, police subsequently arrested him. Kasambara portrayed this attack as politically motivated retribution for his support of social movements mobilizing against the state.[111] In a radio interview, Minister of Information Patricia Kaliati stated, "We are aware that Kasambara and his friends were demanding sex from the men he is alleging were trying to attack him."[112] She also claimed that police arrested Kasambara "because man sleeping with a fellow man is illegal."[113] Casting Kasambara as a spurned lover who used violence when men denied his sexual advances, Kaliati exploited politicized homophobia to deflect attention away from the men Kasambara claimed were sent to murder him. In this way, politicized homophobia became instrumentalized to neutralize political opponents. It also illustrates how politicized homophobia does not require self-identified

---

[109] Momin Rahman, *Homosexualities, Muslim Cultures, and Modernity* (New York: Palgrave Macmillan, 2014), 66.

[110] Frank Namangale, "Kasambara Sues IG, 10 Others," *Nation*, February 23, 2012, 2; Caroline Somanje, "Police Detain Kasambara," *Nation*, February 14, 2012, 1–2.

[111] I discuss this social movement mobilization in more depth in Chapters 3 and 4.

[112] "Kaliati's Sex Assault Claims on Kasambara Rubbished," *Nyasa Times*, February 14, 2012, www.nyasatimes.com/kaliatis-sex-assault-claims-on-kasambara-rubbished/.

[113] Ibid.

queers as targets of politically motivated hatred. As a modular discursive threat, politicized homophobia is portable to and malleable in different sociopolitical contexts and can be used to vilify political opponents who have nothing to do with LGBT advocacy.

Third, politicized homophobia may unfold as a preemptive strategy. In this mode, politicized homophobia acquires a preemptive, "anticipatory" quality intended to deter and foil nascent LGBT organizing or to squelch political opposition.[114] In postwar Liberia, politicized homophobia emerged in 2012 amid rumors that a US-based LGBT rights group would give large sums of money to elected officials if they passed pro-LGBT rights legislation.[115] At the time, no legitimate organization had mobilized publicly in favor of LGBT rights.[116] In response to rumors about Western gay rights activists' attempts to influence Liberian law and politics, lawmakers introduced new punitive measures for those arrested for violating the antisodomy statute. Christian and Muslim leaders organized the New Citizens Movement (NCM), an antigay organization that sought to deter LGBT rights activism from taking root in the country. Making homophobic threats, NCM launched a campaign to preempt the legalization of same-sex marriage and emergence of LGBT organizing.[117]

An example of reactive and preemptive politicized homophobia occurred in Côte d'Ivoire, a Francophone West African nation in which same-sex sexual behavior is illegal only if it occurs in public. Although antihomosexuality laws can be valuable resources for those

---

[114] Meredith L. Weiss, "Prejudice before Pride: Rise of an Anticipatory Countermovement," in *Global Homophobia: States, Movements, and the Politics of Oppression*, edited by Meredith L. Weiss and Michael J. Bosia (Urbana: University of Illinois Press, 2013), 147. See also, Currier and Cruz, "The Politics of Pre-Emption."

[115] Currier and Cruz, "The Politics of Pre-Emption."

[116] Archie Ponpon launched the Movement for the Defense of Gay and Lesbian Rights in Liberia (MODEGAL) in 2012, but LGBT activists affiliated with an HIV/AIDS NGO doubted Ponpon's sincerity in launching MODEGAL, as he, according to these activists, had not sought input from LGBT Liberians about his group's activities. Therefore, these LGBT activists considered MODEGAL to be an illegitimate organization. Ashley Currier and Joëlle M. Cruz, "Religious Inspiration: Indigenous Mobilisation against LGBTI Rights in Postconflict Liberia," in *Public Religion and the Politics of Homosexuality in Africa*, edited by Adriaan van Klinken and Ezra Chitando (New York: Routledge, 2016), 153.

[117] Currier and Cruz, "The Politics of Pre-Emption"; Currier and Cruz, "Religious Inspiration."

who deploy politicized homophobia, politicized homophobia can emerge in contexts in which no antisodomy laws are in effect or have recently been repealed. Despite the absence of antisodomy laws, politicized homophobia emerged unexpectedly in 2013 in Côte d'Ivoire after Alternative Côte d'Ivoire, a local LGBT rights NGO, accepted US $50,000 from the French embassy.[118] After staff and volunteers at Alternative shared photographs on social media from the ceremony during which the French ambassador pledged funds to Alternative Côte d'Ivoire, some Ivoirian journalists downloaded these images and used them to claim that the French embassy was paying the NGO to advocate for the legalization of same-sex marriage. France's legalization of same-sex marriage in May 2013 and US President Barack Obama's call for African leaders to respect LGBT rights during his 2013 visit to Senegal fueled this conspiracy theory.[119] Ivoirian President Alassane Ouattara subsequently stated that same-sex marriage had no place in Côte d'Ivoire. Politicized homophobia seemed to inflame social homophobia when antigay vigilantes ransacked the homes of LGBT activists and the office of Alternative Côte d'Ivoire in 2014. Ivoirian LGBT activists asked United Nations (UN) officials and the Ivoirian government to investigate these attacks, resulting in the posting of UN peacekeepers and Ivoirian military outside of the NGO's office in Abidjan.[120]

Politicized homophobia ≠ sex panic. In this book, I decline to treat politicized homophobia as a sex panic. Characterizing politicized homophobia as a "sex panic"[121] can undermine theoretical approaches that treat it as a strategy in two ways. First, given the

[118] Ashley Currier and Matthew Thomann, "Gender and Sexual Diversity Organizing in Africa," in *Understanding Southern Social Movements: A Quest to Bypass Northern Social Movement Theory*, edited by Simin Fadaee (New York: Routledge, 2016), 87–103.

[119] Adam Nossiter, "Senegal Cheers Its President for Standing Up to Obama on Same-Sex Marriage," *New York Times*, June 29, 2013, A6.

[120] Matthew Thomann, "The Price of Inclusion: Sexual Subjectivity, Violence, and the Nonprofit Industrial Complex in Abidjan, Côte d'Ivoire," Ph.D. dissertation (Department of Anthropology, American University, Washington, DC, 2014), 183–187.

[121] Irvine, "Transient Feelings," 9. For Gayle S. Rubin, sex panics become a "'political moment' of sex" when social anxieties "attach to some unfortunate sexual activity or population." Gayle S. Rubin, "Thinking Sex: Notes for a Radical Theory of the Politics of Sexuality," in her *Deviations: A Gayle Rubin Reader* (Durham, NC: Duke University Press, 2011), 168.

historical legacy of racist portrayals of African sexualities and enduring Afro-pessimism, the term "sex panic" can unfairly emphasize
irrationality in involving politicized homophobia in African societies
that Western elites, diplomats, and politicians often view as mired in a
premodern cultural sensibility. Although my definition of politicized
homophobia accommodates irrationality and illogic within homophobic discourse and action, I do not portray those who deploy politicized
homophobia as crazy or irrational, as doing so would contradict my
understanding of it as a deployable strategy. Instead, I follow Harri
Englund's contextualized approach to collective responses to social
problems in Malawi. Englund shows how Malawians identified
witchcraft as a social problem in the early 2000s. Parents kept children
home from schools, fearing that kidnappers would abduct and dis-
member children in witchcraft rituals. Foreign observers could have
dismissed parents' actions in response to their perceptions of witchcraft
as a social problem as irrational and at odds with national modernity.
Contesting interpretations that cast Malawians' actions as absurd,
Englund argues that protecting their children from witchcraft was
logical.[122] Explaining the collective concern motivating parents'
actions, he is careful not to feed into Afro-pessimist perspectives that
treat Malawians as dupes of harmful cultural traditions; Malawian
parents' efforts to protect their children were in step with societies
around the world that cherish and value children's lives. Conceptualizing homophobia as a strategy that political elites deploy is important
because not all Africans agree with politically motivated sex panics.

Second, the sex-panic framework can obscure the role that social
movements play both as targets of politicized homophobia and as
actors working to reshape contemporary discourses about sexual
norms and rights. For instance, Nancy M. Whittier does not use a
moral-panic approach in her research on mobilization against child
sexual abuse in the United States. She is uncomfortable with this
framework's tendency to insinuate that irrationality overwhelms
people and sidelines evidence of groups mobilizing against an issue
that they view to be a pressing social problem. According to Whittier,
"[p]anics—in which people are mindlessly swept up in the group—are

---

[122] Harri Englund, *Prisoners of Freedom: Human Rights and the African Poor*
(Berkeley: University of California Press, 2006).

not very good explanations for human behavior."[123] She also claims that the moral-panic perspective positions social movement actors "as emerging as a result of the moral panic, rather than as influencing changing views of the issue."[124] Whittier reverses this dominant causal chain in her research, thereby illuminating how sexuality movements shape and produce what scholars dub "sex panics." Avoiding sex-panic terminology permits scholars to parse actors' intentions, in cases in which such attribution is possible. It allows me to give voice to Africans who actively engage in antihomophobic resistance.

The Architecture of Politicized Homophobia

Although politicized homophobia is a strategy that can surprise observers when political elites use opportunities or events unrelated to sexual diversity and human rights to promote homophobic views, it has a familiar architecture. In general, politicized homophobia articulates disgust for same-sex sex, although this disgust might not focus explicitly on the nature of same-sex sex. Politicized homophobia often relies on and replicates essentialist understandings of race and gender in an effort to police sex, sexuality, and political opponents. It can also manifest anxiety about the nation's future; in this sense, politicized homophobia defends and polices a nationalist, heteronormative future. Those who deploy homophobia might disapprove of how (seemingly) distant same-sex sexual practices are from heteronormative social arrangements; this disapproval objects to perceived interruptions to the transmission of cultural values and ideas. In this section, I preview antihomosexuality logics that, when deployed alone or with other logics, combine to make politicized homophobia flexible and portable.

Homosexuality is un-African. One of the most common antihomosexuality discourses is the notion that homosexuality is "un-African," a reference to the supposed cultural, national, and racial inauthenticity of same-gender-loving Africans.[125] This logic

---

[123] Nancy Whittier, *The Politics of Child Sexual Abuse: Emotion, Social Movements, and the State* (New York: Oxford University Press, 2009), 130.

[124] Ibid., 217.

[125] For more about homosexuality-is-un-African discourses, see Currier, *Out in Africa*; Marc Epprecht, *Heterosexual Africa? The History of an Idea from the Age of Exploration to the Age of AIDS* (Athens: Ohio University Press, 2008); Epprecht, *Hungochani*; Hoad, *African Intimacies*.

reproduces the assumption that sexual identity is linked to sexual behavior.[126] One variant of this antihomosexuality logic interpreted the public invisibility of homosexual-, lesbian-, or gay-identified people as confirmation that homosexuality was absent in Malawi. Benjamin Banda, a lawmaker representing Mzimba South, claimed, "If we do not see homosexuality in Malawi, then it does not happen and should not be created."[127] The invisibility of homosexuality in Malawian society fueled speculation that same-sex sexualities were foreign, Western, and un-African.

Some attributed the presence of homosexuality in Malawi to Western cultural influence. Responding to rumors about the legalization of homosexuality, Willie Chaponda, a Christian minister, argued in 2005, "Not everything from the West is good," insinuating that the presence of homosexuality in Malawi was due to Western influence.[128] In 2005, at a Malawi Law Commission meeting held to review the constitution, Paramount Chief Themba Chikulamayembe of Rumphi also espoused this view, blaming "TV channels" for the "erosion of Malawi culture."[129] He also assumed that same-sex relationships were incompatible with Malawian cultural traditions: "Culturally a girl is prepared to look after her husband since her tender age. When a man marries his fellow man, who prepares them for that type of marriage"?[130] Although he reproduced essentialist understandings of women caring for men in opposite-sex marriages, Paramount Chief Chikulamayembe wondered about the possible success of same-sex marriages, if Malawian cultural practices did not prepare young people for such relationships. In a sense, his comment made room for teaching young people about same-sex marriages alongside opposite-sex marriages. Some traditional leaders, such as Chief Kaomba of Kasungu, appreciated the malleability of local culture, "meaning that we should be flexible to adopt new ideas."[131] However, Chief Kaomba

---

[126] Foucault, *The History of Sexuality, Volume 1.*
[127] Charles Mpaka, "Waiting in a Homosexual Closet," *Daily Times*, April 15, 2007, 14.
[128] Olivia Kumwenda, "Clergy Warns on Gaiety," *Nation*, April 8, 2005, 2.
[129] McDonald Bamusi, "Increase in Rape Cases Blamed on Traditions," *Daily Times*, December 18, 2005, 2.
[130] Ibid.
[131] Jacob Jimu, "Homosexuality under Scrutiny," *Weekend Nation*, April 9–10, 2005, 25.

interpreted homosexuality as a practice that would "destroy our culture," a concern about cultural continuity.[132]

One variant of "homosexuality-is-un-African" discourse attributes the arrival of same-sex sexualities in Malawi to LGBT rights organizations funded by Northern donors. In a series of in-depth news articles on homosexuality published in 2012, Bright Mhango included examples of this perspective. He quoted Traditional Authority Mkumbira of Nkhata Bay as advising "Malawians against adopting every Western lifestyle that they encounter," implying that "homosexuality comes from the West."[133] Others suspicious of the growing visibility of same-sex sexualities in Malawi ascribed the fact that "gays are a new phenomenon" to the emergence of "pro-gay campaigners such as the Centre for Development of People (CEDEP) and Centre for Human Rights and Rehabilitation (CHRR)," organizations that "get their funding from the West."[134] According to this logic, LGBT rights organizations preceded and precipitated the public visibility of gender and sexual dissidents and also contributed to the "conversion" of young Malawians into "homosexuals," an argument I explore later.

Some African LGBT activists state that "homophobia is un-African," a reversal of the claim that "homosexuality is un-African."[135] Gaurav Desai expresses precisely this point: "it was not *homosexuality* that was inherited from the West but rather a more regulatory *homophobia*."[136] The assertion "homophobia is un-African" treats homophobia as a foreign ideology introduced by European settlers and colonial laws and practices. To confirm that homophobia is un-African, activists refer to antisodomy laws as a suite of homophobic laws and practices inherited from colonial predecessors.[137] This construction posits that colonial homophobia continues unchanged as postcolonial homophobia. Although this claim suggests that hostility toward same-sex

---

[132] Ibid.

[133] Bright Mhango, "Are Gays Born or Made?" *Weekend Nation*, August 18, 2012, 22.

[134] Ibid.

[135] Currier, *Out in Africa*; Vasu Reddy, "Homophobia, Human Rights, and Gay and Lesbian Equality in Africa," *Agenda*, 50 (2001): 83.

[136] Gaurav Desai, "Out in Africa," in *Postcolonial, Queer: Theoretical Intersections*, edited by John C. Hawley, (Albany: State University of New York Press, 2001), 148; emphasis original.

[137] Ashley Currier, "Decolonizing the Law: LGBT Organizing in Namibia and South Africa," *Studies in Law, Politics, and Society*, 54 (2011): 17–44.

sexualities persists unchanged from the colonial era into the present, in fact, some African nationalist movements revised and revived colonial antihomosexuality practices and laws when they came to power after independence, proving to former colonial rulers that they were even more committed to nationalist heteronormativity than colonialists were.[138] When lawmakers strengthen antisodomy laws with colonial origins, it makes sense for scholars to treat contemporary homophobias as hybrid or emergent indigenous ideologies and practices, rather than as unchanging *postcolonial* homophobias wherein "post" signifies the continuity of colonial homophobias. Treating contemporary politicized homophobias as hybrid entities also makes sense if one considers the "paradox" of the "excessive disorderliness of postcolonies on the one hand and their fetishism of the law on the other."[139] In other words, politicized homophobias result from the confluence of local and transnational discourses and practices.

National readiness and issue ranking. Some elites claimed that certain social issues were more important than decriminalizing same-sex sex, an example of issue ranking, or they argued that Malawi was not ready to confront LGBT rights, a national-readiness logic. Invoking the issue-ranking logic that Malawi had more pressing problems than the status of sexual minorities, Jika Nkolokosa wrote in a 2005 editorial:

Just when I was getting used to the idea that Malawians have very severe problems to worry about before they have the luxury of worrying about the problems of more affluent societies, I learn that one of our pressing issues is to decide whether to allow or not same-sex marriages.[140]

Nkolokosa asserted that the "average" Malawian worried about how to "put together a meal ... for the day's sole meal" and would not

---

[138] Currier, "Political Homophobia."

[139] Jean Comaroff and John L. Comaroff, "Preface," in *Law and Disorder in the Postcolony*, edited by Jean Comaroff and John L. Comaroff (Chicago: University of Chicago Press, 2006), viii. Jean Comaroff and John L. Comaroff characterize this paradox as descriptive of sociopolitical reality in many postcolonies; however, their engagement with this paradox does not descend into Afro-pessimist musings that portray the African continent as mired in hopeless, insuperable misery.

[140] Jika Nkolokosa, "We'll Talk Gay on the Right Day," *Daily Times*, February 2, 2005, 8.

"earnestly take part in a debate on whether to sleep around with people of the same sex."[141]

The national-readiness logic relied on and reproduced collective amnesia about the existence of same-sex sexual practices in Malawian society. This "postcolonial amnesia" is a "process of selectively memorizing certain aspects of a past while ignoring such aspects [that] are politically inconvenient to those who control the mechanisms to create a hegemonic vision of society."[142] National-readiness arguments extended homosexuality-is-un-African logic that same-sex sexualities had no origins or place in Malawian cultural practices because European colonialism, foreign tourists, and Northern countries allegedly imported these practices into Malawi. In response to Northern donors' insistence that Malawian state actors implement and respect LGBT rights, those who invoked the national-readiness logic defended the government's refusal to honor LGBT rights because this action would necessitate nationwide deliberation about gender and sexual minority rights, a conversation for which, they argued, undereducated Malawians were unprepared.

Often, national-readiness and issue-ranking logics reinforced one another. Critics were adamant that Malawians were not ready for debates about same-sex sexualities, relationships, and marriage. According to this logic, Malawi was unprepared to address same-sex sexualities, relationships, and marriage; citizens needed more time to adjust to the reality of sexual diversity before tackling questions related to sexual minority rights. In addition, critics ranked other social problems as more urgent than homosexuality. Heinrich H. Dzinyemba railed against attempts in 2005 to "saddle the legislature with a debate on homosexuality when there are already a lot of issues which need to be looked into seriously."[143] Combining both strands, Unandi Banda contended in an editorial that "our society is conservative and as such radical policy issues like homosexual[ity] should not be advanced now at the expense of basic policy issues." For Banda, programs for

---

[141] Ibid.

[142] Saskia Eleonora Wieringa, "Postcolonial Amnesia: Sexual Moral Panics, Memory, and Imperial Power," in *Moral Panics, Sex Panics: Fear and the Fight over Sexual Rights*, edited by Gilbert Herdt (New York: New York University Press, 2009), 208.

[143] Heinrich H. Dzinyemba, "Homosexuality Is Unnecessary and Undesirable," *Malawi News*, February 19–25, 2005, 6.

improving road safety deserved attention over "advocating for homosexuality ... My plea to colleagues who have appetite for homosexuality talk is, can you suspend your agenda for the next 100 years? Maybe [at] that time it will make sense."[144] Such arguments reproduced tenets of modernization theory that held that countries in the global South were behind industrialized nations in the global North in terms of economic, political, and social development.[145] Those who subscribed to this theory assumed that Malawi would and should become modernized following the paths taken by Northern countries, a position that implied that Malawi would eventually embrace gender and sexual diversity. Marshaling modernization theory, antigay opponents contended that now was not the time to contemplate gender and sexual diversity.

Homosexual "reproduction." Narratives about proliferating homosexuality and multiplying gay-identified Africans speculated about how "homosexuals" converted heterosexuals into same-sex-loving people. Rejecting activists' argument that decriminalizing same-sex sex was consistent with the principles of Malawi's emerging democracy, Imraan Shareef, a member of parliament, contended in 2005, "Democracy should go with morals and respecting rights of other people ... Something that corrupts morals, like homosexuality should not exist."[146] He assumed that same-sex sexualities involved corruption and conversion and suggested that sexual minorities lured heterosexuals into homosexuality, destabilizing heterosexuals' moral compass.

Conversion narratives also used tropes about homosexual "infection" and predation. Predation narratives sometimes conflate homosexuality with criminality, casting gay men as sexually abusing boys. Some observers endorsed the notion that lesbians and gay men indoctrinated susceptible youths into same-sex sexual practices. This

---

[144] Unandi Banda, "Rights in Malawi," *Nation*, January 24, 2007, 20.

[145] For critiques of modernization theory in relation to gender and sexual diversity in the global South, see M. Jacqui Alexander, *Pedagogies of Crossing: Meditations on Feminism, Sexual Politics, Memory, and the Sacred* (Durham, NC: Duke University Press, 2005), and Sean Chabot and Jan Willem Duyvendak, "Globalization and Transnational Diffusion between Social Movements: Reconceptualizing the Dissemination of the Gandhian Repertoire and the 'Coming Out' Routine," *Theory & Society*, 31, no. 6 (2002): 699.

[146] Suzgo Khunga, "Legalise Homosexuality, Parliament Asked," *Sunday Times*, November 20, 2005, 3.

viewpoint emerged in cases involving men accused of sexually abusing young men or adolescent boys. Commenting on the 2002 conviction of a British man, Richard Hayles, a teacher, for sexually assaulting homeless youth, the *Nation's* editor argued that it was not the boys' sexual abuse by an adult, but their introduction to homosexuality, that was the most unfortunate consequence of the case. According to the editor,

Children learn from adults. Adults are their role models. The most despicable aspect of the teacher's acts, therefore, is negative teaching. To them, the experience he has exposed ... them to will stick into their minds as a normal way of life. As they grow old, they will want to practise it on others.[147]

From the editor's viewpoint, the boys' sexual victimization irrevocably converted them into homosexuals who would inevitably abuse boys later. Sexually abused homeless youth were beyond saving, according to this logic, because what would become most salient in these youths' lives was the sexual abuse they suffered, which made them "gay."

Ethnic extinction. A stock argument against homosexuality and gay rights constructed same-sex sexualities as contributing to the extinction of Africans, Malawians, and indigenous culture. Tapping into conspiracy theories, some antigay critics claimed that Western donors' support for gay rights would lure scores of Malawians away from procreative, heterosexual relationships. For example, a letter condemning the Malawi Human Rights Resource Centre's attempt to convince lawmakers to include a sexual-orientation nondiscrimination clause in the constitution in the mid-2000s, a case I examine in the next chapter, portrayed homosexuality as "go[ing] against the sustenance of the human race because people of the same sex have no capacity for procreation."[148] This position not only interrogated sexual minorities' capacity for reproduction but also expressed anxiety about population extinction, especially because African countries have long been targets of population-control policies.[149] To justify his position, the author also pointed to Christianity and Islam's rejection of homosexuality.

---

[147] "Be Vigilant against Abuse of Children," *Nation*, January 23, 2002, 10.
[148] Francis Makanda Banda, "On Legalising Homosexuality," *Daily Times*, February 23, 2005, 8.
[149] See Amy Kaler, "The Moral Lens of Population Control: Condoms and Controversies in Southern Malawi," *Studies in Family Planning*, 35, no. 2 (2004): 105–115.

Some Malawians viewed homosexuality as leading to perilously declining birth rates and even ethnic extinction. Effie Pelekamoyo, the executive director of the Family Planning Association of Malawi, expressed concern that men would seek sexual satisfaction with other men. She asked, "What is wrong with men having sex with a woman? If men continue to have sex with men, how will our nation have children?"[150] Pelekamoyo treated same-sex relationships as new fads that would entice men away from sexual congress with women. Central to her objection was a worry that same-sex relationships would endanger the continuity of families, ethnic groups, and the nation.

Gay rights = same-sex marriage. Many debates about homosexuality assumed that demands for decriminalizing same-sex sex doubled as a campaign for the legalization of same-sex marriage. In 2004, D. D. Phiri, an editorial columnist for the *Nation*, wrote disapprovingly of the legalization of same-sex marriage. He emphasized the importance of social conformity in Malawian society because "to be counted as a fellow human being you must behave like other human beings."[151] Conformity with the principle of "*umunthu* (Malawian) or *ubuntu* ... set[s] you apart from animals."[152] For Phiri, same-sex-loving people who "transgress common morality, *umunthu* the natural behavior of humans ... have no inherent rights to dignity and equality."[153] In his view, it made sense that sexual nonconformity resulted in social ostracism. Taking an absolutist stance, Phiri claimed that same-sex marriage could never become legal in Malawi because rights "should be interpreted so as to conform to cultural values and to what members of the community regard as naturally good."[154] In a subsequent column, Phiri remarked that some "think we are in the twilight of the conventional marriage and family when they learn of same sex marriages."[155] Debates about permitting same-sex marriages in Malawi also emerged after the contentious marriage-equality campaign in South Africa in 2005 and 2006.[156] Commenting on the legalization of same-sex

---

[150] Charles Mkula, "Gays: Malawi's Dangerous Society," *Sunday Times*, October 11, 2009, 11.

[151] D. D. Phiri, "Human Rights and Morality," *Nation*, March 30, 2004, 8.

[152] Ibid.   [153] Ibid.   [154] Ibid.

[155] D. D. Phiri, "Marriage and Divorce," *Nation*, September 14, 2004, 7.

[156] Melanie Judge, Anthony Manion, and Shaun de Waal, eds. *To Have and to Hold: The Making of Same-Sex Marriage in South Africa* (Johannesburg: Fanele, 2008).

marriage in South Africa, Phiri pitied South Africans who were so worn out by apartheid "discrimination" that they had a distorted sense of human rights, which included LGBT rights in the postapartheid era.[157] He regarded the legalization of same-sex marriage as giving "homosexuals respectability," which he interpreted as a sign of national decline.[158]

Frequently, antigay opponents mixed different arguments when they rejected same-sex sexualities. Beginning his antigay screed with an objection to same-sex marriage on the principle that it was a "new concept" that contravened "the cultural values, norms, and dignity of Malawians," Jeffrey Kanyinji combined Christian and psychological discourses to justify repudiating same-sex sexualities in 2006: "Homosexuality is a psychological problem affecting people in the West which should not be normalised in the name of human rights in Malawi. This is a satanic right that is being turned into human right."[159]

Apprehension about the legalization of same-sex relationships also triggered questions about reshaped gender relations between women and men. Some traditional leaders were anxious about gay rights because they thought that "by accepting any same-sex relations, the traditional domination of men over women shall be altered."[160] According to this argument, accepting same-sex sexualities would unsettle gender and sexual norms, creating an opportunity for women and men to reimagine gender relations in Malawi. By this logic, advocating for sexual minority rights constituted an opportunity for women's and LGBT rights organizing, but no women's rights NGOs exploited this opportunity, likely due to women's rights activists' fears of retribution or personal antigay prejudice.

Homosexuality = prosperity. Some homophobic logics equated same-sex sexualities with economic prosperity, which amounted to "gay for pay" arguments.[161] These logics played out in different registers. At the individual level, some Malawians harbored the notion that having same-sex sex would yield payment. In a news article covering the arrests and sentencing of Malawian men for sodomy, a man convicted

---

[157] D. D. Phiri, "Moral Decline," *Nation*, November 21, 2006, 10.   [158] Ibid.
[159] Jeffrey Kanyinji, "Big No to Homosexuality," *Daily Times*, January 1, 2006, 15.
[160] Jimu, "Homosexuality under Scrutiny," 25.
[161] For more about gay-for-pay logic, see Currier, *Out in Africa*, 124, 129, 131–132.

of raping a boy in 2005 stated, "I was told that if I have sex with a boy I would become rich."[162] In this way, some Malawians conflated gayness with affluence. This perception had material consequences for LGBT people. For instance, when an unnamed gay man sought legal assistance after being assaulted for being gay, "many lawyers refused to represent" him.[163] "The one who accepted told me to give him about $20,000. This is because there is a perception that we [gays] have a lot of money."[164] As I document in Chapter 5, would-be blackmailers and extortionists targeted gay and bisexual men, based on the perception that they were wealthy. In this way, money and sex were impossible to disentangle.

The logic that equated same-sex sexualities with economic prosperity also emerged in national and transnational politics. As I discuss in Chapter 2, some Northern donors began insinuating that if the government did not free Chimbalanga and Monjeza, they would suspend development aid to Malawi. At the same time, public scrutiny of Northern donor funding of human rights and LGBT rights NGOs intensified. In this climate, the link between gay rights and economic prosperity became cemented. A leading LGBT rights activist quoted by Crystal Biruk stated, "The donors have loved MSM [men who have sex with men] since [the trial] ... LGBT equals money now."[165] Voicing opposition to the possible legalization of same-sex marriage, leading human rights activist Vera Chirwa portrayed some gay rights supporters as being enticed by "monetary gains."[166] She claimed, "I do not know why some people support [homosexuality], maybe they want to be funded. We should not sell our nation because of [poverty]: if we do not have money let's just work harder."[167] Chirwa's comment exemplified the viewpoint that political leaders should not betray Malawian heteronormative practices in exchange for donor funding. Like Chirwa, Mark Kambalazaza, an evangelical Christian minister,

---

[162] Francis Machado, "5 Years in Jail for Sodomy," *Daily Times*, February 25, 2005, 4.

[163] Edwin Nyirongo, "Gay Men Claim Ill-Treatment," *Nation*, December 14, 2015. http://mwnation.com/gay-men-claim-ill-treatment/.

[164] Ibid.

[165] Crystal Biruk, "Studying Up in Critical NGO Studies Today: Reflections on Critique and the Distribution of Distributive Labour," *Critical African Studies*, 8, no. 3 (2016): 295.

[166] Taweni Kalua, "Vera against Gay Marriages," *Nation*, August 27, 2007, 4.

[167] Ibid.

alleged that LGBT rights supporters were "doing it purely for the sake of getting donor money into the country."[168] Speculation that some Malawians supported LGBT activists only to elicit Northern donor funds motivated such gay-for-pay arguments.

Organization of the Book

The politicization of same-sex sexualities in Malawi began in 2004–2005 when a human rights organization, the Malawi Human Rights Resource Centre (MHRRC), promoted the decriminalization of same-sex sex, which prompted swift antigay reprisal and resulted in the production of politicized homophobia. Unlike other accounts that treat the Chimbalanga and Monjeza case as the genesis of public homophobia in the country, Chapter 1, "The Politicization of Same-Sex Sexualities in Malawi," locates the origins of the politicization of homosexuality in the mid-2000s in MHRRC's failed attempt to persuade lawmakers to add a sexual-orientation nondiscrimination clause to the constitution and to decriminalize same-sex sex. Using an analysis of newspaper articles and interviews with activists, I first show how public concerns about same-sex sexualities remained largely dormant between 1995 and 2004, but these concerns emerged in 2004 when MHRRC promulgated sexual minority rights. However, when Malawian media publicized MHRRC's recommendation early in 2005, news commentators and political elites besmirched MHRRC's reputation and agitated against homosexuality. Around the same time, homosexuality also became a divisive issue within the Malawian Anglican church when a diocese selected a British clergy member as its bishop. The ensuing controversy involved allegations that the bishop-elect was gay and endorsed gay rights. Both episodes in the mid-2000s cemented opposition to homosexuality in both political and religious discourses, resulting in the simultaneity of politicized and religious homophobias in subsequent episodes. Although political and public attitudes toward same-sex sexualities were overwhelmingly negative, some journalists, religious leaders, and activists supported sexual minority rights. I also discuss the rise of LGBT organizing initiated by the Centre for the Development of People (CEDEP).

[168] "Kambalazaza Denounces Gay Marriages," *Weekend Nation*, February 10–11, 2007, 12.

Following my reconstruction of the emergence of politicized homophobia, in the second chapter, "Trials of Love: The Rise of Politicized Homophobia," I illuminate how the 2010 trial of Chimbalanga and Monjeza operated as a "political spectacle" that magnified antipathy toward homosexuality and LGBT rights. The trial ensured that homophobia became a fixture in Malawian sociopolitical discourses. Concentrating domestic attention on same-sex intimacy, the trial accelerated the construction of same-sex sex and sexualities as monumental social problems in need of policing and resulted in the escalation of antigay intolerance into reactive politicized homophobia, a discourse that political elites were subsequently able to mobilize against their opponents. International outcry about the prosecution, conviction, and sentencing of the couple contributed to the rise of reactive politicized homophobia, as state leaders defended the sovereign right to charge and prosecute sexual minorities who violated the antisodomy law. In this chapter, I also trace the trial's consequences in the form of the "sexualization of politics," specifically in the form of concern about the sexual vulnerability of homeless youth. In addition, I document the trial's mostly negative effects on individual gender and sexual minorities and human and LGBT rights NGOs, drawing from interviews with LGBT people and HIV/AIDS, human rights, LGBT rights, and women's rights activists and analysis of newspaper coverage of the trial.

As Chapter 2 shows how different political elites became involved in perpetuating homophobia, in Chapter 3, "The Repressive 'Wedge' Politics of Politicized Homophobia," I assert that politicized homophobia became a key strategy for leaders interested in bolstering their grip on the state. After the trial's political spectacle, the government targeted social movements critical of Mutharika's leadership for repression. This chapter demonstrates how Mutharika's government wielded proactive politicized homophobia as an instrument to discipline social movements and to turn Malawians against NGOs. Using data collected from Malawian newspaper articles, I situate contemporary wariness of NGOs amid historic state hostility toward NGOs in the country. Civil society's criticisms of widespread corruption, fuel and electricity shortages, and food scarcity increased in 2010 and 2011, erupting into nationwide protests on July 20, 2011. Government authorities brutally put down the July 20 protests and subsequently harassed and attacked leading civil society activists. Politicized homophobia constituted part of the discursive arsenal political elites used to deter ordinary Malawians from participating in the July 20 protests and to portray NGOs as willing to pander to unseemly Western (sexual) interests, such as promoting gay rights, in exchange for donor funding. Interviews with HIV/AIDS, human rights, LGBT rights, and women's rights activists reveal how the government used politicized homophobia as a tool of repression to silence their criticism of Mutharika's regime.

Whereas I argue in Chapter 3 that state leaders used politicized homophobia as a strategy to discipline social movements that opposed Mutharika's rule, in Chapter 4, "Arrested Solidarity: Why Some Movements Do Not Support LGBT Rights in Malawi," I track the effects of politicized homophobia on HIV/AIDS, human rights, LGBT rights, and women's rights NGOs. Politicized homophobia generated deep divisions among these movements, as activists contemplated the costs associated with publicly championing LGBT rights and criticizing Mutharika. In spite of the presence of inter-movement support for LGBT rights in Malawi, pro-LGBT activists in some movements experienced limits on when and how they could express their solidarity. Foreign donors pressured some activists to express public support for LGBT rights. Other activists identified factors, such as Malawians' unpreparedness for debates about sexual diversity and the existence of issues more urgent than LGBT rights, as obstacles to displays of support for LGBT rights. Using interviews with HIV/AIDS, human rights, LGBT rights, and women's rights activists, I explain activists' difficulties in being seen as promoting LGBT rights and same-sex sexualities in Malawi.

Building on findings in Chapter 4 that demonstrate how politicized homophobia disadvantaged different social movements, Chapter 5, "Under Duress: Sexual Minorities' Perceptions about the Effects of Politicized Homophobia," identifies multiple ways that politicized homophobia also harmed sexual minorities. My main motivation in this chapter is not to portray lesbian, gay, and bisexual (LGB) people as helpless victims of overlapping politicized, religious, and social homophobias. Instead, to combat the "ethical loneliness"[169] that arises when members of marginalized groups are continually unable to share

---

[169] Jill Stauffer, *Ethical Loneliness: The Injustice of Not Being Heard* (New York: Columbia University Press, 2015), 1–2.

their experiences of suffering, I document the wide range of indignities that LGB people ascribed to politicized homophobia and how layered politicized, religious, and social homophobias curtailed sexual minorities' expressions of agency. These indignities included: unwanted public visibility; antigay prejudice in their families and communities; the threat of arrest; forced outing, blackmail, and extortion; interactions with healthcare providers; rape and unwanted sex; antigay harassment and violence; and antigay vigilantism. I use eighty interviews that Malawian research assistants and I conducted with LGB Malawians in 2014 to analyze the negative outcomes that research participants perceived stemmed from politicized homophobia.

In the conclusion, "The Reach and Limits of Politicized Homophobia," I address both why scholars should be careful not to exaggerate the dangers posed by politicized homophobia, which can reproduce Afro-pessimist representations of Africans as homophobes, and why politicized homophobia remains an enduring problem for Malawian gender and sexual minorities. First, I frame my discussion of politicized homophobia's limits within a context of resisting Afro-pessimist portrayals of politicized homophobia as imperiling African gender and sexual minorities. Such misrepresentations sometimes inadvertently depict these national contexts as hopelessly homophobic and imagine LGBT Africans as living in unending misery. Recognizing the boundaries and limits of politicized homophobia enables scholars and activists to diagnose its reach without resorting to racist, Afro-pessimist mischaracterizations of gender and sexual diversity politics in African countries. Second, I offer an ethnographic account of an LGBT rights activist's trouble with the law, after police arrested him on charges of violating the antisodomy law. His arrest coincided with CEDEP and CHRR's observance of the International Day Against Homophobia and Transphobia (IDAHOT) in May 2014. The chapter ends with a brief discussion of how LGBT rights activists are trying to overturn the sodomy convictions of men in same-sex relationships and to decriminalize same-sex sex.

1 | The Politicization of Same-Sex Sexualities in Malawi

While same-sex sexualities were politicized in the 1990s in Namibia, South Africa, Zambia, and Zimbabwe, this phenomenon did not materialize in Malawi at the same time, likely because politicians and Malawian citizens were adjusting to life in a newly democratizing country after the end of President Hastings Kamuzu Banda's authoritarian regime.[1] Social movements focused on ensuring that the promise of democratization was fulfilled under President Bakili Muluzi's leadership, rendering political discussions about gender and sexual minorities mostly invisible.[2] In 1995, Zimbabwean President Robert Mugabe began publicly vilifying gender and sexual minorities and lesbian and gay activists.[3] Within two years of Mugabe's initial antigay outburst in 1995, same-sex sexualities became politicized in Namibia and Zambia. Namibian President Sam Nujoma unleashed antigay vitriol in 1996, prompting the formation of The Rainbow Project (TRP), an LGBT rights organization.[4] TRP and Sister Namibia (a lesbian-inclusive feminist organization) countered state-sponsored antigay threats in the late 1990s and early 2000s.[5] In 1998, Zambians formed the Lesbian, Gay, Bisexual, and Transgender Association

---

[1] Englund, *Prisoners of Freedom*; Resnick, "Two Steps Forward."

[2] Boniface Dulani, "Nurtured from the Pulpit: The Emergence and Growth of Malawi's Democracy Movement," in *Movers and Shakers: Social Movements in Africa*, edited by Stephen Ellis and Ineke van Kessel (Boston: Brill, 2009), 138–155.

[3] Engelke, "We Wondered"; Epprecht, *Hungochani*; Keith Goddard, "A Fair Representation: GALZ and the History of the Gay Movement in Zimbabwe," *Journal of Gay and Lesbian Social Services*, 16, no. 1 (2004): 75–98; Hoad, *African Intimacies*.

[4] Currier, "Political Homophobia"; Robert Lorway, *Namibia's Rainbow Project: Gay Rights in an African Nation* (Bloomington: Indiana University Press, 2014).

[5] Ashley Currier, "The Aftermath of Decolonization: Gender and Sexual Dissidence in Postindependence Namibia," *Signs: Journal of Women in Culture and Society*, 37, no. 2 (2012): 441–467; Currier, *Out in Africa*.

(LEGATRA) and publicized their intent to register the organization with the state.[6] When foreigners offered funding to support LEGATRA's LGBT organizing, state leaders responded with "anti-lgbt threats."[7] LEGATRA foundered within a year of its launch.[8] As activists secured LGBT rights gains in South Africa, such as a sexual-orientation nondiscrimination clause in the constitution and the right to marry, opposition to same-sex sexualities manifested in urban townships, rural areas, and political parties, sometimes as violent homophobia and transphobia targeting African gender and sexual minorities.[9] Yet Malawians were more focused on democratizing and building civil society than on gender and sexual minority rights in the 1990s and early 2000s.

In this chapter, I demonstrate how same-sex sexualities became politicized in Malawi and document responses to this politicization, including sympathetic responses to sexual diversity and LGBT organizing. I contend that the politicization of homosexuality transformed into politicized homophobia in Malawi in the mid-2000s due to two factors. First, the growing public visibility of NGOs understood to be "promoting" same-sex sexualities and gay rights prompted antihomosexual scorn.[10] NGOs' perceived involvement in legalizing same-sex sex made them prime targets of politicized homophobia, as political elites were able to target specific NGOs thought to be promulgating gay rights and gender and sexual diversity. In some cases, political elites targeted particular NGOs, but such targeting could become more indiscriminate, trapping NGOs perceived to be beholden to Northern donors. Second, disagreements about leadership within the Malawian Anglican church transformed antihomosexual religious stances into publicly recognizable religious homophobia. In turn, religiously

---

[6] Hoad, *African Intimacies*, 83–84.

[7] Mark Ungar, "State Violence and Lesbian, Gay, Bisexual, and Transgender (lgbt) Rights," *New Political Science*, 22, no. 1 (2000): 75.

[8] Adriaan van Klinken, "Homosexuality, Politics and Pentecostal Nationalism in Zambia," *Studies in World Christianity*, 20, no. 3 (2014): 264.

[9] Currier, *Out in Africa*, 51–88; Nonhlanhla Mkhize, Jane Bennett, Vasu Reddy, and Relebohile Moletsane, *The Country We Want to Live In: Hate Crimes and Homophobia in the Lives of Black Lesbian South Africans* (Cape Town, South Africa: HSRC Press, 2010).

[10] I use the terms "gay rights" and "sexual minority rights" interchangeably in this chapter to denote the specificity of Malawians' perceptions about the emergence of gay rights advocacy at the time. Gender minority rights did not manifest publicly in the mid-2000s.

motivated objections to homosexuality and gay rights became usable material in subsequent deployments of politicized homophobia.

I begin by reviewing the nature of infrequent news reports about gender and sexual diversity between 1995 and 2005 in Malawi. Then, I discuss two cases that contributed to the politicization of homosexuality. In a bold move, the Malawi Human Rights Resource Centre (MHRRC), a human rights NGO, recommended adding a sexual-orientation nondiscrimination clause to the constitution and decriminalizing sodomy in 2004. However, when media reported MHRRC's suggestion early in 2005, news commentators and political elites besmirched MHRRC's reputation and mobilized against homo-sexuality. In addition, homosexuality became a divisive issue within the Malawian Anglican church when a diocese selected a British clergy member as its bishop in 2005–2006. The ensuing controversy involved allegations that the bishop-elect was gay and endorsed gay rights. Both episodes in the mid-2000s cemented opposition to homosexuality as a fixture in political discourse.[11] Although the politicization of homo-sexuality began in the mid-2000s, negative discourses about same-sex sexualities did not completely silence gender and sexual minorities and their allies. I also profile sympathetic responses to gender and sexual diversity and the rise of LGBT organizing, chiefly in the guise of Centre for the Development of People (CEDEP) and Centre for Human Rights and Rehabilitation (CHRR).

Homosexuality in the Public Sphere between 1995 and 2004

Between 1995 and 2004, same-sex sex concerned police and prison officials as a criminal offense, but same-sex sexualities barely registered for most journalists, politicians, and citizens. Sporadic news reports confirmed the existence of same-sex sexualities in Malawi but did not accumulate into a mobilizable discourse against same-sex sexualities. Coverage treated same-sex sexualities and gender diversity as oddities, aberrant practices to be deplored, or acts to be ignored. In the mid- and late 1990s, when newspapers published stories about gender diversity,

---

[11] Jessie Kabwila refers to these episodes in her analysis of antihomosexuality discourse in Malawi. Jessie Kabwila, "Seeing beyond Colonial Binaries: Unpacking Malawi's Homosexuality Discourse," in *Queer African Reader*, edited by Sokari Ekine and Hakima Abbas (Dakar, Senegal: Pambazuka, 2013), 377–392.

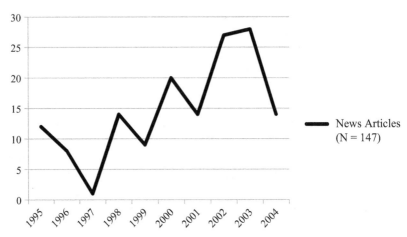

Figure 1.1 Articles mentioning gender or sexual diversity, 1995–2004

same-sex sexualities, or LGBT organizing, these reports came from Northern or other African countries, such as Zimbabwe, whose president was cracking down on LGBT activism.[12] There was little original reporting about indigenous same-sex sexualities in Malawi in this ten-year period.

Of the 1,921 Malawian newspaper articles published between 1995 and 2016 that mention gender and/or sexual diversity, only 147 articles were published between 1995 and 2004.[13] In other words, only 13 percent of the articles mentioning gender and/or sexual diversity were published between 1995 and 2004. Figure 1.1 displays a line graph showing the frequency of articles published in Malawian print newspapers between 1995 and 2004. In 1995, newspapers published twelve articles dealing with gender and/or sexual diversity. The number of articles mentioning gender and/or sexual diversity between 1995 and

[12] Silvia Aloisi, "Gay-Bashing Continues in Africa," *Daily Times*, October 6, 1999, 9; "First Lesbian Priest Comes Out," *Nation*, March 21, 1995, 5; "Gays in Botswana Are Upset," *Daily Times*, December 19, 1995, 9; Wanjira Kiama, "Where Are Kenya's Homosexuals?," *Nation*, November 18, 1998, 5; "Mugabe Lashes Out at Gays, US Leaders," *Malawi News*, August 19–25, 1995, 3; "Sebokolo – Man or Woman," *Daily Times*, December 6, 1995, 14; Emelia Sithole, "Angry Crowd Trashes Gay Stand at ZIBF," *Daily Times*, August 5, 1996, 4.

[13] The Malawian newspapers from which I collected articles mentioning gender and sexual diversity include the *Daily Times*, *Malawi News*, and the *Nation*. *Nyasa Times* did not publish online news articles between 1995 and 2004.

2004 peaked in 2002 (N = 27) and 2003 (N = 28) with reporting about the case of a British man convicted of sexually abusing homeless adolescent boys.[14]

The relative infrequency of news accounts about gender or sexual diversity between 1995 and 2004 demonstrates that same-sex sexualities were not politicized in this period. Politicization depends on the public visibility of same-sex sexualities, specifically the visibility of same-sex sexualities in the media.[15] Media visibility can hasten the politicization of homosexuality by concentrating public attention on negative portrayals of sexual diversity. News media circulate (mis)-information about same-sex sexualities, contributing to the accumulation of negative discourses about same-sex sexualities. The aggregation of negative discourses about same-sex sexualities in the news media both accompanies and fuels the politicization of same-sex sexualities.

When newspapers published accounts about gender or sexual diversity, these reports were not always welcome. Some readers harbored suspicions that disseminating information about same-sex sexualities promoted and foisted same-sex sexual practices on innocent Malawians. In 2002, an NGO objected to the *Nation* publishing articles about the "experience of homosexuals in Europe."[16] An "open minded observer" penned a letter that dismissed the unnamed NGO's concerns that "such a publication was tantamount to encouraging the practice of homosexuality in this country."[17] The letter

---

[14] In November 2001, Richard Hayles, a British man and teacher at a Blantyre high school, was arrested on charges that he had molested "street children," whom Hayles had invited to live at his residence on school grounds. Brian Ligomeka, "British National Arrested for Sodomy," *African Eye News Service*, November 21, 2001, http://allafrica.com/stories/200111210116.html. Hayles' conviction on three counts of sodomy resulted in twelve years in prison with hard labor, but because the sentences were to run concurrently, he would only serve five years. Frank Namangale, "Briton Gets 12 Years for Sodomy," *Daily Times*, January 23, 2002, 1. President Bakili Muluzi pardoned Hayles in 2003, and Hayles was subsequently deported. Frank Namangale, "Muluzi Pardons British Sodomite," *Daily Times*, May 20, 2003, 1.

[15] Mwikya, "The Media, the Tabloid"; Vasu Reddy, "Perverts and Sodomites: Homophobia as Hate Speech in Africa," *Southern African Linguistics and Applied Language Studies*, 20 (2002): 174; Strand, "Homophobia as a Barrier."

[16] Open-minded Observer, "Homosexuality Is Happening," *Nation*, September 18, 2002, 13.

[17] Ibid. I was unable to identify the NGO that issued the press release or to locate the press release that criticized the *Nation* for publishing stories about sexual minorities in other countries.

writer rejected the argument that circulating information about same-sex sexualities amounted to inciting people to engage in same-sex sex. The author stated,

Surely, informing people of what is going on in other parts of the world is not to encourage that behaviour. Logically speaking, if the newspaper carries a feature on HIV/AIDS is that to say it is promoting HIV/AIDS behaviours? ... The problem with prejudiced views against a group of people is that common sense can be ship wrecked [sic] against the rocks of prejudice. Homosexuality is happening and people need to be informed. We cannot turn a blind eye to world events and not publish stories for the national interest and information.[18]

The letter's author supported reporting about sexual diversity because it was newsworthy. The author also acknowledged the presence of same-sex sexualities in Malawian society, recognition that constituted the starting point for affirmative discourses about sexual diversity.

When same-sex sexualities received media attention between 1995 and 2004, this coverage focused mostly on sodomy arrests[19] or sex in prisons.[20] Such news coverage negatively depicted same-sex sexualities, reinforcing the supremacy of heteronormative sexual

---

[18] Ibid.

[19] McDonald Chapalapata, "Tourist Arrested for Abuse," *Daily Times*, July 20, 2000, 1; "Homosexual Jailed," *Daily Times*, July 30, 1998, 2; Peter Makossah, "Man Rapes Fellow Man," *Weekend Nation*, January 18–19, 2003, 3; Peter Makossah and Denis Mzembe, "Man Rapes Boy, 15," *Nation*, October 3, 2003, 3; Malawi News Agency, "4 Prisoners Rape Fellow Inmate," *Daily Times*, January 7, 2000, 2; Malawi News Agency, "Man Gets 9 Months for Sodomy," *Daily Times*, October 10, 2000, 4; Chikumbutso Mtumodzi, "Asian Arrested for Oral Sex," *Daily Times*, April 28, 1998, 2; Silvester Nyoni, "30 Months IHL for Indecent Assault," *Daily Times*, August 25, 2000, 3.

[20] "4 Prisoners Rape Fellow Inmate," 2; Joseph Chimbuto, "Homosexuality Hits Hard at Chichiri Prison," *Daily Times*, June 3, 2003, 5; Paul Kalizang'oma, "Consider Prisoners with Condoms," *Nation*, May 24, 2004, 15; Gabriel Kamlomo, "Prisoners' Plight: Who Will Listen?," *Nation*, June 3, 1998, 15; Joseph Langa, "Prison Illtreatment Irks Prison Reform Committee," *Daily Times*, February 7, 2000, 4; Peter Makossah, "Jails Fertile Ground for Homosexuality," *Nation*, October 22, 2003, 3; Limbani Moya, "Sickness and Death in Jail," *Malawi News*, June 6–12, 1998, 9; Dennis Mzembe, "Homosexuality Still a Scourge in Prisons," *Nation*, August 9–10, 2003, 3; Frank Namangale, "Homosexuality Worsens HIV/AIDS Cases in Prisons," *Daily Times*, May 28, 2003, 11; George Ntonya, "Good Prison Conditions a Far Cry," *Nation*, December 19, 2000, 11; Penelope Paliani, "Amnesty International Petitions Government over Prison Sodomy," *Daily Times*, January 8, 2001, 2; Penelope Paliani, "Incredible Tales of Juvenile Prisoners," *Daily*

arrangements in Malawi. On rare occasions, when news reports mentioned homosexuality or sodomy specifically, such mentions were coupled with other sex crimes. For instance, a police spokesperson affirmed that Malawians reported 283 sexual offenses in 1998.[21] Most offenses involved rape and defilement charges.[22] According to the police spokesperson, "[r]arely do we get figures on sodomy, incest and bestiality," although he characterized sexual offenses "as a significant social problem."[23]

Occasional news stories treated gender diversity and same-sex sexual practices as anomalies or novelties.[24] In a feature about incest and child sexual abuse, a journalist interviewed a woman from Blantyre who attributed instances of "incest and lesbianism" to poverty and inadequate living quarters, suggesting that the close proximity of women to one another promoted sex between them.[25] An in-depth report on gender atypicality appeared in the Malawian press in 1996. The story featured an adolescent girl playing soccer on a boys' team. The girl stated, "I wish I were a boy. Boys have many interesting things to do."[26] The story mentioned that she "likes wearing trousers and cutting her hair short just like boys do."[27] Although the journalist intimated nothing different about the girl's physiological development, the fact that she played with and dressed like boys violated local gender norms, a novelty the journalist found worthy of a news story.

One Malawian activist recalled that "homosexuality, you know, gays" first drew public attention in 2000.[28] Jeremiah, a human rights activist, referred to news coverage extrapolated from an NGO report[29]

Times, August 2, 2001, 13; Kennedy Simeza, "Foleni," *Malawi News*, February 24–March 1, 1996, 10.

[21] Cheu Mita, "283 Sexual Offences Last Year," *Nation*, February 18, 1999, 3.

[22] Defilement cases involved adults who sexually abused girls.

[23] Mita, "283 Sexual Offences," 3.

[24] "Woman Gives Birth to Hermaphrodite," *Daily Times*, June 1, 2000, 3; "Woman Transfigures," *Daily Times*, November 9, 2000, 4.

[25] Edward Chimwaza, "Relation Connotation Main Cause of Incest, Child Abuse," *Malawi News*, June 13–19, 1998, 9.

[26] Portia Chinyama, "I Should Have Been a Boy," *Nation*, September 20, 1996, 15.

[27] Ibid.

[28] Jeremiah, human rights activist, interview with the author, Lilongwe, Malawi, July 14, 2012.

[29] This report addressed sex and HIV/AIDS transmission in Malawian prisons. Dorothy Jolofani and Joseph DeGabriele, *HIV/AIDS in Malawi Prisons: A Study of HIV Transmission and the Care of Prisoners with HIV/AIDS in Zomba, Blantyre, and Lilongwe Prisons* (Paris: Penal Reform International, 1999).

that there was a growing community of lesbians and gay men in Malawi.[30] Some human rights NGO representatives interpreted the confirmation of the presence of lesbians and gay men in Malawi as initiating conversations about sexual rights. Forecasting the rise of LGBT rights NGOs in the country, Shyley Kondowe, the executive director of the Malawi Institute for Democratic and Economic Affairs, affirmed that lesbians and gay men were "free to associate" and form NGOs.[31] Kondowe even speculated that same-sex relationships might be legal under the "marriage by repute" statute, which recognizes common-law relationships.[32] An unnamed lawyer claimed that same-sex sex was legal in Malawi, as "for as long as it is not forced on anyone, conscential [sic—consensual] homosexuality is not illegal. It would be against human rights to prosecute them."[33]

In contrast, Martin Nkuna, a trainer with CHRR, an NGO that eventually defended LGBT rights in Malawi, decried the possibility of gay rights taking hold in Malawi.[34] Projecting an understanding that the sociopolitical majority determines the content of human rights, Nkuna explained,

My own view is that if society is against such behaviour, you cannot say freedoms are being violated. The constitution is the aspirations of the people. If Malawians say no to lesbians and gays, whether human rights condoned that or not, that's it.[35]

Much like CHRR staff sentiments in 2000, the MHRRC board rejected same-sex sexualities and LGBT organizing as "new phenomen[a]," according to Jeremiah. He stated that the MHRRC "board was a little bit resistant ... [O]ur board has got ... academics ... lawyers, ... judges, ... and those other respectable individuals" who offered "resistance" not only to homosexuality but also to the possibility of MHRRC advocating for LGBT rights. Board members' opposition likely stemmed from the concern that it would be unseemly for Malawians to see those holding positions of influence and privilege

---

[30] Gabriel Kamlomo, "Gays, Lesbians Surface in Malawi," *Daily Times*, August 24, 2000, 2.
[31] Ibid.   [32] Ibid.   [33] Ibid.
[34] In the late 2000s, CHRR emerged as an NGO defender of LGBT rights in Malawi, alongside CEDEP. Both CEDEP and CHRR are presently the leading LGBT rights defenders in the country.
[35] Kamlomo, "Gays, Lesbians Surface," 2.

"encouraging" same-sex sexual practices. Board members' concerns subsequently materialized when MHRRC publicly advocated for LGBT rights in 2005, a year in which same-sex sexualities became politicized.

Gays in the Constitution? The Politicization of Homosexuality in Malawi

The politicization of homosexuality emerged when political elites had a target, MHRRC, to blame for "promoting" homosexuality in the country. In 2004, MHRRC proposed that lawmakers decriminalize same-sex sex.[36] MHRRC's recommendation for reforming the constitution was innocuous, but when newspapers seized on this suggestion in 2005, political elites and news commentators turned to antigay vitriol. Critics blamed MHRRC for introducing homosexuality into the country through surreptitious means, namely through constitutional reform. MHRRC's defense of same-sex sexualities ushered in the politicization of same-sex sexualities. Political elites could attribute the sudden media visibility of same-sex sexualities to local human rights activists submitting to the will of Northern governments and pushing "un-African" practices and values on Malawians.

In 2004, Malawian lawmakers redrafted the constitution. MHRRC responded to the Malawi Law Commission's invitation for submissions from NGOs about constitutional changes they wanted. Recommending many amendments that would improve the constitution's protection of minority groups, MHRRC submitted a "Draft Proposals for Constitutional Amendments" document to the Malawi Law Commission in September 2004. In addition to endorsing the abolition of

---

[36] In a 2017 essay, David John Frank and Dana M. Moss claim that Malawian lawmakers criminalized sex between women in 2000. David John Frank and Dana Moss, "Cross-National and Longitudinal Variations in the Criminal Regulation of Sex, 1965–2005," *Social Forces*, 95, no. 3 (2017): 959, 960. Frank and Moss based this conclusion on a 2000 Malawi Law Commission report recommending that lawmakers criminalize sex between women. In actuality, lawmakers amended the penal code to criminalize sex between women in 2010, a move that came to light in 2011 when President Bingu wa Mutharika assented to it. Agnes Mizere, "Malawi Violating Human Rights Obligations – ICJ," *Daily Times*, February 11, 2011, 3. I thank Tara McKay for bringing this to my attention.

the death penalty and provision of free, compulsory primary schooling for all Malawian children, MHRRC proposed ending legal discrimination against "homosexuals" by amending Section 20 of the constitution.[37] Noting that repealing the antisodomy statute in the penal code would not go far enough in protecting same-sex-loving people from discrimination, MHRRC also suggested amending the constitutional ban on discrimination so that it would become a sexual-orientation nondiscrimination clause. MHRRC's proposed change to Section 20 reads: "(1) Discrimination of persons in any form is prohibited and all persons are, under any law, guaranteed equal and effective protection against discrimination on grounds of race, colour, sex, *including sexual orientation*, language, religion, [. . .]."[38]

When lawmakers were drafting the new constitution in 1994, after the first democratically held elections in Malawi, they debated what the nondiscrimination section should cover. According to Jeremiah,

---

[37] MHRRC, "Draft Proposals for Constitutional Amendments: Submission to the Law Commission," September 2004, Word document, 5.

[38] Ibid., emphasis added. The following is MHRRC's recommendation in its entirety (emphasis added):

IX. The Ban on Discrimination [Section 20 (1)]

Penalties for homosexual practices provided for in Malawi's Penal Code still violate every person's right to freely choose his or her sexual orientation, which is a recognised international human rights standard: The Human Rights Committee set up under the ICCPR, for instance, has considered that sexual orientation is included in the concept of "sex" – and therefore protected from discrimination – within the meaning of Art. 26 ICCPR (cf. amongst others Steiner/Alston: *International Human Rights in Context*, 2nd ed., p. 833). Furthermore, Art. 17 ICCPR protects individual privacy, which includes, one could argue, the private freedom of sexual orientation. These provisions are translated into the Malawian Constitution through Sections 20 and 21 respectively, so that the whole matter merely could be considered a problem of the Penal Code's compliance with both international norms and the Constitution. However, awareness of this fact does not seem to be very high in our society, so that additional constitutional emphasis on *the right to freely choose one's sexual orientation* might be necessary to ultimately eliminate any penalties for homosexual practices from the Penal Code, thereby ending the unconstitutional legal discrimination of homosexuals. Therefore, Section 20 (1) should be amended as follows:

(1) Discrimination of persons in any form is prohibited and all persons are, under any law, guaranteed equal and effective protection against discrimination on grounds of race, colour, sex, *including sexual orientation*, language, religion, [. . .].

lawmakers "had to insert that word 'sex.' You can't discriminate [against] a human being because of sex." Yet the term "sex" was not fixed, as Jeremiah noted.

So the issue here is: how do we interpret, how do we categorically look at sex? Is it just because of a penis and a vagina? Is it sexual intercourse? Is it a man and a woman? If you talk of a man and woman, yes, those are gender matters, but how do we look at the sex itself? There was that contestation. And if it's the sex, there's [a] section in the penal code ... [that] only talks of the human behavior of a man sleeping with another man.

In its submission, MHRRC skillfully exploited the indeterminacy of the meaning of "sex" in Section 20. Making the case for the amendment to Section 20, MHRRC argued that lawmakers should interpret the term "sex" in the nondiscrimination reference as applying not only to gender but also to sexual orientation, although the antisodomy law at the time applied only to sex between men.[39] Justifying this broad interpretation, MHRRC cited the international human rights precedent set by the International Covenant on Civil and Political Rights (ICCPR) Human Rights Committee's interpretation of "sex" as including sexual orientation. In its submission, MHRRC suggested that the fact that the penal code was not in "compliance with both international norms and the Constitution" necessitated modifying the nondiscrimination clause to include sexual orientation.[40] Constitutional protection for the "right to freely choose one's sexual orientation" might be the only way to "ultimately eliminate any penalties for homosexual practices from the Penal Code, thereby ending the unconstitutional legal discrimination of homosexuals."[41]

MHRRC's language of "choice" can be construed one of two ways. First, MHRRC's submission promoted a social-constructionist understanding of sexual orientation and identity. Promulgating individuals' right to privacy, MHRRC contended that people should be able to "choose" their "sexual orientation" free from state or institutional intervention. This idea contravened later essentialist collective action frames in Malawi that portrayed same-sex sexualities and gender variance as genetic. According to the essentialist position, lesbian,

---

[39] I discuss how lawmakers criminalized sex between women in Chapter 4, note 60.

[40] MHRRC, Draft Proposals, 5.   [41] Ibid.

gay, and bisexual people were "born that way"; they did not (and could not) "choose" to be gay.[42] Second, MHRRC's use of "choice" could refer to individuals' declaration of a sexual minority identity. This interpretation disentangles sex acts from sexual identities, much as that queer-theoretical approaches to same-sex sexualities separate sexual behavior from sexual identities.[43] Identifying as a "lesbian" is not evidence that one is in a sexual relationship with a woman; instead, "lesbian" expresses a woman's sexual attraction to other women.

MHRRC's action was bold and unprecedented in 2004, as no Malawian NGO had so directly defended sexual minority rights before. MHRRC's spokesperson advised Malawians to "accept that there were gays and lesbians in their community and they needed to be allowed to come out in the open and live freely."[44] Yet several months passed before news about MHRRC's defense of sexual minority rights circulated throughout the country.[45] A human rights activist familiar with MHRRC's action attributed the revelation of its submission to the Malawi Law Commission to a position that MHRRC's "communications officer" maintained "on the issues of rights, ... Section 20, ... [and] homosexuality."[46] MHRRC's communications officer reportedly insisted, "'Homosexuality is not a sin ... So we need to afford [sexual minorities] the respect and the dignity that they require.' That's

---

[42] Tom Waidzunas, *The Straight Line: How the Fringe Science of Ex-Gay Therapy Reoriented Sexuality* (Minneapolis: University of Minnesota Press, 2015); Suzanna Danuta Walters, *The Tolerance Trap: How God, Genes, and Good Intentions Are Sabotaging Gay Equality* (New York: New York University Press, 2014).

[43] Nikki Sullivan, *A Critical Introduction to Queer Theory* (New York: New York University Press, 2003).

[44] Kabwila, "Seeing beyond Colonial Binaries," 384.

[45] It is unclear why it took six months for Malawian journalists to learn of MHRRC's recommendation that the constitution contain a sexual-orientation nondiscrimination clause in the organization's submission to the Malawi Law Commission in September 2004. MHRRC's submission is a thirteen-page document, and the first and only mention of homosexuality occurs on page five. It is possible that this suggestion initially attracted no attention in 2004 because the submission deals with many other issues, including children's rights, social welfare, vocational education, economic and social rights, death penalty abolition, and elected officials' terms.

[46] I do not identify this research participant by name, gender, or NGO affiliation or state when or where this interview occurred to protect this person's identity.

where it caused kind of a fire [with newspapers] saying, [the] 'Resource Center is supporting homosexuality.'"[47]

When Malawian journalists broke the news about MHRRC's submission in 2005, MHRRC's proposal for amending Section 20 elicited tremendous backlash from a range of groups, including Pentecostal leaders, NGOs, and Rastafarians.[48] Willie Chaponda, the president of the Pentecostal and Charismatic Network International, invoked a "slippery slope" argument suggesting that soon, sexual minorities would be "crying loudly to have bestiality legalized."[49] Chaponda also rejected the call to decriminalize homosexuality in the so-called Christian nation of Malawi, ruminating that taking this step would "create a sinful nation in the name of human rights."[50] Some objectors insinuated that amending the constitution would signal a weakened, "feeble" state that would let "human rights organizations ... promote homosexual practices under the guise of prompting ... basic values or basic human rights."[51] This logic generated a hyperbolic future in which state recognition of gender and sexual minority rights would confirm Malawi as a "weak" African state, a radical revision of how scholars use this term to classify governments in terms of their strength or fragility.[52] In an editorial, Heinrich H. Dzinyemba rebuffed MHRRC's claim that the penalties for sodomy prosecutions "violated every person's right to freely choose his or her sexual orientation ... Instead the MHRRC should ask the Malawi Law Commission to review the law relating to homosexuality so that the legislature makes it further stiff."[53] Dzinyemba's rejoinder constituted a predictable

[47] Ibid.
[48] Tiwonge Kampondeni, "Rastas against Homosexuality," *Daily Times*, March 11, 2005, 4; Frank Namangale, "Churches, NGO Slum Homosexuality Proposal," *Daily Times*, February 3, 2005, 4.
[49] Namangale, "Churches, NGO Slum," 4.   [50] Ibid.
[51] Dzinyemba, "Homosexuality Is Unnecessary," 6.
[52] For a definition of weak states, see Robert I. Rotberg, "The Failure and Collapse of Nation-States: Breakdown, Prevention, and Repair," in *When States Fail: Causes and Consequences*, edited by Robert I. Rotberg (Princeton, NJ: Princeton University Press, 2004), 4–5. Some scholars treat Malawi as a weak or "fragile" democracy due to the legacy of Banda's authoritarian regime and the nation's indebtedness to multilateral lending agencies. Many postcolonial scholars recognize former colonies' debt burdens to Northern donors and multilateral lending agencies as continuing colonialism. For example, see Patrick Bond, *Against Global Apartheid: South African Meets the World Bank, IMF, and International Finance*, 2nd edn (New York: Zed, 2003).
[53] Dzinyemba, "Homosexuality Is Unnecessary," 6.

antigay backlash that often accompanies public proposals for gay rights in that it recommended increasing penalties for those convicted of sodomy.

Some critics speculated that MHRRC defended gay rights because staff were "homosexuals, hence their shamelessness in lobbying for such an inhuman proposal."[54] Gay- and lesbian-baiting was a staple of homophobic political threats intended to isolate and weaken the influence wielded by NGOs, which political opponents and feminist activists in other African countries have experienced.[55] In addition, critics inverted the trope of human rights, casting MHRRC's recommendation as "inhuman." A theater troupe even pilloried MHRRC's petition in a play, *False Prophets*. Gertrude Kamkwatira, the director of the Wanna Do Ensemble Theatre portrayed MHRRC's action as misguided, stating,

The NGOs talk so loud as if they are holier than thou but there is no impact from what they talk about. They spend donor money on silly issues like homosexuality. If there are homosexuals in these NGOs they should come out in the open.[56]

Kamkwatira's comments reflect a common suspicion that NGOs were engaging in deceitful activities, such as advocating for sexual minority rights, possibly because NGO staff were gay.[57] This speculation about NGOs also reflects the perception that "human rights NGOs [were] elitist and greedy."[58] According to this logic, sexual minority rights would benefit a minority of Malawians, and human rights NGO leaders who promoted gay rights were likely gay and stood to gain personally from the passage of such legislation. Like Kamkwatira, Chief Mgabu of Chikwawa asserted that some NGOs did not

[54] Tione P. Zagwazatha, "Homosexuality Madness," *Daily Times*, February 4, 2005, 8.
[55] See Currier, "Political Homophobia"; Cynthia Rothschild, *Written Out: How Sexuality Is Used to Attack Women's Organizing* (New York: IGLHRC and Center for Women's Global Leadership, 2005).
[56] Karen Msiska, "Wanna Do Takes NGO Ills to Stage," *Nation*, March 16, 2005, 25.
[57] In Chapter 3, I elaborate on suspicions that political elites and ordinary Malawians harbored about NGOs.
[58] Englund, *Prisoners of Freedom*, 121.

comprehend "democracy. Democracy does not mean promoting every-thing."[59] Other opponents suggested that gay rights activists might meet with an unfortunate demise, a veiled threat of violence targeting those who would contemplate defending sexual diversity.[60]

Leaders of different NGOs expressed their disdain for MHRRC's action, isolating MHRRC within civil society. No NGO defended MHRRC's recommendations around expanding sexual minority rights, indicating that NGO leaders were unwilling to endorse LGBT rights publicly. Reverend Ian Longwe, the director of the Forum for Peace and Reconciliation, depicted MHRRC as "an agent of ungodli-ness." Referring to debates about same-sex marriage in the United States, he suggested that Malawi "should be on alert with the gay community who declared war on [the] USA," an exaggerated charac-terization of LGBT organizing in the United States, which some scholars have critiqued for succumbing to neoliberal individualism.[61] Longwe suggested that gay militancy would emerge in the country, necessitating vigilance on the part of ordinary Malawians. The call to provide sexual minorities with constitutional protections was trans-lated into support for gay rights and the legalization of same-sex marriage, an issue that citizens and lawmakers in the United States and European nations were debating in 2004 and 2005.[62]

Women's rights activists criticized MHRRC's defense of sexual minority rights as well. The NGO Gender Network's Task Force on Participation of Women in Politics and Decision-Making decried MHRRC's promulgation of gay rights as "a rotten and immoral ideology." Deploying gender-complementary logic,[63] Reen Kachere, the task force's chairperson, claimed, "Men and women are supposed to coexist and as such, the task force can't encourage men to have sex

---

[59] Jacob Jimu, "Homosexuality under Scrutiny," *Weekend Nation*, April 9–10, 2005, 25.

[60] Peter Qeko Jere, "Homosexuality and the Bible," *Daily Times*, July 9, 2006, 7.

[61] Namangale, "Churches, NGO Slum," 4. For critiques of US LGBT organizing, see Lisa Duggan, *The Twilight of Equality? Neoliberalism, Cultural Politics, and the Attack on Democracy* (Boston: Beacon Press, 2003) and Jane Ward, *Respectably Queer: Diversity Culture in LGBT Activist Organizations* (Nashville, TN: Vanderbilt University Press, 2008).

[62] M. V. Lee Badgett, *When Gay People Get Married: What Happens When Societies Legalize Same-Sex Marriage* (New York: New York University Press, 2009).

[63] Chris Brickell, "The Sociological Construction of Gender and Sexuality," *The Sociological Review*, 54, no. 1 (2006): 99.

with fellow men. We ... shall not be part of this barbaric act."[64] Invoking gender complementarity indicated the task force's allegiance to heteronormative arrangements in Malawi. Women's rights NGOs continued to distance their work from sexual minority rights in the years after this episode, a development I discuss in Chapter 4.

Author Stanley Onjezani Kenani also slammed MHRRC, an organization he previously "held ... in high esteem," for proposing the decriminalization of same-sex sex, a "not only nauseating but also unbelievable" prospect. In a letter to the editor, Kenani chastised MHRRC: "MHRRC is playing Judas Iscariot of our culture here. Suggestions that kickback[s] from influential homosexuals the world over cannot be overruled. But the dignity of our people must not suffer under these inducements." Comparing MHRRC to Judas Iscariot, the biblical figure who betrayed Jesus Christ for thirty silver coins and initiated the actions leading to Christ's death, Kenani implied that MHRRC was peddling its legal influence in exchange for donor funding, specifically from "influential homosexuals the world over." Kenani admonished MHRRC to "[f]ind a better way of spending donor money" to introduce "fundamental" rights in Malawi first. "When everyone is satisfied that all the basic rights are in place, we can start asking donors to help us introduce homosexual rights in Malawi."[65] Kenani's criticism invoked several common tropes used in politicized homophobia. First, Kenani expressed wariness about the influence of foreign "homosexuals" on Malawian politics. He raised the suspicion that LGBT activist organizations in the global North were funneling money to African countries in an effort to convert Africans into "homosexuals." Second, he conflated legal and social acceptance of homosexuality with economic prosperity in the form of donor funding if Malawian lawmakers decriminalized same-sex sex. Third, he engaged in issue ranking when he called for establishing

---

[64] Reen Kachere, "No to Homosexuality," *Nation*, February 14, 2005, 19.

[65] Stanley Onjezani Kenani, "Away with Homosexuality," *Nation*, February 4, 2005, 15. Kenani penned a short story, "Love on Trial," which was shortlisted for the 2012 Caine Prize for African Writing. The short story fictionalizes the case of two African gay men arrested for their sexual relationship; the story was presumably based on the 2010 prosecution of Tiwonge Chimbalanga, a transgender woman, and Steven Monjeza, a cisgender man, for violating the antisodomy law, which I discuss in the next chapter. Stanley Onjezani Kenani, "Love on Trial," in *The Caine Prize for African Writing 2012*, edited by Caine Prize (Oxford: New Internationalist, 2012), 49–66.

"fundamental" rights in Malawi before tackling gay rights. Finally, he portrayed gay rights promoters as national traitors willing to abandon African heteronormative principles for the opportunity to advance economically.

Other critics echoed arguments made by Kenani. In a letter to the editor, Burnet Msika, Chrispine Ngwena, and Baxter Chimlambe exhibited outrage over MHRRC's "weird proposal" and invoked President Robert Mugabe's decade-old allegation that homosexuals were worse "than pigs and dogs," arguing, "Even dogs do not practice homosexuality so why should we be inferior to dogs?" The letter's authors also suggested that human rights NGOs have run out of issues to pursue, an offshoot of issue ranking: "Having felt they have exhausted their objectives and to avoid closing down their organisations, they are running wild, championing useless and unheard of motions or causes that are in direct conflict with not only our culture but also biblical precepts."[66] Such objections paired concerns about betraying the heteronormative African nation with claims that same-sex sexualities contravened Christian doctrine. In addition, these concerns fueled suspicion that NGOs would latch on to any issue in a desperate bid to stay in business.

Criticism of MHRRC disappeared from newspapers later in 2005, although the question of decriminalizing same-sex sex and legalizing same-sex marriages did resurface. A group of Malawians in South Africa pushed lawmakers to repeal Sections 153 and 156 of the penal code, which governed same-sex sexualities. Calling themselves the "Lesbian and Gay Movement of Malawi (LGMM)" – the first time an organized group publicly identified itself as a Malawian lesbian and gay movement organization[67] – the group declared that without the decriminalization of same-sex sex, "lesbians and gay individuals shall continue to be treated unfairly, harassed, persecuted in silence, paid less, sacked and falsely accused," outlining how homophobia hemmed in same-sex-loving Malawians. Like other short-lived African LGBT

[66] Burnet Msika, Chrispine Ngwena, and Baxter Chimlambe, "MHRRC under Fire," *Nation*, February 9, 2005, 15.

[67] Idriss Ali Nassah characterized LGMM as having a "Yeoville, South Africa," address, which raised questions about LGMM's national authenticity; Nassah implied that it was odd for a "Malawian" lesbian and gay rights organization to operate out of South Africa. Idriss Ali Nassah, "Things Stranger than Fiction," *Sunday Times*, November 20, 2005, 4.

activist groups, LGMM disappeared from view after this announcement.[68] Imraan Shareef, a Malawian lawmaker, rejected calls for decriminalizing same-sex sex, stating, "Democracy should go with morals and respecting rights of other people. It's what Malawians have to adhere to. The amendment should not be allowed and MPs should not be tempted to amend the sections."[69]

Toward the end of 2006, at an open session inviting Malawians to submit recommendations for legal reform, MHRRC and the Student Law Society of Malawi asked lawmakers serving on the Legal Affairs Committee to add a sexual-orientation nondiscrimination clause to the constitution, renewing MHRRC's original recommendation to the Malawi Law Commission in September 2004.[70] Despite the overwhelmingly negative response to their initial efforts to secure sexual minority rights, MHRRC staff were undeterred. Specifically, MHRRC and the Student Law Society of Malawi asked lawmakers to amend Section 20 of the constitution to "respect and protect homosexuals." Lawmakers offered different reasons for refusing the request. Benjamin Banda, MP for Mzimba South, stated that there was no need for such an amendment because no research proved the existence of sexual minorities in the country, perpetuating the myth that same-sex sexualities were un-African; "it could not, therefore, be legalised in Malawi just because it has been made legal elsewhere in the world." This logic rejected the idea that international norms recognizing sexual minority rights established legal precedents that Malawi should follow. Offering a rejoinder to the notion that a legal amendment was unnecessary because no sexual minorities existed in Malawi, representatives from the Student Law Society contended that it would be impossible to prove the presence of sexual minorities because it meant "catching people in the act" of having sex, an activity that should be afforded privacy. Adden Mbowani, MP from Nkhotakota South, rejected homosexuality, asserting that it was "immoral" and "stupid" because

---

[68] See Ashley Currier and Joëlle M. Cruz, "Civil Society and Sexual Struggles in Africa," in *The Handbook of Civil Society in Africa*, edited by Ebenezer Obadare (New York: Springer, 2014), 337–360; Currier and Thomann, "Gender and Sexual Diversity Organizing in Africa."

[69] Khunga, "Legalise Homosexuality." All citations in this paragraph come from this source.

[70] Marcus Muhariwa, "Parliamentary Committee Rejects Homosexuality," *Sunday Times*, December 17, 2006, 2.

"two people of the same sex cannot have sex and be accepted in society." Mbowani pointed to Christian and Muslim denunciation of same-sex sexualities to support his viewpoint. Atupele Muluzi, the chairperson of the Legal Affairs Committee, confirmed that lawmakers would probably not change their position on homosexuality, meaning that parliamentarians would not consider reforming the antisodomy law any time soon.[71]

Citing research conducted by unnamed NGOs, Justin Dzonzi, an MHRRC spokesperson, suggested that middle- and upper-class Malawians were engaging in same-sex sex "because of their interaction with people of other cultures."[72] According to this logic, class privilege and higher levels of educational attainment exposed affluent people to liberal attitudes about sexuality, supposedly enhancing their interest in same-sex sex. In turn, they circulated ideas about same-sex sexualities among fellow Malawians. Dzonzi defined homosexuality as "preferring men even where one has an opportunity to be with a woman."[73] He excluded sex between incarcerated men from this definition, insinuating that all incarcerated men were heterosexual by default but only had sex with other men "because they are deprived of female company."[74] Such logic perpetuated assumptions that same-sex sex occurred in prison only because presumably heterosexual incarcerated men had no sexual access to women.[75]

After submitting suggestions to the Malawi Law Commission, MHRRC's communications officer defended these recommendations in response to mostly negative reactions to gay rights. The communications officer explained that "gays and lesbians existed in Malawi and that his organization wanted them to come out to fight for their rights."[76] MHRRC's director also defended the organization's submission to MHRRC executive board members, in light of the controversial suggested amendment to Section 20. A human rights activist familiar with MHRRC's defense of gay rights recalled that the director at the time,

a human rights lawyer ... had to tell the board, "We are here not looking at individuals. We are here looking at human rights matters and what the laws tell us to do. So, we found that it was irregular. That is why we came up with

---

[71] Ibid.   [72] Ibid.   [73] Ibid.   [74] Ibid.
[75] See Kunzel, *Criminal Intimacy.*   [76] Namangale, "Churches, NGO Slum," 4.

critiques, critiques for the best interest, not of the organization, but the best interest of the law, as well as law enforcers."

MHRRC's submission was not simply about sexual minority rights; it involved correcting the constitution so that it contained no contradictions on human rights. MHRRC supported harmonizing all laws pertaining to human rights. The same activist explained how the communications officer's comments "caused kind of a fire [with newspapers] saying, 'Resource Center is supporting homosexuality.'" The board of trustees

made [MHRRC's] director apologize in the papers. He wrote … a press release to say that what [the communications officer] was saying was not representative of the views and feelings of Malawi Human Rights Resource Centre board and staff. And they actually stopped [the communications officer] from saying anything about Malawi Human Rights Resource Center in the papers or anywhere else.

In effect, the board gagged the communications officer as punishment for tarnishing MHRRC's reputation. According to the human rights activist and newspaper coverage in 2005, the suggested amendment to Section 20 was unpopular with Malawians, which "forced" the board to "restructure" MHRRC. Some MHRRC staff involved with drafting the submission to the Malawian Law Commission found their positions revised in ways that amounted to demotions, an example of the board retaliating against those thought to be promoting sexual minority rights. The human rights activist likened these changes at MHRRC as a tacit edict to staff: "don't talk too much about homosexuals." The edict worked. Since MHRRC's proposed amendment to Section 20, the organization has not taken a public position on homosexuality. MHRRC became a human rights organization that steers clear of the politics of same-sex sexualities publicly.

In the first public example of the politicization of same-sex sexualities, a few features stand out. After an NGO defended sexual minority rights while recommending changes to the Malawian constitution, news media exploited MHRRC's suggestion, giving political elites, including elected officials, religious leaders, and prominent activists the opportunity to comment on same-sex sexual practices and gay rights. Political elites reached consensus in their disapproval of homosexuality and gay rights. Although subsequent groups appealed to lawmakers to decriminalize same-sex sex in 2006, their calls never gained traction. This episode contributed to the political consolidation of opprobrium toward same-sex sexualities and produced reactive politicized homophobia. In fact, growing opposition toward same-sex sexualities and fears about the legalization of same-sex marriage propelled the Malawi Law Commission in 2007 to recommend that the constitution should "expressly prohibit same sex marriages" because same-sex marriages "undermine the institution of marriage" and because the "nation is not ready for same sex relationships," an example of the national-readiness trope.[77]

The Rise of Religious Homophobia in Malawi

Not only did requests to decriminalize same-sex sex begin to saturate political discourses in 2005–2006, but the politicization of homosexuality also surfaced in Christian congregations in Malawi. Growing objections to same-sex sexualities within the Anglican Church in the late 1990s and early 2000s manifested in occasional columns from Christian ministers about the "sin"[78] of homosexuality or same-sex sex as the "misuse" of sex.[79] In an early isolated case of religious homophobia, Malawian ministers organized to oppose a discussion

---

[77] The Malawi Law Commission suggested an amendment to Section 22 (3) of the constitution that read: "All men and women have the right to marry and found a family and a marriage shall be celebrated between a man and a woman." Malawi Law Commission, *Report of the Law Commission on the Review of the Constitution*, Law Commission Report No. 18, 2007, 32. In 2015, lawmakers took preemptive action to prevent marriage equality and passed the Marriage, Divorce, and Family Relations Act, although no activist group had demanded access to same-sex marriage. The act defines marriage as involving one cisgender man and one cisgender woman. See Thom Chiumia, "Malawi Marriage Bill Spurns Same-Sex Liaisons," *Nyasa Times*, February 17, 2015. www.nyasatimes .com/malawi-marriage-bill-spurn-same-sex-liasons/. Although women's and children's rights activists praised the act for raising the minimum age for boys and girls to marry to eighteen, the act prohibits same-sex marriage and forbids transgender people, particularly those who have undergone gender-confirming surgery, from "marrying a person, prior to that sex-changing surgery [who] was of the same sex [as] them." See Naith Payton, "Malawi's New Anti-LGBT Law Comes into Effect," *Pink News*, April 17, 2015. www.pinknews.co.uk/2015/04/ 17/malawi-anti-lgbt-law-signed-in/.

[78] Saustin Kazgeba Mfune, "On Homosexuality," *Weekend Nation*, August 16–17, 2003, 6; Saustin Kazgeba Mfune, "On Homosexuality," *Weekend Nation*, August 23–24, 2003, 6.

[79] Aubrey Mataka, "Sex and the Bible," *Weekend Nation*, July 10–11, 2004, 6.

of "gay groups on the agenda" at the 1998 meeting of the Fellowship of Councils of Churches in Eastern and Southern Africa. A Church of Central African Presbyterian (CCAP) Blantyre Synod representative stated, "I do not think our church can discuss gays favourably because we don't recognize [gays] in the church."[80] A Church of Nazarene representative concurred that "[g]ay people are not recognised in our international church."[81] The Malawian Law Society (MLS) chairperson asserted that "gayism is not allowed in Malawi. There is a provision in the penal code which states that it is an offence to be gay in Malawi. This means these people are not recognised in Malawi."[82] One newspaper reader sympathized with Christian leaders' positions that same-sex sexuality is "obviously an abnormality and therefore, not human" but called on them to grapple with homosexuality as both a social and "spiritual problem" worthy of clerics' attention.[83]

Malawian Christian leaders' antigay contempt mirrored developments within African Christian churches at the 1998 Anglican Conference of World Bishops.[84] Leading African Anglican clerics registered their disapproval of homosexuality, which the international press covered.[85] Anglican debates about homosexuality erupted in Malawi, a country with nearly two million Anglicans, and had the potential to stir up political debate about protecting African Christianity from the

[80] Lizzie Nyirenda, "Churches Condemn FOCCESA Inclusion of Homosexuals," *Daily Times*, May 6, 1998, 3.

[81] Ibid.

[82] Ibid. The MLS spokesperson erroneously conflated the illegality of same-sex sex with gay identity, a common misperception. In countries like Malawi, same-sex sex is against the law; however, identifying as lesbian, gay, or bisexual is not illegal. MLS changed its position on same-sex sexuality after the Chimbalanga and Monjeza trial. See "Lawyers Urged to Promote Rights," *Daily Times*, June 26, 2012, 2.

[83] Maxwell Ng'ombe, Sr., "Church Leaders Decision Was Wrong," *Daily Times*, May 27, 1998, 8.

[84] For accounts and analyses of how homosexuality was politicized at the Lambeth conference, see Miranda K. Hassett, *Anglican Communion in Crisis: How Episcopal Dissidents and Their African Allies Are Reshaping Anglicanism* (Princeton, NJ: Princeton University Press, 2007), 71–101, Hoad, *African Intimacies*, 48–67, and Bart Luirink and Madeleine Maurick, *Homosexuality in Africa: A Disturbing Love* (Soesterberg, Netherlands: Uitgeverij Aspekt, 2016), 113–128.

[85] Gustav Niebuhr, "Anglican Conference Takes Tough Line on Homosexuals," *New York Times*, August 6, 1998, A12.

unsavory direction Western Christianity was taking.[86] In 2003, Malawian Anglican dioceses debated the election of openly gay Gene Robinson as bishop in the United States. Threatening to sever ties with the Episcopal Church of the United States, Malawian Anglican Archbishop Bernard Malango joined other Anglican leaders in "minister[ing] against homosexual marriages," a show of antigay unity that was poised to give African Anglicans more power within the Anglican system.[87] Following the lead of Peter Akinola, a Nigerian Anglican bishop, some African Anglican leaders deliberated about whether to refuse funding from Western churches that condoned the "ordination of gay bishops" in 2004.[88] This emerging position established a connection between development assistance, albeit in religious funding circles, and support for gay rights. In addition, African Anglican bishops stated that they would stop sending African clergy to study theology at Western universities and probe the possibility of initiating a "separate, 'African' theology rejecting gay clergy and same-sex marriages."[89]

Tension around gay rights became public in July 2005 when Anglican parishioners in the Lake Malawi Diocese elected Nicholas Paul Henderson, a white British man, as their next bishop. Henderson had worked with the diocese for eighteen years. Motivated by parishioners' speculation about Henderson's background, Bishop Malango investigated and subsequently refused to install Henderson, "a liberal British vicar," as bishop "because of his support for gay rights."[90] Rumors about Henderson's support for gay rights metamorphosed into speculation that he was gay, a common development when antigay critics wonder why presumably heterosexual people would endorse gay rights.[91] In a letter addressed to Henderson, Bishop Malango inquired

---

86 Felix Malamula, "Anglicans Say No to Bishop-Elect," *Nation*, December 2, 2005, 3.

87 Malawi News Agency, "Malawi Anglicans Denounce Gay Bishop Appointment," *Daily Times*, August 11, 2003, 1, 3; Wadza Otomani, "Primates to Commission Anti-Gay Anglican Bishop," *Daily Times*, September 4, 2003, 5.

88 "Anti-Gay Bishops May Say No to US Funds," *Nation*, April 14, 2004, 7.

89 "African Bishops Break from West Seminaries," *Weekend Nation*, November 6–7, 2004, 5.

90 Taonga Batolo, "Clergy Say Big 'No' to Homosexuality," *Daily Times*, December 11, 2005, 5.

91 Sangwani Mwafulirwa, "I Am Not Gay, Says Anglican Bishop," *Sunday Times*, September 18, 2005, 13.

about rumors that Henderson "currently live[d] with [or had in the past lived with] a male lodger," insinuating that two men, who were not blood relations, would only cohabit if they were in a same-sex relationship and not for financial reasons.[92] Some Lake Malawi Diocese members lodged a complaint claiming that it "would be hypocritical for Malango to accept Henderson who [has] openly shown support for gays when Central Africa and the African Primates (a grouping of bishops) have vehemently challenged western liberal theologies, including recognition of same-sex relationships."[93] Ultimately, the Anglican Church of Central Africa rejected Henderson as the Lake Malawi Diocese bishop.[94]

Discontent among parishioners grew when Malango announced that Henderson would make a "private" visit to the diocese early in 2006.[95] So divided was the congregation that the two "factions, one for the pro-gay priest [Henderson] and the other one against, now have mass at different times on Sundays, suggesting some support for people with same-sex desires."[96] Opponents of Henderson's appointment as bishop claimed that his visit sowed confusion in the diocese, leading parishioners to doubt Malango's resistance to Henderson. Contrary to Malango's announcement that Henderson was visiting Malawi in an unofficial capacity, Lake Malawi Diocese officials welcomed Henderson upon his arrival at the Kamuzu International Airport in Lilongwe. In a public statement, Henderson disputed that he was gay or had endorsed gay rights in the past.[97] Henderson stated, "I have absolutely nothing whatever to do with the gay movement. I have been linked to the gay movement because I was once the general secretary and lately

[92] Maxwell Ng'ambi, "Pro-Gay Bishop Rejected," *Daily Times*, December 2, 2005, 3.

[93] Ibid., 2–3.

[94] Taonga Batolo, "Clergy Say Big 'No' to Homosexuality," *Sunday Times*, December 11, 2005, 5.

[95] Bright Sonani, "Malango Okays Pro-Gay Bishop Visit," *Nation*, February 10, 2006, 2.

[96] Daveson Nyadani, "Same-Sex Sexuality and HIV/AIDS: A Perspective from Malawi," in *From Social Silence to Social Science: Same-Sex Sexuality, HIV & AIDS, and Gender in South Africa*, edited by Vasu Reddy, Theo Sandfort, and Laetitia Rispel (Cape Town: HSRC Press, 2009), 139.

[97] Bright Sonani, "I'm Not Gay – Rejected Bishop," *Nation*, February 13, 2006, 1, 3.

the chairman of a theological society, which is a legal theological society, which discusses many issues including the gay issue."[98]

Henderson's supporters rejected a retired Zambian bishop, James Mwenda, as a replacement and filed an injunction to prevent the diocese from installing him.[99] In Nkhotakota in July 2006, Henderson's supporters mounted a "roadblock" to thwart Mwenda's installation. A machete-wielding attacker ordered supporters to dismantle the roadblock, but the group fought him off and retired to the church. Subsequently, "two Muslim young men ... hired by another Bishop who supports Mwenda" invaded the church and "started threatening people," according to one news account.[100] Some opposed to installing Henderson as a bishop invoked a "gay-for-pay" argument and suggested that Henderson's supporters "are misguided because of the love of money. What they want from this pro-gay Bishop is favours from him."[101] This argument implied that supporters hoped that Henderson's nationality would translate into economic prosperity for the diocese. Henderson's liberal positions on gay rights and other social issues would presumably convince Westerners to invest in business opportunities in the diocese. Although the episode echoed similar debates among African Anglican leaders and had lingering effects on the diocese, it remained contained and involved a diocese removed from Blantyre and Lilongwe.[102] Like African Anglican leaders, other Christian clergy in Malawi, such as those with the Presbyterian Church, voiced disapproval of the ordination of gay clergy.[103] Nevertheless, this episode constituted the merger of political and religious opposition to homosexuality, a unity evident in later episodes of politicized homophobia.

---

[98] Peter Gwayazani, "Anglican Bishop Denies Being Gay," *Daily Times*, February 13, 2006, 3.

[99] Anthony Kasunda, "Anglican Bishop's Offices Still Closed," *Daily Times*, March 7, 2006, 2; Anthony Kasunda, "High Court Throws Out Anglican Case," *Daily Times*, May 26, 2005, 1, 3.

[100] Deborah Nyangulu, "Hooligans Attack Anglican Church," *Daily Times*, July 3, 2006, 2.

[101] Bob Mzunga, "Anglican Bishops Should Stand Firm," *Daily Times*, March 8, 2006, 8.

[102] Edwin Nyirongo, "Court Throws Out Anglican Church Case," *Nation*, May 13, 2009, 3.

[103] Edyth Betha, "Gay Clergy: What the Local Church Says," *Weekend Nation*, July 8–9, 2006, 12.

Public Sympathy for LGBT People and Rights in Malawi

Antipathy toward same-sex sexualities and sexual minority rights abounded in Malawian newspaper accounts. Rarely did Malawians publicly express sympathy for LGBT people and rights. Yet it is important to document the infrequent instances in which Malawians offer public support for LGBT rights or social acceptance of LGBT people because they countered widespread assumptions that Africans are homophobes. For instance, some political and religious elites admitted the existence of sexual minorities in the country.[104] An anonymous person interviewed by a journalist acknowledged that same-sex sexuality is a "social reality in Malawi. There are some who are married to people of opposite sex but are homosexuals at heart. They are afraid to come out into the open because they fear rejection and ostracism."[105]

Although many journalists expressed their displeasure for homosexuality in editorials, the occasional column displayed some sympathy for lesbian and gay organizing and gay rights. For instance, in 2005, Idriss Ali Nassah recounted the hostility that GALZ experienced in 1996 when members exhibited organizational materials at the Zimbabwe International Book Fair in Harare. Nassah explained that "GALZ survived [the] gratuitous violence" resulting from President Robert Mugabe's antigay threats and had enjoyed a growing membership in the intervening years. Describing GALZ's offices as "run like an elite country club – with no raised voices, with soft music, no threats, no uncouth behavior and no coarse language," he stated that GALZ was more professional "than the fanatics who had hounded them out" of the 1996 fair.[106] Nassah depicted GALZ's mobilization in the face of state repression with some compassion.[107] An editorial by Yolamu Nyoni classified those who criticized homosexuality as "immoral" as being "hypocritical" and "uninformed." Invoking sexual minorities'

---

[104] Olivia Kumwenda, "Clergy Warns on Gaiety," *Nation*, April 8, 2005, 1–2.

[105] Jimu, "Homosexuality under Scrutiny," 25.

[106] Idriss Ali Nassah, "Things Stranger than Fiction," *Sunday Times*, November 20, 2005, 4.

[107] Nassah's tone hardened when telling readers to "prepare for a battle for the bitter end because to expect Malawians to welcome homosexuals with open arms in their midst is no different from believing in the fairy tale of the Mermaid." Nassah, "Things Stranger than Fiction," 4.

right to privacy, Nyoni queried, "[W]ho are we therefore to deny others their right to choose for themselves?"[108] In addition to MHRRC's support for decriminalizing same-sex sex and affording sexual minorities the right to privacy, Nyoni's commentary constituted an early defense of sexual minority rights. Other pundits advised newspaper readers to prepare for the eventuality of lesbian and gay organizing in Malawi instead of "just dismissing it with a cultural answer."[109]

Early LGBT Organizing in Malawi

In Malawi, a group of gay and bisexual men and allies formed the Centre for the Development of People (CEDEP) in late 2005 in Blantyre, Malawi's commercial capital in the heavily populated Southern region, to advocate for the inclusion of men who have sex with men (MSM) as a target population in national HIV/AIDS programs.[110] Benjamin, a cofounding member and CEDEP officer, asserted that the inspiration for CEDEP stemmed from a collective interest to create a "movement that is going to give a voice to ... other [sexual minorities] who are not able to speak out."[111] In a 2007 interview, Gift Trapence, then-director of operations at CEDEP, indicted HIV/AIDS organizations that "have very nice policies" of including MSM "on paper but it's only for them to get funds."[112] Trapence's comments pointed to the hypocrisy of NGOs that claimed to include gender and sexual minorities in their advocacy work but only viewed them as useful in terms of generating income from donors for the organization. As Richard, a cofounding CEDEP member, explained:

There were some insinuations from the [AIDS] program implementers saying that they cannot implement programs targeting MSM because the people do not exist, so they took that as an excuse of not doing anything ... so we

---

[108] Yolamu Nyoni, "Legalise Homosexuality," *Daily Times*, January 1, 2006, 15.

[109] Godfrey Mapondera, "Any Malawians Who Are Gays?" *Sunday Times*, November 27, 2005, 24.

[110] Nyadani, "Same-Sex Sexuality and HIV/AIDS." I do not intend for this discussion of early LGBT organizing in Malawi to be exhaustive. Forthcoming research from Crystal Biruk and Alan Msosa historicizes LGBT organizing in Malawi.

[111] Benjamin, interview with the author, June 27, 2012, Blantyre, Malawi.

[112] Charles Mpaka, "Q & A Saturday: Gift Trapence," *Malawi News*, April 14–20, 2007, 5.

thought, "How can they say that people do not exist when we know [they exist]?" Some of them are our friends. Some of them are amongst us. So let's come up with something to mobilize the community.[113]

Cofounding members decided that they had to register CEDEP with the government to gain access to donor and government funds.

Like LGBT activist organizations in other African nations, cofounders believed that they should register CEDEP as a human rights organization and not as an LGBT organization, given the newness of the LGBT rights movement in the country and presence of social homophobia in Malawi.[114] Although CEDEP was a "human rights" organization on paper, staff devoted the minimal resources they had to HIV/AIDS education and advocacy. To avoid additional scrutiny, the group also adopted a nondescript name, as Moses, a cofounding member of CEDEP, explained.[115] Richard stated that activists were worried about political persecution and selected "Centre for the Development of People" as a name so that "we would not be labeled or identified as ... gay."[116] Activists hoped that an innocuous name would protect CEDEP from harassment. LGBT activists in other African countries have used similar naming strategies with success.[117]

Once established as a human rights organization, CEDEP organizers decided that they had a responsibility not only to sexual minorities but also to other vulnerable communities, such as sex workers and prisoners. Like other Malawian organizations, CEDEP focused on funding proposals, education, and outreach and relied heavily on networks of volunteers to conduct work outside the office.[118] Founding members' prior experience working in HIV/AIDS organizations also promoted CEDEP's alignment with public-health practices and technologies. As Thomas, a founding CEDEP member, explained:

---

[113] Richard, interview with the author, June 28, 2012, Blantyre, Malawi.
[114] Currier and Cruz, "Civil Society and Sexual Struggles in Africa."
[115] Moses, interview with the author, July 2, 2012, Lilongwe, Malawi.
[116] Richard, interview with the author, June 28, 2012, Blantyre, Malawi.
[117] Currier and Cruz, "Civil Society and Sexual Struggles in Africa"; Marc Epprecht, "Sexual Minorities, Human Rights, and Public Health Strategies in Africa," *African Affairs*, 111, no. 443 (2012): 223–243.
[118] Susan C. Watkins and Ann Swidler, "Working Misunderstandings: Donors, Brokers, and Villagers in Africa's AIDS Industry," *Population and Development Review*, 38, no. S1 (2013): 197–218.

Most of the politicians have been arguing to say homosexuality does not exist in Malawi ... So, we thought the best way to bring this to them is by conducting research. So, just in 2006, the first activity that we did was to do ... a KAP study: knowledge, attitude, and practices of men who have sex with men in Malawi ... because there was not any other data around in Malawi, not anywhere. So, that was the first data. That was the first statistics. That was the first evidence that people [homosexuals] exist.[119]

In collaboration with Malawian researchers at the University of Malawi and a Zambian researcher at the University of Zambia, the KAP study identified about 100 MSM within a month in Lilongwe and in the Southern region.[120] In a 2009 news interview, Trapence explained that MSM "are all over and they cut across society and demographics. From a villager to those in high office and religious leaders, [MSM] are there, it's happening."[121] Such research opportunities reflected CEDEP's commitment to a public-health strategic orientation, as CEDEP staff and leaders invested heavily in accruing expertise in all areas of HIV/AIDS advocacy, including research.[122]

By establishing the "real" presence of (male) homosexuality in Malawi, this initial, small-scale study executed by CEDEP reinvigorated debate about the criminalization of same-sex sex and created a context in which personal, albeit anonymous, testimonials of LGBT Malawians became possible.[123] CEDEP organizers continued conducting research on how HIV/AIDS impacted MSM. Dr. Eric Umar, a psychologist involved in CEDEP's research, stated that these studies

---

[119] Thomas, interview with the author, June 27, 2012, Blantyre, Malawi. See also Charles Mpaka, "Homosexuality in Malawi Real – Research," *Daily Times*, July 7, 2007, 2.

[120] P. R. T. Ntata, A. S. Muula, and S. Siziya, "Socio-Demographic Characteristics and Sexual Health Related Attitudes and Practices of Men Having Sex with Men in Central and Southern Malawi," *Tanzania Journal of Health Research*, 10, no. 3 (2008): 124–130.

[121] Felix Mponda, "Malawi Has 10,000 Gays – Expert," *Malawi News*, September 26–October 2, 2009, 3–4.

[122] Ashley Currier and Tara McKay, "Pursuing Social Justice through Public Health: Gender and Sexual Diversity Activism in Malawi," *Critical African Studies*, 9, no. 1 (2017): 71–90.

[123] Mpaka, "Homosexuality in Malawi," 2; Charles Mpaka, "Waiting in a Homosexual Closet," *Sunday Times*, April 15, 2007, 14; Mwiza J. Nkhata and Mandala Mambulasa, "Should the Law Legalize Homosexuality?" *Daily Times*, February 4, 2007, 12–13.

were trying to help MSM "practice safe sex so that HIV does not spill over from the gay community to the general public."[124] Leaders obtained funding from foreign donors to rent a house in Blantyre for use as the organization's office. Organizers managed to hire an "office administrator" and an "accountant" and purchased a TV and "videos from friends on MSM" that they screened during "seminars and roundtable discussions to just see what other people in other places are doing," according to Blessings, a cofounding member of CEDEP.[125]

With time, CEDEP officers helped engender receptive attitudes among a few National AIDS Commission (NAC) officials. Blessings explained that eventually, "we were being invited [by NAC] every year to present at national conferences." According to Blessings, NAC officials found CEDEP's work with MSM to be so compelling that

if you read [NAC] work plans ... since 2006, you'll notice that in all the major national plans on HIV and AIDS they mention working with MSM and all that. They were actually literally copying and pasting some of the statements that were in [CEDEP] reports into their policy documents.

CEDEP initiated HIV/AIDS advocacy in the mid- and late-2000s at a time when sexual diversity received only occasional, negative scrutiny from political officials. The episodic nature of early antihomosexual scorn enabled CEDEP to work with LGBT people unnoticed. However, the arrests and prosecution of Tiwonge Chimbalanga and Steven Monjeza for sodomy in December 2009 turned same-sex sexualities into a "very explosive and divisive issue" throughout 2010, resulting in NAC's distancing from CEDEP for a time, according to Blessings.

Participating in Chimbalanga and Monjeza's defense constituted a turning point, a moment when "new directions" in organizations emerge, for CEDEP.[126] CEDEP's immersion in the couple's legal defense initiated a new pathway for strategic action, leading the organization in the direction of expanded social-justice advocacy.[127] In one sense, CEDEP was beginning to inhabit more fully the human rights

---

[124] Mponda, "Malawi Has 10,000 Gays," 3.

[125] Blessings, interview with the author, July 4, 2012, Lilongwe, Malawi.

[126] Kathleen M. Blee, *Democracy in the Making: How Activist Groups Form* (New York: Oxford University Press, 2012), 70.

[127] Currier and McKay, "Pursuing Social Justice."

role that founders had created for the NGO. However, CEDEP's growing recognition within Malawi as a respected NGO earned it the wrath of President Bingu wa Mutharika's administration and the ruling political party, the Democratic People's Party (DPP). State leaders' threats failed to deter CEDEP officers, as I discuss in subsequent chapters.

From the Politicization of Homosexuality to Politicized Homophobia

When does politicized homosexuality become politicized homophobia? The politicization of homosexuality first circulated (mis)information about gender and sexual diversity. In this way, (mis)information about same-sex sexualities began saturating social and political discourses. In the context of an African society undergoing rapid sociopolitical change, information about "new" sexual practices like same-sex sex generated concerns from different cultural and political elites, such as religious leaders, politicians, and traditional authorities. Responses to these "new" sexual practices became overwhelmingly negative. As elites voiced their anxieties about same-sex sexualities, these anxieties flooded social and political discourses, agglomerating into politicized homophobia.

In the mid-2000s, politicized homosexuality metamorphosed into politicized homophobia in Malawi for two reasons. First, as NGOs perceived to endorse gay rights and same-sex sexualities ascended to public visibility, they became targets of antigay vituperation. Sometimes, political elites directed antihomosexual scorn at particular NGOs, such as MHRRC. As subsequent chapters will show, this targeting became more diffuse, entrapping NGOs portrayed as doing Northern donors' bidding. Second, antihomosexual religious positions solidified into religious homophobia and became fodder for later episodes of politicized homophobia.

Public spectacles can also facilitate the transition of the politicization of homosexuality into politicized homophobia. As I discuss in the next chapter, the arrest, trial, and sentencing of Tiwonge Chimbalanga and Steven Monjeza for violating the antisodomy law became a national and international spectacle attracting attention from local NGOs, such as CEDEP, international human and LGBT rights organizations, Northern donors, and foreign political leaders. International scrutiny fueled politicized homophobia during and after the trial. In particular, Malawian political elites chafed at Northern donors' suggestion of tying development aid to the Malawian government's position on LGBT rights. Politicized homophobia accelerated by the trial ensnared LGBT rights organizations and gender and sexual minorities.

2 | Trials of Love
The Rise of Politicized Homophobia

Homosexuality began saturating political discourses in 2005 in Malawi, beginning with the publicity given to MHRRC's support for a sexual-orientation nondiscrimination clause in the constitution and conflicts within an Anglican diocese over the election of a bishop reported to support gay rights. However, the 2010 prosecution of Tiwonge Chimbalanga and Steven Monjeza concentrated the nation's attention on same-sex sexualities and gender variance in an unprecedented way. The arrests of Chimbalanga, a transgender woman, and Monjeza, a cisgender man, highlighted the criminalization of same-sex sex and provided President Bingu wa Mutharika's government with a convenient platform for escalating the politicization of homosexuality into reactive politicized homophobia with potent consequences for gender and sexual minorities in Malawi, consequences that still reverberate in people's lives.[1]

The trial constituted a historic political spectacle in Malawi, generating awareness about same-sex relationships and serving as an anchor for reactive politicized homophobia as Northern donors pressured Mutharika's administration to release the couple. The trial's "political spectacle" hinged on publicly exposing Chimbalanga and Monjeza's "private life." Although the trial portrayed Chimbalanga and Monjeza both as men, misgendering Chimbalanga in the process, it allowed prosecutors, political elites, and Malawian observers to ponder Chimbalanga's identity as a woman. In turn, the construction of Chimbalanga and Monjeza's love as a perverse oddity served as the ground for inflaming political elites' attitudes toward LGBT rights and gender and sexual diversity.[2] "Political spectacle" refers to the

---

[1] Crystal Biruk offers a thorough analysis of the trial, particularly how witnesses understood Chimbalanga and Monjeza's relationship and interpreted Chimbalanga's femininity. Biruk, "Aid for Gays."

[2] Murray Edelman, *Constructing the Political Spectacle* (Chicago: University of Chicago Press, 1988), 99.

"production of meanings through a display of political power such that transgression and disciplining of the other are seen as the exercise of legitimate power."[3] News coverage of the trial helped transform same-sex sexualities into what Ken Plummer calls public "sexual prob-lem[s]," inciting debate about same-sex sexualities in the public sphere and making them "issue[s] that society must deal with."[4] Debate about how to manage same-sex sexualities falls within the category of the "incitement to discourse" that produces controlling images of same-sex sexualities in Malawi.[5] The trial as spectacle became much more than determining whether Chimbalanga and Monjeza had sex with each other; it served as an informal referendum on the future of same-sex sexualities in Malawi. As a spectacle, the trial focused national and international attention on the constructed peculiarity of same-sex sex, ignoring the loving relationship between Chimbalanga and Monjeza and the fact that their relationship did not fit squarely within the "same-sex" relationship paradigm. The trial politicized same-sex sex and homophobia and generated unprecedented social concerns about same-sex sex and sexualities, construing them as social problems. "Problems create authorities to deal with them, and the threats they name are often personified as enemies."[6] Within the trial's discursive arena, gender and sexual minorities and LGBT rights activists emerged as enemies and threats and government officials as authorities capable of neutralizing these threats. As a political spectacle, the trial saturated cultural and political discourses with information about same-sex sexualities. As the trial and ensuing international attention surprised political elites, these developments converged to produce reactive pol-iticized homophobia in Malawi.

That the trial constituted a political spectacle is evidenced in the increase of news articles mentioning gender or sexual diversity between 2005 and 2010.[7] Figure 2.1 illustrates the surge in publications

---

[3] Shirin M. Rai, "Feminizing Global Governance," in *Gender and Global Politics in the Asia-Pacific*, edited by Bina D'Costa and Katrina Lee-Koo (New York: Palgrave Macmillan, 2009), 100.

[4] Ken Plummer, "The Sexual Spectacle: Making a Public Culture of Sexual Problems," in *Handbook of Social Problems: A Comparative International Perspective*, edited by George Ritzer (Thousand Oaks, CA: Sage, 2004), 523.

[5] Foucault, *The History of Sexuality*, 17.

[6] Edelman, *Constructing the Political Spectacle*, 121.

[7] I collected articles from the *Daily Times*, *Malawi News*, and *Nation* published between 2005 and 2009. When I began this project in 2011, I began collecting

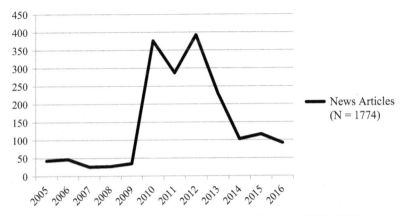

Figure 2.1 Articles mentioning gender or sexual diversity, 2005–2016

focusing attention on the trial. News publications mentioning gender or sexual diversity remained well under 100 for each year between 2005 and 2009, the year in which Chimbalanga and Monjeza were arrested. With the trial, news publications mentioning gender or sexual diversity in 2010 (N = 376) increased more than tenfold from 2009 (N = 35). Newspapers covered all aspects of the arrests, trial, sentencing, and pardons of Chimbalanga and Monjeza.

As a process, the politicization of homosexuality unfolds unevenly and unpredictably, generating competing meanings and urgency for state intervention in homosexuality. Politicized homophobia spilled over into other pressing social problems, entrapping other vulnerable populations, such as homeless youth, into the web of speculation about so-called aberrant sexual practices in the country. In this way, sex infused politics through the sexualization of politics.

Sometimes, debates about sex and sexualities surprise political elites. When conjecture about same-sex sexualities overtakes political discourse, the sexualization of politics can arise. I use the "sexualization of politics" approach to identify when anxieties about sexual communities, practices, and identities spill over into political debate and

articles from *Nyasa Times*; at the time, the online publication's archive only went back to 2010. Therefore, I only have one article from the *Nyasa Times* published in 2010. In 2011, I began systematically gathering articles mentioning gender or sexual diversity from the online repositories of all four publications. When microfilm of more recent years became available, I replaced screenshots of online news articles with copies of original newspaper articles.

trigger new or dormant apprehensions.[8] Some scholars use the term "sexualization of politics" to discuss sexual politics or processes of the politicization of (homo)sexuality more generally.[9] However, I use the term specifically to refer to circumstances in which the treatment of same-sex sexualities as a social problem unexpectedly spills over into other social problems, blurring the lines between different sexual practices and communities. Sexualization traps different vulnerable communities and links them to same-sex sexual practices, tarnishing them with the same stigmatizing brush that affects gender and sexual minorities. In other words, the "sexualization of politics" perspective reflects how discourses of sexuality can unexpectedly engulf political deliberation.

In this chapter, I reconstruct the arrests, trial, and convictions of Chimbalanga and Monjeza and the corresponding rise in reactive politicized homophobia and trace the trial's effects on gender and sexual minorities and NGOs sympathetic to LGBT rights. I also document how politics during the trial became sexualized when political elites diverted attention to the sexual vulnerability of homeless youths.[10] Next, I show how the trial created an opportunity for CEDEP, CHRR, and other organizations to hone their advocacy for gender and sexual minorities yet narrowed the spaces of anonymity that provided gender and sexual minorities freedom and refuge from notoriety. I use interview evidence given by LGB people who were almost unanimous in their agreement that the trial generated unwanted negative visibility for them. The politicized homophobia that the trial intensified also produced adverse outcomes for human rights and LGBT rights NGOs.

---

[8] Irvine, "Transient Feelings."

[9] For examples, see Barbara Bompani and Caroline Valois, "Sexualizing Politics: The Anti-Homosexuality Bill, Party-Politics, and the New Political Dispensation in Uganda," *Critical African Studies*, 8, no. 2 (2016): 1–19; Claire Laurier Decoteau, "The Crisis of Liberation: Masculinity, Neoliberalism, and HIV/AIDS in Postapartheid South Africa," *Men and Masculinities*, 16, no. 2 (2013): 139–159; Valerie Sperling, *Sex, Politics, and Putin: Political Legitimacy in Russia* (New York: Oxford University Press, 2015), 4.

[10] In Chapter 5, I discuss LGB Malawians' perceptions of the effects that politicized homophobia had on their lives and communities.

The Engagement and Arrests

Toward the end of December 2009, Tiwonge Chimbalanga and Steven Monjeza became engaged at the Mankhoma Lodge in Blantyre in a public engagement ceremony known as *chinkhoswe*[11] in Chichewa.[12] Monjeza explained that he met Chimbalanga at church five months earlier. "I have never been interested in a woman, [and] neither has Chimbalanga."[13] Since Chimbalanga worked at the lodge, the owners allowed the couple to hold the ceremony there. Hundreds attended the ceremony. Journalist Caroline Somanje describes how the couple wore "traditional matching outfits" as they celebrated their engagement "under two tents."[14] According to Somanje, guests gawked at Chimbalanga because "his female dressing and make-up did little to disguise his masculinity."[15] Chimbalanga identified as a woman, and coworkers knew her as a woman; her feminine gender presentation aligned with her identification as a woman. The article portrayed the "inquisitive crowd" as "more amused than supportive."[16]

The day after Somanje reported on the engagement ceremony, police arrested the couple for "engaging in an indecent act."[17] Police interpreted the engagement ceremony as confirmation that Chimbalanga and Monjeza had consummated their relationship, which police construed as a same-sex relationship. Davie Chingwalu, the police spokesperson for the Southern Region, held out the possibility that the

---

[11] Joe Mlenga defines *chinkhoswe* as a "prenuptial traditional ceremony in Malawi that involves the kith and kin of two people, hitherto between a man and woman. Gifts are exchanged and advice given to the lovers, and in some societies the event is a substitute of exchanging marriage vows in a church. In such a scenario, couples go straight to live together as a family after the *chinkhoswe*. *Chinkhoswe* is an open and public ceremony, though some hold it privately in the confines of their homes." See Joe Mlenga, "How Sociology Enriches Human Rights: The Case Study of Malawi's First Openly-Gay Couple," in *Beyond the Law: Multi-Disciplinary Perspectives on Human Rights*, edited by Frans Viljoen (Pretoria, South Africa: Pretoria University Law Press, 2012), 103.

[12] For a detailed account of the *chinkhoswe* from Chimbalanga's perspective and her life since the trial, see Mark Gevisser, "Love in Exile," *Guardian*, November 27, 2014, www.theguardian.com/news/2014/nov/27/-sp-transgender-relationship-jail-exile-tiwonge-chimbalanga.

[13] Caroline Somanje, "Gays Engage," *Nation*, December 28, 2009, 2.

[14] Ibid., 1.   [15] Ibid., 2.

[16] Caroline Somanje, "Blantyre Gay Couple Arrested," *Nation*, December 29, 2009, 2.

[17] Ibid.

prosecutor could charge them under Section 156 of the Penal Code, which reads:

Any male person who, whether in public or private, commits any act of gross indecency with another male person, procures another male person to commit any act of gross indecency with him, attempts to procure the commission of any such act by any male person with himself or with another male shall be guilty of a felony and be liable to imprisonment for five years with or without corporal punishment.[18]

Interested bystanders congregated outside the courthouse and generated commotion consistent with a "circus" as they ogled the "gay lovers"[19] who were charged with three separate counts: two counts of buggery (which was spelled as "puggery" in the initial account, suggesting that the journalist was unfamiliar with the term) that violated Section 153 of the Penal Code and occurred when Monjeza had sex with Chimbalanga and Chimbalanga "allowed Monjeza to have sex with him"; and one count of "gross indecency" resulting from the couple cohabiting as "husband and wife."[20] The fact that Malawians left work and gathered to witness the couple as they were escorted to and from the courthouse evidenced ordinary people's growing interest in gender and sexual diversity.[21]

In the days after Chimbalanga and Monjeza's arrests, journalists interviewed people about their attitudes toward gay rights. Some interviewees supported gay rights. Triza Chiduka, a woman from Lunzu, endorsed giving sexual minorities "freedom to operate" because "Malawi is a democratic country which needs to entrench democratic values." She recommended that Malawi should emulate "countries such as South Africa where homosexuality is legal if it is to be recognised as a country that follows principles of democracy." She envisioned Malawi's future as a "recognized" progressive democracy as one that hinged on enshrining and respecting gay rights. Invoking

---

[18] Ibid.

[19] Caroline Somanje, "Gay Couple in Court Today," *Nation*, December 30, 2009, 2.

[20] Caroline Somanje, "Gay Couple Charged with Three Counts," *Nation*, December 31, 2009, 2.

[21] I thank Tara McKay for pointing out that those who congregated outside the courthouse to catch a glimpse of the couple left work, an important consideration in a country in which poverty and underemployment remain major concerns.

the liberal-democratic principle of individual rights, Gift Dafuta, a man from Ndirande, argued that sexual minorities should be able to "exercise their rights and they should not be infringed upon in any way."[22]

Chimbalanga and Monjeza's arrests elicited much media coverage in Malawi and internationally, including calls for their release from police custody[23] and privately expressed concerns about the government permitting the trial to continue.[24] News coverage turned the couple's public appearances into spectacles of gender and sexual nonconformity for Malawian readers. Somanje described how the police "tried in vain to shield the lovebirds who turned into celebrities overnight with their unusual tale of gay union."[25] The reporter recognized the genuine affection that Chimbalanga and Monjeza displayed for one another but seemed puzzled by their public declaration of joining their lives together. Their arrival at the courthouse aroused the curiosity of Blantyre residents who attempted to catch a "glimpse" of the "handcuffed couple … during a cat-and-mouse chase that lasted close to 45 minutes."[26] Somanje portrays Chimbalanga, "the wife," as seeking the attention of others when she "turned the court corridors into a modelling show as he catwalked alongside the husband who was the complete opposite as he shied away from media cameras and the jeering crowd."[27] Curious onlookers congregated outside the courthouse and

---

[22] Eliah Nthara, "Mixed Views on Legalising Homosexuality," *Nation*, January 4, 2010, 4. All quotations in this paragraph come from this source.

[23] Caroline Somanje, "Amnesty Wants Gays Released," *Nation*, January 8, 2010, 1–2.

[24] Leaked cables between the US embassy in Malawi and State Department confirmed a private meeting that Mutharika convened on January 18, 2010, with key foreign diplomats. At this meeting, the German ambassador raised concerns about the prosecution of Chimbalanga and Monjeza and inquired whether the government would assess the "constitutionality" of laws governing same-sex sexualities. Government representatives defended the antisodomy laws, while Mutharika vehemently deplored same-sex sexualities. See Tara McKay, "Invisible Men: Constructing Men Who Have Sex with Men as a Priority at UNAIDS and Beyond," PhD dissertation (Los Angeles: University of California, Los Angeles, Department of Sociology, 2013), 134, and United States Government, "10LILONGWE37, Malawi: Donors to Rare Tour D'Horizon with President Mutharika," WikiLeaks, January 19, 2010, http://wikileaks.org/cable/2010/01/10LILONGWE37.html.

[25] Somanje, "Gay Couple Charged," 2.   [26] Ibid.

[27] Somanje, "Amnesty Wants Gays Released," 1–2.

police station "singing wedding songs" and jeered at the couple who were being transported to court proceedings.[28]

News reports sensationalized Chimbalanga's gender presentation as being out of step with heteronormative behavior, while the state's prosecution of Chimbalanga both interpellated her as a man and made space for contemplating her life as a Malawian woman. Additional reporting detailed Chimbalanga's gender identity as a woman. An acquaintance of Chimbalanga's claimed that she hid her male sex when working at the lodge and that she disrobed to prove her femaleness. According to the acquaintance, Chimbalanga undressed in front of her and two friends and revealed "ladies' underpants, which was yellow. He suppressed the manhood between his legs and insisted that he was female until I asked him to spread his legs and boom! Down it dangled to everyone's shock."[29] Such testimony depicted Chimbalanga as a misgendered curiosity deserving of social ostracism and contempt. Crystal Biruk discusses how Chimbalanga performed womanhood in her community.

Tiwonge was a proper woman in many ways – attending church regularly and seeking to follow traditional womanly protocols for a proper engagement and marriage to Steven. Retrospectively, then, we might read the series of acts recalled during the trial – a pastor's agreement to take on a role as a traditional marriage counsellor (ankhoswe) to the couple when asked by Steven, the engagement photographer's willingness to serve as a marriage advocate for Tiwonge, the loaning of zitenje to Tiwonge by [another woman], the admission of Tiwonge into a church congregation as a woman, and her employment in women's work at a lodge – as individual acts that accumulatively verified Tiwonge as a "woman" in her community. Indeed, locally, Tiwonge was known by the nickname "Auntie Tiwo."[30]

In a variety of ways, Chimbalanga's community recognized and welcomed her as a woman, yet news media and many Malawians treated her as an oddity.

---

[28] Caroline Somanje, "'Aunt Tiwo,' Monjeza Denied Bail for Safety," *Nation*, January 5, 2010, 2–3.

[29] Caroline Somanje, "'Aunt Tiwo' Concealed Status for Money – Witness," *Nation*, January 12, 2010, 2.

[30] Biruk, "Aid for Gays," 458. A *zitenje*, also known as a wrapper, is a piece of fabric that many Malawian women wrap around their abdomens to fashion a skirt. Zitenje is sometimes spelled "chitenje."

The prosecutor alleged the following about the couple's relationship: (1) Monjeza committed "buggery," a violation of Section 153a; (2) Chimbalanga let Monjeza have sex with her, a violation of Section 153c; and (3) the couple committed "gross indecency" when they "lived together as husband and wife," a violation of Section 156. Prosecutors cited the couple's five-month cohabitation as evidence of their sexual intimacy.[31] When Chimbalanga and Monjeza were charged with two counts of violating the antisodomy statute and one count of gross indecency, Dickens Mwambazi, the prosecutor, argued for their indefinite "remand," fearing that the couple might "tamper with evidence."[32] Mwambazi supported subjecting Chimbalanga and Monjeza to invasive medical examinations that were supposed to confirm whether they had had sex with each other, examinations that positioned both Chimbalanga and Monjeza as men.[33] With what evidence did Mwambazi fear that the couple would tamper? Did Mwambazi believe that they would destroy evidence confirming their love relationship or related to their sexual relationship? Mauya Msuku, a defense lawyer, expressed incredulity at Mwambazi's request: "How can [Chimbalanga and Monjeza] tamper with evidence when they don't even know which doctor will examine them or the witnesses?"[34] Msuku argued that Chimbalanga and Monjeza had the right to bail and that government prosecutors wanted to deny them bail so that they could build their case while the arrested couple remained jailed. Msuku claimed that the "State should have done its homework before arresting the two, otherwise we assume there is no offence. The approach to arrest and investigate later is unsafe."[35] Ultimately, the magistrate declined to release the couple on bail in the interest of keeping them safe, away from hostile antigay spectators,

---

[31] Ibid., 456. [32] Somanje, "Gay Couple Charged," 2.

[33] As in some other African nations, Malawian law enforcement officers sometimes forced men and transgender women suspected of violating antisodomy laws to undergo intrusive anal examinations. According to a 2016 Human Rights Watch report, when police do not know how to proceed with antisodomy arrests and prosecutions, they are often "at a loss as to how to find 'proof' to help convict those who had been denounced for same-sex conduct but had not been caught in the act"; in such cases, they resort to "anal examinations." See Human Rights Watch, "Dignity Debased: Forced Anal Examinations in Homosexuality Prosecutions," July 12, 2016, www.hrw.org/report/2016/07/12/ dignity-debased/forced-anal-examinations-homosexuality-prosecutions.

[34] Somanje, "Gay Couple Charged," 2. [35] Ibid.

given the attention that their arrests had elicited inside and outside of Malawi.[36] After denying the couple bail, the magistrate allowed Chimbalanga to speak on the issue of bail because "the court wanted not to be seen to be oppressing anyone."[37] Chimbalanga stated,

People who used to come and visit us are no longer coming to see us; we are suffering the place [jail] is not good. We are Malawians and we cannot run away. Even the security they are talking about, no one can harm us; we are safe.[38]

Chimbalanga testified to the bleak jail conditions and isolation she and Monjeza experienced while being confined without bail.

The Prosecution and Reactive Politicized Homophobia

Journalists covered the trial's phases in detail, from arrest to sentencing. At a February 2010 evidentiary hearing, those charged with assessing the mental competency of Chimbalanga and Monjeza affirmed they found "nothing mentally wrong with the suspects," a declaration that challenged popular opinion that they had psychological disorders.[39] News media sensationalized the trial, which drew local and international onlookers. News coverage addressed how Chimbalanga and Monjeza were subjected to invasive physical examinations to ascertain whether they had anal sex and to verify whether Chimabalanga was a "woman."[40] These examinations generated the possibility of considering Chimbalanga as both a man and a woman, destabilizing the state's construction of her fixed gender identity as a man. Such intrusive examinations legitimize the state's power to compel queer bodies to produce evidence of "homocriminality," a term Amar Wahab uses to signify how queer people only become legible in

---

[36] Caroline Somanje, "There Are Many Gays in Malawi," *Nation*, January 1, 2010, 3.

[37] Wezzie Nkhoma-Somba, "Lawyer's Licence Affects Gays Case," *Daily Times*, February 4, 2010, 3.

[38] Nkhoma-Somba, "Lawyer's Licence," 3.

[39] Max Mpotazingwe, "Gay Case Ruling March 22," *Daily Times*, February 19, 2010, 3.

[40] Frank Namangale, "Aunt Tiwo's Fate March 22," *Nation*, February 19, 2010, 2.

postcolonial states' legal frameworks as "criminals."[41] State-sponsored disciplining of gender and sexual dissidents also buttressed Mutharika's regime, which could paint any group that would dare to question their actions as traitors to heteronormative nationalism.

Upholding the political spectacle, news stories revealed public fascination with the mechanics of same-sex sex, an example of how producing knowledge about same-sex sexualities is part of the function of the politicization of homosexuality. For instance, stories related how Chimbalanga narrated to examiners how she and Monjeza "had anal sex."[42] Chimbalanga "played the role of a wife," and Monjeza "play[ed] the role of a husband," a gendered depiction of same-sex sex.[43] However, the "details" of how precisely Chimbalanga and Monjeza had sex "were too explicit to be published."

During the prosecution, journalists commented on Chimbalanga's gender identity and performance. Occasional stories identified Chimbalanga as a "bride," certifying her gender identity as a woman.[44] In a story about the couple's decision not to call witnesses for their defense, the journalist noted,

As usual a crowd of people gathered at the court to see the couple and some were peeping through the window as proceedings were underway.

It took the Police Mobile Force Officers who were providing security at the court to chase the crowd. Chimbalanga popularly known as Aunt Tiwo continued amazing people as he continued displaying his effeminate flirting characteristics.[45]

This representation of Chimbalanga objectified her feminine gender presentation, interpreting her preference for skirts over trousers as curious signs of gender variance. Monjeza's attire and gendered behavior were apparently heteronormative enough not to warrant commentary. As Malawians continued to gather outside the courthouse to observe Chimbalanga, the crowds affirmed how the trial functioned as a political spectacle.

---

[41] Amar Wahab, "Homophobia as the State of Reason: The Case of Postcolonial Trinidad and Tobago," *GLQ*, 18, no. 4 (2012): 488.

[42] Taonga Sabola, "All Eyes on Malawi as Court Sentences Gay Couple," *Nation*, May 20, 2010, 6.

[43] Namangale, "Aunt Tiwo's Fate," 2.

[44] Nkhoma-Somba, "Lawyer's Licence," 3.

[45] Theresa Chapulapula, "Gays Remain Silent," *Daily Times*, April 7, 2010, 3.

As the trial proceeded, pundits commented disapprovingly on Chimbalanga and Monjeza's relationship. Some speculated that the couple staged a public engagement ceremony "for money," an example of the argument that homosexuality amounted to economic prosperity.[46] Steven Nhlane stated that it was possible that

someone ... promised them huge amounts of money to test the waters [on the legality of homosexuality]. He or she must have convinced them that after the Chinkhoswe, they would be arrested, prosecuted, convicted, and sentenced. They would serve jail. Finish the sentence. Come out of prison and find their largesse. Then live happily ever after – after properly [getting] married, of course.

Nhlane concludes that the couple must be "crazy," as "no sane person living a normal life would stoop so low even if lured by whatever amount of money as to pretend to be gay, risk arrest and prosecution and conviction and imprisonment."[47] Such news commentary kept toxic ideas about same-sex sexualities in the public eye, disseminating the political spectacle of the trial throughout the country.

In the first few months of 2010, donors and activists from all over the world voiced opposition to the government's prosecution of Chimbalanga and Monjeza.[48] Frank Kufakwandi, the local representative of the African Development Bank and chairperson of the Common Approach to Budgetary Support (CABS) organization of donor countries, admitted, "The current issue of homosexuals in Malawi has raised a lot of international concern, ... and Malawi needs to handle the issue with care."[49] Frazer Nihorya, the deputy minister of finance, dismissed CABS's warning, reminding newspaper readers that the "public in Malawi is still debating on the issue of homosexuals because it is a new phenomenon in the country. It is the popular opinion of Malawians which will influence government's position on

---

[46] For instance, see Somanje, "'Aunt Tiwo' Concealed Status for Money – Witness," 2.

[47] Steven Nhlane, "Chileka 'Lovebirds' Are Sick," *Malawi News*, January 2–8, 2010, 15.

[48] Mike Chipalasa, "Norway Comments on Gay Arrest," *Daily Times*, March 8, 2010, 3; Emmanuel Muwamba, "African NGOs Want Gay Suspects Released," *Nation*, February 1, 2010, 2.

[49] Thom Khanje, "Donors Speak on Gay Rights," *Daily Times*, March 17, 2010, 1.

the matter."[50] Nihorya's statement grounded the government's response in public opinion, which seemed overwhelmingly against same-sex sexual practices and gay rights. Other government officials remained confident that donors would not withdraw funding because of the government's antihomosexuality position.[51] Donors' warnings put government officials on edge. A lawmaker railed against donors' interference in national affairs, exclaiming, "Malawi is not for sale."[52] As the trial acquired significance in transnational diplomatic and activist circuits, it became imbued with additional layers of meaning. Public speculation about whether politicians would accede to foreign pressure to suspend the trial in exchange for donor funding inspired and invigorated debates that Malawi was "for sale." The trial became an international political spectacle.

Donors' endorsement of LGBT rights also contributed to the subsequent formation of a short-lived antigay movement group, a sign that opposition to same-sex sexualities was gaining traction in the country. A "group of concerned citizens" formed the "Anti-Gay Movement," a grassroots group.[53] Invoking the trope of predatory homosexuality, organizer Grandy Chikweza asserted the need for the group in response to the fact "Malawian children have been exposed to homosexuality" through news coverage of the trial.[54] Chikweza objected to the increasing public visibility of same-sex sexualities on the grounds that it would tempt youth into seriously contemplating the viability of same-sex relationships; this objection mirrored concerns that emerged in 2002 about the *Nation* publishing occasional reports about lived gender and sexual diversity in Northern countries.[55] Preempting the emergence of queer communities also motivated the group's formation. Deploying a wave metaphor to rally support for the group, Chikweza lamented, "This homosexuality wave is moving very fast in Africa and it will come to our shores very soon, so there is

---

[50] Ibid., 3.
[51] Karen Msiska, "Kandodo Upbeat on Donor Funding," *Daily Times*, April 2, 2010, 3.
[52] Kondwani Munthali, "Mulanje MP Blasts Gay Advocates," *Weekend Nation*, January 30, 2010, 4.
[53] Suzgo Khunga, "Anti-Gay Movement Formed," *Daily Times*, March 30, 2010, 3.
[54] Ibid.   [55] I discuss this example in Chapter 1.

need to prepare."[56] A few days after news of the Anti-Gay Movement's launch broke, organizers held a press conference in Lilongwe asking opponents of homosexuality to wear purple as a way to indicate how many Malawians despised same-sex sexual practices. The group also warned donor countries not to "put undue pressure on Malawi to adopt cultures that are alien to the country."[57] Group leaders promised to embark on "campaigns to school Malawians on the evils of homosexuality and to ensure that Malawians stop talking about homosexuality once and for all."[58] After this press conference, the Anti-Gay Movement disappeared from view. Perhaps, widespread opposition to homosexuality made this group superfluous, hastening its demise, or Malawians were busy following other pressing priorities.

The trial also presented religious officials with the opportunity to advertise their views on homosexuality publicly. The Malawi Council of Churches (MCC) lent public support to the government's refusal to submit to donor requests that Chimbalanga and Monjeza's trial be suspended. Bishop Joseph Bvumbwe, MCC board chairperson, offered a concrete example of how aid conditionality – donors' promise of funding under the condition that the government cultivated a pro-gay-rights position – was impacting local churches. According to Bvumbwe, "some donor church partners which bless same-sex partnerships have stopped funding several local churches that are vocal against homosexuality."[59] This evidence confirmed for many that Westerners were working to impose their values on Malawians and that if they did not follow Western wishes, the country would lose much-needed development aid.

Responses to Convictions, Sentencing, and Pardons

A crowd composed of foreign activists and journalists, local activists from CEDEP and CHRR, and interested local onlookers descended on the courthouse in Blantyre on May 19, 2010, to hear the ruling about the fate of the "famous gay couple." Barbara Mchenga, a prosecutor,

---

[56] Khunga, "Anti-Gay Movement Formed," 3.

[57] Deborah Nyangulu-Chipofya, "No to Gays in Malawi – Movement," *Daily Times*, April 9, 2010, 1.

[58] Ibid., 3.

[59] Agnes Mizere, "Churches Challenge Donors on Gays," *Daily Times*, March 19, 2010, 3.

lobbied for a conviction and harsh sentence, arguing that public attention to same-sex sexualities generated by the case would leave a "scar" on the nation; a severe sentence might warn young people about the dangers of same-sex relationships. Mchenga exploited the trial as a political spectacle as she urged the magistrate to convict the couple. The couple's lawyer, Mauya Msuku, claimed that because Chimbalanga and Monjeza were first-time offenders, the criminal code did not require the court to sentence them to prison time. In Msuku's view, the couple had already served time, as they had spent the last five months in jail.[60]

Spending more than two hours reading his ruling, Chief Resident Magistrate Nyakwawa Usiwa Usiwa convicted Chimbalanga and Monjeza on May 19, 2010, on all charges of "indecency and puggery [sic]."[61] The magistrate sentenced Chimbalanga and Monjeza to fourteen years in prison, the harshest penalty allowed under the penal code.[62] The sentence elicited condemnation from many world leaders, including from South African President Jacob Zuma, who issued a statement at the behest of southern African Anglican bishops but declined to ask for the couple's release.[63] Asserting this case represented the "'first and worst' of its kind" in Malawi, Usiwa Usiwa justified why he gave the couple fourteen years in prison with hard labor, the maximum sentence that he could assign. Invoking a national-readiness argument, Usiwa Usiwa explained that "society" was not "ready ... to see its sons getting married to other sons or conducting engagement ceremonies"; he added that he did not believe that Malawians wanted to see "its daughters marry each other."[64] He meant the harsh penalty as a "scaring sentence" so that others would not practice same-sex sex.[65]

The "scaring sentence" served as state repression against not only Chimbalanga and Monjeza but also same-sex-loving people. Police spokesperson Davie Chingwalu viewed the verdict and sentence as a

---

[60] Theresa Chapulapula and Wezzie Nkhoma-Somba, "Gays Guilty," *Daily Times*, May 19, 2010, 1. All quotations in this paragraph come this source.

[61] Ibid., 1.

[62] Wezzie Nkhoma-Somba, "Gays Get 14 Years," *Daily Times*, May 21, 2010, 1, 3.

[63] Suzgo Khunga, "Gay Couple Pardoned," *Sunday Times*, May 30, 2010, 1, 3; Dumbani Mzale, "Norway Tells Malawi to Respect Vulnerable Groups," *Nation*, May 20, 2010, 3.

[64] Nkhoma-Somba, "Gays Get 14 Years," 1.   [65] Ibid.

victory and affirmed that the police would continue enforcing antisodomy laws.[66] In reports about the sentence, some journalists quoted
President Mutharika as saying that homosexuality "is evil and very
bad before the eyes of God. It is against moral[ity] and our cultural
values," one of his first public antigay statements.[67] Minister of Information and Civic Education Reckford Thotho viewed the verdict as
"cause for rejoice for Malawians."[68] Msuku, the couple's lawyer,
promised to appeal the sentence. When asked who was paying his
legal fees, Msuku claimed that the expenses he had incurred (and
would incur) were "minimal" and that he required no "sponsor" for
his services.[69] He represented Chimbalanga and Monjeza "because
I have a heart for my clients which I believe anyone can do."[70]

The prosecution and convictions of Chimbalanga and Monjeza
exposed contradictions in the government's antihomosexuality position. On the one hand, most police, prosecutors, and lawmakers
favored enforcing antisodomy laws to send the message to Malawians
and the world that Mutharika's government would not yield to
Western sexual decadence. On the other hand, the government implemented a National HIV/AIDS Policy that "included a full paragraph
on the need to address HIV among MSM [men who have sex with
men]."[71] Dr. Mary Shawa, the secretary for HIV, AIDS, and Nutrition
in the Ministry of Health, a government official who had reversed her
past stances on same-sex sexualities,[72] recognized sexual minorities as

[66] Ibid.   [67] Nkhoma-Somba, "Gays Get 14 Years," 1, 3.
[68] Dickson Kashoti, "UK, US Condemn Gays' 14-year Sentence," *Daily Times*,
      May 21, 2010, 3.
[69] Wezzie Nkhoma-Somba, "Gays to Appeal," *Daily Times*, May 27, 2010, 1, 3.
[70] Ibid.   [71] McKay, "Invisible Men," 132.
[72] Shawa's comments on same-sex sexualities varied over time. Before police
      arrested Chimbalanga and Monjeza in 2009, Shawa endorsed integrating men
      who have sex with men (MSM) into national efforts to stop the HIV/AIDS
      epidemic. Reuters, "Gay Rights Way to Fight AIDS in Malawi – Official,"
      Nation, September 15, 2009, article on file with author. After the couple's arrest,
      in 2010, Shawa reversed course and stated that it would be hypocritical for the
      government to single out sexual minorities in HIV/AIDS education and
      prevention programs: "You can't say you're providing service to homosexuals
      who are visibly not acceptable by both law and cultural values and traditions of
      the people of Malawi. Won't people say government is insane?" Grey Kasunda,
      "Homosexuality Is Alien to Malawi," *Nation*, January 8, 2010, 4. Two months
      later, Shawa confirmed that NAC served MSM under programs targeting
      "multiple concurrent sexual partners." Caroline Somanje, "Govt's HIV
      Prevention Strategy Recognises Gay Relationships," *Nation*, March 9, 2010, 3.

a population vulnerable to HIV/AIDS.[73] Shawa also affirmed the need to study what percentage of MSM were HIV-positive, suggesting that the estimate of 21 percent was too low.[74] This official recognition of the need to incorporate MSM into HIV/AIDS education and prevention programs contradicted the ruling government's resolute antihomosexuality position.[75]

Responses to the convictions and sentences contributed to the trial's ongoing political spectacle. Many Christian and Muslim leaders and traditional authorities embraced the verdict and harsh sentence, arguing that it would discourage sexual minorities from pursuing same-sex relationships.[76] Sheik Yusuf Kanyamula, the chairperson of the Muslim Association of Malawi (MAM), called for the court to add several more years to the couple's sentences and suggested that the

---

In 2011, Shawa advised NGOs not to "use HIV and AIDS to advocate [for] gays." Bright Sonani, "'Gays Vital in HIV Fight,'" *Nation*, April 27, 2011, 3. In 2012, she stated, "Homosexuality in Malawi is illegal. Secondly within our culture, people of the same sex marrying or being involved in sexual exploits is not normal. It is absolutely unacceptable." Anthony Kasunda, "Govt's Gay Hypocrisy," *Nation*, February 24, 2012, 3.

[73] James Chavula, "Embracing the Gay Phenomenon," *Nation*, January 11, 2010, 21; Bright Sonani, "Gays Vital in HIV Fight," *Nation*, April 27, 2011, 3; Bright Sonani, "Recognise Gays in AIDS Fight – Shawa," *Nation*, September 16, 2009, 2.

[74] Suzgo Khunga, "Bingu Stops Comments on Gays," *Daily Times*, June 3, 2010, 1, 3.

[75] Not all HIV/AIDS experts and workers were eager to embrace MSM in their work. Anne Esacove documents hostile attitudes Malawian HIV/AIDS workers held toward male-male sex. "Men's same-sex desire and activity are … construed as deviant and dangerous (in the same category as sex workers and drug users) and unnatural (i.e., situation). The overwhelming silence also reinforces the myth that identities and sexualities based on same-sex desire do not exist in Africa. This, in turn, limits HIV-prevention efforts aimed at men who have sex with other men and supports repressive anti-homosexuality sentiment and legislation." In addition, silence about sexual diversity in HIV/AIDS work "desexualizes women" and sublimates "women's same-sex desire … There is not a single reference to women having sex with other women in the industry interviews and the policy documents do not include special discussions or make reference to women having sex with other women in general discussions of risk or prevention." Anne Esacove, *Modernizing Sexuality: US HIV Prevention in Sub-Saharan Africa* (New York: Oxford University Press, 2016), 26.

[76] Samuel Chibaya, "Chiefs Hail Usiwa Usiwa," *Nation*, May 23, 2010, 4.

death penalty for homosexuality, as sanctioned by the Q'uran, was warranted.[77] Sheik Jaarfar Kawinga, also of MAM, averred, "We are not a country which does filthy things."[78] Some NGO leaders also welcomed the sentence. Billy Banda, executive director of Malawi Watch, supported the sentence but worried that it would provoke a response abroad because the trial garnered international scrutiny. He warned the "international community" not to use "homosexuality as a condition" for releasing development aid to Malawi.[79]

Local LGBT and human rights activists bemoaned the lengthy sentence and explored the possibility of appealing Usiwa Usiwa's ruling.[80] Trapence, CEDEP's executive director, characterized the fourteen-year prison sentence as "unrealistic and one of the harshest ever to be handed on two consenting adults ... Even in a defilement case [involving the sexual abuse of girls], nobody has been given 14 years."[81] However, Trapence recognized that the verdict was "expected because the two were practically already convicted through the media, judging from comments raised by politicians and others."[82] Trapence's comment captured the role of political spectacle in generating reactive politicized homophobia. Along with Malawian LGBT and human rights activists, American and British lawmakers and activists criticized the conviction and "retrogressive" sentence.[83] A British gay rights activist promised to assist Chimbalanga and Monjeza with securing asylum in the country of their choosing.[84]

Most Malawians accepted the maximum sentence the couple received.[85] Some interpreted the sentence as deterring others from seeking out same-sex relationships. In addition, others speculated that the couple staged an engagement ceremony after receiving encouragement from "nongovernmental organisations which are championing

---

[77] Theresa Chapulapula and Wezzie Nkhoma-Somba, "Ruling Excites Clergy," *Daily Times*, May 21, 2010, 3. MAM's support for the death penalty resurfaced in 2014, which I discuss in the concluding chapter.

[78] Paida Mpaso, "Religious Leaders Support 'Gay' Ruling," *Nation*, May 23, 2010, 1.

[79] Chapulapula and Nkhoma-Somba, "Ruling Excites Clergy," 3.   [80] Ibid.

[81] Caroline Somanje, "14 Years IHL!," *Nation*, May 21, 2010, 2.   [82] Ibid.

[83] Kashoti, "UK, US Condemn," 3.

[84] Caroline Somanje, "Pardoned Monjeza, Chimbalanga Offered Asylum," *Nation*, June 1, 2010, 3.

[85] Vales Mchila, "Malawi Has Rights, Too," *Daily Times*, May 24, 2010, 9; Fletcher Simwaka, "Reasoning beyond 13," *Daily Times*, May 28, 2010, 5.

gay rights."[86] One letter to the editor thanked the magistrate for meting out a harsh sentence in defense of the country's heteronormative "values ... donor aid or no donor aid."[87] The letter's author disparaged Malawians who claimed that "whatever comes from the West is the best. They go to the extent of reminding us of our poverty and how we depend on donor aid ... [W]e should never sacrifice the values that define us as a nation because of donor aid which has dirty preconditions," a clear sexualization of donor aid.[88] Other people cited the importance of upholding the magistrate's sentence as a way to defend the nation's sovereignty. One man questioned, "What is democracy if we can't be allowed to make our own decisions as a country?"[89] One pundit criticized LGBT rights activists for promoting a "universal culture that regulates the sense of right or wrong" and ignoring that "almost all nations ... have their own ways of defining human wrongs and human rights."[90] Such commentary partially blamed LGBT rights activists for generating visibility for same-sex sexualities in countries in which same-sex sex is outlawed.

Reacting to the convictions of Chimbalanga and Monjeza, some ordinary Malawians worried that same-sex marriage would ruin their marriage prospects, skewing the local marriage market. One woman questioned: "If men marry each other who will marry me?"[91] This woman speculated that legalizing same-sex marriage would entice men to marry another man. Another woman observed, "There are many women in the country waiting for such men to marry them."[92] Opponents who employed this marriage-market logic typically assumed that men were sexually fickle, beguiled into sexual novelty.[93] After the trial,

---

[86] Eliah Nthara, "Court Right to Impose 14 Years on Gays," *Nation*, May 24, 2010, 4.

[87] Clement Kana, "Thumbs Up for Usiwa Usiwa!," *Nation*, May 28, 2010, 15.

[88] Ibid.

[89] Fatsani Gunya, "Donors, Rights Groups Wrong to Condemn Gays Sentence," *Nation*, May 27, 2010, 6.

[90] Taonga Sabola, "Righting Human Wrongs," *Nation*, May 27, 2010, 15.

[91] Chapulapula and Nkhoma-Somba, "Ruling Excites Clergy," 3; Bartholomew Kawina, "More Support 14-Year Gays Sentence," *Nation*, May 26, 2010, 6.

[92] Kawina, "More Support 14-Year Gays Sentence," 6.

[93] Emmie Chanika, John L. Lwanda, and Adamson S. Muula, "Gender, Gays, and Gain: The Sexualised Politics of Donor Aid in Malawi," *Africa Spectrum*, 48, no. 1 (2013): 96.

one man asked, "These men are insane, why would they want to marry each other when women are there to marry?"[94]

The sentence cast a pall over HIV/AIDS advocacy in the country. The executive director of UNAIDS, Michel Sedibé, expressed concern that the sentence would drive sexual minorities "underground," worsening the HIV/AIDS epidemic. Sedibé explained that sexual minorities act as "vector[s] of transmission because they don't have access to services, treatment or preventive measures."[95] Sexual minorities slipped into anonymity and invisibility to preserve their safety, but their invisibility, a result of their social and political ostracism, contributed to the HIV/AIDS public-health crisis in Malawi, according to Sedibé's logic. This interpretation indirectly blamed sexual minorities for passing HIV to unsuspecting same-sex partners; if they braved the withering consequences of homophobia to visit a clinic and receive medical care, they would behave responsibly and protect themselves and others from the depredation of HIV/AIDS.

Not all Malawians embraced the harsh sentence.[96] In one letter to the editor, the author deployed a national-readiness argument that "Malawi is not ready for homosexuality" but claimed that the "sentence [should] have been less than 14 years" while

there are rapists, murderers, and other criminals roaming our streets. If such people go to court they will only be given a few years in jail, yet they violated other people's lives, but the gay couple practised sodomy in the confines of their homes and did not disturb anyone's life.[97]

Other Malawians shared the letter writer's views that the fourteen-year sentence was "excessive."[98] A right-to-privacy argument bolstered some opinions. One woman from Lilongwe stated that the couple "should have been left alone because they are adults and, therefore, are responsible for their choices. If what they did is a sin, then it is

---

[94] Chapulapula and Nkhoma-Somba, "Ruling Excites Clergy," 3.

[95] Suzgo Khunga, "UNAIDS, Global Fund Bosses Discuss Gays with Bingu," *Daily Times*, May 26, 2010, 4. All quotations in this paragraph come from this source.

[96] Majono, "14 Years of 'Hell on Earth,'" *Sunday Times*, May 23, 2010, 10. See also, Luntha Chalira, "Mixed Views on 14-Year Sentence," *Nation*, May 25, 2010, 4; Gunya, "Donors, Rights Groups Wrong," 6; Kawina, "More Support 14-year Gays Sentence," 6.

[97] James Chalera, "Gay Ruling Too Harsh," *Nation*, May 23, 2010.

[98] Chalira, "Mixed Views on 14-Year Sentence," 4; Kawina, "More Support 14-Year Gays Sentence," 6.

between them and their God and who are we to cast stones at them?"[99]
This woman also applauded donors' criticism of the sentence, stating,
"Donors have the right to speak on the matter because they pump their
money in various areas such as good governance and rule of law."[100]
One editorial objected to the sentence, citing how a long prison term
would harm Chimbalanga psychologically, although the editorial's
author interrogated her gender identity:

What ... would a 14-year jail term achieve to [sic] someone like "Aunt
Tiwo"? The man practically thinks he is a woman; dresses and walks like a
lady and is gender disoriented ... How would confining such a man to
14 years in an environment where homosexuality is said to be ripe supposed
to help solve anything? Won't that make the problem worse?[101]

The editorial suggested that a long prison sentence would not only hurt
Chimbalanga mentally but also encourage the same-sex relationship to
continue in prison.[102]

Ten days after their sentencing, Mutharika pardoned Chimbalanga
and Monjeza, a move that outraged and puzzled many Malawians.[103]
The pardons extended the trial's political spectacle. While United

---

[99] Gunya, "Donors, Rights Groups Wrong," 6.   [100] Ibid.
[101] Onaliyera, "Why Being Lenient on Defilers?," *Sunday Nation*, May 23, 2010.
[102] Two criticisms of the prison sentence are worth singling out. First, one
anonymous author of a letter to the editor identified as gay and employed a
born-this-way argument to encourage Malawians to abandon "homophobia,"
"stigma," and "hate speeches." The newspaper published the letter writer's
email address. See "Give Gays a Break," *Sunday Times*, May 23, 2010, 6.
   Second, an isolated criticism of the sentence highlighted the antisodomy law's
colonial origins, while reminding readers of the love Chimbalanga and
Monjeza had for each other.

To the critics of the 14-year sentence it is love which is on trial and the
conviction of the two gays is ... proof that people can be punished for simply
loving each other, thanks to an old colonial rule framed by Britons at the time
they were colonizers of Malawi, then Nyasaland.

MANA and Times Reporters, "Linking Aid to Gay Rights Is Absurd," *Daily
Times*, May 24, 2010, 3. This analysis came close to calling for decriminalizing
same-sex sex, which would constitute an act of legal decolonization. For
southern African LGBT activist arguments about decolonizing the law through
decriminalizing same-sex sex, see Currier, "Decolonizing the Law."
[103] Luntha Chalira, "Mixed Views on Presidential Pardon," *Nation*, May 31,
2010, 4; Fatsani Gunya, "More Speak on Presidential Pardon," *Nation*, June 1,
2010, 4; Bartholomew Kawina, "Balaka Differs on Gays Pardon," *Nation*,
June 3, 2010, 6.

Nations (UN) Secretary-General Ban Ki-moon visited Malawi in May 2010, he urged Mutharika to pardon the couple. When Mutharika pardoned the couple, he explained that he did not "condone their actions," vilifying Chimbalanga and Monjeza's relationship as "disgusting, demeaning, and a disregard of our culture, religion, and laws."[104] Regarding their trial as just, Mutharika insinuated that Chimbalanga and Monjeza became engaged in a public ceremony with the purpose of "caus[ing] stress and challeng[ing] our laws."[105] He issued the pardon because "he refused to allow the two gays to taint Malawi's democratic image to the outside world."[106] According to Mutharika, the trial's political spectacle compelled him to pardon the couple as a way to rehabilitate Malawi's reputation in international diplomatic and human rights circles.

News coverage portrayed the pardon as Mutharika relenting to "pressure" from the UN and Western countries.[107] According to one report, "[t]here were fears that if [Malawi] had not bowed down to international pressure to release the two, it would have lost out [on] aid as most donors perceived the two arrest[s] and sentencing as a violation of human rights."[108] When announcing the pardon, Mutharika emphasized that he still objected to homosexuality but pardoned Chimbalanga and Monjeza on "humanitarian grounds," a possible attempt at pacifying international donor and activist audiences. In his own speech, Ban referred to a conversation he had with Mutharika about "the issue of gays," commending the president's decision to pardon the couple.[109] Ban mentioned that he would later talk with lawmakers about reforming antisodomy laws.

CEDEP and CHRR leaders welcomed the pardon. Referring to the high-profile nature of the case, Undule Mwakasungula, CHRR's executive director, argued that sexual minority rights were on the "'international agenda and Malawi can't run away from it.'"[110] Mwakasungula was right. The state's prosecution of Chimbalanga and Monjeza captured the attention of Malawians, international donors, and Western activists, igniting a public debate about

---

[104] Caroline Somanje, "Bingu Blasts Donors on Gays," *Nation*, June 3, 2010, 1.
[105] Suzgo Khunga, "Gay Couple Pardoned," *Sunday Times*, May 30, 2010, 1.
[106] Ibid., 3.   [107] Khunga, "Gay Couple Pardoned," 1.   [108] Ibid., 3.
[109] Ibid.
[110] "Rights Groups, Lawyer Welcome Gays' Pardon," *Sunday Times*, May 30, 2010, 3.

homosexuality and unleashing reactive politicized homophobia. Yet it was unclear how the state should proceed after the pardon. Antisodomy statutes in the penal code contradicted the constitution's prohibition of discrimination on the basis of sex, prompting the need for the "harmonisation" of sex laws.[111] "[I]nternational scrutiny" would inevitably result if the government mistreated sexual minorities, according to one editorial.[112] "We will still have problems if some homosexuals come out in the open because our laws will not tell us exactly what to do with them."[113] The politicized homophobia stemming from the trial's spectacle was unlikely to abate if LGBT rights advocacy continued.

The pardon surprised many lawmakers and NGO leaders. The Malawi Law Society portrayed the pardon as possibly illegal and cautioned the president about "willy-nilly decid[ing] to pardon."[114] Linda, a prominent Malawian women's rights activist, commented on how Mutharika pardoned the couple "without consulting the ministers [in] his cabinet."[115] Lucy, a human rights activist, construed Mutharika's pardons as stemming from his prior employment at the UN.

It was definitely a challenge for the president because ... he worked in the UN structures. So he knew well what those people were getting to. And I think that's the reason why he had to resort to a pardon. He [used to work] for the UN ... I mean, we [NGOs] made a lot of noise. We were up in arms and whatever, but [Mutharika] was quiet throughout. And it only took Ban Ki-moon flying in for a few hours to convince this guy, and wam-bam, they were pardoned.[116]

In an interview, Jerry, a local activist and pundit, interpreted the fact that "two gay men dared to engage" and their subsequent conviction as "one of the blessings in this country now" because the government's handling of the case revealed "exactly how non-democratic we are."[117] Although Jerry ignored the indignities Chimbalanga and Monjeza

---

[111] "Our Laws Need Harmonisation," *Sunday Times*, May 30, 2010, 4.
[112] Ibid.   [113] Ibid.
[114] Caroline Somanje, "Law Society Faults Bingu on Gays Information Directive," *Nation*, June 4, 2010, 2.
[115] Linda, interview with the author, June 25, 2012, Blantyre, Malawi.
[116] Lucy, interview with the author, July 3, 2012, Lilongwe, Malawi.
[117] Jerry, interview with the author, July 3, 2012, Lilongwe, Malawi.

suffered throughout the trial and their incarceration, he viewed the case as showing how Mutharika's administration rejected principles of democratic governance, evidence of mounting authoritarianism.

In the days after issuing the pardon, Mutharika's antigay vituperation became more pronounced. Unhappy with the continued media attention on his decision to pardon the couple, Mutharika issued a government-wide moratorium on discussing the case.[118] He wanted the government's silence on gay rights to set a "trap" for donors "to see what they want us to do next."[119] Although Mutharika hoped that the moratorium would make "donors ... feel ashamed" for manipulating him into doing their bidding by pardoning Chimbalanga and Monjeza, he stipulated that the pardon had ended the public visibility and fascination the trial generated for gay rights.[120] He seemed to view the moratorium as slowing or ending the political spectacle that the trial had created in relation to same-sex sexualities. The pardons allowed Mutharika to regain control of the national narrative about morality so that "the two gays" could not "taint Malawi's democratic image to the outside world."[121] This statement confirmed Mutharika's concern about Malawi's international reputation. Implicit in his formulation is the association of democracy and national sovereignty with heteronormative morality, an equation out of step with international norms linking LGBT rights with democratic engagement.

Consistent support from political elites for the arrests, prosecution, convictions, and sentencing of Chimbalanga and Monjeza and accompanying denunciations of same-sex sexualities escalated the politicization of same-sex sexualities into reactive politicized homophobia. The trial served as a stage for political elites to rehearse their collective distaste for same-sex sexualities, portray same-sex sexualities as foreign and dangerous to Malawian culture, and contain or eliminate same-sex sexualities from society. As political spectacle, the trial became a common referent in subsequent discourses of politicized homophobia.

---

[118] Somanje, "Bingu Blasts Donors," 2; see also, Suzgo Khunga, "Bingu Stops Comments on Gays," *Daily Times*, June 3, 2010, 1, 3.
[119] Khunga, "Bingu Stops Comments," 1, 3.   [120] Ibid.   [121] Ibid.

Consequences of Politicized Homophobia during and after the Trial

After Chimbalanga and Monjeza were arrested, local newspapers ran a series of stories about how older Malawian men or male tourists offered homeless boys money for sex. State officials suggested "sweeping street children" away to juvenile detention centers as a way to protect them from the lures of homosexuality and commercial sex work.[122] Their recommendation activated cultural frames that portrayed street children as criminals in training and in need of correction administered by the state. The politicized homophobia that originated with the arrests of Chimbalanga and Monjeza metamorphosed into state officials' concern with the social problems associated with homeless youth; state officials helmed debates about restoring heteronormative social order. Many gender and sexual minorities in Malawi also experienced stress as the trial of Chimbalanga and Monjeza unfolded in Blantyre and in the media nationwide. In addition, LGBT and human rights NGOs experienced adverse consequences related to their defense of gender and sexual minority rights. In this section, I document the consequences produced by politicized homophobia that different social movements and LGB Malawians experienced during and after the trial.

Sexualization of Politics: Same-Sex Sexualities and Homeless Youth

In the weeks following the arrests of Chimbalanga and Monjeza for violating the antisodomy law, public fascination with same-sex sexualities saturated media discourses as Malawian newspapers linked homosexuality to homeless youth, described in the media as "street children." News stories alternately depicted homeless male youth as vulnerable to sexual predators and as criminals in need of incarceration.[123] Coverage of homosexuality and homeless youth metamorphosed into the sexualization of politics, as journalists, activists, and

---

[122] Deogratias Mmana, "Children's Court to Join Govt in Relocating Street Children," *Weekend Nation*, January 30, 2010, 6.

[123] Suzgo Khunga, "Ministry Warns Defiant Children," *Sunday Times*, April 4, 2010, 2; Agnes Mizere, "Sodomised Orphan Appeals for Justice," *Sunday Times*, April 4, 2010, 2.

political elites weighed in on the burgeoning social problem of youth being drawn into same-sex relationships. Through the sexualization of politics, journalists shared graphic, even-prurient discussions of how older men cajoled homeless boys into same-sex sexual liaisons. Pre-occupations with details about boys' sexual vulnerability generated the suggestion of a misguided campaign to sweep homeless youth off the street and into reformatory centers, which would serve as temporary jails. The trial's political spectacle indirectly contributed to the con-struction of homeless boys' sexual vulnerability as an urgent social problem in need of containment.

Portrayed as a social blight, homeless male youth reported having sex with men and other boys after the arrests of Chimbalanga and Monjeza. A *Weekend Nation* article covered the story in January 2010 and referred to the nation's attention to the trial. At the begin-ning of the article, which spills across four pages, boys between the ages of eight and sixteen confessed to having sex with other homeless boys and with older Malawian and foreign men in exchange for food, money, and gifts. The journalist accessed these homeless boys through a children's rights NGO, Step Kids Awareness (STEKA), run by God-knows Maseko.[124] Boys offered narratives of both coerced and con-sensual same-sex sex."[125] One boy related how other boys "entice us with food ... Some of us accept to eat the food and do it [have sex]. Sometimes they just force themselves into us."[126] Another boy claimed that other boys "forced me one day to do it [have sex]" and later was taken to the hospital.[127] Yet another boy referred to others as "cute prey" and submitted to another boy's sexual advances in exchange for the ability to "warm" himself at the other boy's "fire. Refusing would mean that he would burn me with burning plastic paper."[128] Sleeping in insecure places also rendered boys vulnerable to sexual coercion; some were forced to use sex in negotiations for sleeping space. Another story featured testimony from a fourteen-year-old homeless boy: "Ordinary Malawian men, especially beggars and touts, are raping boys. When begging for money we need a place to sleep on the streets

---

[124] For a profile of Maseko, see "From Victim to Father of Street Kids," *Nation*, January 27, 2013, http://mwnation.com/from-victim-to-father-of-street-kids/.
[125] Deogratias Mmana, "Exposed: Street Children Homosexually Abused," *Nation*, January 9, 2010, 3.
[126] Ibid., 3.   [127] Ibid., 2.   [128] Ibid., 2.

so they force us to have anal intercourse."[129] Money figured prominently in these boys' narratives of sexual vulnerability and violation. Narratives reproduced in news accounts also recycled the familiar trope that same-sex sexualities could generate temporary financial security for homeless youth.

Homeless youth's poverty placed them in situations in which they faced two undesirable choices: reject unwanted same-sex sexual advances and be subjected to ongoing hunger and vulnerability or comply with an older, affluent man's request for sex and receive money, gifts, and/or a place to sleep. Maseko, STEKA's director, deplored the "pathetic situation that the boys are introduced to homosexuality as young as eight years. What kind of citizens are we grooming?"[130] Instead of interpreting homeless boys' participation in same-sex sex as evidence of their vulnerability to manipulation and abuse and of the need for interventions that address poverty, Maseko focused only on the perceived oddity of same-sex sexual practices. He ignored young people's sexual vulnerability and blamed them for continuing same-sex sexual practices in the country. Echoing a common suspicion about the intentions of activists who endorsed gay rights, Maseko attributed the sexual abuse of homeless boys to "human rights activists" who endorse

the freedom to sodomise boys ... I fear for this younger generation. Street kids are getting used and want to try it on others so we are building a society of gays. They will end up thinking it is a normal thing.[131]

Maseko's commentary came during Chimbalanga and Monjeza's trial. Within this political context, he viewed the growing public visibility of LGBT rights activism as popularizing same-sex sexual practices and even enticing youth into them. As same-sex sexualities saturated public discourses and cultural imaginary, Maseko characterized "Malawi as a likely breeding ground for homosexuality."[132]

Preempting same-sex sexualities from taking root in the country motivated government officials' plan to round up homeless youth. Some government ministers, such as Patricia Kaliati, the minister of gender, child, and community development, endorsed plans to "sweep all the street children off the streets ... [and] send them to

---

[129] Mizere, "Sodomised Orphan," 2.   [130] Mmana, "Exposed," 3.
[131] Mizere, "Sodomised Orphan," 2.   [132] Ibid.

reformatory" centers.[133] Even magistrates supported this plan. Esmie Tembenu, a child justice court magistrate, approved of the plan and offered to provide guidance and necessary documents for the venture.[134] Ordinary people also commended the plan.[135] Ultimately, the plan shifted blame for homeless youths' vulnerability to sexual abuse away from structural conditions that reproduced homelessness, including poverty and lack of access to adequate education and jobs, to youths' irresponsibility. Removing them from the streets swept the social problem of young people's homelessness out of public view.

The Trial's Effects on Sexual Minorities in Malawi

Many LGB people believed that the trial generated unwanted, unintentional visibility for gender and sexual minorities in Malawi.[136] Most LGB people interviewed for this project contended that before the trial, most Malawians either were unfamiliar with or maintained silence about homosexuality, but the trial "sparked the whole thing," according to Silas, a twenty-four-year-old bisexual man.[137] Silas shared a vignette about a gay man who "used to wear women's clothes" and "used to dance"; town residents "would just laugh and say, 'The guy is a comedian.'" He went on,

However, this man was sleeping with other men, but he was not bringing that in the open. People never suspected it and never talked about it. To them he was just an entertainer; they would just take him as a normal person. When he takes off those [women's] clothes, he puts on manly clothes; people would respect him.[138]

---

[133] Eliah Nthara, "Address Plight of Street Children," *Nation*, January 11, 2010, 4; Joseph Claude Simwaka, "Government to Rid City Streets of Children," *Nation*, March 12, 2010, 3.

[134] Mmana, "Children's Court," 6.

[135] Grey Kasunda, "Malawians Want Kids Off Streets," *Nation*, January 12, 2010, 4.

[136] For more on how LGBT people viewed the trial as a transformative event for gender and sexually diverse people, see Crystal Biruk, "Life Stories in Context: Being Lesbian, Bisexual, and Gender-Nonconforming in Malawi," in *Proudly Malawian: Life Stories from Lesbian and Gender-Nonconforming Individuals*, edited by Makhosazana Xaba and Crystal Biruk (Braamfontein, South Africa: 2016), 14–27.

[137] Silas, interview with Malawian research assistant, April 29, 2014, Lilongwe, Malawi.

[138] Ibid.

According to Silas, other residents regarded this unnamed gay man's gender nonconformity as not constituting sexual nonconformity. Writing in 2006 before Chimbalanga and Monjeza's trial, Jessie Kabwila Kapasula affirms that "cross-dressing … is seldom linked to homosexuality" in Malawi.[139] Silas insisted that after the trial, it would have been impossible for this gay man to wear women's clothing in public without arousing suspicion. He referred to the media's obsession with Chimbalanga's gender identity as a woman as initiating the conflation of gender nonconformity with sexual nonconformity.[140]

The trial's political spectacle spilled over into some sexual minorities' lives. On the one hand, the trial generated awareness about gender and sexual diversity for many Malawians, enabling families and friends to have frank conversations about the subject. Stanley, a gay man and CEDEP staffer, opined that the trial inaugurated the ability of ordinary people to speak publicly about same-sex sexualities. Talk about same-sex sexualities "trickled down to our families … Children could talk about it, and men, women, husbands, and wives would talk about it."[141] Open discussions about gender and sexual diversity was one positive outcome of the politicization of same-sex sexualities. For some ordinary Malawians, such as those living in rural areas, the trial acquainted them with lived sexual minority identities, such as "gay" identities," and same-sex sexual practices, although how heterosexual people viewed "gay" identities and same-sex sexual practices varied greatly.

On the other hand, the trial and accompanying politicized homophobia imbued most conversations with negative portrayals about same-sex sexualities. Some LGB Malawians suggested that politicized homophobia triggered or even aggravated social homophobia within families and communities. For Deborah, a twenty-seven-year-old lesbian, the trial made ordinary Malawians suspicious of women or girls who were close to one another. She stated that people recall, "I've

---

[139] Jessie Kabwila Kapasula, "Challenging Sexual Stereotypes: Is Cross-Dressing 'Un-African'?," *Feminist Africa*, 6 (2006): 68.

[140] See Amanda's narrative in *Queer Malawi*. CEDEP, *Queer Malawi: Untold Stories* (Johannesburg, South Africa: Gay and Lesbian Memory in Action, 2010).

[141] Stanley, interview with the author, July 9, 2012, Lilongwe, Malawi.

never seen this person with a guy or being in a relationship with a guy."[142] When friends or acquaintances saw Deborah with "girls, they start[ed] suspecting" that she was a lesbian. She attributed the timing of such suspicions to the trial and "coming out of Tiwonge – it's when these people start thinking that these girls are like this [lesbian] also."[143] Rebecca, a thirty-two-year-old bisexual woman, affirmed Deborah's perceptions about the trial sensitizing Malawians to the existence of male and female same-sex sexualities in their society. Before the trial, Malawians "never knew that women, they do such things, too. After realizing that [women] do [have same-sex sex]," lawmakers amended the penal code in 2011 so that the antisodomy law applied both to women and men; women arrested under the antisodomy law were eligible for "imprisonment."[144] In these ways, the trial popularized same-sex sexualities and widened Malawians' understandings of them.

Verbal harassment of people perceived to be gender or sexual minorities increased after the trial and elites' deployment of politicized homophobia. Thomas, an LGBT rights activist who worked at CEDEP, shared an example of verbal insults that he witnessed one evening.

> I was drinking with a friend, and that friend was obvious. He was used to cross-dressing, dressing like a woman ... Some guys came, you know. Then they confronted him saying, "You ugly people. You are such people that we do not want."[145]

Thomas attributed the verbal insults in part to the visibility of his friend's gender variance, which the harassers interpreted as gayness. For Thomas, intense public scrutiny of homosexuality associated with the trial made "the issue ... hot because we were debating it, and everyone was talking about it."[146] As a result, if passersby "see you associating with maybe MSM or if they realize that you are an MSM, then they will attack at you with their verbal accusations."[147] Thomas believed that these sentiments trickled down from political elites who tacitly signaled to gender and sexual minorities, "We don't want you.

---

[142] Deborah, interview with the author, April 27, 2014, Lilongwe, Malawi.
[143] Ibid.
[144] Rebecca, interview with the author, April 29, 2014, Lilongwe, Malawi.
[145] Thomas, interview with the author, June 27, 2012, Blantyre, Malawi.
[146] Ibid.   [147] Ibid.

You should be dead."[148] For some LGBT people, the trial generated unwanted visibility for them in their communities; visibility as suspected gender and sexual dissidents rendered them vulnerable to persecution and violence.

The trial also inflamed the emotions of ordinary Malawians who targeted perceived gender and sexual minorities. Roger, a bisexual man and CEDEP officer, acknowledged the prevalence of violence in some communities as a way to resolve arguments. According to Roger, the trial of Chimbalanga and Monjeza heightened people's emotions. He recalled becoming embroiled in a dispute that ended with violence.[149] One night in 2010, he visited a club where "people were discussing homosexuality," likely in relation to the ongoing trial. Club patrons solicited Roger's input on their discussion, but he ignored their requests for his opinion. Roger stated, "I didn't want to come into the issue but they ... managed to push me into" the conversation.[150] Later that night,

somebody called my name and said, "You are a homosexual. You don't pretend as if you are not." And I felt, "No, this was just too much." I had to answer back. I said, "So what? How does that affect you as a human being if I am a homosexual? Do I do it with your brother?"[151]

Roger's confirmation of his sexuality and challenge to club patrons' invasion of his privacy escalated the tension. Roger related how "these people became so violent. I was slapped, and I was like, 'Why do you want to fight me?'"[152] He called a fellow CEDEP officer and friend who happened to be nearby and "rushed into the whole commotion" to help him. Roger speculated that if he had not defended himself, he would have been "beaten by the mob ... People were trying to prompt mob justice. That's what they wanted; that's what they wanted because it was easier for them to mobilize people to hit somebody else because of [his] sexual orientation."[153] Roger's friend helped defuse the situation and escorted him to safety. Roger suffered a bruised face from the altercation.

Although I am unable to measure directly how the politicized homophobia accompanying the trial generated or exacerbated social or familial homophobia, many LGB people and allies perceived that it

[148] Ibid.
[149] Roger, interview with the author, May 23, 2014, Blantyre, Malawi.
[150] Ibid.   [151] Ibid.   [152] Ibid.   [153] Ibid.

generated negative material and social consequences for them. In turn, sexual minorities tried to make strategic choices that insulated them from these perceived negative outcomes. I explore dimensions of the perceived consequences of politicized homophobia on LGB people in Chapter 5.

The Trial's Effect on Human and LGBT Rights NGOs

CEDEP officers used the trial to edge forward with LGBT rights advocacy, while being careful not to draw political ire. They carefully managed their public visibility as many other African LGBT activist organizations do.[154] CEDEP officers sought to balance their commitment to advocating for Chimbalanga and Monjeza and LGBT rights, while ensuring the safety of staff and constituents. Days after the couple's arrests, Trapence, CEDEP's executive director, asked the government to stage a national referendum on decriminalizing same-sex sex, arguing that the country "cannot run away from the fact that we have homosexuals in our midst ... We need to rest this debate once and for all and we can do this through consensus."[155] He presented a national referendum as an opportunity for Malawian citizens to deliberate the place of sexual diversity in society and law.[156] Other human rights NGOs endorsed a national referendum. Speaking days after prosecutors charged the couple early in 2010, Justin Dzonzi, who moved on from MHRRC to become the executive director of Justice

---

[154] See Currier, *Out in Africa.*

[155] "CEDEP Wants Homosexuality Referendum," *Daily Times*, January 7, 2010, 4.

[156] Trapence subsequently reversed his position supporting a national referendum on decriminalizing same-sex sex. In 2012, when DPP leaders demanded a national referendum on "gay rights laws," Trapence and CHRR's executive director, Undule Mwakasungula, dismissed the idea and faulted DPP leaders for using LGBT rights as a "springboard to re-launch its otherwise tattered political image ... The call is not only misguided and misinformed but also retrogressive." Bright Sonani, "Activists Trash DPP Stand on Gay Laws," *Nation*, August 7, 2012, 3. In 2013, in response to political leaders endorsing a nationwide referendum, Trapence asserted, "[I]t is wrong and unheard of for a nation to float an issue that is protected by the Constitution for a referendum." Rex Chikoko, "Peter, Atupele for Vote on Gays," *Nation*, October 7, 2013, 2; "Constitution Clear on Gay Rights, Politicians Aren't," *Daily Times*, November 19, 2013, article on file with author; Timothy Mtambo and Gift Trapence, "On UDF, DPP Referendum Proposal," *Weekend Nation*, October 12, 2013, 7.

Link, asserted that the only way to handle the question of decriminalizing same-sex sex was to put it to a vote of Malawians. Making a peculiar contention that "[d]emocracy is a dictatorship of the majority," he suggested that citizens had to voice their opinions about gay rights by voting in a "referendum."[157] This logic contradicts the viewpoints of some African LGBT rights activists who claim that no one has any business voting on LGBT rights in particular and minority rights in general.[158] Dzonzi affirmed that decriminalization would not resolve the question of gay rights in the country; instead, additional questions like whether lesbians and gay men could adopt children would emerge.[159]

"Trouble started" for CEDEP, according to Blessings, a former CEDEP officer, after Chimbalanga and Monjeza became engaged, and then, national attention focused on same-sex sexualities.[160] Benjamin, a current CEDEP officer, reported that some politicians believed "we [at CEDEP] were trying to test the government on how they are going to react on such issues" of decriminalizing same-sex sex and had encouraged Chimbalanga and Monjeza to hold their engagement ceremony.[161] However, CEDEP became involved in the couple's defense by asking one of their "lawyers to just represent the guys so that at least they don't seem to be abandoned. So we deployed one of our lawyers" to coach them on the necessity of not "opening your mouth because ... we noticed that Tiwonge was very loudmouth[ed]."[162] CEDEP officers were concerned that the couple might further incriminate themselves, generating additional unwanted political scrutiny and public visibility for the NGO. Another example of state-sponsored

---

[157] Grey Kasunda, "Referendum, Solution to Homosexuality," *Nation*, January 5, 2010, 4.

[158] In 2013, an International Lesbian and Gay Human Rights Commission (IGLHRC) representative warned Malawian leaders not to allow citizens to vote on a national referendum on sexual minority rights. Damian Ugwu, IGLHRC's Africa regional coordinator, stated, "Sexual minorities do not need new rights. All they ask for is that the state treats them as the rest of its citizens. They want to be free from discrimination, extortion, arbitrary arrest, and violence. They want to love and be loved." Anthony Kasunda, "Referendum on Same Sex Wrong," *Nation*, October 25, 2013, 3.

[159] Kasunda, "'Referendum,'" 4.

[160] Blessings, interview with the author, July 4, 2012, Lilongwe, Malawi. See also, Chanika, Lwanda, and Muula, "Gender, Gays, and Gain."

[161] Benjamin, interview with the author, June 27, 2012, Blantyre, Malawi.

[162] Blessings, interview with the author, July 4, 2012, Lilongwe, Malawi.

harassment of LGBT rights activists during the trial came when a young man was arrested for hanging "Gay Rights Are Human Rights" posters on a major road; he was charged with "conduct likely to cause breach of peace."[163] Eventually, he pleaded guilty to the charge.[164] This arrest squelched public support for LGBT rights and sympathy for Chimbalanga and Monjeza.

CEDEP officers and staff were vulnerable to the effects of politicized homophobia, particularly when others knew that they worked or volunteered at CEDEP. Those who worked at CEDEP offices were particularly vulnerable. Roger related how CEDEP's offices were ransacked and burglarized more than once.[165] Interpreting the office raids as intended to intimidate LGBT activists, Charles, a CEDEP officer, explained that attackers' "intention was not to steal ... No, they just came to leave a message ... 'You guys need to stop the work that you're doing.'"[166] CEDEP's Blantyre office aroused the suspicion of neighbors who began inquiring about "what sort of programs are we doing because it seems like they see a lot of homosexuals around the offices."[167] Roger failed to "convince" neighbors that the CEDEP office was not a meeting place for LGBT people. Soon after, people broke into CEDEP's office; CEDEP staff believed that young men hired by the ruling party were responsible for the burglary. After Roger reported the burglary, police asked him to come to the local station where they arrested him. Incredulous about being arrested after reporting a burglary, he inquired about the charges. Police claimed, "You know, you've been found with pornographic materials which [is] against the [law], and we are throwing you into a jail [cell]."[168] The alleged "pornographic materials" were queer films and books and HIV/AIDS educational materials, some of which contained nudity for educational purposes, not for titillation. Roger recalled that he "couldn't believe it was me [being] ... detained."[169] A few hours later, senior police officers questioned him. During the exchange with police

---

[163] Caroline Somanje, "Police Arrest Man for Pasting Gay Rights Posters," *Nation*, February 2, 2010, 3.

[164] Caroline Somanje, "Gay Posters Campaigner Given Community Service," *Nation*, February 8, 2010, 3.

[165] See also, McKay, "Invisible Men," 134.

[166] Charles, interview with the author, July 3, 2012, Lilongwe, Malawi.

[167] Roger, interview with the author, May 23, 2014, Blantyre, Malawi.

[168] Ibid.   [169] Ibid.

officers, Roger defended himself and refused to acknowledge state representatives' accusations about CEDEP's LGBT rights advocacy. He asked police:

How could you intercept an individual [based on what you found in CEDEP's office]? CEDEP is not a person. CEDEP is an office. If you found something pornographic in nature, can I see anything of that nature because I don't remember stocking anything pornographic in our offices?[170]

After the interrogation, an officer asked Roger, "Why are you doing this?"[171] He interpreted the question to mean: "Are we [CEDEP] promoting homosexuality? Are we really involved in homosexuality issues?"[172] The officer pressed Roger to confirm that CEDEP advocated for LGBT rights and people. Instead, Roger explained that CEDEP's "issues are to do with HIV/AIDS and human rights."[173] Framing CEDEP's work in terms of less stigmatized advocacy, Roger emulated stances favored by some African LGBT activists who cast LGBT organizing as human rights or public-health interventions.[174] Police released Roger on bail and required him to report to the station once a week.

Police proceeded with their investigation and eventually searched a CEDEP colleague's home. Roger recalled that police "said they were searching for anything that is to do with homosexuality."[175] Attributing the ongoing investigation to politicized homophobia, he explained,

[At] that time, we were experiencing state-propelled homophobia where we felt [homophobia] was being promoted by the state [and was] threatening . . . the rights of the LGBT people in Malawi . . . It was horrible because everybody felt insecure.[176]

In response to the insecurity produced by politicized homophobia, the burglary of CEDEP's office, and ongoing police investigation, CEDEP officers closed the office for a short time as they contemplated their

---

[170] Ibid.   [171] Ibid.   [172] Ibid.   [173] Ibid.
[174] Patrick Awondo, "The Politicisation of Sexuality and Rise of Homosexual Movements in Post-Colonial Cameroon," *Review of African Political Economy*, 37, no. 125 (2010): 315–328; Currier and Cruz, "Civil Society and Sexual Struggles in Africa"; Currier and Thomann, "Gender and Sexual Diversity Organizing in Africa"; Epprecht, "Sexual Minorities, Human Rights."
[175] Roger, interview with the author, May 23, 2014, Blantyre, Malawi.
[176] Ibid.

next steps. According to Roger, officers relocated the NGO's head-quarters away from Blantyre to Lilongwe. Although CEDEP moved its Blantyre office to another neighborhood, it was still vulnerable to burglary. Roger stated that one office location "was broken into about almost every day. And then we said, 'There is no way we can be here.'"[177] At another time, CEDEP officers discovered "posters on the doors [that read], 'No, no homosexuality here. You guys have to move out.'"[178] Insecurity followed CEDEP officers who were vulnerable to harassment, violence, arrest, and detention.

The trial heightened CEDEP's international visibility as officers attended HIV/AIDS conferences and meetings of LGBT activists, which generated both positive and negative consequences. As CEDEP's international profile grew, representatives from international human and LGBT rights organizations began "calling to just curiously ask, 'What are you doing about this case, and what is your role in the case?,'" as Blessings explained.[179] Others wanted to know "how were the couple being treated in prison."[180] Such inquiries emboldened CEDEP officers who interpreted these questions as recognition that the NGO was well poised to advance LGBT rights in Malawi. According to Blessings,

> that's when we thought, "Okay, some people are interested in us playing a role in this." So we just jumped in. It wasn't something formal ... [P]eople knew we're directly involved in advocating for rights of minority people. So they expected an automatic involvement with the case.[181]

However, some CEDEP staff and members wondered if it was appropriate for the NGO to become involved with the defense because Chimbalanga and Monjeza "were not ... CEDEP members. They were just another couple," Blessings recalled.[182] CEDEP officers recognized that as the only NGO representing gender and sexual minorities in Malawi, CEDEP had an obligation to support the couple during the trial. As I discuss in Chapter 4, a women's rights NGO experienced scrutiny from an international donor who queried why the NGO had not assisted Chimbalanga and Monjeza, a development that illustrates NGOs' vulnerability to donor demands. If CEDEP officers had not assisted the incarcerated couple, the NGO could have

---

[177] Ibid.   [178] Ibid.
[179] Blessings, interview with the author, July 4, 2012, Lilongwe, Malawi.
[180] Ibid.   [181] Ibid.   [182] Ibid.

encountered similar queries from donor agencies that might withdraw future funding.

International LGBT rights organizations like the International Lesbian and Gay Human Rights Commission (IGLHRC) consulted CEDEP about the couple's detention, and IGLHRC staff inquired what solidarity actions would support the couple.[183] This consultation positioned CEDEP as the national arbiter on LGBT rights in Malawi. According to Ryan R. Thoreson,

throughout the arrest, detention, and trial of the couple, CEDEP remained IGLHRC's trusted source of information about their well-being, Chimbalanga's preferred name and gender identity, and the desirability of possible interventions. It was CEDEP who called for a letter-writing campaign to the couple in prison; brokers at IGLHRC obliged by launching a postcard campaign at the annual Celebration of Courage gala.[184]

CEDEP funneled information about the trial and atmosphere in Malawi surrounding LGBT rights to international allies. As a result, CEDEP representatives received invitations to attend international meetings at which activists discussed LGBT rights. Later in 2010 at an event recognizing LGBT Pride, US Secretary of State Hillary Rodham Clinton thanked CEDEP for its path-breaking work in making HIV/AIDS services available to LGBT people and for defending LGBT rights "often in unfriendly, even dangerous circumstances."[185]

CEDEP staff and members agreed that the trial catapulted the NGO into the public and media spotlight. In other words, CEDEP became part of the political spectacle surrounding the trial. For Stanley, the magistrate's sentencing of Chimbalanga and Monjeza, who were "first-time offenders," to fourteen years in prison was "really unfair," as the magistrate intended the harsh sentence to "make sure that nobody else gets into that again [by] scaring everyone" away from same-sex relationships.[186] The trial also aggravated negative public perceptions of NGOs. Benjamin likened the trial's effect to turning the government and general public against NGOs that endorsed LGBT

---

[183] In 2015, IGLHRC changed its name to OutRight Action International.

[184] Thoreson, *Transnational LGBT Activism*, 147.

[185] Agnes Mizere, "Clinton Praises Local Gay Activists," *Sunday Times*, June 27, 2010, 3.

[186] Stanley, interview with the author, July 9, 2012, Lilongwe, Malawi.

rights. Because CEDEP routinely submitted human rights reports to the UN, "we've been persecuted here in Malawi," Benjamin explained.[187] International scrutiny angered government officials, especially as

donor countries . . . were not happy with Malawi persecuting the activists . . . So, most of the donor governments give out a few conditions to say, "You don't judge who is to enjoy these human rights, because it's universal. So, everybody should enjoy it. So, if you do not do that, if you do not respect people's dignity, if you do not respect people's rights, then we pull out funding."[188]

According to Benjamin, international pressure and threats to withdraw funding contributed to the antigay backlash that targeted gender and sexual minorities, LGBT rights NGOs, and their allies. Mutharika's administration used international criticism of Malawian governance to foment distrust of CEDEP and CHRR. Benjamin explained

the government was at CEDEP's neck . . . preaching now to the people, "You see? . . . CEDEP has gone to Geneva to report that we don't want gay marriages in Malawi. That's why [Northern governments] have pulled out the funding." So, it was like putting the people, the public, against CEDEP.[189]

In some cases, Mutharika himself resorted to "screaming and talking on different podiums on how CEDEP and CHRR are trying to push this [LGBT rights] agenda [on] the Malawi people."[190] Beatrice, a lesbian and CEDEP member, lamented how Mutharika's government was "misguiding the people" by insinuating that CEDEP only defended LGBT rights because "they just want the money from the donor[s]."[191] The government's repression of CEDEP, CHRR, and other NGOs critical of his government intensified between 2010 and 2012, as I discuss in Chapter 3.

Some pundits expressed indignation about LGBT rights organizations remaining hidden until Chimbalanga and Monjeza's prosecution. Edward Chisambo wondered,

[W]hen did the NGOs know that there was a society of homosexuals in this country whose rights had to be protected? If they did, why did they not

---

[187] Benjamin, interview with the author, June 27, 2012, Blantyre, Malawi.
[188] Ibid.   [189] Ibid.   [190] Ibid.
[191] Beatrice, interview with the author, July 7, 2012, Lilongwe, Malawi.

promote this culture and encourage openness among the gays so that people could stop looking at it as weird?[192]

He indicted activists for not publicizing evidence of same-sex sexualities and LGBT people in the country sooner. This logic also partially blamed LGBT activists for not fostering dialogue about same-sex sexualities earlier in Malawi's history as a way to prepare Malawians for sexual diversity. Countering Chisambo's logic, Trapence affirmed that "there will always be gays in Malawi."[193] Convictions for sodomy would not prevent gay men from "expressing their sexual orientation" and love for other men, according to Trapence.[194] Following other Malawian pundits who decried Northern meddling in Malawian politics, Chisambo charted an indigenous pathway for LGBT rights:

Whatever will happen about gays the truth is that this strange phenomenon in most of Africa let alone Malawi has come to stay although it would take a lot of convincing and millions of Kwacha to persuade a society that has always seen homosexuality as evil. Britain and America should let Africans solve this problem themselves for once.[195]

Although Chisambo did not embrace sexual diversity in Malawi, he believed that foreigners should not force LGBT rights on sovereign African nations. His position made room for indigenous LGBT rights advocacy that would make Malawi more hospitable for gender and sexual dissidents.

After the trial, some CEDEP members and officers wanted to "shrug off the notoriety they endured during the trial and return to their work" around HIV/AIDS, a pathway that did not materialize.[196] For other activists, the trial tinged public suspicion about NGOs with politicized homophobia. Sarah, a human rights activist, deplored how newspapers "turned to say all NGOs are" endorsing same-sex sexual practices "because the donors who are giving them money," asked these NGOs "to deal with issues of homosexuality, which was

---

[192] Edward Chisambo, "Gay Issues Refusing to Die," *Malawi News*, May 15–21, 2010, 14.
[193] Caroline Somanje, "There Are Many Gays in Malawi," *Nation*, January 1, 2010, 3.
[194] Ibid.   [195] Chisambo, "Gay Issues Refusing to Die," 14.
[196] Thoreson, *Transnational LGBT Activism*, 147.

not the case for each and every NGO."[197] Sarah's NGO did not "do that."[198] Staff at her NGO "know it's a human rights issue, but" the government

was brutal in … disregard[ing] several other important issues which Malawi was facing at that point in time. Their idea was to turn the public against civil society to say that "civil society is not good. They're in partnership with the donors … So don't follow them." So it was like creating enem[ies] … between civil society and people at [the] grassroots.[199]

Portrayals of NGOs as money-grubbing organizations willing to carry out nefarious Northern plans to destabilize indigenous gender and sexual norms benefited the government, as media and political elites subjected NGOs to continuous scrutiny. In other words, political elites translated the international scrutiny they experienced into intense surveillance of NGO activities, which I discuss in more detail in the next two chapters.

Conclusion

After the presidential pardon, Chimbalanga and Monjeza still appeared in news stories as objects of popular fascination. Despite the difficulties they experienced stemming from their arrests and pros- ecution, the couple declared their love for each other publicly and asked journalists and the public to "respect … our privacy and dignity … We need to think of our future and reposition ourselves after the most stressful period in our lives."[200] Rejecting transphobic caricatures of her, Chimbalanga criticized news media for "wreck[ing] my life with your exaggerated reporting on me. You particularly mocked me in different cartoons. I am fed up with all this and would like to get a job after losing the good one I had. I want to earn my living without interference."[201] The couple eventually parted ways, perhaps due to the strain caused by relentless public scrutiny.[202] Before her

---

[197] Sarah, interview with the author, July 4, 2012, Lilongwe, Malawi.
[198] Ibid.   [199] Ibid.
[200] Kondwani Munthali, "Leave Us Alone – Aunt Tiwo," *Nation*, June 3, 2010, 2; Caroline Somanje, "I Still Love Aunt Tiwo – Monjeza," *Nation*, May 31, 2010, 1–2.
[201] Caroline Somanje, "Chimbalanga Says Not Bitter with Monjeza," *Nation*, June 9, 2010, 2.
[202] "Monjeza Dumps Aunt Tiwo for a Woman," *Nation*, June 8, 2010, 1–2.

departure from Malawi, Chimbalanga asked media to refrain from publishing her picture in stories about same-sex sexualities, alleging they were "trying to dig a grave and bring out the corpse" by linking the trial and pardons to LGBT politics in the country.[203]

It is unclear whether either Chimbalanga or Monjeza has fared better in the years since the trial. Both were "excommunicated" from the church where they had worshipped.[204] In 2013, Monjeza served jail time for stealing a mobile telephone and bag of maize.[205] In 2015, Caroline Somanje, the journalist who first broke the story about the couple's engagement ceremony, profiled Monjeza's desperate circumstances. Monjeza told Somanje, "I am pleading with you to write another story about the hardships I am going through ... I was chased from my home ... Getting a job has proved a trial as I remain a black sheep."[206] Monjeza's marriage to a woman also did not pan out.[207] With the assistance of Gender DynamiX, a transgender rights organization based in South Africa, Chimbalanga resettled in that country.[208] For a time, Chimbalanga worked as an intern at Gender DynamiX and Iranti-Org.[209] Since her arrival in South Africa, Chimbalanga has been attacked on five separate occasions and struggled to achieve a sense of personal security.[210] However, in 2014, Chimbalanga revealed that she had found love there.[211] Chimbalanga and Monjeza have never been able to escape the political spectacle the trial engendered.

---

[203] Emma Makhumula, "'Stop Associating Me with Monjeza," *Daily Times*, December 6, 2010, 2.

[204] "Church Disowns Gay Couple," *Nation*, January 14, 2012, http://mwnation.com/church-disowns-gay-couple/.

[205] Caroline Somanje, "Monjeza Released from Jail," *Nation*, November 22, 2013, http://mwnation.com/monjeza-released-from-jail/.

[206] Caroline Somanje, "Ed's Note: Monjeza Needs 'Help,'" *Nation*, March 8, 2015, http://mwnation.com/eds-note-monjeza-needs-help/.

[207] Ajussa Leonard, "After Being Gay: Monjeza Cries Out!," *Nation*, March 16, 2015, http://mwnation.com/after-being-gay-monjeza-cries-out/.

[208] ANP/AFP, "No Regrets for Malawian Jailed for Gay Wedding," Radio Netherlands Worldwide, December 9, 2012, article on file with author.

[209] Gevisser, "Love in Exile."

[210] Gevisser, "Love in Exile"; Emilie Iob, "Challenges Remain for LGBT in South Africa," *Voice of America*, May 1, 2013, https://sg.news.yahoo.com/no-regrets-malawian-jailed-gay-wedding-045851350.html/.

[211] Frank Namangale, "Aunt Tiwo Finds New Love," *Nation*, October 26, 2014, http://mwnation.com/aunt-tiwo-finds-new-love/.

The trial as political spectacle sparked reactive politicized homophobia, consolidating tropes vilifying same-sex sexualities, gender and sexual minorities, and LGBT rights advocates. Whereas earlier reporting on trials of men arrested for sodomy received little fanfare, Chimbalanga and Monjeza's audacity in holding a traditional wedding-engagement ceremony to formalize their love and partnership triggered a series of events culminating in a spectacle to which Malawians and academics alike commonly refer in discussions of homophobia and criminalization of same-sex sexualities on the African continent.[212] The trial acted as a vehicle for transforming the politicization of same-sex sexualities into politicized homophobia. The trial concentrated national and international attention on same-sex sexualities and layered additional meanings on to same-sex sexual practices and LGBT rights advocacy. The intense scrutiny accompanying the trial enabled Malawian political elites to rehearse discursive opposition to same-sex sexualities and LGBT rights, which they repackaged into antigay threats and actions as NGOs continued to criticize Mutharika's authoritarian leadership. Mutharika's administration depicted NGOs that disapproved of his leadership as advancing LGBT rights, as the government and ruling party sought to neutralize these NGOs.

The politicization of homosexuality does not always remain contained and confined to specific episodes. It can spiral into the sexualization of politics that ensnares different vulnerable populations and those perceived to be government opponents. Manufacturing a social problem in need of urgent redress, political elites suspected homeless boys and young men of being victims of (homo)sexual predators, who then turned into predators. Political elites' views shifted from sympathizing with homeless youth to implicitly blaming them for their vulnerability. Within discourses of politicized homophobia, there can be great variation in interpreting the causes and consequences of same-sex sexualities and allocating blame for persisting same-sex relationships and LGBT rights advocacy.

---

[212] For recent examples of analyses and mentions of the trial, see Epprecht, *Sexuality and Social Justice in Africa*, 2–3; Neville Hoad, "Queer Customs against the Law"; *Research in African Literatures*, 47, no. 2 (2016): 9–11; and Matt Richardson, *The Queer Limit of Black Memory: Black Lesbian Literature and Irresolution* (Columbus: Ohio State University Press, 2013), 165–166.

Chimbalanga and Monjeza were not the only Malawians hurt by the trial. Gender and sexual minorities understood politicized homophobia as a strategy to "scapegoat" LGBT people.[213] In this way, politicized homophobia was a convenient way for Mutharika and his administration to "cover up [their] own weaknesses with one thing [they] felt is going to get sympathy from the public."[214] Political elites' reliance on politicized homophobia grew in 2011 and 2012, as NGOs remained unrelenting in their criticism of Mutharika's authoritarian government.

[213] Stanley, interview with the author, July 9, 2012, Lilongwe, Malawi.
[214] Ibid.

3 | The Repressive "Wedge" Politics of Politicized Homophobia

After the trial of Tiwonge Chimbalanga and Steven Monjeza, politicized homophobia in Malawi became more pernicious and proactive between 2010 and 2012. During President Bingu wa Mutharika's second term as president, NGOs, including CHRR and CEDEP, leading LGBT rights organizations, began making demands that the government correct the authoritarian direction of Mutharika's leadership and respond to mounting socioeconomic problems, such as electricity, fuel, and foreign currency shortages. When Mutharika and his administration refused to act on a list of NGO demands, NGO leaders planned protests throughout the country. NGOs mobilized thousands of people to participate in ill-fated street protests on July 20, 2011, dubbed the "July 20 protests."[1] Police used violence to disperse and punish protestors; police repression resulted in the deaths of nineteen protestors and bystanders and gunshot injuries of fifty-eight people.[2] Mutharika responded to the protests by threatening to "smoke ... out"[3] activist leaders in 2011 and promising "critics that they will feel the heat" in 2012.[4] State leaders claimed that the July 20 protests were really about legalizing same-sex sex, not about improving economic, social, and political problems plaguing the country. The deployment of politicized homophobia against

---

[1] For a timeline of the events preceding and following the July 20 protests, see Diana Cammack, "Malawi in Crisis, 2011–12," *Review of African Political Economy*, 39, no. 132 (2012): 375–388.

[2] Mabvuto Banda, "Malawi Report Says 19 Killed, 58 Shot in Protests." Reuters, August 15, 2011.
www.reuters.com/article/2011/08/15/ozatp-malawi-protests-idAFJOE77E0N 920110815.

[3] Madalitso Musa, "Group Urges Bingu against Hate Speech," *Daily Times*, August 15, 2011, 4.

[4] "Trouser Attacks: How It All Began," *Nation*, January 22, 2012.
http://mwnation.com/trouser-attacks-how-it-all-began/.

118

protesting NGOs ensnared a variety of organizations, engendering deep divisions between them.

This chapter shows how President Mutharika and members of his government used proactive politicized homophobia to repress domestic NGOs. State actors deployed politicized homophobia both to discredit NGOs that openly criticized their undemocratic leadership, including those that did not work on LGBT rights, and to drive a "wedge" between NGOs, generating divisions among social movements.[5] Multiple forms of repression, including politicized homophobia, converged in the July 20 protests, making it an excellent case for understanding how politicized homophobia operates as state repression. Although much research demonstrates how discursive threats and other forms of repression can constrain feminist and queer organizing,[6] little scholarship traces the effects of different forms of repression – specifically, politicized homophobia – on divisions within and among social movements. This chapter remedies this oversight, explaining how politicized homophobia functioned as a wedge to splinter apart Malawian social movements.

To understand how politicized homophobia shatters tenuous alliances between social movements, I first address how the sociopolitical climate primed state leaders' use of proactive politicized homophobia and then explain how state leaders wielded it to punish upstart social movements. After conceptualizing politicized homophobia as repression and NGOs as targets of scrutiny of African political elites, I discuss historic hostility toward NGOs in Malawi. Social and state antagonism toward NGOs provided part of the political groundwork for state repression of social movements critical of Mutharika's leadership. Next, I enumerate how the Mutharika administration deployed

---

[5] Amy Lind and Christine Keating, "Navigating the Left Turn: Sexual Justice and the Citizen Revolution in Ecuador," *International Feminist Journal of Politics*, 15, no. 4 (2013): 515–533.

[6] Jill M. Bystydzienski, "The Feminist Movement in Poland: Why So Slow?," *Women's Studies International Forum*, 24, no. 5 (2001): 501–511; Lynette J. Chua, "Pragmatic Resistance, Law, and Social Movements in Authoritarian States: The Case of Gay Collective Action in Singapore," *Law & Society Review*, 46, no. 4 (2012): 713–748; Laurie Essig, "'Bury Their Hearts': Some Thoughts on the Specter of Homosexuality Haunting Russia," *QED: A Journal of GLBTQ Worldmaking*, 1, no. 3 (2014): 39–58; Janet Elise Johnson and Aino Saarinen, "Twenty-First Century Feminisms under Repression: Gender Regime Change and the Women's Crisis Center Movement in Russia," *Signs*, 38, no. 3 (2013): 543–567; Ungar, "State Violence."

different forms of state repression, including politicized homophobia, to target NGOs that planned the July 20 protests. I devote some detail to covering the events leading to and the day of the July 20 protests. I end the chapter by charting how repression in the guise of politicized homophobia contributed to the fracturing of alliances between NGOs and outlining the personal costs that Malawian LGBT rights defenders suffered.

Politicized Homophobia as Repression

Politicized homophobia can function as state repression, a hostile response to social movements that are antagonistic to the state.[7] State-sponsored repression is intended to provoke immediate, profound consequences, such as movement demobilization or withdrawal. In general, repression can involve attacks on activists in the form of violence and detention and on organizations as property destruction. In addition, repression as discursive threats can "silence or eradicate oppositional ideas."[8] In some cases, state leaders or other social groups deploy "ridicule, stigma, and silencing," forms of discursive threats, to inhibit feminist and LGBT movement mobilization.[9] Examples include publicly shaming or smearing the reputation of movement organizations.

Repression can unfold in direct and indirect ways. Direct repression takes the more conventional form of "shows and/or uses of force," whereas indirect repression like channeling attempts to "affect the forms of protest available, the timing of protests, and/or flows of resources to movements."[10] In Malawi, repression took both direct and indirect forms. Direct state repression of oppositional social

---

[7] For a discussion of repression, see Jennifer Earl, "Political Repression: Iron Fists, Velvet Gloves, and Diffuse Control," *Annual Review of Sociology*, 37 (2011): 261–284; Jennifer Earl, "Tanks, Tear Gas, and Taxes: Toward a Theory of Movement Repression," *Sociological Theory*, 21, no. 1 (2003): 44–68; Abby Peterson and Mattias Wahlström, "Repression: The Governance of Domestic Dissent," in *The Oxford Handbook of Social Movements*, edited by Donatella della Porta and Mario Diani (New York: Oxford University Press, 2015), 634–652.

[8] Myra Marx Ferree, "Soft Repression: Ridicule, Stigma, and Silencing in Gender-Based Movements," *Research in Social Movements, Conflicts, and Change*, 25 (2004): 88.

[9] Ibid., 89.   [10] Earl, "Tanks, Tear Gas," 48.

movements entailed police violence, arrests of NGO leaders, and discursive threats. Indirect state repression turned social movements against one another, as state leaders and other political elites deployed politicized homophobia. NGOs that had nothing to do with sexual rights were accused of encouraging homosexuality in Malawi because they were critical of Mutharika's administration or had joined the NGO coalition calling for immediate state reforms.

As a form of state repression, politicized homophobia drove a wedge between different Malawian social movements. As a "wedge issue," the unpopular subject of homosexuality becomes a discursive weapon elite actors can use to coerce activists into distancing their movements from defenders of sexual diversity.[11] Antigay opponents in different countries have portrayed same-sex sexualities, gender diversity, and LGBT rights campaigns as undermining gender and sexual norms, religious ideals, and national political stability.[12] Typically, opponents employ sexual minority rights as a wedge issue for political gain, including winning an election, deflecting attention away from state actors' deceit, and reducing attention paid to a controversial issue. In this way, antigay opponents may proactively use same-sex sexualities and LGBT rights to divide social movements.[13] In Malawi, LGBT rights and same-sex marriage became issues that divided NGOs.

Politicized homophobia in Malawi functioned as a wedge through the use of discursive threats. Although politicized homophobia can take the form of state-sponsored violence, it often materializes as discursive threats to deter criticism of or organized opposition to state policies.[14] Some research suggests that discursive threats can "legitimize" repression, such as state-sponsored violence, particularly in contexts in which public opinion is firmly against a social movement and

[11] Lind and Keating, "Navigating the Left Turn." See also, Gilbert Herdt, "Introduction," in *Moral Panics, Sex Panics: Fear and the Fight Over Sexual Rights*, edited by Gilbert Herdt (New York: New York University Press, 2009), 23.

[12] Currier, *Out in Africa*; Tina Fetner, *How the Religious Right Shaped Lesbian and Gay Activism* (Minneapolis: University of Minnesota Press, 2008); Smith, *New Right Discourse on Race and Sexuality*; Arlene Stein, *The Stranger Next Door: The Story of a Small Community's Battle over Sex, Faith, and Civil Rights* (Boston: Beacon Press, 2002).

[13] Amy Lind and Christine Keating also refer to this strategy as "pinkwedging." Lind and Keating, "Navigating the Left Turn," 518.

[14] Anna Gruszczynska, "Sowing the Seeds of Solidarity in Public Space: Case Study of the Poznan March of Equality," *Sexualities*, 12, no. 3 (2009): 312–333.

the cause for which the movement advocates.[15] This is certainly the case for homosexuality in Malawi. According to Afrobarometer survey data from 2014 to 2015, 89 percent of Malawians "strongly dislike" homosexuals.[16] Given the level of antihomosexual opprobrium in Malawi, same-sex sexualities were an easy target for the state. With public sentiment overwhelmingly against sexual dissidents, there has been palpable social and state-sponsored hostility toward gender and sexual diversity rights defenders. As I discuss in Chapter 2, CEDEP has been the target of police raids and burglaries. In 2013, thieves broke into CEDEP's Lilongwe office, after tying up the security guard, and stole computers, printers, and other equipment. Gift Trapence, the executive director of CEDEP, stated, "We are hoping it's a mere robbery. But as an institution, CEDEP has been targeted in the past" by police and antigay opponents.[17] Malawian activists allied with the "unpopular" LGBT movement were vulnerable to different "kinds of repression at the same time: state repression ... and exclusion from the political and social environment."[18]

Repressive discursive threats from the state convinced some activist leaders to compromise their positions on sexual rights, to side completely with the state and elites against LGBT rights, or to distance themselves from movements championing LGBT rights. The prospect of gaining favor with elites or lessening state repression directed at their organizations induced some leaders to pressure other NGOs to stop making demands and engaging in collective action. These compromised movements sought to undo the "negative radical flank effect,"[19] which refers to unfavorable outcomes associated with being

---

[15] Annette Linden and Bert Klandermans, "Stigmatization and Repression of Extreme-Right Activism in the Netherlands," *Mobilization*, 11, no. 2 (2006): 214.

[16] 4 percent "somewhat dislike" homosexuals, 1 percent do "not care" about homosexuals, 2 percent "somewhat like" homosexuals, 3 percent "strongly like" homosexuals, and 1 percent do not know if they like or dislike homosexuals. Boniface Dulani, Gift Sambo, and Kim Yi Dionne, "Good Neighbours? Africans Express High Levels of Tolerance for Many, But Not for All," *Afrobarometer Dispatch*, 74 (2016): 26. http://afrobarometer.org/publications/tolerance-in-africa/.

[17] Suzgo Khunga, "Thugs Target CEDEP, Steal Office Equipment," *Nation*, October 14, 2013, 3.

[18] Linden and Klandermans, "Stigmatization and Repression," 226.

[19] Herbert H. Haines, "Black Radicalization and the Funding of Civil Rights: 1957–1970," *Social Problems*, 32, no. 1 (1984): 32.

perceived as extremists.[20] As Malawian political elites used politicized homophobia proactively to malign either specific NGOs supporting LGBT rights or NGOs collectively, some NGO leaders publicly discredited and shamed LGBT rights organizations, distancing their organizations from sexual diversity activism. Thus, some social movements became repressive agents by disciplining other movements, indirectly carrying out the state's repressive agenda.

State and Social Suspicion of NGOs

State antipathy toward specific domestic NGOs inculcated a sociopolitical environment that encouraged media, citizens, politicians, and religious leaders to vilify NGOs, particularly those critical of Mutharika's governance.[21] Malawian NGOs that became targets of state and social hostility were typically those that worked on issues associated with social movements, such as respecting human rights, improving the rule of law, and strengthening democratic institutions. Domestic NGOs with paid staff, formal rules, and bureaucratic procedures differed from grassroots community-based organizations that worked almost exclusively at the local level, sometimes in concert with NGOs.[22] As in other African countries, "[r]elationships between contemporary ... governments" and NGOs in Malawi "have been largely adversarial and imbued with mutual mistrust."[23] This is not to say that political elites and ordinary Malawians uniformly disapproved of all NGOs. However, many Malawians were skeptical of NGOs they perceived to have close ties to Northern donors. This skepticism emerged from a fundamental irony. Without foreign

---

[20] Whereas some scholars use the negative radical flank effect to discuss how moderate movement organizations may discipline and exclude extremist organizations in the same movement, I have adapted this concept to reflect how movements in the same coalition may disparage and sideline unpopular or "extremist" movements.

[21] Although Mutharika's government disparaged international NGOs, such as Amnesty International, that criticized his leadership, in this chapter, I focus on attacks leveled by his administration against domestic NGOs.

[22] Susan Cotts Watkins and Ann Swidler, *A Fraught Embrace: The Romance and Reality of AIDS Altruism in Africa* (Princeton, NJ: Princeton University Press, 2017), 46–48.

[23] Grace Chikoto-Schulz and Kelechi Uzochukwu, "Governing Civil Society in Nigeria and Zimbabwe: A Question of Policy Process and Non-State Actors' Involvement," *Nonprofit Policy Forum*, 7, no. 2 (2016): 137.

donor funding, most NGOs would not exist; therefore, NGOs were ethically dubious from their inception, according to some Malawians. As Susan Cotts Watkins, Ann Swidler, and Thomas Hannan explain, a "key problem for foreign donors is that they cannot actually reach their intended beneficiaries directly, but rather have to act through an 'aid chain'" of NGOs.[24] NGOs channel funds from Northern donors to Malawian beneficiaries.[25] Although NGO activities can and do benefit ordinary Malawians, NGOs' public reputations as currying favor with Northern donors enhance widespread misgivings about these organizations.

As the state engaged in democratizing activities, NGOs proliferated in the 1990s and 2000s in Malawi.[26] However, NGO "activities were competitive rather than coordinated" in this neoliberal economic system, leaving some constituents to wonder whom NGOs were supposed to represent, as NGOs vied for precious foreign donor funding.[27] Many Malawian NGOs functioned as *intermediaries ...* between the needs of the state and the needs of ordinary people," delivering social services to underserved populations and pressuring state leaders to curtail economic malfeasance and to implement social-justice reforms.[28] Although many NGOs served Malawians, they also engaged in strategies that enlarged their scope of action to the transnational arena, notably by procuring Northern donor funding, participating in international conferences, and consulting with foreign diplomats. In this way, social movement mobilization within Malawi also doubled as transnationalization.[29]

Financial necessity partly motivated NGOs' transnationalization because leaders sought ways to become "sustainable" without having to rely on funders' assistance. Participating in a transnational public

---

[24] Susan Cotts Watkins, Ann Swidler, and Thomas Hannan, "Outsourcing Social Transformation: Development NGOs as Organizations," *Annual Review of Sociology*, 38 (2012): 287.

[25] Adam Branch and Zachariah Mampilly, *Africa Uprising: Popular Protest and Political Change* (New York: Zed, 2015), 76–77.

[26] Englund, *Prisoners of Freedom*.

[27] Peter Dwyer and Leo Zeilig, *African Struggles Today: Social Movements since Independence* (Chicago: Haymarket Books, 2012), 135.

[28] Ibid., 157; emphasis original.

[29] Marie-Emmanuelle Pommerolle, "The Extraversion of Protest: Conditions, History, and Use of the 'International' in Africa," *Review of African Political Economy*, 37, no. 125 (2010): 264–265.

sphere rendered some NGOs vulnerable to intranational critique, as some political elites and ordinary Malawians viewed NGOs as agents serving Northern donors, not Malawians in need. In skeptics' eyes, the "NGO presence in Africa can reasonably be seen, for good or ill, as the latest successor of earlier colonial penetrations."[30] Suspicion motivated many elites' and Malawians' unfavorable views of NGOs, generating the seeds for the political repression of different NGOs and oppositional social movements.

Hostility toward NGOs in Malawi

Since Malawi's democratic transition away from the authoritarian rule of Hastings Kamuzu Banda in 1994, NGOs supported Bakili Muluzi (1994–2004) and Bingu wa Mutharika (2004–2012) in their first terms but developed a contentious relationship with each president in their second terms when the president and cabinet ministers began governing undemocratically.[31] Political and public suspicions about NGOs began circulating during Muluzi's first term in office and persisted throughout Mutharika's presidency.

Criticisms of NGOs tended to cluster into four categories. First, some observers worried about proliferating NGOs. The multiplication of NGOs threatened to engender competition in NGO circles for limited donor funding and support.[32] Other critics expressed concern about significant overlap between NGO and government mandates.[33] Second, some critics alleged that NGOs were established so that founders could line their own pockets.[34] In 2006, an unnamed diplomat accused NGO leaders of trying to defraud donors: "Most of them are obsessed with posh 4X4 vehicles and build mansions at the expense

---

[30] Ann Swidler, "Syncretism and Subversion in AIDS Governance: How Locals Cope with Global Demands," *International Affairs*, 82, no. 2 (2006): 282.

[31] Jerry, interview with the author, July 3, 2012, Lilongwe, Malawi. See also, Dwyer and Zeilig, *African Struggles Today*, 137, 139, and Englund, *Prisoners of Freedom*.

[32] "Government Asked to Finance Civil Society," *Daily Times*, March 6, 2002, 2.

[33] Emily L. Nkamanga, "Keep an Eye on NGOs," *Nation*, May 19, 1995, 9.

[34] Giles Likongwe, "Government Should Inspect NGOs," *Daily Times*, February 19, 1997, 9; Tamanda Matebule, "CONGOMA Accuses NGOs of Misusing Donor Aid," *Daily Times*, September 11, 2001, 2; Henry Mchazime, "Government Slams NGOs," *Daily Times*, October 11, 2010, 3; "NGO That Covers Nefarious Activities," *Malawi News*, January 11–17, 1997, 8.

of suffering Malawians meant to benefit from developmental projects."[35] Such accounts portrayed NGO leaders as motivated by personal greed instead of a commitment to serve Malawians.

Third, some critics accused NGOs of lacking accountability to the public, government, and donors. Rural community members voiced concerns about advocacy and development NGO representatives' disregard for local priorities, which might be for a clinic, not for a series of workshops.[36] Fourth, many criticisms of NGOs concentrated on their political activity.[37] Critics charged some NGOs of being neocolonial agents "infiltrating ... Malawi society and destabilising it so that right wing elements in certain countries can say 'we told you so: Africans are not ready to rule themselves.'"[38] Apprehension about NGOs' loyalties and stances toward the government set the stage for repression targeting NGOs and social movements critical of the government's direction.

Beginning in the mid-1990s, some lawmakers and NGO leaders themselves sought to limit NGO activities – an example of channeling, a form of indirect repression. In 1995, NGOs began taking steps to regulate themselves to achieve "openness and transparency."[39] In the late 1990s, the Council for Non-Governmental Organisations (CONGOMA) instituted a "Code of Conduct" for NGOs, a form of NGO surveillance of other NGOs.[40] Some NGO leaders supported these efforts.[41] Other NGO representatives objected to CONGOMA's seeming collaboration with the government and state leaders'

---

[35] Caroline Somanje, "Malawi NGOs Are Gold Diggers, Says Diplomat," *Malawi News*, August 12–18, 2006, 3.

[36] Sam Banda, Jr., "NGOs Told to Act, Not Workshop," *Daily Times*, November 5, 2007, 2; "Don't Impose Projects on People – ADRA," *Daily Times*, April 27, 2010, 4; Temwani Mgunda, "NGOs: Achievers or Deceivers?," *Daily Times*, April 7, 2006, 27; Harold Ngalawa, "NGOs Are Dictators," *Daily Times*, July 1, 1997, 3.

[37] Cydric Damala, "Government's Threats to Ban Some NGOs Are a Timely Disciplinary Measure," *Sunday Times*, March 28, 2010, 8; "Government Asked to Finance Civil Society," 2.

[38] Giles Likongwe, "Government Should Inspect NGOs," *Daily Times*, February 19, 1997, 9.

[39] "NGOs Set New Rules," *Daily Times*, May 22, 1995, 1.

[40] Akimu Kaingana, "NGOs to Adopt Strict Code," *Daily Times*, March 27, 1997, 2; Aubrey Mchulu, "NGOs Launch Code of Conduct," *Daily Times*, May 27, 1997, 2.

[41] Aubrey Mchulu, "Law for NGOs Credibility, Integrity," *Nation*, June 4, 1996, 1.

"directive that [government] should be informed on any developments relating to donor aid."[42] Lawmakers proposed a bill about NGO regulation in 1996. In 1998, some human rights NGO leaders claimed that lawmakers and CONGOMA excluded them from discussions about the proposed legislation; CONGOMA's executive director dismissed these concerns, alleging that dissenting NGOs were not aligned with the umbrella body or had not attended planning meetings.[43] In 1999, CONGOMA directed NGOs not to engage in "partisan" politics.[44]

News commentators interpreted the NGO bill as the government's attempt to punish NGOs for taking away donor funds.[45] Muluzi's government reacted unfavorably when NGOs asked donors to pressure the government to change its policies toward and treatment of certain populations,[46] exemplifying the "boomerang" model of NGO activism in bringing international pressure to bear on governments engaging in human rights abuses or authoritarian governance.[47] After lawmakers passed the NGO bill in 2001, some NGOs became more openly critical of the law,[48] which gave the "state the final say in defining legitimate organizations."[49] During Muluzi's second term in office, government officials harassed NGOs perceived to be "indulging [in] politics" and targeted advocacy NGOs.[50] At a 1999 meeting of regional leaders, Muluzi warned NGOs that behaved as "political partners" that "[i]f they do not change their attitude then African governments will react," a veiled threat of repression.[51] NGO leaders did not react well to threats of repression.[52] Emmie Chanika, the

[42] "NGOs Worried with Government Move," *Nation*, December 20, 1996, 3.
[43] Victoria Msowoya, "Non Governmental Organisations Cry Out," *Daily Times*, April 1, 1998, 11.
[44] Bright Sonani, "NGOs Not for Politics," *Daily Times*, July 20, 1999, 3.
[45] "NGOs a Nightmare to Government," *Daily Times*, March 16, 2001, 15.
[46] "Government Condemns NGOs," *Daily Times*, December 21, 2001, 1.
[47] Margaret E. Keck and Kathryn Sikkink, *Activists beyond Borders: Advocacy Networks in International Politics* (Ithaca, NY: Cornell University Press, 1998), 12–13.
[48] Pilirani Semu, "NGOs Gang Up against Law," *Nation*, September 25, 2001, 1–2; Pilirani Semu, "NGOs to Fight for New Law," *Nation*, February 9, 2001, 1.
[49] Englund, *Prisoners of Freedom*, 97.
[50] Mabvuto Banda, "NGOs Condemn Muluzi's Statement," *Daily Times*, October 6, 1999, 3.
[51] Aubrey Mchulu, "Muluzi Warns NGOs," *Nation*, October 6, 1999, 1.
[52] Banda, "NGOs Condemn," 3.

executive director of the Civil Liberties Committee (CILIC) and CONGOMA board member, challenged government officials' expectations that NGO leaders and staff should remain nonpartisan. She stated, "We are citizens of Malawi first before becoming NGO leaders and as every other citizen we have a right to have political leanings since we also have a right to vote."[53]

Some NGO leaders and foreign donors supported Mutharika at the start of his first term.[54] Malawi's economic fortune improved in Mutharika's first term because of "renewed emphasis on civil service integrity, better fiscal policy due to the appointment of an experienced macroeconomist as Minister of Finance and Mutharika's personal commitment to improving the state's performance."[55] Mutharika's administration was also credited with engineering an "economic success story, underpinned by a popular agricultural subsidy that took Malawi from a 43 percent food deficit to a 53 percent food surplus nation. During this time, Malawi's economy grew at an average rate of 7 percent per annum."[56] In his first term as president, "Mutharika was feted domestically and internationally for implementing developmentalist policies" that jumpstarted the country's economy.[57] Yet when Mutharika's commitment to stopping corruption evaporated, NGOs began criticizing Mutharika's leadership at the start of his second term as president. According to Jerry, "when it comes to [the] second term, that's when the issues of greed started coming [up]."[58] Jerry was referring to NGO leaders' allegations of corruption and financial mismanagement in Mutharika's administration.

Mutharika's growing displeasure with donor criticism erupted in 2011. In March, he lambasted donors for agreeing with NGOs'

[53] Pilirani Semu, "Future for NGOs Bleak – CONGOMA," *Nation*, August 17, 2001, 2.

[54] Lucy, interview with the author, July 3, 2012, Lilongwe, Malawi. See also, Resnick, "Two Steps Forward," 115–118.

[55] Diana Cammack and Tim Kelsall, "Neo-Patrimonialism, Institutions, and Economic Growth: The Case of Malawi, 1964–2009," *IDS Bulletin*, 42, no. 2 (2011): 93.

[56] Kim Yi Dionne and Boniface Dulani, "Constitutional Provisions and Executive Succession: Malawi's 2012 Transition in Comparative Perspective," *African Affairs*, 112, no. 446 (2012): 112–113.

[57] Clive Gabay, "Two 'Transitions': The Political Economy of Joyce Banda's Rise to Power and the Related Role of Civil Society Organisations in Malawi," *Review of African Political Economy*, 41, no. 141 (2014): 376.

[58] Jerry, interview with the author, July 3, 2012, Lilongwe, Malawi.

criticisms of his administration.[59] He railed against donors: "What is your agenda in Malawi? Let me remind you that you came here and signed protocol agreements with the government of Malawi of which I am the leader. Now, why do you divert [funds] and start working with NGOs?"[60] Mutharika's criticism of NGOs converged with his increasing scorn for donors; he viewed the former as luring Northern donors away from the state, generating unwanted competition for donor funds. His disapproval of donors deteriorated into name-calling when he blasted "stupid Europeans" for "listening to 'stupid [nongovernmental] organisations.'"[61] Mutharika's disposition toward European donors turned hostile when he expelled British High Commissioner Fergus Cochrane-Dyet after the online leak of a cable in which Cochrane-Dyet described Mutharika as an autocrat.[62] In turn, Great Britain dismissed Malawi's government representative to the country.[63] Ordinary Malawians, church and NGO leaders, and donor representatives bemoaned these developments as endangering donor aid.[64] In conjunction with his increasingly authoritarian leadership, Mutharika's views on donors and NGOs continued to worsen. Although donor influence had the potential to undermine or strengthen NGOs' criticism of Mutharika, the president exploited NGOs' dependency on donor funding to tarnish their reputations.

[59] About 40 percent of the government's budget came from donor funding, according to a 2011 news report. Suzgo Khunga, "Malawi Expels British Envoy," *Daily Times*, April 28, 2011, 3–4.

[60] Wycliffe Njiragoma, "Bingu Blasts Donors," *Daily Times*, March 21, 2011, 1.

[61] Phillip Rukunuwa, "Hold Your Breath, Mr. President," *Daily Times*, May 11, 2011, 8.

[62] Suzgo Khunga, "Malawi Expels British Envoy," *Daily Times*, April 28, 2011, 3–4; Agnes Mizere and Suzgo Khunga, "Envoy Was Not Deported," *Sunday Times*, May 1, 2011, 1, 3.

[63] Dickson Kashoti, "Expelled Malawi Envoy Jets In," *Daily Times*, May 4, 2011, 1, 3.

[64] Dickson Kashoti, "Expulsion of British Envoy Unfortunate – EU," *Daily Times*, May 9, 2011, 2; Suzgo Khunga and Macdonald Thom, "Bishop Bvumbwe Warns on UK Ties," *Daily Times*, April 29, 2011, 3; Simeon Maganga, "Government Must Apologise to Britain," *Daily Times*, April 22, 2011, 1, 3; Karen Msiska and Suzgo Khunga, "Synod Condemns Government on UK Envoy Expulsion," *Daily Times*, May 2, 2011, 3; Madalitso Musa, "Malawians, EU Fault Government on UK Envoy," *Daily Times*, April 29, 2011, 3; Wycliffe Njiragoma, "Britain Warns Malawi Government," *Daily Times*, April 20, 2011, 1, 3.

The Run-Up to the July 20 Protests

NGO leaders grew increasingly unhappy with Mutharika's authoritarian leadership during his second term in office. As activists' criticisms of Mutharika mounted, some prominent activists received threats from state and ruling party leaders, some of which materialized in violence.[65] The government used multiple forms of repression to deter NGO leaders from mobilizing against Mutharika's rule. For instance, the office and home of Undule Mwakasungula, CHRR's executive director, were ransacked.[66] State and ruling party leaders and other elites dismissed some threats and attacks as staged by NGOs trying to "buy public sympathy" – an example of ridicule, a form of discursive repression.[67]

Some scholars and activists suspected that Mutharika's commitment to democracy was insincere. Clive Gabay claims that Mutharika's "erraticism had been apparent since his days as Secretary General of the Common Market for Southern and Eastern Africa (COMESA) in the 1990s."[68] For instance, Isaac, a human rights activist, speculated that growing up "under colonialism" made Mutharika mistrust Western governance, a sentiment that Linda, a women's rights activist, shared.[69] Linda conjectured that "having worked in the World Bank, [Mutharika] suffered racism. So, I think he never got over it. That's the psychology of a typical man who suffered critical racism."[70] She believed that after leaving the World Bank, Mutharika "wanted to use his ... personal power to fix those people" who mistreated him.[71] Employing a logic similar to that identified by Linda, Isaac explained the seeds of Mutharika's antipathy toward democracy:

---

[65] Anthony Kasunda, "Mwakasungula Gets Death Threats," *Nation*, March 25, 2011, 1–2; Frank Namangale, "Rights Activists Raise Death Threats Alarm," *Nation*, March 2, 2011, 1–2.

[66] Bright Sonani, "Police Invade Undule's Karonga Home," *Nation*, March 14, 2011, 3; Bright Sonani, "Thugs Attack Undule's Offices," *Nation*, March 4, 2011, 1–2.

[67] Bright Sonani, "Government Says NGOs Staged Attack on Undule," *Nation*, March 10, 2011, 2.

[68] Gabay, "Two 'Transitions,'" 376.

[69] Isaac, interview with the author, July 11, 2012, Lilongwe, Malawi.

[70] Linda, interview with the author, June 25, 2012, Lilongwe, Malawi.   [71] Ibid.

he criticized the idea of democracy as a concept because he received it as a Western concept. What he wanted to develop was an African form of governance – whatever that meant – in order for Africans to develop their countries. And from that point on, you could see a slow progression towards dictatorship in his pronouncements, in his close relationship with [Zimbabwean President] Robert Mugabe and dictators like [Sudanese President Omar] al-Bashir, and also [in] his decision to align Malawi more close[ly with] communist China.[72]

Mutharika's leadership offered multiple warning signs of his administration's lack of democratic transparency. According to Isaac, Mutharika "progressively trampled on fundamental freedoms slowly, by criticizing the press, by deriding civil society for their actions, for what he called spearheading a gay agenda. So he wanted to … cultivate a mood of criticism" that turned "local communities" against NGOs that Mutharika portrayed as "protecting the gay agenda in order to trample on Malawi's traditional values."[73] Mutharika's administration positioned LGBT rights as an unwelcome development in Malawi and depicted NGOs critical of the government as "protecting the gay agenda," a move intended to discredit oppositional NGOs publicly.[74] One defender of Mutharika's leadership joined Mutharika in portraying a wide swath of NGOs as "agitating for gay rights … Surely, this tendency cannot be anything but a manifestation of bad will on the part of leaders of the said NGOs who instead of sweating for the wellbeing of the people they target, they are busy tussling it out against their own beneficiaries in partnerships with external advocates for gay rights."[75] Portraying oppositional NGOs as prioritizing LGBT rights above other issues enabled Mutharika and political elites to cast NGOs as betraying the heteronormative nation and interests of Malawians in need of crucial social services. The government, ruling party, and other elites wielded politicized homophobia to turn public opinion against defiant NGOs and to engender irreconcilable divisions among social movements. Despite the fact that most NGOs opposing Mutharika's leadership did not work on LGBT rights, politicized homophobia operated as a means to discipline and divide social movements.

Mutharika's administration enacted several measures that consolidated his power, weakened democratic institutions, and contributed to

---

[72] Isaac, interview with the author, July 11, 2012, Lilongwe, Malawi. [73] Ibid.
[74] Ibid. [75] Damala, "Government's Threats to Ban," 8.

the repressive sociopolitical environment. These measures included: an amended Police Act; Penal Code Section 46, which threatened the press with censorship; and a law that redesigned the country's flag with little input from ordinary Malawians.[76] First, after the Police Act's passage, some activists expected that police would deny their requests to stage demonstrations. According to Isaac, "police act in cahoots with the government" and "would ordinarily not accept a demonstration spearheaded by civil society, unless it was a pro-government agenda [or] a safe agenda [having] ... to do with food."[77] Second, Isaac pointed out that Section 46 was another repressive constraint on social movements. Section 46 "empower[s] a minister to close down" newspapers "perceived to be anti-government," which Isaac believed dealt "a heavy blow" to the Malawian press.[78] Curtailing press freedom "contributed to this downward slide of [the] ... work of civil society," shrinking the democratic space from which NGOs could criticize the government, according to Isaac.[79] Third, a crisis over academic freedom at Chancellor College contributed to activists' consternation over the sociopolitical climate in the country.[80] Fourth, the DPP-led government surreptitiously "set up a presidential advisory board where they co-opted some members of civil society who sort of softened their approach to activism. So that also divided civil society," Isaac related.[81] NGO leaders who accepted an appointment to this advisory board diluted their resistance to the government.

In response to Mutharika's authoritarianism and shortages of basic necessities, NGO leaders decided to draft a petition listing their state-directed grievances. In 2009 and 2010, during Mutharika's second term in office, Malawi experienced significant shortages of foreign currency, electricity, and fuel, which NGO leaders attributed to poor leadership, corruption, and financial mismanagement. Activists

---

[76] Cammack, "Malawi in Crisis," 377. See also, Resnick, "Two Steps Forward," 127–133.

[77] Isaac, interview with the author, July 11, 2012, Lilongwe, Malawi. Food scarcity was a social and economic problem that galvanized many Malawians. It would have made little sense for the government to ban a protest related to food security because it affected so many Malawians.

[78] Isaac, interview with the author, July 11, 2012, Lilongwe, Malawi.   [79] Ibid.

[80] Government officials accused a Chancellor College professor of using a lesson about the Arab Spring to provoke students into mobilizing against Mutharika's administration. Cammack, "Malawi in Crisis," 377.

[81] Isaac, interview with the author, July 11, 2012, Lilongwe, Malawi.

became outraged, as Justice, a CONGOMA staff member, indicated, because "there [was] a shortage in the country to a level that has never happened before. So we started talking publicly trying to change the government's . . . view. The government was not listening."[82] Unhappy with Mutharika's refusal to listen to alternative viewpoints, activists developed a "20-point petition because we felt that . . . having failed to dialogue with the president, [it] was important to . . . come up with a position that speaks to the concerns of Malawians."[83] The petition enumerated activists' grievances, which included the following issues: shortages of fuel, electricity, and foreign currency; the academic-freedom crisis; and Mutharika's administration's financial mismanagement, political corruption, disregard for the rule of law, refusal to hold local elections, and general belligerence.[84]

Activists planned to stage "a demonstration. This demonstration was supposed to take place in February 2011, but the government did not give us permission to conduct that demonstration. Instead, the president called for a meeting with the civil society leaders" at that time, Justice explained.[85] At the meeting, activists delivered the presentation, giving the president the opportunity to respond to their grievances. Isaac attended the meeting at which Mutharika pledged to listen to NGOs' grievances and related that activists informed the president that

Malawi was on a downward slope towards dictatorship, and we demanded that the twenty-point petition be responded to immediately by government. Of course, [for] some of the issues, we knew the solutions were long term, but we thought it would be important for the government to make its position known on the issues and to give a timeframe on when those issues would be resolved, for example, the fuel crisis and other issues . . . We said to give us a timeframe when fuel will be available. We said, "Give us a timeframe when forex [foreign currency] will be available," but then on other issues we said, "We're not going to negotiate on . . . Section 46. We need a repeal immediately. We need a repeal of certain sections of the Police Act."[86]

---

[82] Justice, interview with the author, July 9, 2012, Lilongwe, Malawi.
[83] Davis, interview with the author, July 10, 2012, Lilongwe, Malawi.
[84] I distilled this list of grievances from NGOs' submitted petition to Mutharika, which was posted to Vince Kumwenda's blog (http://vincekumwenda.blogspot .com/2011/07/petition-presented-to-malawi-president.html).
[85] Justice, interview with the author, July 9, 2012, Lilongwe, Malawi.
[86] Isaac, interview with the author, July 11, 2012, Lilongwe, Malawi.

Isaac recalled that the "meeting did not end well. The president, visibly angry, banged the table and so on," expressing anger at activists' temerity in confronting him with their grievances.[87] Isaac remembered activists telling Mutharika, "'As civil society, we're not going to back down.' So we said given the president's volatile personality, we need to mobilize the whole nation to show the discontent of citizens."[88]

As NGOs organized a response to Mutharika's refusal to engage with their demands, same-sex sexualities remained in the spotlight. In May 2011, CONGOMA representatives advised Mutharika not to use homosexuality "to divert attention from real issues affecting the country," evidence of activists' awareness that Mutharika and his comrades used politicized homophobia as repression.[89] CONGOMA representatives reassured Mutharika's government that "advocating for minority rights [was] not a priority [for CONGOMA] as homosexuality—practised by a minority—remain[ed] illegal in the country."[90] In their efforts to persuade Mutharika to respond to NGOs' grievances, CONGOMA representatives deployed issue ranking, which suggested that there were more pressing matters than LGBT rights; in turn, this ploy perpetuated politicized homophobia. Mutharika continued attacking sexual minorities, addressing one political party rally, "You will never see dogs marry each other. These people [sexual minorities] want us to behave worse than dogs. I cannot allow it."[91] At an event celebrating the elevation of chiefs one month later, Mutharika reproached NGO leaders for "selling the country by getting money to champion foreign cultures" and practices like same-sex sexualities.[92] Deploring LGBT rights as an aid conditionality, Mutharika stated, "Yes, we rely on donors but what is happening is like giving a beggar more money than he or she usually gets and spit[ting] on him or her. Sometimes it is fair to tell them to take their money so that we keep our culture."[93] The journalist who penned this story recognized the government's politicized

---

[87] Ibid.   [88] Ibid.

[89] Kondwani Munthali, "Slow Down Mr. President – NGOs," *Nation*, May 6, 2011, 2.

[90] Ibid., 1.

[91] Kondwani Munthali, "Gays Worse Than Dogs – Bingu," *Nation*, May 16, 2011, 2.

[92] Edwin Nyirongo, "NGOs Selling Malawi for Money – Bingu," *Nation*, June 8, 2011.

[93] Ibid.

homophobia as intended to discredit NGOs defending LGBT rights; he stated, "Government spin doctors have recently intensified the campaign to isolate NGO leaders that want government to remove laws that make same-sex relationships illegal."[94] In a repressive move, police also confiscated "cloth inscribed with messages promoting gay rights," which CEDEP and CHRR arranged to be produced in neighboring Tanzania.[95] State leaders' ongoing deployment of politicized homophobia ensured that they could quickly and proactively employ it as a repressive instrument.

The July 20 Protests

When Mutharika took no action on NGO grievances, activists obtained police permission to hold protests in Blantyre, Lilongwe, and Mzuzu, on July 20, 2011. In the days preceding the protests, DPP youth cadets "brandish[ed] ... machetes and metal bars" in Blantyre's business district in an effort to dissuade people from taking part in the protests.[96] An observer commented on the panga-wielding DPP youth cadets: "Where is democracy when you see people carrying such dangerous weapons in the streets in party cars without being apprehended? Whatever they threaten us with, we will still march because this is our country and we have the right to voice our concerns when things are not okay."[97] NGO leaders called attention to a "DPP plot to attack [the protests], create mayhem, and block roads designated for" protests in different cities.[98] DPP leaders authorized "sympathizers" to stage "pro-government demonstrations," and NGO leaders warned the government that the pro-government counterprotests had the potential to "spark violence."[99]

---

[94] Ibid.

[95] Frank Namangale, "Police Seize Gay Campaign Cloth," *Nation*, May 18, 2011, 3. See also, Thokozani Chenjezi, "People Impound CHRR, CEDEP Cloth," *Daily Times*, May 20, 2011, 4.

[96] Madalitso Musa, "Bingu Okays Demonstrations: DPP Cadets Terror on the Loose," *Daily Times*, July 20, 2011, 1.

[97] Ibid.

[98] Kondwani Munthali, "There's Plan to Attack Demos, Arrest Leaders – NGOs," *Nation*, July 19, 2011, 2.

[99] Kondwani Munthali and Anthony Kasunda, "PAC, MHRC Caution Government on Violence," *Nation*, July 19, 2011, 1.

Police used violence to disperse and repress protestors on July 20.[100] Challenging the government exacted a steep toll on some activists. On July 20, 2011, police attacked Daniel, a human rights activist, and others in Lilongwe.[101] Between twenty and thirty activist colleagues, including prominent human rights activists, gathered at a church, waiting to see if they would be allowed to hold the protest as planned. A private citizen filed a court injunction preventing the protests from taking place, generating confusion among would-be marchers.[102] Almost one year after the July 20 protests, Davis, a human rights activist, expressed surprise that "even after we had acquired the permission to hold peaceful demonstrations," Mutharika's "regime used a supporter ... to get an injunction last minute, which created chaos because Malawians couldn't understand why the injunction" was in place.[103] Because Davis and other NGO leaders were "law-abiding citizens," they knew that they could not "proceed with the demonstrations."[104] They informed protest organizers throughout the country about the need to halt the demonstration because of the injunction.

The church seemed like a safe place for activists to wait. Daniel recalled thinking, "Maybe [the police] cannot invade a church, okay, because it is a sacred place."[105] After a few hours, the police stormed the church and "rounded ... up" activists.[106] "They made us lie on the ground. So we lay on the ground."[107] The police then asked activists to get up and move toward "big police vans ... known for violence."[108] The police "started beating us [with nightsticks] on 20th of July."[109] Davis attributed the outburst of violence to the president who "directed [DPP youth] cadets ... to beat any person who goes in the streets."[110] Daniel explained that police "received a message [to] leave" activists, who drove themselves to the hospital.[111] Yet their

---

[100] Daniel Wroe, "Donors, Dependency, and Political Crisis in Malawi," *African Affairs*, 111, no. 442 (2012): 135–144.

[101] Daniel, interview with the author, July 9, 2012, Lilongwe, Malawi.

[102] Bright Sonani, "Court Reverses Injunction, LL Marches in Afternoon," *Nation*, July 21, 2011, 3.

[103] Davis, interview with the author, July 10, 2012, Lilongwe, Malawi.

[104] Ibid.

[105] Daniel, interview with the author, July 9, 2012, Lilongwe, Malawi.

[106] Ibid.   [107] Ibid.   [108] Ibid.   [109] Ibid.

[110] Davis, interview with the author, July 10, 2012, Lilongwe, Malawi.

[111] Daniel, interview with the author, July 9, 2012, Lilongwe, Malawi.

route to the hospital was circuitous because "most of the roads were closed," due to the protest, an irony Daniel found amusing.[112]

Police violence erupted in other cities as well. Some protestors allegedly torched police cars and tires in an effort to block major roads. Mutharika blamed street violence and looting on NGOs. He stated, "The information that we have is that the arsonists and looters had pre-assigned targets to attack and were being directed to such looting locations through cell phones and hostile radio stations. This action was clearly criminal and not political."[113] Much to the disappointment of activist leaders, Mutharika scheduled a public lecture for July 20, instead of responding to NGOs' demands. Daniel recalled that as the protests turned violent, the president opted to give a "public lecture. He was saying that he wants to teach Malawians on good governance at his state house," a claim that NGO leaders found ludicrous.[114] "[W]hile we [were] organizing demonstrations, the party followers, the sympathizers, went to the state house for a public lecture."[115] After the president learned that "the towns are burning" and "people are rioting," he "cut short the public lecture," Daniel recalled.[116]

Mutharika's government claimed that NGOs brought state repression on themselves. Mutharika himself warned both NGOs and opposition political parties about the serious consequences of trying to stage a coup. He stated,

The demonstrations were a ploy by John Tembo, Undule Mwakasungura [sic], Rafiq Hajat, Cassim Chilumpha, [Reverend Macdonald] Sembereka, Joyce Banda, and Ralph Kasambara to overtake my government which flopped. But they should know that this is a serious offence ... what Honourable Tembo, Mwakasungura [sic], Joyce Banda, and others should know is that the souls of those who died in the riots of Wednesday, July 20, will haunt them.[117]

[112] Ibid.

[113] Wycliffe Njiragoma, "Bingu Responds to July 20 Petition," *Daily Times*, August 15, 2011, 1.

[114] Daniel, interview with the author, July 9, 2012, Lilongwe, Malawi.

[115] Ibid.   [116] Ibid.

[117] John Tembo ran for president against Mutharika in 2004 and 2009 and lost. Undule Mwakasungula was CHRR's executive director and coordinator of the Human Rights Consultative Committee. Rafiq Hajat was the executive director of the Institute for Policy Interaction (IPI). Cassim Chilumpha was the vice president of Malawi during Mutharika's first term as president until he was accused of treason for conspiring to assassinate Mutharika; during 2011, he

Voice Mhone, CONGOMA's executive director, condemned Mutharika for blaming police violence on NGOs: "[W]e expected him to lead the nation in mourning the deaths of ... fallen friends and not inciting hostilities towards NGO leaders. The President must not use the souls of those who passed away as a campaign tool."[118] Newspaper editors joined the chorus of those calling for Mutharika and his administration to deescalate their repression. A *Malawi News* editorial asserted, "Government has been blaming everybody—from donors, gay rights activists, civil society, to opposition parties—for everything that has not been right ... in this country ... Government should get out of the denial state it is in ... It is time it stopped looking for scapegoats for everything it has done wrong, or failed to do right."[119]

State repression of NGO leaders persisted after the July 20 protests. After the furor over the protests subsided, NGO leaders planned "to hold a peaceful ... demonstration" in August in the form of a "vigil," Davis related.[120] Mutharika warned that authorities would not

sit idle and watch. Those who are responsible [for the anarchy], the government will find you, wherever you are hiding ... If you decide to go on the streets on the 17th [of August], I will find you there. I will not allow the country to be run by NGOs. Which elections elected Undule Mwakasungula, [Voice] Mhone, or [Rafiq] Hajat?[121]

Mutharika continued to name and blame certain NGO leaders for inciting opposition against his administration. However, the vigil "never took place" because Mutharika's administration learned about it and "instructed the Malawi army to come in and fight the protestors," Davis explained.[122] NGO leaders "decided to call off the vigil.

was the elected legislative representative for Nkhotakota South. Reverend Macdonald Sembereka was the executive director of Malawi Network of Religious Leaders Living or Personally Affected by HIV and AIDS (MANERELA+). In 2011, Joyce Banda was the vice president of Malawi. Ralph Kasambara was a former attorney general of the country and activist. Lucas Bottoman, "Bingu Warns Demo Organizers," *Malawi News*, July 23–29, 2011, 3.

118 Ibid., 7.   119 "Stop the Blame Game," *Malawi News*, July 23–29, 2011, 4.
120 Davis, interview with the author, July 10, 2012, Lilongwe, Malawi.
121 Dickson Kashoti and Simeon Maganga, "No Demos, Bingu Warns," *Daily Times*, August 12, 2011, 1. Also, see note 117 in this chapter.
122 Davis, interview with the author, July 10, 2012, Lilongwe, Malawi.

So what we did was that we advised the citizens to hold the vigil in their homes."[123] Due to activists' unrelenting pressure on the government to initiate reform, the government increased threats against activists, even "victimizing some of us," according to Davis.[124] Mutharika claimed that activists were trying to "overthrow [the] government," an allegation used to justify state retaliation against NGO leaders.[125] One leader shared a harrowing story of being accused of treason.[126] During a "live radio debate [about] … 'where has Malawi gone wrong and what needs to be done?,'" government spokespeople alleged that, by challenging the government, he had "committed treason" and "should be very mindful of the consequences of that." In response to this threat, which "was live," the activist leader knew that

Malawians were listening, and I told them [the listeners], "If I die, they should hold these two guys accountable." … Soon after the interview, … I got an anonymous call … He said, "Who do you think you are? Do you have the energy to fight this government?"

When the activist leader pressed the stranger for his identity, the caller elaborated on his threat: "'No, you don't need to know the caller, but you must know that you're being followed. We are actually following every detail, every movement that you are making' … He told me that I will be the sacrificial lamb for all the people who are opposing [Mutharika's] regime." Mutharika's threats of violence against protest organizers persisted, and he warned activists: "I will smoke you out."[127]

Whereas some activists experienced threats from unknown sources, other activists suffered far worse consequences as NGO leaders promised to stage a follow-up protest on September 21, 2011. To deter the mass protests that occurred July 20, 2011, Mutharika issued threats suggesting he was willing to wage "war." He claimed that he authorized a "committee on dialogue" as a conciliatory sign, but the frustration he conveyed about NGO leaders refusing to participate in the talk was far from mollifying.

---

[123] Ibid.   [124] Ibid.   [125] Ibid.
[126] To protect this research participant's identity, I provide no identifying details about the nature of his advocacy work.
[127] Madalitso Musa, "Group Urges Bingu against Hate Speech," *Daily Times*, August 15, 2011, 4.

What the hell do you want? If you are not ready for the talks, make your position known. Inform me of the day that we can start war ... [I]f my opponents want "war," so be it. I will take them head-on. Let this country go on fire if you want but enough is enough, I cannot tolerate this anymore.[128]

Activists viewed Mutharika's pugilistic threats warily, and some retreated from public engagements.

State repression continued for several months after the July 20 protests. DPP youth cadets allegedly set fire to the office of the Institute for Policy Interaction (IPI) in Blantyre in September 2011. Davis recalled a presidential spokesperson claiming that Rafiq Hajat, IPI's executive director, "was trying to destroy evidence because he ... mismanaged funds," an example of repressive rhetoric alleging the NGO's improper use of donor funds.[129] Soon thereafter, the home of Reverend Macdonald Sembereka, the leader of the Malawi Network of Religious Leaders Living or Personally Affected by HIV and AIDS (MANERELA+), a pro-LGBT rights organization, was "torched."[130] Within a few days of the arson at Sembereka's home, Mwakasungula found a "poster pasted on his house ... written 'house [for] sale,'" which Davis interpreted to mean: "We know where you live."[131] News coverage confirmed that "for sale" signs appeared at Mwakasungula's home and at the CHRR office.[132] Around the same time Mwakasungula found a threat at his home, Wapona Kita, a human rights lawyer assisting NGO leaders, also discovered "a poster pasted on his car written 'car for sale,' and they included [his mobile] number," Davis shared.[133] Fearing for their personal safety and that of their families, some activist leaders went into hiding in Malawi, moving from safe house to safe house to evade attacks from the police, military, or DPP youth cadets. Several weeks after the attacks, Isaac recalled several strangers who "started shouting [and] banging on the

---

[128] Caroline Kandiero, "Bingu Makes War Threats," *Daily Times*, August 26, 2011, 1. All quotations in this paragraph come from this source.

[129] Davis, interview with the author, July 10, 2012, Lilongwe, Malawi.

[130] Madalitso Musa, "Rev. Sembereka's House Torched," *Sunday Times*, September 12, 2011, 1, 3.

[131] Davis, interview with the author, July 10, 2012, Lilongwe, Malawi.

[132] Suzgo Khunga, "'For Sale' Posters Pasted at Undule's Home, Office," *Daily Times*, March 6, 2012, 3.

[133] Davis, interview with the author, July 10, 2012, Lilongwe, Malawi.

gate ... So I called the police. They said, 'Well, there's nothing we can do.'"[134] Fearing that these strangers would return and harm his family, Isaac felt that he had no other choice but "to go into hiding for about three or four days with the family. It was terrible, terrible."[135] Others, like Mwakasungula and Hajat, fled the country until the political atmosphere quieted down.[136]

Threats to activists' personal safety prompted some activists to scale back their mobilization efforts. After the July 20 protests, Patricia, an activist who worked at an NGO working to improve healthcare provision and access, felt that her security had been compromised. She confessed, "It became very difficult, you know? Because of the security threats. So, even [for] me, my waking hours became very unpredictable because I was not sure if I'm safe working from home or if I'm safe working in the office."[137] Like Patricia, other activists either directly involved with or on the margins of the July 20 protests faced threats from the police and government.

Threats from the police and DPP youth cadets did not deter some activist leaders from pressing forward with the grievances articulated in the petition they presented to the president. According to Davis, "things didn't change" after July 20. "As civil society, we maintained our opposition" to the government. Like other social movements cornered by government repression, human rights organizations, including that helmed by Davis, "mobiliz[ed] international support." Davis enumerated NGO leaders' efforts to catapult Malawi's devolving governance issues into international prominence. With other NGO leaders, Davis represented Malawian NGOs at an "international conference for human rights defenders" and updated meeting attendees about state repression in Malawi. NGO leaders also met with and lobbied European parliamentarians. On this international outreach tour, NGO leaders "met the Minister of Foreign Affairs for [the] Irish government" along with representatives from Amnesty International and Transparency International, an international NGO that monitors governments' corruption around the world. For Davis, "these

---

[134] Isaac, interview with the author, July 11, 2012, Lilongwe, Malawi.
[135] Ibid.
[136] "Malawi Activists 'in Hiding after Mutharika Threat,'" *BBC*, July 25, 2011, www.bbc.co.uk/news/world-africa-14276599.
[137] Patricia, interview with the author, July 13, 2012, Lilongwe, Malawi. All quotations in this paragraph come from this source.

platforms" enabled NGO leaders to publicize what they "were going through in Malawi." NGO leaders also elicited regional support from the Southern Africa Human Rights Defenders' Forum. Additionally, activist leaders aired their grievances with the United Nations and African Union, hoping that these supranational bodies would influence Mutharika. Although Davis believed that this outreach "helped to bring the issues to the international domain," not even a "statement by the United Nations" budged Mutharika from his defiant position, which constituted a reversal of his accession to UN wishes, when, in 2010, he pardoned Chimbalanga and Monjeza, a move recommended by UN Secretary-General Ban Ki-moon. Therefore, "things didn't improve. The president remained militant." Mutharika continued to claim that NGOs were "working with misguided international bodies whose intention is to overthrow his regime, and he will use what it takes to protect himself."[138] In particular, Mutharika's administration became confrontational with Northern governments that rescinded promises to deliver development aid because they objected to the government's authoritarian tactics.

To subvert and constrain social movements, state officials offered lucrative government positions to some NGO leaders. Alice, an activist working at a human rights NGO, explained that state leaders "were literally trying to buy members of civil society to their side." She suggested that in exchange for jobs, former NGO leaders were supposed to inform the government of NGOs' plans. Alice stated that insider information would give the government "adequate grounds" to place NGO leaders under "house arrest." Rumors of the government "buying" leaders circulated among NGOs. Alice mentioned that the government recruited a senior staff member from a prominent human rights organization to work for Mutharika's administration. She portrayed this individual as a lackey who "used to back up whatever economic statement or policy [President] Bingu [wa Mutharika] would make, whether it was good or bad. So he would actually be talking on TV and saying that that is good." According to Alice, the strategy of luring NGO leaders away from their jobs was part of the government's larger plan "to turn the public against civil society to say that 'civil society is not good. They're in partnership with the donors . . . So don't

---

[138] Davis, interview with the author, July 10, 2012, Lilongwe, Malawi. All quotations in this paragraph come from this source.

follow them.' So it was like creating an enemy of very bad relationships between civil society and people at grassroots."[139]

Another repressive tactic entailed isolating and portraying NGOs as enemies of the state. Bessie Chirambo, the president's advisor on NGOs, negatively portrayed NGOs critical of Mutharika's leadership as "bark[ing] at anything including flies. These NGOs have become monotonous with their requests to government and as government we have become deaf to them. If they really care about people they should ... not take people to the streets to demonstrate where they get killed."[140] Her statement squarely blamed NGOs for the deaths resulting from the July 20 protests and confirmed that the government was ignoring NGO demands for economic, political, and social change. Going on the offensive, Mutharika claimed that these organizations "were alien to Malawi, were working with [what] he called 'power-hungry politicians,' and [were] not patriotic."[141] NGO leaders like Davis believed that Mutharika's xenophobic characterization of NGOs "had the potential to incite Malawians to rise against us."[142] In addition to deploying xenophobic allegations that NGOs actively undermined Malawian social and political institutions, Mutharika's administration and political party mobilized politicized homophobia to corral and silence social movements during and after the July 20 protests.

The Deployment of Politicized Homophobia during and after the July 20 Protests

With looming mass protests in urban areas, state leaders portrayed the planned July 20 protests as an attempt by NGOs to force the government to decriminalize same-sex sex, an example of the government's effort to use politicized homophobia proactively to drive a wedge between social movements. In turn, NGOs were supposed to pressure LGBT rights organizations into suspending their advocacy. In these ways, politicized homophobia functioned as a tool of state repression

[139] Alice, interview with the author, July 4, 2012, Lilongwe, Malawi. All quotations in this paragraph come from this source.

[140] Jacob Nankhonya, "NGOs 'Bark Like Dogs,'" *Sunday Times*, February 26, 2012, 3.

[141] Davis, interview with the author, July 10, 2012, Lilongwe, Malawi.

[142] Ibid.

during and after the July 20 protests. Although one could argue that it makes more sense to analyze politicized homophobia as part of the regime's broader efforts to stifle democratic dissent associated with the July 20 protests, I find it important to emphasize how politicized homophobia operated as a political strategy that elites hoped would contain NGOs the regime depicted as trying simultaneously to oust the government and to decriminalize same-sex sex. Using politicized homophobia, the government sought to suppress the democratic exchange of ideas and grievances and to mobilize public opinion against sexual diversity. State leaders hoped politicized homophobia would silence NGOs calling for democratic accountability and respect for Malawians' rights and ultimately "depoliticize social protest."[143]

NGOs became targets of the government's repressive campaign of politicized homophobia when several human rights activists expressed solidarity for LGBT rights. According to Isaac, "there was a very bold attempt by Malawi's small gay community to fight for their rights," which human rights NGOs supported.[144] As "human rights activists we said ... 'We're just saying these people have rights. Let us debate the issue as Malawians.'"[145] Instead, Mutharika publicly claimed that these NGOs were "against Malawian traditional values ... They speak about governance, but their actual objective is to promote gay rights in Malawi."[146] Jackson, a former CEDEP employee, notes that the media helped stoke opposition to organizations' defense of LGBT rights. Malawian journalists reported that "NGOs were advocating for gay marriages," insinuating that organizations like CHRR and CEDEP had staged the engagement ceremony between Chimbalanga and Monjeza as a ruse to initiate public debate about the legalization of same-sex marriage.[147]

Operating as a "scavenger ideology," politicized homophobia discouraged some Malawians from participating in the mass protest that elites tried to portray as an underhanded effort to legalize same-sex marriage.[148] In an editorial, political scientist Blessings Chinsinga recalled how the government characterized the "July 20 demonstrations ... as a façade for promoting gay rights when the

---

[143] Mbembe, "On Politics as a Form of Expenditure," 319.
[144] Isaac, interview with the author, July 11, 2012, Lilongwe, Malawi.
[145] Ibid.   [146] Ibid.
[147] Jackson, interview with the author, July 4, 2012, Blantyre, Malawi.
[148] Mosse, "Racism and Nationalism," 164.

people of this country had credible governance, human rights, economic and social concerns that needed urgent government attention."[149] Senior Chief Kaomba, an influential traditional leader, claimed that July 20 protest organizers wanted "Malawi to allow men [to] marry fellow men that is why they are marching."[150] Along with traditional leaders from Kasungu, Vuwa Kaunda, a government spokesperson, alleged that NGOs were agitating for "gay rights."[151] Hetherwick Ntaba, Mutharika's spokesperson, implored protest organizers to reveal whether money they had received from Northern donors was "funding . . . the July 20 demonstrations."[152] According to Ntaba, this admission would "assure Malawians that one of the issues Malawians will be demonstrating for will not be the advancement of gay rights in the country."[153] A government-controlled entity, the Malawi Broadcasting Corporation (MBC) also represented the "demonstrations as a gay rights event," disseminating false information to Malawians.[154] Repudiating Ntaba's insinuation that activists' demands motivating the July 20 protests were illegitimate, Reverend Sembereka characterized the government's "gimmick" of deploying politicized homophobia as "distracting Malawians from real issues that rob them of their hard-won democracy and rights."[155] Sembereka also demanded that the government furnish evidence that NGOs had received "'huge' sums of money from gay rights bodies outside the country."[156]

Some activists conjectured that elites exploited rural Malawians' low levels of literacy when deploying politicized homophobia. Jeremiah, a human rights activist, theorized that Mutharika, the DPP, and his supporters used homosexuality "to rally the support from the people who are ignorant. Because 65% of Malawians, they're illiterate.

---

[149] Blessings Chinsinga, "Of Gay Rights and Section 65," *Sunday Times*, June 10, 2012, 7.

[150] Wisdom Chimgwede, "The Only July 20, 2011," Zodiak Online, July 18, 2011, article on file with author.

[151] Ibid.

[152] Bright Sonani, "Government Using Gay Issues to Distract Malawians – HRCC," *Nation*, July 14, 2011, 3.

[153] Ibid.

[154] Kondwani Munthali, "Police Used Lethal Force – Report," *Nation*, August 16, 2011, 2.

[155] Ibid.   [156] Ibid.

Thirty-five percent are the ones who are knowledgeable. And most of the people living in the villages, 85% of our population is in the villages. So the level of illiteracy is very high in the villages. So, it is easier for the government to convince the majority" about the supposed danger of homosexuality.[157] Jeremiah speculated that government officials used politicized homophobia as a ruse, "instead of solving the problems: economic, social, cultural."[158] Similarly, Michael, an HIV/AIDS activist and Christian minister, asserted that the "government wanted to capitalize on the ignorance of the masses" about homosexuality as a way to distance the government from "mainstream human rights issues."[159] Tapping into citizens' religious zeal, political elites used homosexuality as a ruse to divide NGOs, inviting ordinary Malawians to criticize NGOs that supported decriminalizing same-sex sex.

When deploying repressive homophobic rhetoric, political elites constructed Northern donors as sponsoring LGBT rights organizing in Malawi.[160] NGOs that received donor funding became morally and politically suspect in statements politicians made. Jeremiah explained that politicians' message was: "Let us get rid of the donors because they're giving money to these few NGOs to advance their goal of homosexuality ... [P]eople should represent our government against the donors because the NGOs are supporting homosexuality."[161] Viewing NGOs as little more than puppets doing the bidding of donors, politicians characterized donors and NGOs as enemies of Malawian society. Jeremiah scoffed at how the government convinced rural Malawians that "those few NGOs, which were ... fighting for the rights of gays" were pressing the government to allow "men [to] marry men, women [to] marry women, and the villagers were

---

[157] Jeremiah, interview with the author, July 14, 2012, Lilongwe, Malawi. Jeremiah's estimates are not far off. The United Nations Educational, Scientific, and Cultural Organization (UNESCO) Institute for Statistics reports a literacy rate for Malawians over fifteen as being 62.14 percent in 2015. UNESCO Institute for Statistics, "Malawi." http://uis.unesco.org/en/country/mw. The United Nations Development Programme (UNDP) affirms Jeremiah's citation that about 85 percent of Malawians live in rural areas. UNDP, "About Malawi." www.mw.undp.org/content/malawi/en/home/countryinfo.html.

[158] Ibid.

[159] Michael, interview with the author, July 4, 2012, Lilongwe, Malawi.

[160] See also, Biruk, "Aid for Gays."

[161] Jeremiah, interview with the author, July 14, 2012, Lilongwe, Malawi.

believing" the message.[162] The "'who will marry us' argument"[163] swept some women's rights NGOs into the antigay camp, as their leaders speculated about who would marry women, a tactic that exploited poverty as a ruse in antigay mobilization.[164] While organizations, politicians, and religious leaders were "running away from the civil rights organizations," according to Jeremiah, Malawians were "looking at us as if we [were] enemies of the state and enemies of the citizenry. So that is the way the government was manipulating, using the agenda of those few NGOs that were fighting for rights of these people we call minorities." Jeremiah believed that by scapegoating organizations championing LGBT rights, the government was "twisting the truth." These actions were characteristic of a "sick government" using "propaganda" to divide social movements.

Some activists held that the government authorized repressive action against vocal NGOs because state leaders viewed these NGOs as dangerous political rivals. Gideon, a former human rights activist, believed that "the DPP government thought the only way to defeat civil society, which had grown in strength more than the opposition political parties, was to talk about the gay rights issues." Through repetition, elites sought to associate NGOs exclusively with LGBT rights, impugning NGOs' reputations in the process. Gideon explained that "the DPP government" depicted "civil society as promoting minority rights, gay rights issues, knowing the majority of Malawians would not accept at least for now that gay rights should be part of our [society] or that same-sex marriages should be part of our society now."[165]

Mutharika's administration exaggerated the place that LGBT rights had among Malawian social movements. Of the more than 400 NGOs registered with CONGOMA that operated in Malawi, Justice observed that only "three or four NGOs" advocated for LGBT rights. Blaming LGBT rights organizations, Justice attributed state repression to upstart NGOs that "were so vivid in" their support of LGBT rights

---

[162] Ibid.

[163] This argument refers to antigay assumptions that the newness of homosexuality would entice heterosexual Malawians into same-sex relationships, producing a shortage of people to marry.

[164] Chanika, Lwanda, and Muula, "Gender, Gays, and Gain," 99.

[165] Gideon, interview with the author, July 12, 2012, Lilongwe, Malawi. All quotations in this paragraph come from this source.

that these NGOs ignored that the "whole society doesn't want to hear about [gay rights]." As a result, LGBT rights was a "good whip ... for the government to use in castigating" and repressing NGOs, and "the government used" LGBT rights "for propaganda" to discredit a broad swath of organizations.[166] According to Justice, if organizations had refrained from pushing for LGBT rights, the state would have had little ammunition against NGOs critical of Mutharika's administration. Justice held LGBT rights organizations accountable for the state repression of NGOs.

Politicized homophobia contributed to fracturing among social movements, a consequence of repression. Organizations defending "minority rights" – an umbrella concept NGOs used to group prisoners, LGBT people, and sex workers – were at odds with NGOs whose leaders favored taking a more conciliatory tone with Mutharika's repressive administration and asked pro-LGBT organizations to suspend their pro-LGBT advocacy.[167] NGO leaders who favored compromise wanted to stop state repression directed at their groups. Benjamin, a CEDEP officer, believed that Mutharika's government was "politicizing the homosexuality issue" to turn "other civil society leaders to rebel against CEDEP and CHRR," the two leading NGOs defending gay rights.[168] Michael asserted,

> Government played a game to divide civil society and they did manage that ... [S]ome of our colleagues [in civil society] were coming to us and saying, "[I]f you want us to join in this fight for broader governance issues, then you better slow down on minority rights."[169]

State leaders' politicized homophobia succeeded in engendering divisions within social movements and enlisted NGOs to use politicized homophobia to police one another. Lucy believed that the government's statements and hostility "fragmented" social movements.[170]

---

[166] Justice, interview with the author, July 9, 2012, Lilongwe, Malawi. All quotations in this paragraph come from this source.

[167] For more information about African sex worker activism, see Mgbako, *To Live Freely in This World*.

[168] Benjamin, interview with the author, June 27, 2012, Blantyre, Malawi.

[169] Michael, interview with the author, July 4, 2012, Lilongwe, Malawi.

[170] Lucy, interview with the author, July 3, 2012, Lilongwe, Malawi. Divisions among NGOs predated the emergence of politicized homophobia. For instance, in 1998, Emmie Chanika, CILIC's executive director, lamented the disorganization and disagreement among some women's rights NGOs. She

She continued, "Already some have even gone on a honeymoon period now."[171] The fragmentation Lucy diagnosed contributed to the demobilization of some NGOs whose leaders and staff decided that challenging the government was no longer worth the effort. Their hibernation in a "honeymoon period" signaled that they were standing down.

Mwakasungula described how these divisions reached CONGOMA. After the May 2011 meeting to which Mutharika invited members of the CONGOMA board, CONGOMA representatives asked the leaders of CHRR and CEDEP to "slow down on advocating for minority rights."[172] In a press conference, Voice Mhone, the chairperson of CONGOMA, stated that NGOs in CONGOMA were disavowing LGBT rights, a sign of acquiescence to state hostility toward civil society. Conflating calls to decriminalize same-sex sex with a nonexistent campaign to legalize same-sex marriage, Justice explained that Mhone also stated, "Yes, gay marriages in Malawi ... are illegal, and for now, let them remain as such."[173] Mhone's statement positioned CHRR and CEDEP as rogue activist organizations advocating for minority rights that threatened Malawian society. Justice suggested that NGO leaders hoped that this statement would convince government leaders to abandon their scapegoating campaign: "Therefore, the government should stop using it as propaganda in hitting all the NGO community. So we presented this position to the president."[174] Government officials "still used" antigay threats against NGOs, according

discussed how women's rights NGOs agreed to stage a protest on a particular day, but there was subsequent disagreement among them. Chanika stated that some NGO representatives "decided to inform the authorities that [the protest] had been postponed, while" the protest was still slated to go forward. Victoria Msowoya, "Our Fellow Women Disappoint Us," *Malawi News*, August 22–28, 1998, 14.

[171] Lucy, interview with the author, July 3, 2012, Lilongwe, Malawi.

[172] Mwakasungula, "The LGBT Situation in Malawi," 375.

[173] Justice, interview with the author, July 9, 2012, Lilongwe, Malawi. Clive Gabay's research with different Malawian NGOs demonstrates that many leaders viewed CONGOMA as "notoriously resistant to political activism, particularly when targeted at the government." Clive Gabay, *Exploring an African Civil Society: Development and Democracy in Malawi, 1994–2014* (Lanham, MD: Lexington Books, 2015), 103–104.

[174] Justice, interview with the author, July 9, 2012, Lilongwe, Malawi.

to Justice, arguing that "these NGOs" were promoting "gay rights."[175] In this example, divisions within civil society around LGBT rights were on public display.

NGOs' positions on LGBT rights varied considerably. Recalling a "general assembly" of NGOs convened by the Human Rights Consultative Committee (HRCC) in February 2011, before Malawians took to the streets on July 20, Gideon, a former human rights activist, mapped out three different positions leaders adopted in response to LGBT rights. The first position involved rejecting LGBT rights. Leaders who adopted this position asserted, "No, as civil society, we shouldn't advocate for Malawi society to embrace gay rights, or gay issues, or same-sex marriages, whatever the difference is." A second group of leaders sided with LGBT rights organizations and "said, 'No, this thing is happening in Malawi. If we are to effectively combat HIV and AIDS, then we cannot throw this issue out of the window.'" A third group favored staking "middle ground." According to Gideon, those who endorsed a moderate position argued,

As civil society, we've got the duty and responsibility to disseminate information ... So, let's simply conduct research and establish the extent to which same-sex marriages have [happened and] how many same-sex relationships are happening in Malawi. If there are people who are in hiding, they are engaging in same-sex relationships in an underground fashion. We need to know that and establish the extent to which [this] is an issue or is a problem in Malawi.

Gideon portrayed these positions matter-of-factly, without indicating whether the debate about civil society's position on LGBT rights was excitable. NGOs ultimately reached no consensus on what a unified position on LGBT rights should be. Gideon remembered that "we got out of that meeting without a clear resolution on this matter, and ... the chairperson for HRCC was ... frustrated. He simply said, 'Let us close this chapter. Let us not discuss this issue anymore. We shall convene a proper assembly to talk about this specific issue later on in the future.'" Gideon associated a "sense of failure" with the assembly because NGO leaders rarely met "to discuss same-sex issues."[176]

---

[175] Ibid.
[176] Gideon, interview with the author, July 12, 2012, Lilongwe, Malawi. All quotations in this paragraph come from this source.

"Vilified": The Costs of Opposing the Government

Acting in solidarity with NGOs defending LGBT rights could exact a toll on individual activists and on organizations. The costs of promoting LGBT rights included the loss of credibility in activist circles, threats of violence against individual activists and their families exemplified in vigilante retribution against NGO leaders in the aftermath of the July 20 protests, and unwanted trouble with the police and government ministries. Michael, an HIV/AIDS activist and a Christian minister, explained that he had "personally been vilified for being in solidarity with the key affected populations from both a religious point of view and from politicians at some point in time." Along with CEDEP, Michael pressed for the inclusion of LGBT persons in HIV/AIDS prevention, education, and treatment programs and in faith communities. Despite Michael's efforts to educate religious leaders about sexuality and HIV/AIDS, his colleagues in the faith-based community rejected his message about embracing gender and sexual minorities. Some of Michael's "peers within the faith community … say I'm promoting gays. And … I was even stopped from celebrating church services because they said I was promoting gay rights."[177] Michael's avowed solidarity with gender and sexual minorities in Malawi resulted in peers objecting to him presiding over religious services in his congregation. Although stories like Michael's are dispiriting, they reflect local conditions for African LGBT organizing.

Activists not in the public eye watched how the police and other government officials treated LGBT rights activists, fearing that the police would turn up at their homes on orders from the government to repress human rights organizations. Hope, an LGBT rights supporter and women's rights activist, stated, "[C]ivil society talk[s] for the ordinary people. Yeah, when issues are not going [well], civil society stands up to say, 'No, we're not supposed to do this. This is not the right way. *This* is the right way." In light of NGOs' trenchant criticism of Malawian political leadership, Hope thought that "sometimes, these human rights activists … are looked at like threats," trying "to overthrow" the government because they criticized the country's direction. Although Hope did not "experience any threats," activists

---

[177] Michael, interview with the author, July 3, 2012, Lilongwe, Malawi. All quotations in this paragraph come from this source.

"sometimes ... have fears of the unknown. Even though something hasn't happened to you, you actually have fears of the unknown."[178]

Malawian citizens and political elites expressed doubt about NGOs. Naysayers voiced an array of objections about NGO activities, from accusing them of fraud to alleging that they were little more than pawns of powerful Northern donors. Widespread complaints about NGOs persisted for more than fifteen years, setting the stage for government officials' efforts to repress oppositional social movements. This resentment and interrogation of NGOs' activities contributed to an environment in which state hostility toward critical NGOs was normalized and even expected in Malawi.

In response to Mutharika's authoritarian governance, NGOs forged a coalition that insisted that Mutharika take action to reinstitute the democratic rule of law and resolve problems, such as electricity, fuel, and foreign currency shortages. When Mutharika did not act on these demands, NGO leaders held protests throughout the country on July 20, 2011. Police used repressive violence against protestors, resulting in many deaths and injuries. To deter Malawians from joining the protests, state leaders claimed that the July 20 protests were an attempt to legalize same-sex sex. In this way, the state deployed politicized homophobia against oppositional NGOs, pitting them against one another. Some activists suffered personally as the government and ruling party sympathizers harassed them. This hostile sociopolitical environment dampened some NGOs' support for LGBT rights.

Threats of repression notwithstanding, CEDEP and CHRR leaders remained vocal critics of Mutharika's leadership. Late in 2011, Mutharika blamed Malawi's political woes on the "work of the devil," logic that leaders of CEDEP and CHRR reversed in a press release that read:

If the problems the country is facing are being caused by Satan, then we believe Satan is using the President because the problems centre on poor economic and political governance led by [Mutharika] as President. As organisations who believe in the above power of the Almighty God, we strongly ask President Mutharika to reject the Satan he is condemning.[179]

---

[178] Hope, interview with the author, July 12, 2012, Lilongwe, Malawi. All quotations in this paragraph come from this source.

[179] Anthony Kasunda and George Singini, "Satan Using Bingu – NGOs," *Nation*, January 2, 2012, 2.

As CEDEP and CHRR leaders continue to critique the government's human rights abuses and demand improved governance in Malawi, they still face criticism from other NGO representatives. According to Timothy Mtambo, CHRR's executive director, Emily Banda, the chairperson of the Non-Governmental Organisation (NGO) Board, hijacked a 2015 meeting of NGO leaders and "started insulting [him] for being a gay rights activist ... [CHRR] officers had to ask her to leave the meeting."[180] A UN representative in Malawi requested that Banda account for denouncing "human rights activists who fight for minority rights," specifically the leaders of CEDEP and CHRR.[181] Public shaming of NGOs that defended LGBT rights continues to constrain the work of organizations like CEDEP and CHRR.

Until his unexpected death in April 2012, President Mutharika portrayed homosexuality as a scourge that would destroy Malawian society. Facing a stagnant economy and corruption charges, Mutharika, other politicians, and religious leaders claimed that sexual minorities and their supporters promoted Western interference in national affairs and had convinced NGOs to overthrow the government in exchange for donor funding. The accession of Mutharika's vice president, Joyce Banda, as president in 2012 did little to blunt levels of politicized homophobia. Despite state leaders' antigay hostility, some sympathetic NGOs, including MANERELA+,[182] publicly defended gender and sexual minorities and LGBT rights. However, activists in different social movements questioned what, if any, public stance they should take on homosexuality and if they should display solidarity with CEDEP and CHRR, the two leading NGOs defending LGBT rights in Malawi. As the next chapter demonstrates, politicized homophobia arrested expressions of solidarity with LGBT rights NGOs and for LGBT rights.

---

[180] Golden Matonga, "UN Summons NGO Board Chair Over Squabble," *Nation*, October 18, 2015, http://mwnation.com/un-summons-ngo-board-chair-over-squabble/.

[181] Ibid.

[182] Deogratias Mmana, "Homosexuals Deserve to Die – Apostle," *Weekend Nation*, April 30, 2011, 3; Kondwani Munthali, "Accept Prostitutes, Gays, Urges Bishop," *Nation*, February 28, 2011, 1–2; Edwin Nyirongo, "Changing Police Perception towards Homosexuality," *Nation*, January 5, 2015, http://mwnation.com/changing-police-perception-towards-homosexuality/; Bright Sonani, "NGOs Attack Church on Gays," *Nation*, February 26, 2011, 3.

4 | *Arrested Solidarity*

Why Some Movements Do Not Support LGBT Rights

LGBT rights NGOs in African nations tend to operate independently of other movements.[1] Yet, in sociopolitical fields hostile to gender and sexual dissidence, LGBT rights NGOs sometimes depend on solidarity partnerships with sympathetic organizations, such as HIV/AIDS, human rights, and women's rights NGOs. In this chapter, I explore the circumstances that impede the possible solidarity partnerships that HIV/AIDS, human rights, and women's rights NGOs can forge with besieged LGBT rights defenders.

When political elites sow divisions between NGOs, which I explain in the previous chapter, they can disappear as the primary agents of politicization. In such instances, activists can become willing or unwitting accomplices in abetting politicians' plans for cultivating disharmony around LGBT rights. In this way, politicized homophobia can involve primary actors who initially deploy antigay discourses and threats and secondary actors who continue politicizing same-sex sexualities. Secondary actors may continue following the antihomosexual scripts created by primary actors, reproducing arguments against homosexuality that primary actors have already introduced. Alternatively, secondary actors may develop additional grounds for rejecting sexual diversity and LGBT rights, taking an antihomosexuality campaign in a new direction. NGO leaders may cooperate with a politicized-homophobia campaign already underway to curry favor with politicians. In other cases, activists' investment in politicizing homophobia exceeds an interest in enhancing their position with the ruling party, influential religious leaders, and traditional leaders; they may activate homophobia because they personally object to same-sex sexualities. Conversely, activists may remain on the sidelines and not voice opposition to the hostility they witness unfolding before them. When activists do not develop a common solidarity around LGBT

[1] Currier and Cruz, "Civil Society and Sexual Struggles in Africa."

154

rights or another issue, they are incapable of banding together and taking advantage of emerging political opportunities.

Despite some intermovement support for LGBT rights in Malawi, pro-LGBT activists in other movements experienced limits on when and how they could express their solidarity. A women's rights activist reported feeling pressure from a foreign donor to express solidarity with LGBT rights NGOs and to take a stand for LGBT rights. If potential local allies feel pressured by donors and foreign observers into publicly displaying solidarity with African LGBT rights NGOs, these performances of solidarity may turn into hollow gestures of goodwill that offer few tangible benefits to LGBT activists and constituents. Other activists cited additional factors as inhibiting displays of support for LGBT rights. These factors included Malawians' unpreparedness for frank discussions about same-sex sexualities and the existence of issues perceived to be more urgent than gay rights. Based on more than fifty interviews I conducted with HIV/AIDS, human rights, LGBT rights, and women's rights activists, I explain how being seen as promulgating LGBT rights and same-sex sexualities in contemporary Malawi complicated their advocacy. In some cases, politicized homophobia rendered solidarity impossible for NGO leaders.

After reviewing theoretical perspectives about cross-movement solidarity, I discuss the obstacles that inhibited activists' public solidarity for LGBT rights.[2] Activists identified several factors confounding or preventing displays of solidarity for LGBT rights and with LGBT rights NGOs. First, politicized homophobia generated high costs for activists contemplating endorsing LGBT rights, leading some activists to temper or withhold public solidarity for LGBT rights. Second, Western donor pressure on NGOs to show visible support for LGBT rights and the decriminalization of same-sex sexual conduct rendered activists vulnerable if they showed no public solidarity for LGBT rights. Third, some activists ranked other issues as more pressing than LGBT rights advocacy; they directed their efforts toward other urgent social problems. Fourth, some activists claimed that Malawians were not prepared for frank discussions about gender and sexual diversity, making public advocacy on LGBT rights premature. Fifth, envy about

[2] Chi Adanna Mgbako explores the potential for solidarity among sex workers' rights movements and LGBT movements in different African continents. When I conducted fieldwork in Malawi in 2012 and 2014, I was unaware of such alliances in Malawi. Mgbako, *To Live Freely in This World.*

the donor funding NGOs had received for LGBT rights programs highlighted resource disparities between NGOs, making some activists envious of and reluctant to work with well-resourced LGBT rights NGOs. At the end of the chapter, I discuss how and why it matters that HIV/AIDS, human rights, and women's rights activists missed the political opportunity to join LGBT rights activists in pressing for the decriminalization of same-sex sexual practices, a legal reform that President Joyce Banda announced as a priority soon after taking office after the death of her predecessor, Bingu wa Mutharika, in 2012.

Looking for Solidarity: Feminist and Social Movement Studies Perspectives

The number of organizations populating a movement affects what actions individual organizations take. When multiple organizations surface within a social movement, the movement tends to undergo diversification.[3] Diversification entails organizations specializing in particular tactics, achieving specific goals, or concentrating their mobilization in a specific geographic area, which Sandra R. Levitsky describes as "niche activism."[4] In some African countries, activists have established multiple organizations within the LGBT movement, including some that specialize in HIV/AIDS work. Diversification can be healthy for social movements, enabling organizations to work with a subset of constituents with multiple grievances. Some Kenyan LGBT rights NGOs "focus on health," while others engage in legal and legislative advocacy.[5] Such specialization means that activists involved with other NGOs do not have to worry about catering to all constituents' needs and interests.[6] Moreover, organization specialization does not necessarily produce factionalism, although specialization can involve disagreement between NGOs about which organization is

---

[3] For an extended discussion of the dynamics of diversification, specialization, and organization population within social movements, see Currier and McKay, "Pursuing Social Justice," 73–78.

[4] Sandra Levitsky, "Niche Activism: Constructing a Unified Movement Identity in a Heterogeneous Organizational Field," *Mobilization*, 12, no. 3 (2007): 272.

[5] Kaitlin Dearham, "NGOs and Queer Women's Activism in Nairobi," in *Queer African Reader*, edited by Sokari Ekine and Hakima Abbas (Oxford: Pambazuka, 2013), 188.

[6] Richard Ssebaggala, "Straight Talk on the Gay Question in Uganda," *Transition* 106 (2011): B–44–B–57.

responsible for certain campaigns.[7] Some movements have an identity that is elastic enough to accommodate differences in organizations' identities, ideologies, goals, and tactics.[8] However, in some African sociopolitical fields, particularly those characterized by antigay repression, only one or two LGBT rights NGOs have emerged, as is the case in Malawi. CEDEP is the leading LGBT rights NGO in the country. Since the Malawian LGBT movement field is relatively underpopulated, CEDEP and CHRR, a partner NGO, are highly visible as LGBT rights defenders and vulnerable to homophobic attacks from political elites. Support from sympathetic NGOs in other movements would help protect LGBT rights NGOs from political attacks.

Feminist and social movement studies scholars agree that cross-movement support, taking the form of coalitions or solidarity actions, often benefits recipient movements.[9] Conventional wisdom holds that when organizations within a movement or across movements pool their resources, organizations learn from one another and benefit from accrued gains in a coalition.[10] Solidarity can act as the social glue that keeps a coalition functioning productively. Recent feminist scholarship defines solidarity as the "principle of mutual support between individuals, groups, and organisations."[11] Citing Jodi Dean's definition of "reflective solidarity," feminist theorist Chandra Talpade Mohanty suggests that "solidarity is always an achievement," as it requires the interaction of stakeholders with different interests to agree temporarily to collaborate collectively on meaningful social change.[12]

Solidarity actions can involve protests in one place that duplicate the demands made by activists elsewhere; a familiar example is the student divestment movement, which demanded that US universities sell their

---

[7] Awondo, "The Politicisation of Sexuality."   [8] Levitsky, "Niche Activism."
[9] Nella Van Dyke and Holly J. McCammon, eds., *Strategic Alliances: Coalition Building and Social Movements* (Minneapolis: University of Minnesota Press, 2010).
[10] Eithne Luibhéid and Sasha Khokha, "Building Alliances between Immigrant Rights and Queer Movements," in *Forging Radical Alliances across Difference: Coalition Politics for the New Millennium*, edited by Jill M. Bystydzienski and Steven P. Schacht (Lanham, MD: Rowman & Littlefield, 2001), 77–90.
[11] Caroline Sweetman, "Introduction, Feminist Solidarity, and Collective Action," *Gender & Development*, 21, no. 2 (2013): 219.
[12] Jodi Dean, *Solidarity of Strangers: Feminism after Identity Politics* (Berkeley: University of California Press, 1996), 142; Chandra Talpade Mohanty, *Feminism without Borders: Decolonizing Theory, Practicing Solidarity* (Durham, NC: Duke University Press, 2003), 7.

stock in companies that did business in apartheid South Africa.[13] Other solidarity actions may include issuing a press release supporting an ally's cause or boycotting products associated with labor violations.[14] Solidarity actions can transform activists and social movements into allies. Writing about people who become LGBT allies, Daniel J. Myers distinguishes between movement beneficiaries and allies. Beneficiary activists are movement constituents who anticipate deriving advantages from movement gains, whereas ally activists do not hold such expectations. Allies face critical decisions about what to tell different audiences about their solidarity. "Should they reveal, in any environment or interaction, that they are aligned with, support, and are active in this movement"?[15] Myers' question raises another: If allies do not reveal their support for a movement, how will others know about their solidarity?

To find evidence of solidarity, scholars and movement observers look for visible displays of intermovement solidarity. Often, activists exhibit or practice solidarity in a moment of attack or hostility, rendering assistance in varied ways. Determining solidarity among social movements depends largely on what observers can see. Visible displays or declamations of support constitute solidarity. Ally activist organizations come to the public defense of weaker, bullied organizations at press conferences or in press releases distributed to news outlets. Invested observers assume that this cycle will repeat in the event of future hostility. In politically fluid contexts, activists may not develop or sustain solidarity agreements that continue over time. Activists negotiate solidarity cautiously and contextually, calculating how promises they make in the present may affect or compromise their actions in the future.[16]

---

[13] Sarah A. Soule, "Situational Effects on Political Altruism: The Student Divestment Movement in the United States," in *Political Altruism? Solidarity Movements in International Perspective*, edited by Marco Giugni and Florence Passy (Lanham, MD: Rowman & Littlefield, 2001), 161–176.

[14] Ethel C. Brooks, *Unraveling the Garment Industry: Transnational Organizing and Women's Work* (Minneapolis: University of Minnesota Press, 2007).

[15] Daniel J. Myers, "Ally Identity: The Politically Gay," in *Identity Work in Social Movements*, edited by Jo Reger, Daniel J. Myers, and Rachel L. Einwohner (Minneapolis: University of Minnesota Press, 2008), 170.

[16] Dennis J. Downey and Deana A. Rohlinger, "Linking Strategic Choice with Macro-Organizational Dynamics: Strategy and Social Movement Articulation," *Research in Social Movements, Conflicts, and Change*, 28 (2008): 3–38.

The Impossibility of Public Solidarity Produces Political Restraint

The criminalization of same-sex sex and politicized homophobia prevented some activists from showing solidarity for LGBT rights. In this context, exhibiting support for LGBT rights publicly became both practically and politically impossible for some NGOs. Joseph, an activist working with the Malawi Network of People Living with HIV/AIDS (MANET+), explained that the criminalization of same-sex sex complicated HIV/AIDS NGOs' efforts to serve sexual minorities. Since same-sex sex was "illegal," Joseph stated that some NGOs "don't want to be seen as investing in something that is illegal."[17] Yet, according to Joseph, many HIV/AIDS activists acknowledged that "HIV prevalence is actually high among the homosexuals, but if it's not controlled, it means the spread will also be high. Okay, it has been a very complicated situation."[18] Research estimates that approximately 21 percent of men who have sex with men (MSM) in Malawi are HIV positive.[19] Occupying a paradoxical position, HIV/AIDS activists grappled with the reality that excluding sexual minorities from HIV/AIDS programs endangered their lives, but antigay political elites could view advocacy that included sexual minorities as endorsing "illegal" activities.

For activists sympathetic to the marginalization Malawian gender and sexual dissidents experienced, endorsing LGBT rights or the decriminalization of same-sex sex could expose them to criticism. As Joseph explained, NGOs adopted different positions on homosexuality. He stated, "One position is to fight for legalization to make homosexuality legal in Malawi, and I think that's the trend maybe our colleagues at CEDEP and CHRR will be taking."[20] Despite activists' bravery in defending LGBT rights, political and religious

---

[17] Joseph, interview with the author, July 12, 2012, Lilongwe, Malawi.

[18] Ibid.

[19] Heather Fay, Stefan D. Baral, Gift Trapence, Felistus Motimedi, Eric Umar, Scholastika Iipinge, Friedel Dausab, Andrea Wirtz, and Chis Beyrer, "Stigma, Health Care Access, and HIV Knowledge among Men Who Have Sex with Men in Malawi, Namibia, and Botswana," *AIDS and Behavior*, 15, no. 6 (2011): 1088–1097.

[20] Joseph, interview with the author, July 12, 2012, Lilongwe, Malawi.

leaders viewed homosexuality "as something very alien that is not Malawian."[21] Deploying a variation of "homosexuality-is-un-African" discourse, political elites staked a moral position that generated public resistance to the aims of pro-LGBT rights NGOs.[22] Aware of disdain for same-sex sexualities, MANET+ activists had "not advocated for legalization. Our position has been we have to put the resources and the programs where it matters. Now if there is evidence that HIV is high among homosexuals, then we have to do something. They have to access the services."[23] Although activists at MANET+ would not publicly demand the decriminalization of sodomy, they drew the line at discriminatory practices that compromised gender and sexual dissidents' health.

The existence of pro-LGBT rights NGOs also released organizations like MANET+, which served HIV-positive Malawians, from "advocating for legalization because we know there are others, not that it's bad, but we know there are other organizations that are better placed" to call for the decriminalization of same-sex sex, according to Joseph.[24] Claiming that few NGOs were qualified to champion LGBT rights, Joseph applied the "niche activism" concept to describe a loose solidarity that emerged organically among a network of sympathetic NGOs.[25] Knowing that other NGOs were working to legalize same-sex sexual practices absolved activists involved with NGOs that lacked legal expertise from launching decriminalization campaigns. Ultimately, this logic could backfire if many activists wrongly perceived that others were advancing LGBT rights, when in reality, no group was pursuing such a campaign.

Given MANET+ activists' reticence about supporting decriminalization openly, they opted to use their expertise in healthcare provision and HIV/AIDS to press government officials to honor their commitment to include sexual minorities in HIV/AIDS prevention, education, and treatment efforts. Using the cover of healthcare and HIV/AIDS treatment, Joseph explained that MANET+ told government officials that

Malawi's a signa[tory] for universal access to HIV prevention, treatment, care, and support. And, in that declaration, it talks about ensuring that

---

[21] Ibid.   [22] Currier, *Out in Africa*, 121–122.
[23] Joseph, interview with the author, July 12, 2012, Lilongwe, Malawi.
[24] Ibid.   [25] Levitsky, "Niche Activism."

everyone has access to services regardless of their sexual orientation. So, what we've been doing is just to remind the government of its commitment and obligation.[26]

According to this logic, the government already promised to provide services to all Malawians in need of them, and sexual minorities counted as Malawians. Joseph bluntly stated, "Let them not be denied services because they are homosexuals."[27] For MANET+, arguing for including LGBT people in HIV/AIDS service provision is a "more acceptable way" of engaging in pro-LGBT advocacy "than saying, 'Let's legalize homosexuality.'"[28] This position has insulated MANET+ from antigay hostility. The NGO had "not received any negative feedback on the issue that we've been doing on homosexuality."[29] MANET+ modeled a restrained form of public solidarity for LGBT rights.

The Costs of Absent Solidarity

Activists with MANET+ reported no antigay backlash for the NGO's inclusion of sexual minorities in HIV/AIDS advocacy. What might happen if activists were not seen supporting LGBT rights? If activists publicly endorsed LGBT rights, they faced hostility locally from political, religious, and traditional leaders but could reap benefits from foreign donors that might reward their NGOs' support with additional resources. In contrast, if activists delayed or withheld public support for LGBT rights, they could avoid hostility from local political, religious, and traditional leaders but encounter disapproval from representatives of foreign donors who expected HIV/AIDS, human rights, and women's rights NGOs to sanction LGBT rights.

This dilemma emerged for a women's rights NGO as politicized homophobia intensified in 2010 and 2011. During a visit involving a representative from a donor agency funding a project that educated rural Malawian women, Linda, a women's rights activist, shared that the representative asked why the NGO had not been publicly visible in 2010 after the arrests of Chimbalanga and Monjeza for violating the antisodomy statute. Linda recalled, "So, as soon as we sat down, she

---

[26] Joseph, interview with the author, July 12, 2012, Lilongwe, Malawi.
[27] Ibid.   [28] Ibid.   [29] Ibid.

says, 'What happened with the homosexuality case?'"[30] This inquiry
occurred during a monitoring and evaluation visit, imbuing the question with a disciplinary quality. Linda's response could influence future
support the donor agency rendered. When Linda sought to clarify the
parameters of the donor representative's question, the representative's
tone became "different."[31] The representative explained that leading
LGBT rights activists had stated that Linda and her NGO "were not
supporting" Chimbalanga and Monjeza.[32] The evidence the representative proffered of Linda's alleged lack of support was the women's
rights NGO's public invisibility. Linda disagreed with how the representative equated the NGO's invisibility with a lack of solidarity for
LGBT rights. Linda stated, "Come on. They [CHRR and CEDEP] were
in the forefront. We were in the back going like this [clapping her
hands in applause]. If they thought that my presence is important, like
I should be visible, they could have approached me" and invited her
NGO to join a coalition publicly criticizing the prosecution of Chimbalanga and Monjeza.[33] Objecting to the representative's insinuation
that her NGO's absence constituted homophobic prejudice, Linda
claimed, "I don't remember" voicing opposition to the case, but she
did "remember saying, 'Let's support it, but don't attach donor aid
to'" demands for the release of Chimbalanga and Monjeza or for the
decriminalization of same-sex sex, which would amount to "a new
form of neocolonialism."[34] Linda's concern about tying development
assistance to LGBT rights mirrored that of other African LGBT activists who objected to donors' withdrawal of aid from countries like
Malawi and Uganda in which gender and sexual dissidence was punished.[35] The representative asked Linda directly, "So, are you opposed
[to homosexuality]?"[36] Linda worried that if the representative interpreted her NGO's invisibility as lack of support for the LGBT rights

---

[30] Linda, interview with the author, June 25, 2012, Blantyre, Malawi.   [31] Ibid.

[32] Ibid. Apart from Linda's interview, I found no evidence that LGBT rights
activists complained to foreign donors about the lack of women's rights NGOs'
solidarity for LGBT rights publicly. However, in interviews, a few LGBT rights
activists explained that women's rights NGOs had offered little public support
for LGBT rights.

[33] Ibid.   [34] Ibid.

[35] "African Statement in Response to British Government on Aid Conditionality,"
in *Queer African Reader*, edited by Sokari Ekine and Hakima Abbas (Dakar,
Senegal: Pambazuka, 2013), 209–210.

[36] Linda, interview with the author, June 25, 2012, Blantyre, Malawi.

advocacy undertaken by CHRR and CEDEP, the representative might recommend diverting funding away from her organization.

Yet invested observers, such as this donor representative, could not see behind-the-scenes agreements that activists had forged. Activists from different movements may reach a temporary agreement that particular NGOs will take the lead on one campaign or crisis, while other organizations wait in the wings. On the ground, activists do not necessarily expect colleagues to voice support on every single public campaign. To distant observers who expect activists to be seen supporting particular issues, NGOs' invisibility seems confusing. Distant observers are unsure of the reason for activists' invisibility, but they may inappropriately attribute animosity to allies' absence, which seems to have occurred in the case of the representative evaluating Linda's NGO.

Defending her NGO's reputation and justifying her organization's invisibility in relation to politicized homophobia, Linda stated that, in January 2012, two years after the arrests of Chimbalanga and Monjeza, her NGO was busy responding to a spate of public sexual assaults on women by male street vendors who forcibly removed women's clothing.[37] Linda explained, "We had a trousers issue. Women were being stripped ... naked recently."[38] News coverage after one attack alleged that a young man snapped the exposed "G-string panties" of a young woman at a Lilongwe market, "inciting many people to join him [in] harassing the woman."[39] Sexual assaults of women wearing leggings, pants, and shorter skirts occurred in other cities and towns in Malawi. Activists organized women throughout Malawi to boycott men vendors in the "Lelo nkugule, Mawa undivule" campaign, which meant "Today, I buy from you; tomorrow you undress me?"[40] During the campaign against these sexual assaults, women's rights NGOs were "in the forefront," according to Linda.[41]

---

[37] Linda's use of the 2012 strip assault campaign to explain why her NGO did not display public solidarity for LGBT rights seemed disingenuous, particularly because this campaign occurred almost two years after Chimbalanga and Monjeza's trial.

[38] Linda, interview with the author, June 25, 2012, Blantyre, Malawi.

[39] "Trouser Attacks: How It All Began," *Nation*, January 22, 2012, http://mwnation.com/trouser-attacks-how-it-all-began/.

[40] "US Commends Joyce Banda's 'Bold Actions,'" *Nyasa Times*, May 22, 2012, www.nyasatimes.com/us-commends-joyce-bandas-bold-actions/.

[41] Linda, interview with the author, June 25, 2012, Blantyre, Malawi.

Other human rights NGOs "were in the back[ground], and they were supporting. But they were not the face of the campaign. Every campaign has a face. So, my colleagues were like, 'Yes, we're with you on this one. We're with you.'"[42] Linda stressed the difference between manifesting public support for an NGO's campaign and silently standing with the NGO. She articulated this distinction more forcefully when discussing the gendered dynamics of the prosecution of Chimbalanga and Monjeza, noting that

> they're men. They are not women. Thank you. Yeah, Tiwonge and Steven, it was a man's issue, so, me, I felt [CEDEP and CHRR were] at the forefront; that's great. You know, [the] next time they try and prosecute a lesbian, I'll be in the forefront defending this particular person.[43]

Although Linda claimed to support LGBT rights and promised to aid any lesbian arrested on suspicion of having sex with another woman, she felt that her NGO did not have to mount a public defense of Chimbalanga and Monjeza as aggrieved members of the Malawian LGBT community.

Linda cited the gender of Chimbalanga and Monjeza in justifying her NGO's public invisibility during their trial. In this particular case, defending sexual minorities was a "man's issue" because two "men," "not women," were in the dock.[44] Like local journalists and the judicial system, Linda characterized Chimbalanga as a gay "man," not as a transgender woman in need of legal services, despite Chimbalanga's repeated self-identification as a woman in the media.[45] By upholding a binary understanding of "women" and "men," Linda contributed to the silencing of transgender persons in Malawi who would benefit from her NGO's legal services precisely if they were persecuted because of their gender variance.[46] Ignoring Chimbalanga's gender identity is an example of how transgender women and men

---

[42] Ibid.   [43] Ibid.   [44] Ibid.

[45] Frank Namangale, "Aunt Tiwo Is a Man – Doctor," *Nation*, January 28, 2010, 3.

[46] Jessie Kabwila outlines how visible gender nonconformity is not necessarily linked to sexual diversity. She explains that cross-dressing has become a way for Malawian entertainers to boost their popularity. In addition, at some funerals, female mourners may dress like men, and male mourners may dress like women. Kabwila's commentary indicates that historically there has been space in Malawi for cross-dressing. Kabwila, "Seeing beyond Colonial Binaries."

remain sidelined in some African feminist movements.[47] This gender
binary also promotes the supremacy of "gay" and "lesbian" concerns
in the "LGBT" movement imaginary, marginalizing transgender persons and gender variance.[48]

LGBT rights activists involved with CEDEP noted that some prominent women's rights activists maintained "positive attitudes" toward
gay rights.[49] However, pro-LGBT feminist activists, with the exception
of Jessie Kabwila, had not "come out" to talk about their stance,
according to Moses, a CEDEP officer.[50] Their absence when lawmakers amended the antisodomy law in 2011 to criminalize sex
between women was notable; this amendment passed with little fanfare
or contestation from LGBT rights or women's rights NGOs. In general,
"the women's movement in Malawi has been silent on the issues; they
haven't commented on" LGBT rights.[51] "Whether you talk about the
gay issues or the lesbian issues, they haven't commented. Even when
the [lesbian] women were arrested in Mulanje, they didn't even comment on that."[52] Moses was referring to the case of an unmarried
market woman arrested on charges in 2009 for allegedly inducing two
teenage girls she employed as domestic workers to have sex with her in
exchange for "fashionable clothes" and "better perks."[53] Police
charged the market woman with "indecent assault."[54] When the
woman was arrested for sexually assaulting the girls, one news report
depicted the woman as "practicing lesbian sex" with and "pull[ing] the
private parts of the girls."[55] The girls stated that they consented to

[47] Zethu Matebeni, "Feminizing Lesbians, Degendering Transgender Men:
A Model for Building Lesbian Feminist Thinkers and Leaders in Africa?," *Souls*,
11, no. 3 (2009): 347–354.
[48] Ashley Currier, "Transgender Invisibility in Namibian and South African LGBT
Organizing," *Feminist Formations*, 27, no. 1 (2015): 91–117.
[49] Moses, interview with the author, July 2, 2012, Lilongwe, Malawi.   [50] Ibid.
[51] Ibid.   [52] Ibid.
[53] MANA, "Woman in Court for Sexually Assaulting Maids," *Nation*, December
10, 2009, 6.
[54] Kandani Ngwira, "Nkando Homophile Arrested," *Sunday Times*, December 6,
2009, 4
[55] Ibid. The news report may refer to the sexual practice of labia stretching or
elongation, which involves routine stretching of the labia minora intended to
enhance the sexual pleasure of women and their (presumed) male sexual partners
after marriage. See Pia Grassivaro Gallo, Debora Moro, and Miriam Manganoni,
"Female Genital Modifications in Malawi: Culture, Health, and Sexuality," in
Circumcision and Human Rights, edited by George C. Denniston, Frederick
Mansfield Hodges, and Marilyn Fayre Milos (New York: Springer, 2009), 83–95.

"sexual relations" with their employer at first, but after their employer dismissed one of them, the girls became angry and reported their "secret sexual relationship" to police.[56] The employer pleaded her innocence at the trial. When she was acquitted on charges of indecent assault, Minister of Gender, Child, and Community Development Patricia Kaliati deplored the trial outcome, stating that her ministry would appeal the ruling; Kaliati banished the "suspected lesbian" from the district she represented.[57] Although Linda claimed that her NGO would come to the aid of lesbians threatened with legal action, the organization failed to defend not only the market woman prosecuted for indecent assault[58] but also two other women purported to be lesbians.[59]

---

[56] MANA, "Woman in Court," 6.

[57] James Chimpweya and Caroline Somanje, "Kaliati Slams Court for Acquitting Lesbian Suspect," *Nation*, January 21, 2010, 2.

[58] Upset that prosecutors could not convict the market woman of sodomy, lawmakers introduced an amendment later in 2010 that criminalized sex between women in response to the state's inability to prosecute lesbians under the gender-specific antisodomy law. Until this amendment, the antisodomy statute only criminalized sex between men. Signed into law by President Bingu wa Mutharika in January 2011, the updated antisodomy statute criminalizes sex between men and sex between women and does not distinguish between consensual and coerced same-sex sex. Resnick, "Two Steps Forward." Endorsing the gender-neutral antisodomy law as progress, George Chaponda, the minister of justice and constitutional affairs, claimed that the old law was unsatisfactory because "it was only mentioning men and government wanted to include women to ensure that homosexuality is criminalized without discrimination" in terms of gender. Justifying the need for this particular law reform, Chaponda invoked the language of gender equality. Feminist activist and scholars would likely interpret this explanation as a perverse application of gender-egalitarian logic, as the law criminalized sex between women, when measures to introduce gender equality were supposed to remove barriers and hardships that women endure. Wanga Gwede, "Malawi Refuses 'Homosexuality' Aid Condition," *Nyasa Times*, February 9, 2011, article on file with author; Kapya J. Kaoma, "The Marriage of Convenience: The US Christian Right, African Christianity, and Postcolonial Politics of Sexual Identity," in *Global Homophobia: States, Movements, and the Politics of Oppression*, edited by Meredith L. Weiss and Michael J. Bosia (Urbana: University of Illinois Press, 2013), 75–102.

[59] In an attempt to provoke President Joyce Banda into taking a position on same-sex sexualities at the beginning of her presidency, a journalist paid two women in 2012 to adopt intimate poses in photographs for a story about "lesbians" getting engaged in secret, evoking Chimbalanga and Monjeza's 2009 engagement ceremony. Clement Chinoko, "Lesbians Engage," *Sunday Times*, May 20, 2012, 1, 3; Wanga Gwede, "Malawi Lesbian Couple Won't Be

Despite the fact that her NGO missed opportunities to assist women accused of being lesbians, Linda's experiences highlight complex reasons why organizations may not engage in public solidarity with LGBT rights NGOs. Acting as an ally did not mean that an NGO would routinely issue a public statement defending LGBT rights. However, according to Linda, the donor funding her NGO assumed that women's rights NGOs were supposed to display public solidarity with groups advocating for LGBT rights. Although outsiders might imagine that particular Malawian NGOs, by virtue of their constituents and grievances, would serve as natural allies for LGBT activists, Linda's presentation of her NGO's relationship with CEDEP and CHRR, the NGOs leading the fight for LGBT rights, suggests that activists continually renegotiated their understandings and partnerships with other NGOs. This negotiation involved identifying which NGOs would be the "public face" of a campaign. If too many NGOs served as "public faces" for a campaign, this could muddy the campaign's message, confusing key audiences. This social movement reality reveals that

Prosecuted," *Nyasa Times*, May 21, 2012, www.nyasatimes.com/malawi-lesbian-couple-wont-be-prosecuted-justice-minister/. Although police spokesperson Davie Chingwalu affirmed that police would investigate the couple because same-sex sex remained illegal, Minister of Justice and Attorney General Ralph Kasambara stated the women would not be prosecuted. Deogratias Mmana and George Singini, "Clerics Query Same Sex Laws," *Nation*, May 22, 2012, 3. A subsequent news article revealed that the "lesbian couple" was "given money to [test] the waters" of public sentiment toward same-sex sexualities, especially since lawmakers had criminalized sex between women the previous year. Green Muheya, "Malawi Lesbian Couple Fake, Lawyer Says No Case," *Nyasa Times*, May 21, 2012, www.nyasatimes.com/malawi-lesbian-couple-fake-lawyer-says-no-case/. Later, the women claimed that the photos of them kissing stemmed from the filming of a play in which they were featured actors and threatened to sue the *Daily Times* for defamation. "Malawi 'Lesbian Couple' Sue for K50, 'It Was Movie Shoot' – Lawyer," *Nyasa Times*, May 23, 2012, www.nyasatimes.com/malawi-lesbian-couple-sue-for-k50m-it-was-movie-shoot-lawyer/. Police arrested Clement Chinoko, the journalist who wrote the initial story about the "lesbian couple" and revealed that DPP representatives promised to pay him for "stir[ring] a hornets' nest for President Joyce Banda and throw her on a collision course with either donors or traditional and religious leaders." The plan's architects hoped that if police arrested the women, foreign donors would condemn Banda's government and harden their stance toward Malawi, or if police did not arrest the women, political elites would interpret this action as support for LGBT rights and incite a torrent of criticism from ordinary Malawians. "Lesbian Story Scheme by DPP, Court Grants Reporter Bail," *Nyasa Times*, May 20, 2012, www.nyasatimes.com/lesbian-story-scheme-by-dpp-court-grants-reporter-bail/.

judging individual NGOs' solidarity for LGBT rights by whether or not they exhibit visible support for LGBT rights campaigns is imprudent. Activists manage and nurture complicated relationships with organizations in different social movements. How activists calculate intermovement solidarity for a particular campaign may differ substantially from the agreements activists make in subsequent partnerships. Local activist solidarities cannot always be deduced through observation from afar.

Issue Ranking

Whereas politicized homophobia made some HIV/AIDS, human rights, and women's rights activists cautious about exhibiting solidarity for LGBT rights, for others, LGBT rights competed with other pressing issues for activists' attention. In some cases, women's rights activists assigned LGBT rights a lower priority than issues related to gender-based violence (GBV). Linda mentioned that sexual assaults on women occupied her NGO at the beginning of 2012, illustrating the point that activists responded to what they deemed as the most urgent issues first. Activists ranked problems facing the movement or NGO and made strategic choices about the issues they should tackle, which could create cascading effects that distanced organizations from LGBT rights solidarity. Activists could also assign LGBT rights a lower priority due to personal antigay prejudice. Conversely, activists might regard LGBT rights compassionately but face difficult decisions about apportioning organizational resources and activist energies; subsequent decisions made based on past issue ranking could set organizations on a path leading them further away from defending LGBT rights.

Benjamin, a former activist with CEDEP, discussed how activists ranked issues. Offering a hypothetical example, Benjamin narrated how NGO leaders conversed about their priorities at a meeting when "they do not realize that there is a representative from CEDEP" in attendance.[60] If gay rights appeared as an agenda item, "they will talk in a way that you could tell that they are not for the agenda item, or they want that agenda [item] to come last. They are like, 'We have so many things to talk about or to handle that we are wasting time talking

---

[60] Benjamin, interview with the author, June 27, 2012, Blantyre, Malawi.

about'" gay rights.[61] In Benjamin's experience, these leaders perceived gay rights as "petty issues" threatening to distract them from crises, such as medicine and foreign currency shortages, which were "the imminent things ... that were supposed to be addressed forthwith."[62] Leaders argued that "issues to do with MSM ... come last" and assumed that gay rights was "a minority issue. It's just a few, one, or two, or three people who are concerned with this issue. So, why should the whole nation be talking? Why should we waste resources on addressing issues [that] are only affecting a handful of people?"[63] According to Benjamin, although NGO leaders "understand these issues," they ranked them as less important; therefore, NGO leaders believed, "We've got better things to discuss than this issue."[64] Benjamin thought that human rights activists in Malawi viewed gay rights as an indulgence they could not afford. Some Egyptian human rights activists adopted this perspective when justifying their refusal to assist gay men arrested in 2001 on the Queen Boat in Cairo. Some Egyptian activists "reproduced ... prejudices against the rights of ... homosexuals, identifying them with superfluous consumption, waste, luxury, and indulgence."[65]

Issue ranking by NGO leaders emerged in 2010, days after police arrested Chimbalanga and Monjeza. Rafiq Hajat, the executive director of the Institute for Policy Interaction (IPI), claimed that gay rights merited no attention because other matters were more important. Hajat maintained, "The issue has been blown out of proportion. There are crucial issues such as attacks on the Constitution, forex, water and electricity crises, illiteracy and other challenges that we need to focus on as a nation."[66] Hajat worried that if clamoring about gay rights persisted, it would displace bread-and-butter problems facing the nation, problems that concerned most Malawians. According to Hajat, debating whether to decriminalize same-sex sex was "not productive. In fact, it is diverting attention from the critical issues ... I don't think homosexuality can solve the problems of poverty, electricity, water and the like." Like many social movement leaders, Hajat divorced sexual minority rights from tangible inequalities, such as

[61] Ibid.   [62] Ibid.   [63] Ibid.   [64] Ibid.

[65] Paul Amar, *The Security Archipelago: Human-Security States, Sexuality Politics, and the End of Neoliberalism* (Durham, NC: Duke University Press, 2013), 77.

[66] Kasunda, "Referendum, Solution to Homosexuality," 4. All quotations in this paragraph come from this source.

poverty and electrical outages, seeing no linkage between these issues. This viewpoint privileged material inequalities facing the masses above the social and material inequalities affecting a few.

Guided by issue ranking, activists made strategic choices about the social problems they should address. CONGOMA was one group that exercised caution with respect to LGBT rights. According to Justice, CONGOMA was not completely unresponsive to LGBT rights; the group allowed member NGOs to bring their "priorities" to CON-GOMA.[67] In response to CHRR and CEDEP's identification of gay rights as an issue, some NGO leaders seemed willing to allow the issue to remain on the agenda. Yet while CONGOMA worked on "setting our priorities, [LGBT rights] did not get any priority."[68] CONGOMA leaders did not want to alienate faith-based organizations because, according to Justice, if CONGOMA, as an umbrella body, promulgated "gay rights, they retreat, and they pull out ... So we needed to open the whole society."[69] Issues that took precedence over gay rights included "social-economic rights, rights to good living, rights to health," and the "availability" of fuel, "drugs in the hospitals," and "forex so that the businesses can pick up and run the economy."[70] Like Linda, Margaret, an activist affiliated with an NGO promoting Malawians' access to healthcare, distanced her NGO from work on "gay rights" because "we have critical issues that we must focus on: issues of child health, dental health, [and] education, providing [a] wide focus on things that matter."[71] Discounting "gay rights," Margaret believed the matter should not siphon attention away from healthcare.

Other activists viewed gay rights skeptically, worrying that homosexuality would supplant other pressing issues related to GBV. Alice, an activist working at a human rights NGO, pointed out that the political and public obsession with homosexuality kept activists and lawmakers from making progress on eliminating rape and GBV. According to Alice, the fascination with homosexuality stemmed in part from the fact that no high-profile public figure has "come out to say, 'I'm one of them [a homosexual].' They would not. We just suspect or assume that they are. No one has come out."[72] Alice

---

[67] Justice, interview with the author, July 9, 2012, Lilongwe, Malawi.
[68] Ibid.   [69] Ibid.   [70] Ibid.
[71] Margaret, interview with the author, July 13, 2012, Lilongwe, Malawi.
[72] Alice, interview with the author, July 4, 2012, Lilongwe, Malawi.

wondered why sympathetic activists should endorse gay rights, when no gay rights activists identified publicly as lesbian, gay, or bisexual. Challenging the position that only gender and sexual minorities could advocate for themselves, Gift Trapence, CEDEP's executive director, stated that "it does not matter whether he is MSM or not."[73] Instead, what mattered was the activist's continued advocacy.

On the one hand, if no activist defending LGBT rights was "out" as lesbian or gay, it raised ethical concerns for sympathetic activists about whether they should speak for gender and sexual minorities. On the other hand, some activists thought that there were more pressing priorities than LGBT rights. To demonstrate this point, Alice questioned,

So, why should we go there with [LGBT activists]? Malawi has so many problems ... Three or four weeks ago, the president [Joyce Banda] visited ... a location ... She was talking of within a month, 68 girls were raped. Is that not an issue? We are wasting our energies talking about issues of homosexuality.[74]

Framing homosexuality as an issue of privacy that society should not disturb, Alice explained that sexual minorities were "ordinary people ... indulging themselves," but they were not infringing on anyone's "enjoyment of rights. They do it in their own way."[75] Politicizing homosexuality, an issue that Alice did not view as harming anyone, ended up harming defenseless children, in Alice's opinion, because focusing on gay rights siphoned activists' attention away from child sexual abuse. She stated, "We leave out these children who are being abused day in, day out. Is that not an issue to talk about?"[76] Alice believed that social movements and the government were not doing enough to protect children from child sexual abuse.

Citing ongoing religious debates about gay rights, Alice elaborated on how she ranked issues.

There was an article in the papers three weeks ago where they were saying ... that religious leaders are coming together jointly to come up with a communiqué on their observations and what they feel about homosexuality. I said, "These people are wasting their time. Why don't they come out to talk about

---

[73] Mponda, "Malawi Has 10,000 Gays," 4.
[74] Alice, interview with the author, July 4, 2012, Lilongwe, Malawi.
[75] Ibid.　[76] Ibid.

people who are raping girls, who are raping children as young as six months? Is that not an issue? And they're talking about issues of homosexuality, you know. So, for some of us personally, I don't see why we should get involved and get bogged down [with] issues of homosexuality.[77]

Protecting children from sexual violence ranked as an urgent concern for Alice. Instead of marshaling children's vulnerability to disparage homosexuality, as some political elites in Malawi have done, Alice criticized politicized homophobia as diverting women's rights activists away from patriarchal sexual violence that hurt children.[78] In a 2013 editorial, Jimmy Kainja, a Malawian blogger, made a similar point. Lamenting the lack of attention that reports of the sexual abuse of twelve children had received, Kainja queried,

[I]magine the outrage if those reported 12 [child sexual abuse] cases were about homosexual[s]? ... Why do ... harmless adults having sexual relationships with members of the same sex arouse so much anger, hatred and outrage but it is all muted when it comes to child molestation?[79]

Kainja's commentary shows how politicized homophobia hurt not only sexual minorities but also children victimized by sexual abuse. Politicized homophobia siphoned women's rights activists' time and attention away from addressing critical social problems like child sexual abuse. Activists critical of politicized homophobia might support LGBT rights privately and consider doing so publicly in other circumstances, but at this moment, what attracted the derision of Alice and Kainja was how homophobia cluttered the sociopolitical sphere in which Malawian activists operated.

Another issue deserving activists' attention was unsafe abortion, an issue connected to "safe motherhood," a term women's rights activists employed to describe the cluster of issues contributing to maternal mortality. Hope, a human rights activist and LGBT rights supporter, identified "safe motherhood" as "the most important thing we are

---

[77] Ibid.

[78] When Jyoti Puri sought access to crime statistics about the Indian government's enforcement of the antisodomy law, Section 377, she encountered a similar argument from civil servants who argued that crimes against women should merit more attention from her "as a (woman) researcher" than antisodomy cases. Puri, *Sexual States*, 36.

[79] Jimmy Kainja, "Giving Hypocrisy Its Meaning: Child Abuse in a 'God-Fearing' Malawi," *Nyasa Times*, July 31, 2013, www.nyasatimes.com/giving-hypocrisy-its-meaning-child-abuse-in-a-god-fearing-malawi/.

focusing on now ... because some time back when these issues were not looked into, mothers ... were just dying silently."[80] Alice claimed that too many "maternal deaths" were due to "unsafe abortion."[81] In Malawi, "abortion is a crime, and even the one offering abortion is also taken to task."[82] She noted that the "slippery slope" argument leveraged against homosexuality – that legalization and sexual liberalization would entice heterosexuals into same-sex sexual relationships – was also used to discredit abortion.[83] According to Alice, antiabortion opponents will say,

"If we legalize abortion, every woman will be procuring it at any time." You know, that kind of thinking. And it's quite challenging because that's not the way it happens. In other countries, we know very well where [abortion is] legalized, it actually adds value because you actually experience a reduction of deaths in terms of abortion, but I don't know how Malawi would take it.[84]

The slippery-slope argument rang hollow for Alice, who expressed disappointment upon learning of President Joyce Banda's opposition to legalizing abortion. Alice explained that before becoming president in April 2012 after Mutharika's death, Banda had championed the issue of safe motherhood and maternal mortality. Banda's antiabortion stance confused Alice, who remarked, "If she's not for abortion, then how come she claims to be an ambassador of safe motherhood? How are we going to reduce maternal deaths when in Malawi seventeen percent comes from unsafe abortion? Seventeen percent is quite high."[85] Although Alice recognized the similarities between the arguments some Malawian political elites used to oppose decriminalizing abortion and same-sex sex, she ranked unsafe abortion as an issue more pressing than homosexuality, particularly in the lives of Malawian women whom she viewed as in need of fierce advocates.

As many social problems competed for activists' attention in Malawi, activists refused to consider LGBT rights as more pressing than other issues like GBV. It is significant that activists who espoused

---

[80] Hope, interview with the author, July 12, 2012, Lilongwe, Malawi.
[81] Alice, interview with the author, July 4, 2012, Lilongwe, Malawi.   [82] Ibid.
[83] Gary Mucciaroni, *Same Sex, Different Politics: Success and Failure in the Struggle over Gay Rights* (Chicago: University of Chicago Press, 2009).
[84] Alice, interview with the author, July 4, 2012, Lilongwe, Malawi.   [85] Ibid.

this viewpoint did not discuss defending LGBT rights in conjunction
with other social-justice actions, such as advancing children's rights or
addressing GBV. A laser focus on a single issue could trap NGOs into
an unproductive cycle, preventing them from forming coalitions with
other groups that, in turn, could enable them to make gains on their
primary issue. Additionally, a single-issue focus can hasten an NGO's
demise, shrinking the resources available to and volunteers interested
in supporting the organization.[86] Such a focus could generate subsequent, unforeseen problems for NGOs.

National Readiness for Decriminalized Same-Sex Sexualities?

In addition to asserting that certain social problems ranked as more
urgent than LGBT rights, some activists claimed that Malawians were
not ready for the decriminalization of same-sex sex. Gideon noted that
most people "have been ready to demonstrate against civil society on
this ... gay rights issue."[87] Citing Malawians' unpreparedness for a
national debate about LGBT rights and legalizing same-sex sex, certain
activists decided against pursuing public LGBT rights advocacy.
Although activists understood how heteronationalism structured
Malawian sexual ideologies and practices, they evinced little interest
in contesting the heteronationalist status quo.

Favoring a circumspect approach to advocating for gender and
sexual diversity rights in Malawi, Linda encouraged LGBT rights
campaigners to recognize that "Malawians are still learning about
homosexuality. It's a homophobic culture. And, just like any other
culture, you need to be educated to understand the dynamics of homosexuality. Because, for them," homosexuality provided social titillation.[88] Pretending to be a Malawian looking at a newspaper photo of
Chimbalanga and Monjeza in handcuffs, Linda demonstrated how
Malawians perceived gender and sexual dissidents as distant others.
She imitated bystanders staring at the couple whom she portrayed
as gay: "It's like, 'Oh! Look at those two men. They got married.

---

[86] Bob Edwards and Sam Marullo, "Organizational Mortality in a Declining Social
Movement: The Demise of Peace Movement Organizations in the End of the
Cold War Era," *American Sociological Review*, 60, no. 6 (1995): 908–927.

[87] Gideon, interview with the author, July 12, 2012, Lilongwe, Malawi.

[88] Linda, interview with the author, June 25, 2012, Blantyre, Malawi.

Ha-ha.'"[89] Although Linda's commentary depicted Malawians opposed to same-sex sexualities as socially and politically immature, it also suggested that rushing into LGBT advocacy without acknowledging social resistance to homosexuality was a mistake.

Other activists claimed that low literacy levels and lack of access to quality education contributed to Malawians' unpreparedness to discuss same-sex sexualities knowledgeably. Gideon invoked this perception when he explicated how Mutharika's government exploited ordinary Malawians' lack of access to information in an effort to smear NGOs' reputations. Gideon believed that state officials portrayed public debate about same-sex sexualities as inauthentic because NGOs pushed lawmakers to take up gay rights.[90] Gideon explained that the "major weakness of civil society" was that foreign-funded NGOs had thrust same-sex sexualities into public view, instead of waiting for "the majority of the people" to buy "into that kind of thinking."[91] Had Malawians initiated public debates about same-sex sexualities, then sexual diversity would have merited political consideration and social discussion, according to political elites. This logic did not persuade Gideon. His "own assessment" was that state leaders circulated "misinformation. Malawians are not given the right information that can assist them to make their own informed opinions."[92] If information were communicated in a manner easily understood by people throughout the country, Gideon and other activists believed that Malawians might soon be ready to discuss LGBT rights and the inclusion of gender and sexual minorities in legal, social, and political institutions.

Still other activists like Alice believed that Malawians were not prepared for a sober debate about same-sex sexualities. Alice explained, "Malawi may not be ready to deal with such matters, and, for me, yes, we are not yet ready. We have to wait for a while because, if you ask about these views from traditional authorities, they are very, very much opposed."[93] In Alice's experience, traditional leaders, much like political and religious leaders, alleged that homosexuality was absent from Malawian culture. According to Alice,

---

[89] Ibid.
[90] Gideon, interview with the author, July 12, 2012, Lilongwe, Malawi.
[91] Ibid.   [92] Ibid.
[93] Alice, interview with the author, July 4, 2012, Lilongwe, Malawi.

traditional leaders "always say, 'No, it [homosexuality] was not there'"[94] in Malawian society in the past, echoing a variant of "homosexuality-is-un-African" discourse.[95] Alice discussed a meeting in Blantyre attended by traditional leaders who asked her pointedly,

"You, as a human rights person, what are your comments on issues of homosexuality?"

And I said, "For me, homosexuality is as old as prostitution. It's just that now it is coming out and people are debating about it. Otherwise it has been there [in Malawian society]. It's not a recent phenomenon. It is not, but we want to make it to be something which has come from America. No, it's not."[96]

Using traditional leaders' hostility toward homosexuality as a benchmark for citizens' heteronationalist attitudes, Alice believed that Malawian "society is just not yet ready" for a discussion about the merits of decriminalizing same-sex sex.[97]

The strategic choice not to advocate for LGBT rights publicly was practical for activists whose NGOs struggled to serve marginalized constituencies, including girls, women, and HIV-positive persons. Nevertheless, casting the decision not to collaborate with other NGOs on a LGBT rights campaign because Malawi was "just not yet ready" for decriminalized same-sex sexualities fed into developmentalist discourses about sexual politics. Developmentalist discourses portray Western nations as more culturally, politically, socially, and sexually enlightened, while postcolonial nations in the global South are underdeveloped and presently incapable of meeting benchmarks associated with social (and sexual) progress.[98] Although activists like Alice and Linda honestly enumerated what they viewed as cultural, social, and political obstacles to decriminalizing same-sex sex in Malawi, the rationale they offered reinforced a hierarchy of nations based on perceived acceptance of gender and sexual diversity, a hierarchy that benefited Western nations associated with queer tolerance and disadvantaged nations in the global South that purportedly rejected queerness.

---

[94] Ibid.   [95] Currier, *Out in Africa.*
[96] Alice, interview with the author, July 4, 2012, Lilongwe, Malawi.   [97] Ibid.
[98] Alexander, *Pedagogies of Crossing*; Currier, *Out in Africa*, 119–120.

Envy, Money, and Distance

The leading LGBT rights defenders in Malawi, CEDEP and CHRR, have received external funding from foreign donors, generating tensions among less well-resourced NGOs. Some scholars and observers question the ability of NGOs that receive external funding and material support to exercise autonomy.[99] Skeptics suggest that external funding skews the strategic priorities of activists who bend their collective will to implement donors' wishes. From this perspective, activists who seek and accept donor funding risk losing control of how they pursue their goals, particularly if donors ask activists to change their tactics, action priorities, or NGO management. Linda's experiences with an NGO donor match the scenarios described by skeptics of donor funding. The donor representative interrogated Linda about why her NGO had not publicly backed LGBT rights at a time when the representative believed that cross-movement solidarity was crucial. If Linda had obliged the representative's request by publicly supporting and incorporating LGBT rights into her NGO's strategic priorities, she and her colleagues might have had to rearrange the NGO's plans.

Despite the objections raised by skeptics about the ethics and politics of funding social movements in the global South, in reality, many NGOs, particularly LGBT rights NGOs, cannot mount campaigns or implement certain strategies, such as educating constituents about HIV/AIDS and STIs, without donor funding.[100] With external funding, NGOs hire staff, pay for activists' transportation, rent office or meeting space, and purchase materials used in advocacy, such as computer equipment, condoms, lubricants, and educational materials. Membership dues or small donations from constituents do not generate the revenue needed to pay stipends to staff or to buy large quantities of condoms and lubricants. In the past, LGBT rights NGOs around the

---

[99] Haines, "Black Radicalization"; Incite! Women of Color against Violence, ed. *The Revolution Will Not Be Funded: Beyond the Non-Profit Industrial Complex* (Boston: South End Press, 2009).

[100] Currier and Cruz, "Civil Society and Sexual Struggles in Africa"; Timothy Hildebrandt, "Development and Division: The Effect of Transnational Linkages and Local Politics on LGBT Activism in China," *Journal of Contemporary China*, 21, no. 77 (2012): 845–862.

world have encountered obstacles to securing funding for their work.[101] When LGBT rights NGOs lose funding, they often shut down their operation or suspend an activist project.[102]

Funding does not trickle down to all organizations in a social movement or across movements. Therefore, resource inequalities between NGOs can generate enmity among activists who begrudge the good fortune of other organizations. Gideon observed such jealousy in leaders of NGOs that were "grossly underfunded. So, participating in a gay rights campaign would expose an NGO to readily available channels of funds."[103] The "readily available" funds flowing to NGOs like CEDEP and CHRR frustrated the "struggling civil society sector. Even today as we speak, civil society is so grossly underfunded it will talk about anything that comes its way" in the hope that NGOs will receive external funding.[104] Gideon implied that despite the unpopularity of LGBT rights, NGOs desperate for external funding might endorse LGBT rights publicly. Yet the "dilemma is . . . if an NGO is seen to be advancing same-sex relationships in Malawi, it's going to be disowned by the people."[105] In other words, supporting LGBT rights as a way to procure donor funding could backfire for NGOs, making them the subject of homophobic vitriol. Benjamin, a staff member at CEDEP, observed this dynamic in other human rights NGOs. Speaking about an NGO that worked in villages in the Northern region, Benjamin narrated how staff expressed their disgust at the thought of working with CEDEP. Staff viewed CEDEP as a "human rights organization . . . [that] is advocating for same-sex relationships.

---

[101] Julie Moreau and Ashley Currier, "Queer Dilemmas: LGBT Activism and International Funding," in *Queer Development Studies: A Reader*, edited by Corinne Mason (New York: Routledge, 2018), 223–238.

[102] Cymene Howe, *Intimate Activism: The Struggle for Sexual Rights in Postrevolutionary Nicaragua* (Durham, NC: Duke University Press, 2013). Although indigenous philanthropy or fundraising remains isolated and difficult in South Africa, the Other Foundation has emerged as an African "community trust that advances human rights and social inclusion in southern Africa, with a particular focus on lesbian, gay, bisexual, transgender, and intersex (LGBTI) people." The Other Foundation, *Progressive Prudes: A Survey of Attitudes towards Homosexuality and Gender Non-Conformity in South Africa* (Johannesburg, South Africa: The Other Foundation, 2016), 15. http://repository.hsrc.ac.za/bitstream/handle/20.500.11910/10161/9400.pdf?sequence=1&isAllowed=y.

[103] Gideon, interview with the author, July 12, 2012, Lilongwe, Malawi.

[104] Ibid.   [105] Ibid.

As much as we want human rights, we do not want such rights."[106] For some NGO workers, LGBT rights sullied the category of "human rights," making NGOs that championed human rights suspect in the eyes of antigay political elites. Staff at other NGOs coveted the resources that NGOs supporting LGBT rights could marshal, according to some LGBT rights activists. Despite the risks associated with endorsing LGBT rights and staff members' personal prejudices, the reality was that "there is a lot of money . . . around" LGBT rights, according to Gideon.[107] Benjamin related that some NGO leaders envied CEDEP's ability to garner "more resources."[108]

As other scholars have demonstrated, social movements are not devoid of emotions.[109] Activists mobilize varied emotions, such as indignation, despair, and even jealousy, while at other times, they seek to suppress them. As Gideon suggested, envy of other NGOs' resources contributed to some leaders' wary attitudes toward other NGOs and toward supporting LGBT rights. As a result, certain emotions guiding and structuring relations between NGO representatives could produce distance and exacerbate already-existing divisions between NGOs, divisions that had long been simmering within civil society, as Chapter 3 demonstrates.

Missed Opportunity for Pro-LGBT Rights Solidarity

Until his unexpected death in April 2012, President Mutharika portrayed same-sex sexualities as a social and political scourge. The accession of the vice president, Joyce Banda, the leader of the People's Party (PP), to the presidency seemed auspicious to LGBT rights supporters who anticipated that the climate for discussions about decriminalizing same-sex sexualities in Malawi would improve. In her first "State of the Nation" address in May 2012 after becoming president, Banda identified laws criminalizing same-sex sex as "bad laws" in need

---

[106] Benjamin, interview with the author, June 27, 2012, Blantyre, Malawi.
[107] Gideon, interview with the author, July 12, 2012, Lilongwe, Malawi.
[108] Benjamin, interview with the author, June 27, 2012, Blantyre, Malawi.
[109] Erika Summers Effler, *Laughing Saints and Righteous Heroes: Emotional Rhythms in Social Movement Groups* (Chicago: University of Chicago Press, 2010); Deborah B. Gould, *Moving Politics: Emotion and ACT UP's Fight against AIDS* (Chicago: University of Chicago Press, 2009).

of legislative review and repeal.[110] Wapona Kita, a human rights lawyer, welcomed the news, stating that decriminalization was "long overdue."[111] Political scientist Blessings Chinsinga celebrated Banda for "boldly and unequivocally putting the question of gay rights into the public domain for debate," which charted a long-awaited direction away from "her predecessor's [Mutharika's] machinations that exploited the gay rights debate as a shield for ill-governance and executive arrogance."[112]

Banda's tentative support for decriminalizing same-sex sex constituted a political opportunity that LGBT rights supporters could have exploited, yet HIV/AIDS, human rights, and women's rights activists were noticeably absent in 2012 from public debates, apart from CEDEP and CHRR's public statements endorsing the antisodomy law's repeal.[113] For instance, Gift Trapence, CEDEP's executive director, supported rescinding these laws but opposed what he characterized as the "politicisation" of homophobia, which, in his view, "reached its climax when the public media ... peddle misinformation and opposition to rights of minorities."[114] For Trapence, one consequence of politicized homophobia involved "how the issue of decriminalisation of anti-homosexuality laws is mistaken for legalisation of gay marriages."[115] Clarifying that decriminalizing same-sex sexual practices does not automatically legalize same-sex marriage because the "Marriage Act ... recognizes marriage as being between a man and a woman," Trapence explained that many "different steps [must] be taken to reach the level of recognising gay marriages. What is important is not to discriminate against someone based on sexual orientation. This is the issue of equality and that's what we are talking about on the

---

[110] Felix Mponda, "Blues Will Eat Humble Pie," *Daily Times*, May 20, 2012, article on file with author.

[111] "Malawi to End Ban on Homosexual Acts, Says President Banda," *Nyasa Times*, May 18, 2012, www.nyasatimes.com/malawi-to-end-ban-0n-homosexual-acts-says-president-banda/.

[112] Blessings Chinsinga, "Of Gay Rights and Section 65," *Sunday Times*, June 10, 2012, 7.

[113] George Mhango, "Government Has Taken Good Direction on Minority Rights," *Nation*, May 23, 2012, 1, 8; Agnes Mizere, "Review Anti-Gay Laws," *Daily Times*, September 5, 2012, 2. A notable exception is Jessie Kabwila, a feminist English professor at Chancellor College, who was an outspoken supporter of LGBT rights. Edwin Nyirongo, "Homosexuality Not Foreign – Kabwila Kapasula," *Nation*, November 7, 2012, 3.

[114] Mizere, "Review Anti-Gay Laws," 2.   [115] Ibid.

need to repeal the sodomy laws."[116] During CEDEP and CHRR's commemoration of the International Day Against Homophobia and Transphobia in 2012, Trapence stated, "[D]ecriminalisation will not only help people from the misery of having to live a life underground, but also help to stem the continuing HIV epidemic."[117] In addition, decriminalizing same-sex sex could gradually encourage more Malawians to accept LGBT people and recognize that they deserve "protection from discrimination."[118] Ordinary lesbians and gay men wanted the government to decriminalize same-sex sex. Nile Banda, a gay man in his forties, stated in a newspaper interview, "It doesn't make sense for government to arrest two consenting adults for having sex. How I wish one day Malawians woke up and accepted us as human beings—no labels, no conditions."[119]

Before Banda's endorsement of law reform, lawmakers and activists probed the possibility of repealing some of the "bad laws" Mutharika had signed into law in the aftermath of the July 20 protests. NGOs met with government officials in talks mediated by the UN to discuss activists' concerns about Mutharika's undemocratic governance. As talks unfolded over the next few months, LGBT rights defenders, such as CEDEP and CHRR, continued to participate.[120] Around the time that NGOs participated in negotiations with Mutharika's government, UN Secretary General Ban Ki-moon advised African leaders gathered

---

[116] Ibid. The 2015 Marriage, Divorce, and Family Relations Act defined marriage as involving one cisgender man and one cisgender woman, preempting the legalization of same-sex marriage and forbidding transgender people to marry a person of the same sex they were assigned at birth. Thom Chiumia, "Malawi Marriage Bill Spurns Same-Sex Liaisons." *Nyasa Times*, February 17, 2015, www.nyasatimes.com/malawi-marriage-bill-spurn-same-sex-liasons.

[117] A 2011 CEDEP and CHRR study measuring Malawians' attitudes revealed that only "30 percent" of survey respondents believed that LGBT people should be protected from discrimination. Gabriel Kamlomo, "NGOs Decry Homophobia in Malawi," *Daily Times*, May 21, 2012, 4.

[118] Anthony Kasunda, "Accept Sexual Minorities, Malawians Urged," *Nation*, May 17, 2012, 4.

[119] Bright Mhango, "Please Accept Us," *Nation*, August 11, 2012, 21.

[120] CEDEP and CHRR's engagement with broader issues related to democratic governance, economic security, and foreign affairs persist to this day. Gabriel Kamlomo, "CSOs Demand All Inclusive Govt," *Daily Times*, April 11, 2012, 4; Archibald Kasakura, "Contact Group/NGOs Set on Showdown over Timeframe," *Malawi News*, January 28–February 3, 2012, 2–3; Wezzie Nkhoma-Somba, "CHRR, CEDEP against Injunction Bill," *Sunday Times*, June 19, 2012, 3.

at the African Union summit in Addis Ababa, Ethiopia, to "respect gay rights," a suggestion that could be interpreted as recommending the rescission of the antisodomy law.[121] Despite activists' insistence on the antisodomy law repeal, the Malawi Law Commission (MLC) countered that no funds were available to pay for a law review.[122] While newspaper editorials counseled lawmakers to overturn these laws, some activists asserted that the "government should not waste money with the reviewing process but should just take them back to parliament to have them repealed."[123] In May 2012, Minister of Justice and Attorney General Ralph Kasambara promised to remove the "bad laws" review from the MLC and submit these laws to legislators for repeal; he also depicted Mutharika's action to send the bad laws to the MLC for review as an attempt "to buy time" from disgruntled NGOs and opposition political parties.[124]

Observers around the world responded favorably to President Banda's announcement that she favored repealing the antisodomy law during her "State of the Nation" address.[125] Whereas Western observers showered Banda with praise, many Malawians objected to Banda's suggestion that lawmakers rescind the antisodomy law along with other "bad laws."[126] One Malawian thought it was "politically suicidal as people will look at her as a sell out to the donors," a reference to heteronationalist fears that state leaders would comply with donor demands that the state honor LGBT rights in exchange for

[121] "Respect Gay Rights, UN's Ban Tells African Leaders," *Nyasa Times*, January 29, 2012, www.nyasatimes.com/respect-gay-rights-uns-ban-tells-african-leaders/.

[122] Theresa Chapulapula and Simeon Maganga, "No Money for Bad Laws' Review," *Daily Times*, February 3, 2012, 1, 3.

[123] "Bad Laws Should Be Repealed," *Daily Times*, February 3, 2012, 4; Madalitso Musa, "Repeal All Bad Laws – JB Told," *Daily Times*, April 25, 2012, 3.

[124] Theresa Chapulapula, "Govt Acts on Bad Laws," *Malawi News*, May 5–11, 2012, 3.

[125] Simeon Maganga, "UK Engages JB on Human Rights," *Daily Times*, May 31, 2012, 1, 3.

[126] Simeon Maganga, "Petra Queries Homosexuality Legalisation Hastened," *Daily Times*, May 21, 2012, article on file with author; "My Take on Whether It Is Good for Malawi to Support Minority Rights," *Nation*, May 30, 2012, 8; "My Take on Whether Malawians Are Justified to Deny Gay Relationships as a Right," *Nation*, July 11, 2012, 8; "My Take on Whether Same Sex Relationships Should Be Decriminalised," *Nation*, June 20, 2012, 8; "US Commends Joyce Banda's 'Bold Actions,'" *Nyasa Times*, May 22, 2012, www.nyasatimes.com/2012/05/22/us-commends-joyce-bandas-bold-actions/.

development aid.[127] Another editorial characterized Banda's plan for law reform as transforming Malawi from a "God-fearing nation" into a "donor-fearing nation" that would do donors' bidding without question.[128] Some Western diplomats, such as UK diplomats, promised that development assistance was not yoked to gay rights.[129] Religious critics alleged that abandoning antigay laws would "deliberately provoke God" and promised to stage protests if lawmakers acted on Banda's wishes.[130] Other opponents objected to the proposed mechanism for changing the antisodomy law; instead of allowing lawmakers to take action on these laws, they wanted the government to sponsor a national "referendum on whether Malawi should legalise homosexuality."[131] Ken Msonda, the People's Party deputy publicity secretary, defended the proposal to remove antigay laws, stating that the party "shall not entertain or accommodate bad laws, laws that divide us as a nation. We need to move forward. What do we lose as a nation if we tolerate some people that [sic] act [differently]? We have a lot [more] to worry about than this."[132] Although Msonda invoked issue ranking in his endorsement of Banda's plan to repeal bad laws, his statement aligned the new ruling party with a pro-LGBT-rights position for the first time in Malawi's history.[133]

Responding to these criticisms, Banda relented to pressure from different groups opposing decriminalization of same-sex sex and announced that she would not lobby lawmakers to undertake this

---

[127] Golden Matonga, "Malawians See Hope in JB Speech," *Daily Times*, May 21, 2012, article on file with author; Rahul Rao, "On 'Gay Conditionality,' Imperial Power, and Queer Liberation," January 1, 2012, https://kafila.online/2012/01/01/on-gay-conditionality-imperial-power-and-queer-liberation-rahul-rao/.

[128] Yokoniya Chilanga, "Malawi Becoming a Donor Fearing Nation," *Daily Times*, June 11, 2012, 9.

[129] Madalitso Musa, "UK Aid Not Tied to Gay Rights," *Daily Times*, June 1, 2012, 1, 3.

[130] Mmana and Singini, "Clerics Query," 2. See also, Emmanuel Muwamba, "Nkhoma CCAP Synod Warns MPs on Gay Laws," *Nation*, June 3, 2012, 3.

[131] Simeon Maganga, "Let Malawians Vote on Homosexuality," *Daily Times*, June 13, 2012, 2.

[132] Frank Namangale, "It Is Cruel to Jail People for Being Unnatural – PP," *Weekend Nation*, May 26, 2012, 3.

[133] Msonda reversed his tepid support for LGBT rights in 2016, when he recommended instituting the death penalty for "gays." Lucky Mkandawire, "MLS Wants PP's Msonda Probed for Gay Remarks," *Nation*, January 5, 2016, http://mwnation.com/mls-wants-pps-msonda-probed-for-gay-remarks/.

law reform. One columnist depicted Banda's situation as amounting to "dancing an undanceable dance. She is damned if she repeals anti-gay laws and damned if she doesn't."[134] Explaining her evolving position, Banda stated that

as a president I do not make laws. The bill about same sex marriages has not gone to parliament; it is yet to be discussed even at cabinet level. Even if it were tabled for debate, I will not force MPs to pass it. If the people of Malawi do not want same sex marriages MPs will not pass the law.[135]

Admitting the limitations of her office, Banda submitted to antigay political elites' will. Her unfortunate portrayal of decriminalizing same-sex sex as legalizing same-sex marriages gave credence to widespread misperceptions that decriminalization would automatically grant same-sex couples the right to marry.[136] If HIV/AIDS, human rights, and women's rights activists had joined forces with LGBT rights activists to lend support for Banda's important initiative, perhaps they could have persuaded Banda and other PP lawmakers to pursue this law reform. Instead, LGBT rights supporters from CEDEP and CHRR defended the plan to decriminalize same-sex sex largely by themselves.[137] In 2012, Trapence of CEDEP and Undule Mwakasungula of CHRR began writing and publishing weekly columns in the "Sexual Minority Forum" about gender and sexual diversity in the *Weekend Nation* in an effort to educate Malawians about LGBT rights.[138]

---

[134] Chipiri wa Chipiri, "Criticism of JB's Stance on Gay Rights Unfair," *Malawi News*, May 26-June 1, 2012, 7.

[135] Archibald Kasakura, "JB Won't Push MPs on Same Sex Law," *Malawi News*, May 26–June 1, 2012, 2.

[136] Kasambara worked to dispel Banda's conflation of the decriminalization of same-sex sex with same-sex marriage. In an interview the day after Banda's confusing comments, he stated, "The issue is not about allowing or not allowing same-sex marriages ... [W]e have not yet started talking or debating same-sex marriages in Malawi, but we are discussing minority rights of lesbians and gays." Albert Sharra, "We Have Not Yet Started Talking Same-Sex Marriages," *Weekend Nation*, June 2, 2012, 4.

[137] Bright Sonani, "Activists Trash DPP Stand on Gay Laws," *Nation*, August 7, 2012, 3; Bright Sonani, "Activists Want Kalinde to Withdraw Remarks," *Nation*, August 13, 2012, 3; Yvonne Sundu, "Minority Rights Misconception Encouraging AIDS Spread," *Nation*, August 24, 2012, 7.

[138] Undule Mwakasungula and Gift Trapence, "Living Together in Sexual Diversity," *Weekend Nation*, September 22, 2012, 7; Undule Mwakasungula and Gift Trapence, "Overcoming Homophobia May Save Lives," *Weekend Nation*, September 29, 2012, 7; Undule Mwakasungula and Gift Trapence,

After a few months of heated exchanges in the media about the virtues of rescinding the antisodomy law, Banda admitted public defeat and explained why the repeal was unlikely to happen soon.[139] She stated,

Anyone who has listened to the debate in Malawi realises that Malawians are not ready to deal with that right now ... Where Malawi is and most African countries are is maybe where America or the UK was about 100 years ago. The best thing the world can do is to allow each country to take its course, to allow each country to have that debate freely without the pressure of being pushed.[140]

Deploying a national-readiness argument in conjunction with a plea for other countries, funding agencies, and supranational organizations to respect Malawi's sovereignty on debating sex laws, Banda abandoned an ambitious plan to advance LGBT rights as human rights and to roll back autocratic laws and policies implemented by her predecessor. Predictably, foreign donors and UN leaders refused to accept Banda's explanation and implored her to take steps to respect sexual

"Constitutional Rights and Public Opinion on Homosexuality in Malawi, Part 1," *Weekend Nation*, October 13, 2012, 7; Undule Mwakasungula and Gift Trapence, "Homosexuality, Constitutional Rights, and Public Opinion in Malawi, Part II," *Weekend Nation*, October 20, 2012, 7; Undule Mwakasungula and Gift Trapence, "Homosexuality, Constitutional Rights, and Public Opinion in Malawi, Part III," *Weekend Nation*, October 27, 2012, 7; Undule Mwakasungula and Gift Trapence, "Malawi's Homophobic Culture," *Weekend Nation*, November 3, 2012, 7; Undule Mwakasungula and Gift Trapence, "Letter from a Gay Man 'in Hiding,'" *Weekend Nation*, November 10, 2012, 7; Undule Mwakasungula and Gift Trapence, "Church Hypocrisy," *Weekend Nation*, November 17, 2012, 7; Undule Mwakasungula and Gift Trapence, "Is the Church Ignorant of Gay Issues? (Part 1)," *Weekend Nation*, November 24, 2012, 7; Undule Mwakasungula and Gift Trapence, "Politicisation of Gay Issue," *Weekend Nation*, December 8, 2012, 7; Undule Mwakasungula and Gift Trapence, "Anti-Gay Laws Must Be Reviewed!," *Weekend Nation*, December 15, 2012, 7; Undule Mwakasungula and Gift Trapence, "Would Jesus Embrace Homosexuals?," *Weekend Nation*, December 22, 2012, 7; Undule Mwakasungula and Gift Trapence, "MIAA's Statement Is Total Misleading and Fabrication of Facts," *Weekend Nation*, December 29, 2012, 7.

[139] Nick Chakwera, "Vote: No!," *Malawi News*, May 26–June 1, 2012, 11; Bright Sonani, "DPP Cautions Govt on Gay Laws," *Nation*, August 1, 2012, 2.

[140] Emmanuel Muwamba, "JB Says Malawi Unlikely to Repeal Anti-Gay Laws," *Nation*, October 1, 2012, 3.

minority rights.[141] Similarly, some human and LGBT rights activists voiced disapproval with Banda's concession to anti-LGBT positions. Mwakasungula argued that LGBT rights constituted a "human rights issue and you don't just put such matters into the public opinion. The president should not be in a position to promote homophobia against a section of her own people."[142]

In November 2012, Kasambara announced he was temporarily suspending laws governing same-sex sex, a development that Malawian NGOs like CEDEP and CHRR and international NGOs like Amnesty International commended.[143] Kasambara's announcement was met with withering criticism from Malawians, prompting him to deny that he had announced a moratorium at all.[144] The Malawi Law Society decried the moratorium, asserting that this move was both "unconstitutional" and "illegal . . . This means any minister can wake up and start suspending any law."[145] DPP members called for President Banda to fire Kasambara for announcing the moratorium without consulting parliament.[146] While opposition parties criticized Kasambara, Banda confirmed that she would not take a public position on the legality of same-sex sex.[147]

[141] Anthony Kasunda, "Donors Caution on Gay Rights," *Nation*, October 8, 2012, 1–2; Emmanuel Muwamba, "UN Hopes Malawi Will Review Same Sex Laws," *Nation*, December 13, 2012, 2.

[142] Austin Kakande, "CSOs on JB's Neck over Homosexual Laws: She Should Be Last Person to Promote Homophobia – Undule," *Malawi Voice*, October 1, 2012, article on file with author.

[143] Amnesty International, "Suspension of Anti-Homosexuality Laws in Malawi a Historic Step Forward," November 5, 2012, www.amnesty.org/en/news/suspension-anti-homosexuality-laws-malawi-historic-step-forward-2012-11-05; "Malawi Suspends Anti-Homosexuality Laws: 'Police Cannot Arrest Gays for Now,'" *Nyasa Times*, November 5, 2012, www.nyasatimes.com/malawi-suspends-anti-homosexuality-laws-police-cannot-arrest-gays-for-now/; "Undule Mwakasungula Welcomes Government's Move to Suspend Anti-Gay Laws," *Malawi Voice*, November 6, 2012, article on file with author.

[144] Taonga Batolo, "Kamlepo Calls for Anti-Gay Protests: 'Malawi Should Not Allow Homosexuality,'" *Nyasa Times*, November 6, 2012, www.nyasatimes.com/kamlepo-calls-for-anti-gay-protests-malawi-should-not-allow-homosexuality/. Simeon Maganga, "Kasambara Denies Suspending Gay Law," *Daily Times*, November 7, 2012, 3.

[145] Bright Sonani, "Law Society Faults Govt," *Nation*, November 7, 2012, 2.

[146] Chikondi Juma, "DPP Wants Kasambara Fired," *Daily Times*, November 12, 2012, 1, 3.

[147] Chikondi Juma, "JB Will Not Take a Stand on Homosexuality – State House," *Daily Times*, November 16, 2012, 2.

The state's changing positions on decriminalizing same-sex sex confounded many Malawians, some of whom supported holding a national referendum on gay rights.[148] Raphael Tenthani, a *Sunday Times* columnist, expressed bewilderment over state leaders' inability to decide "what stand to take on the controversial homosexual debate. The President and her Attorney General have been all over the place, saying one thing today and the other the next day on the issue." It is worth quoting at length from Tenthani's column because it illustrates the one-step-forward-two-steps-back dilemma of advancing LGBT rights in a sociopolitical environment saturated with politicized homophobia and in a government whose leaders took different positions on decriminalization.

The other day Joyce Banda excited the world when she said she would send all the country's homophobic laws to the cleaners, only to eat her own words when some sections of the self-styled religious nation rose against her stand.

Not to be out-done, her youthful chief legal advisor also made all the right noises about declaring a moratorium on all homophobic laws. But, after making the world headlines, my name-sake Ralph Kasambara struggled to explain himself barely 24 hours later.

I know we, Malawians, tantalise ourselves as a "God-fearing" nation whatever that means. But governing means formulating policies and defending them.

Why are our leaders afraid to take a stand on this "gay" debate and get done with it? Hiding behind a "national debate" does not help. Someone has to lead such a "national debate" for crying out loud.

Take a stand on this issue and defend it; this flip-flopping will not gel with both sides of the divisive debate.[149]

Tenthani's exasperation with the never-ending, "controversial homosexual debate" is clear. He had little patience for politicians' ambivalence about LGBT rights. Trapence lamented that the government was "moving in circles on the issue of legalising gay relationships ... as people's rights are being violated. As a result, opposition parties are

---

[148] George Kasakula, "Can JB Govt Decide on Gays?," *Weekend Nation*, November 10, 2012, 31; Simeon Maganga, "Let Malawians Vote on Homosexuality," *Daily Times*, June 13, 2012, 2; George Mhango, "Govt Should Take a Stand on Gays – Dausi," *Nation*, December 5, 2012, 1.

[149] Raphael Tenthani, "Let's Take a Stand on Gays," *Sunday Times*, November 25, 2012, 2. See also, Raphael Tenthani, "Flip-Floppers," *Sunday Times*, November 11, 2012, 2.

taking advantage of the state's lack of clarity to further confuse the public."[150] According to Trapence, one of the few activists voicing support for LGBT rights publicly, the state's ambivalence created an opening for opposition parties, especially Mutharika's DPP, to use politicized homophobia to criticize Banda's leadership and bolster opposition toward decriminalizing same-sex sex.[151]

Piludzu, the *Sunday Times'* political cartoon, pilloried political parties' reluctance to take on the "gay issue" in 2012.[152] The cartoon features a Malawian man and woman reading a chalkboard with the heading "gay issue" and political parties' positions on the matter.

PP: Parliament debate it
PETRA: West forcing practice on Malawians
DPP: We can mobilise our supporters to protest this
UDF: We will discuss it next year
MCP: Very alien practice

The man queries, "Why is everyone running away from the issue?" The woman replies, "Afraid of losing votes in 2014," referring to the national elections planned for May 2014.[153] The prescient cartoon captured politicians' concerns about coming out on the wrong side of decriminalizing same-sex sex; if they supported decriminalization when most Malawians opposed homosexuality, they risked losing voters' support during the next major election, a position about which Malawian media would remind voters.

If HIV/AIDS, human rights, and women's rights activists had banded together and lent support as a coalition for decriminalizing same-sex sex and suspending the antisodomy law, instead of leaving CHRR, CEDEP, and one or two other sympathetic NGOs alone to respond to these developments, then they might have convinced President Banda and Minister of Justice and Attorney General Kasambara to support rescinding the antisodomy law fully. Instead, opposition political parties filled the vacuum left by NGOs' silence on decriminalizing same-sex sexual practices. As evidenced by my interviews with

---

[150] Archibald Kasakura, "German Govt for Minority Rights," *Daily Times*, November 27, 2012, 4.

[151] Golden Matonga, "DPP Presses Govt on Gays, Abortion," *Daily Times*, November 28, 2012, 1, 3. See also, Frank Namangale, "Petra against Repeal of Same Sex Law," *Nation*, May 21, 2012, 3.

[152] Piludzu, "Gay Issue," *Sunday Times*, November 25, 2012, 5.   [153] Ibid.

activists involved in different social movements, activists' lack of solidarity for LGBT rights made it impossible for them to mobilize around this political opportunity. Activists' personal prejudice, issue ranking, competition among NGOs for funding, and NGOs' involvement with other campaigns prevented HIV/AIDS, human rights, LGBT rights, and women's rights NGOs from creating a coalition capable of taking advantage of this political opportunity. In other words, activists missed this political opportunity. Despite the mixed messages sent by Banda's administration and lack of solidarity from HIV/AIDS, human rights, and women's rights NGOs around LGBT rights, LGBT rights defenders continue to press for the decriminalization of same-sex sexual practices.[154]

Conclusion

HIV/AIDS, human rights, and women's rights activists could face both personal and political consequences for displaying public solidarity for LGBT rights. As I discuss in Chapter 3, Michael's LGBT rights promotion elicited hostility from other Christian ministers, who tried to prevent him from leading services in his church. Many activists I interviewed feared the political costs associated with showing support for LGBT rights, which could include condemnation from political elites and religious and traditional leaders and loss of funding from foreign donors. Such fears kept some activists from displaying solidarity, as in the case of Joseph, an HIV/AIDS activist. For other activists like Linda, a women's rights activist who claimed to support LGBT rights privately, other campaigns kept their NGOs busy; she also explained that she did not want to siphon attention away from NGOs' work by chiming in with public support for LGBT rights. Still other activists objected to supporting LGBT rights openly because they thought the issue was a distraction from urgent social problems or claimed that Malawians were ill prepared to have candid discussions about gender and sexual diversity. Finally, some activists envied the resources NGOs had obtained for their LGBT rights advocacy.

The atmosphere of politicized homophobia in Malawi thoroughly saturated civil society. In one sense, politicized homophobia was

---

[154] Kandani Ngwira, "Malawi's Controversial Gay Law Case Gains High Level Support," *Daily Times*, January 21, 2014, article on file with author.

inescapable. HIV/AIDS, human rights, and women's rights activists had several strategic choices in this environment, all options with negative and positive political consequences. First, HIV/AIDS, human rights, and women's rights activists could publicly oppose politicized homophobia and express solidarity with LGBT rights defenders. By taking this action, they would likely become targets of political elites, exposing their reputations and activities to further criticism. Such criticism could entail being accused of submitting to Western donors' interests, selling out Malawian sovereignty. Conversely, standing up to politicized homophobia could create public reputations for these NGOs as LGBT allies, catching the attention of foreign donors and international LGBT rights NGOs. These actions could yield new opportunities, including material and nonmaterial support, for ally NGOs.

Second, NGOs could quietly agitate against politicized homophobia, insulating themselves from the deleterious effects of being publicly seen as LGBT rights supporters. This position could allow them to render behind-the-scenes support for LGBT people and NGOs. Nevertheless, less visible support for LGBT rights would leave LGBT rights defenders alone and vulnerable in this environment. Third, NGOs could publicly or tacitly endorse politicized homophobia, which offered organizations the opportunity to cozy up to the government and ruling party. Cultivating friendly relationships with state and ruling party officials could afford NGOs that sanctioned politicized homophobia certain access to government resources and other perquisites. In some cases, government officials recruited receptive NGO leaders away from civil society into lucrative government posts.

Fourth, NGOs could withdraw entirely from debates about homosexuality and LGBT rights, sitting on the sidelines while political elites deployed homophobia against NGOs and other opponents. This scenario unfolded in 2012 when HIV/AIDS, human rights, and women's rights activists did not voice support for the decriminalization of same-sex sex. Their support might have swayed lawmakers to consider repealing the antisodomy law. Although retreat might keep NGOs out of the line of fire, donor representatives might deduce that NGO staff held antigay views because they did not oppose politicized homophobia. In other words, shrinking away from debates about politicized homophobia did not inoculate NGOs against suspicion that they tacitly endorsed antigay discourses and activities.

Indeed, NGOs' absence could become conspicuous, if interested observers, such as Western donors and international LGBT rights organizations, expected their presence; Linda's NGO faced this situation. Ultimately, if embattled LGBT rights defenders could not count on support from local NGOs working on similar, overlapping issues, then on whom could they rely?

5 | Under Duress

Sexual Minorities' Perceptions about the Effects of Politicized Homophobia

Politicized homophobia has harmed Malawian sexual minorities. This statement is not new or novel, yet little research documents the consequences of politicized homophobia on lesbian, gay, and bisexual (LGB) people, particularly on LGB people's perceptions that politicized homophobia disadvantages them. Newly generated public visibility stemming from politicized homophobia affected sexual minorities' life trajectories in Malawi in diverse ways. As politicized discourses of same-sex sexualities saturated the public sphere, sexual minorities had to navigate occasionally treacherous social and intimate terrain. Many contended with antigay discrimination, harassment, and violence on top of dealing with inequalities like poverty. Although recent research suggests that social homophobia, particularly interpersonal homophobia between men and boys, may be waning in places in the global North, such as Great Britain,[1] still much research from African,[2]

---

[1] Mark McCormack, *The Declining Significance of Homophobia: How Teenage Boys Are Redefining Masculinity and Heterosexuality* (New York: Oxford University Press, 2012).

[2] Aarmo, "How Homosexuality Became 'Un-African'"; Awondo, "The Politicisation of Sexuality"; Lorway, *Namibia's Rainbow Project*; Mkhize, Bennett, Reddy, and Moletsane, *The Country We Want to Live In*; Zanele Muholi, "Thinking through Lesbian Rape," *Agenda*, 61 (2004): 116–125; Juan A. Nel and Melanie Judge, "Exploring Homophobic Victimisation in Gauteng, South Africa: Issues, Impacts, and Responses," *Acta Criminologica*, 21, no. 3 (2008): 19–36; Graeme Reid and Teresa Dirsuweit, "Understanding Systemic Violence: Homophobic Attacks in Johannesburg and Its Surrounds," *Urban Forum*, 13, no. 3 (2002): 99–126; Adrian D. Smith, Placide Tapsoba, Norbert Peshu, Eduard J. Sanders, and Harold W. Jaffe, "Men Who Have Sex with Men and HIV/AIDS in Sub-Saharan Africa," *The Lancet*, 374, no. 9687 (2009): 416–422; Amanda Lock Swarr, "Paradoxes of Butchness: Lesbian Masculinities and Sexual Violence in Contemporary South Africa," *Signs*, 37, no. 4 (2012): 961–986; Kate Winskell and Gaëlle Sabben, "Sexual Stigma and Symbolic Violence Experienced, Enacted, and Counteracted in Young Africans' Writing about Same-Sex Attraction," *Social Science & Medicine*, 161 (2016): 143–150.

European,[3] and North American[4] contexts illustrates the deleterious effects of anti-queer microaggressions[5] and social homophobia on perceived and actual sexual minorities.[6] These effects can range from hurtful comments about one's appearance and sexual and/or gender identity, job loss, employment and housing discrimination, loss of custody of one's children, queer-bashing, and property damage. However, this research trajectory obscures LGB people's understanding of how the national context, particularly African contexts, gives rise to politicized, social, and religious homophobias. This chapter documents the far-reaching effects of politicized homophobia in the lives of LGB Malawians, particularly in the forms of

---

[3] Phillip M. Ayoub and David Paternotte, eds. *LGBT Activism and the Making of Europe: A Rainbow Europe?* (New York: Palgrave Macmillan, 2014); Graff, "Looking at Pictures of Gay Men"; Ronald Holzhacker, "State-Sponsored Homophobia and the Denial of the Right of Assembly in Central and Eastern Europe: The 'Boomerang' and the 'Ricochet' between European Organizations and Civil Society to Uphold Human Rights," *Law & Policy*, 35, no. 1–2 (2013): 1–28; Koen Slootmaeckers, Heleen Touquet, and Peter Vermeersch, eds. *The EU Enlargement and Gay Politics: The Impact of Eastern Enlargement on Rights, Activism, and Prejudice* (New York: Palgrave Macmillan, 2016); Luca Trappolin, Alessandro Gasparini, and Robert Wintemute, eds. *Confronting Homophobia in Europe: Social and Legal Perspectives* (Oxford: Hart Publishing, 2012).

[4] Warren J. Blumenfeld, ed. *Homophobia: How We All Pay the Price* (Boston, MA: Beacon, 1992); Doug Meyer, *Violence against Queer People: Race, Class, Gender, and the Persistence of Anti-LGBT Discrimination* (New Brunswick, NJ: Rutgers University Press, 2015); C. J. Pascoe, *Dude, You're a Fag: Masculinity and Sexuality in High School* (Berkeley: University of California Press, 2007).

[5] Microaggressions are "subtle and covert acts, often identified as verbal or nonverbal insults" and rooted in racism, sexism, homophobia and/or transphobia. These "brief, 'subtle and stunning' encounters . . . are a frequent occurrence in the lives of subordinated groups and . . . impact views of the self." Janice McCabe, "Racial and Gender Microaggressions on a Predominantly-White Campus: Experiences of Black, Latina/o, and White Undergraduates," *Race, Gender, & Class*, 16, no. 1–2 (2009): 134–135. See also, Derald Wing Sue, *Microaggressions in Everyday Life: Race, Gender, and Sexual Orientation* (Hoboken, NJ: Wiley, 2010).

[6] In the past, research based in contexts in the global North has tended to focus on white, cisgender, middle-class gay men's and lesbians' experiences with homophobic violence. See Douglas Victor Janoff, *Pink Blood: Homophobic Violence in Canada* (Toronto, Canada: University of Toronto Press, 2005) and Gail Mason and Stephen Tomsen, *Homophobic Violence* (Sydney, Australia: Hawkins Press, 1997). For a critique of this scholarly tendency in favor of an intersectional approach to understanding homophobic discrimination and violence, see Meyer, *Violence against Queer People*, 4–13, and Murray, *Homophobias*.

verbal harassment, familial and community rejection, physical and sexual violence, and even attempted murder. This chapter privileges LGB people's perceptions about the impact of politicized, social, and religious homophobias on their lives, social networks, and communities.

Most LGB Malawians interviewed for this project in 2012 and 2014 believed that the climate fomenting politicized homophobia restricted their social mobility and inhibited their abilities to express their gender and sexual identities fully and openly. LGB people's narratives establish a link between the politicized and social homophobias that trapped them. Silas, a twenty-four-year-old bisexual man, explained that "it is very hard with the current situation in our country" because "homosexuality is ... criminalized. So with that kind of environment, there is no way, if you know that your sexual orientation is not heterosexual, [for you to] come in the open."[7] Politicized homophobia and criminalized same-sex sexualities boxed in many Malawian sexual minorities like Silas, preventing them from actualizing their social aspirations.

Politicized homophobia creates social and political conditions that constrain sexual minorities' agency, adversely affecting their sociality. If people have the "capacity to reflect critically" on their condition "but few means by which to change it," they have "some autonomy and limited agency but not an open horizon for fulfilling life goals."[8] Overlapping social, politicized, and religious homophobias along with other forms of sociopolitical marginalization, such as poverty and heteropatriarchy, generate conditions of constrained agency for many LGB Malawians. This is not to say that they are completely powerless; instead, recognizing their constrained agency means acknowledging that LGB people may pivot carefully as they manage the social expectations of different groups to which they belong, such as families and local, national, ethnic, and religious communities, while trying to satisfy their own personal desires. As Carisa Showden argues,

---

[7] Silas, interview with Malawian research assistant, April 29, 2014, Lilongwe, Malawi.

[8] Carisa Showden, *Choices Women Make: Agency in Domestic Violence, Assisted Reproduction, and Sex Work* (Minneapolis: University of Minnesota Press, 2011), 4.

"[a]gency is autonomy plus options; thus, agency includes not only the personal but also the political."[9]

My purpose in this chapter is not to establish a causal argument about politicized homophobia inflaming and aggravating social and familial homophobias. As I discuss in Chapter 2, specifically with respect to Chimbalanga and Monjeza's trial's effects on sexual minorities, it is difficult to develop a definitive causal model tracing the effects of politicized homophobia on LGB Malawians' lives. However, one cannot ignore the abuses and indignities that sexually diverse Malawians have experienced in the last decade.[10] Therefore, my purpose in this chapter is ethical: to amplify the voices of LGB Malawians who attribute their suffering to the rise of politicized, social, and religious homophobias, a maelstrom of homophobias that together can envelop and isolate queer Africans. LGB Malawians do not wither in these circumstances. Demonstrating profound resilience, many of the LGB Malawians interviewed for this study narrated disturbing accounts of abuse and violence, while later reflecting on joyful, loving relationships or safe harbors in which they could open up about their experiences. Not only do I rely on firsthand accounts from LGB people, but I also document and analyze accounts about the consequences of politicized, social, and religious homophobias that LGB people shared with one another. These narratives affected LGB people who heard them from others, and I include them because the people I interviewed thought it was important to relate the experiences of friends and loved ones.

Documenting queer Africans' experiences with social, politicized, and religious homophobia is important for three reasons. First, the act of documenting their experiences gives African sexual minorities the opportunity to articulate what they have experienced in their own words. When LGB people feel socially isolated and disconnected from family and friends because they fear being outed as sexual minorities, they are less likely to disclose these experiences to confidantes. Sharing these experiences can serve as part of the healing and recovery process for some people. Voicing their experiences constitutes an act of agency, albeit a constrained one, for some queers. Second, this documentation

---

[9] Ibid., 1.

[10] For example, see CEDEP, *Queer Malawi* and Makhosazana Xaba and Crystal Biruk, eds. *Proudly Malawian: Life Stories from Lesbian and Gender-Nonconforming Individuals* (Braamfontein, South Africa: MaThoko's Books, 2016).

is important for LGBT and human rights activists in Malawi, who, in turn, can use these findings to lobby lawmakers for changes in laws and policies governing sexual minorities' lives. For almost a decade, CEDEP has supported and participated in research assessing sexual minorities' risks for becoming infected with HIV and other STIs.[11] CEDEP was able to leverage this research to convince the National AIDS Commission to incorporate MSM into HIV/AIDS plans and priorities. As Crystal Biruk and Gift Trapence explain, CEDEP offers staff and volunteers "safety and security trainings," maintains a "toll-free help line" so that gender and sexual minorities can report violence, and assists LGBT people who interact with the police.[12]

Finally, and perhaps most importantly, such documentation serves as a crucial first step in removing sexual minorities from the social isolation they may be suffering. The acts of listening, witnessing, and documenting queer Africans' experiences can guard against "ethical loneliness."[13] Jill Stauffer portrays ethical loneliness as the

isolation one feels when one, as a violated person or as one member of a persecuted group, has been abandoned by humanity, or by those who have power over one's life's possibilities. It is a condition undergone by persons who have been unjustly treated and dehumanized by human beings and political structures, who emerge from that injustice only to find that the surrounding world will not listen to or cannot properly hear their testimony – their claims about what they suffered and about what is now owed them – on their own terms. So ethical loneliness is the experience of having

---

[11] Stefan Baral, Gift Trapence, Felistus Motimedi, Eric Umar, Scholastika Iipinge, Friedel Dausab, and Chris Beyrer, "HIV Prevalence, Risks for HIV Infection, and Human Rights among Men Who Have Sex with Men (MSM) in Malawi, Namibia, and Botswana," *PLoS ONE*, 4, no. 3 (2009): 4–5. doi:10.1371/journal.pone.0004997; Heather Fay, Stefan D. Baral, Gift Trapence, Felistus Motimedi, Eric Umar, Scholastika Iipinge, Friedel Dausab, Andrea Wirtz, and Chis Beyrer, "Stigma, Health Care Access, and HIV Knowledge among Men Who Have Sex with Men in Malawi, Namibia, and Botswana," *AIDS and Behavior*, vol. 15, no. 6 (2011): 1088–1097; Andrea L. Wirtz, Dunker Kamba, Vincent Jumbe, Gift Trapence, Rehana Gubin, Eric Umar, Susanne K. Strömdahl, Chris Beyrer, and Stefan D. Baral, "A Qualitative Assessment of Health Seeking Practices among and Provision Practices for Men Who Have Sex with Men in Malawi," *BioMed Central International Health and Human Rights*, 14, no. 20 (2014): www.biomedcentral.com/1472-698X/14/20.

[12] Crystal Biruk and Gift Trapence, "Community Engagement in an Economy of Harms: Reflections from an LGBTI-Rights NGO in Malawi," *Critical Public Health*, 28, no. 3 (2017): 350.

[13] Stauffer, *Ethical Loneliness*, 1.

been abandoned by humanity compounded by the experience of not being heard. Such loneliness is so named because it is a form of social abandonment that can be imposed only by multiple lapses on the part of human beings residing in the surrounding world.[14]

Ethical loneliness can result when sexual minorities suffer an inability to relay their trauma to others who both recognize the harm they have experienced and consider this harm to be an injustice. To be capable of feeling ethical loneliness, people must apprehend that their trauma occurred partly due to their positions as marginalized sexual minorities or because they experienced antihomosexual oppression. This inability to speak differs from the "condition of inarticulation" that Bernadette Barton documents in the lives of LGB people in the US South. When struggling with the condition of inarticulation, sexual minorities "lack the appropriate tools, especially language, to combat oppression, and be happy, healthy, and self-actualized. They ha[ve] no linguistic framework to explore their identities and sexual feelings."[15] In the case of ethical loneliness, LGB people accept (to some degree) their sexual minority identities and possess the requisite capacity and willingness to articulate the harm they have suffered as sexual minorities.

When explaining LGB people's experiences with harassment and violence that they attribute to the rise in politicized homophobia, I identify and discuss the strategies that LGB people create and develop to survive homophobic and transphobic discrimination, harassment, and violence.[16] Sexual minorities in Malawi developed different ways to negotiate predicaments associated with politicized, social, and religious homophobias. Documenting these strategies enables me to emphasize LGB people's capacity to weather social and political turbulence stemming from politicized homophobia, while identifying its injurious effects. Detailing LGB people's strategies for withstanding homophobia affirms their resilience and avoids portraying Malawian sexual minorities as helpless victims. It is important to highlight LGB people's resilience to avoid reproducing racist portrayals of queer Africans only as pitiable victims. In this chapter, I discuss how sexual

---

[14] Ibid., 1–2.

[15] Bernadette Barton, *Pray the Gay Away: The Extraordinary Lives of Bible Belt Gays* (New York: New York University Press, 2012).

[16] I recognize that some LGB people may be targets of transphobic harassment, due to perceived gender nonconformity.

minorities dealt with the following experiences linked to politicized homophobia that constrained their agency: unwanted public visibility; antigay prejudice in their families and communities; the threat of arrest; forced outing, blackmail, and extortion; discriminatory inter-actions with healthcare providers; rape and unwanted sex; anti-queer harassment and violence; and antigay vigilantism.

Unwanted Visibility

At a 2012 workshop sponsored by CEDEP and CHRR, noted feminist academic Jessie Kabwila recommended that sexual minorities should become publicly visible "in a Malawian way, and not the western style of coming out as gay."[17] The "Malawian way" in Kabwila's view involved "targeting villages throughout the country and not having a poster-person-approach as a symbol of gays."[18] She advised sexual minorities to practice culturally and ethnically appropriate ways to disclose their sexual identities publicly because "one could pay dearly for coming out in the open. We need to protect the person. Exposing them gives advantage to opponents because there is a target for them to hit."[19] Kabwila's commentary captures the dilemma that many sexual minorities confronted. They carefully managed their gendered and sexual visibility to insulate themselves from homophobic and trans-phobic harm. Before the prosecution of Chimbalanga and Monjeza in 2010, few Malawians were familiar with same-sex sexualities, according to Justin, a thirty-one-year-old gay man. Justin recalled, "During that time, [LGB] people were living in a very great secret. If you are doing that homosexual or gay relationship, we were just doing so that the people were not knowing [about same-sex relation-ships]."[20] To preserve their anonymity, some sexual minorities crafted gender and sexual strategies.

Some LGB people modified their gender presentations to avoid unwanted scrutiny of and inquiries about their gender and sexuality. Gender-nonconforming LGB people faced dilemmas associated with keeping others from figuring out their sexual minority identities.

---

[17] Agnes Mizere, "Where Are the Gays? – Chief Asks," *Sunday Times*, October 14, 2012, 4.
[18] Ibid.   [19] Ibid.
[20] Justin, interview with the author, May 11, 2014, Mzuzu, Malawi.

Grace, a twenty-three-year-old lesbian, described how she moved from contexts that required gender normativity to spaces in which she could more freely express her masculine gender presentation.

I am a girl, ... but I dress like a young man. If, in our community, we have a funeral, then I dress like a girl putting on *zitenje*. I dress like that, and I behave as a girl. I stay [on] the women's side at the funeral. I do not ... put on trousers [there]. If I [dress] like that [in a feminine way], then it means I am hiding my identity. If I dress like a man, that means I am telling the people [that I am a lesbian] ... When I am in the midst of LGBT people, then I show that I am one of them [by adopting a masculine style].[21]

Grace followed ethnic gender norms that required her to wear *zitenje* like other women and to remain with women during the funeral procession she mentioned.

Whereas Grace worked to "cover" her lesbian identity and masculine gender presentation by enacting feminine behaviors, Deborah, a twenty-seven-year-old lesbian, dispensed with attempts to pass as a gender-normative woman.[22] Deborah explained that because she preferred wearing "flat shirts" and "trousers" over dresses and "high heels," she believed her gender presentation prevented her from "completely hid[ing]" her sexuality.[23] She attributed the prevalence of heteronormative gender norms as guiding people's expectations for women to be feminine. She described gender-conforming women as "do[ing] what all the girls do. Wear dresses. Carry handbags. Put on high heels, which to me, I can't do it because someone wants me to do it. I have to do things that I feel I'm comfortable with."[24] Her gender nonconformity, however, exposed her to social scrutiny and speculation about her gender presentation. Family, friends, and even strangers felt emboldened to comment on people's gender nonconformity and to pressure Deborah and other gender-diverse people to abandon their nonheteronormative gender presentations.

Most LGB people socialized with other gender and sexual minorities, but some instituted and followed rules for such

---

[21] Grace, interview with the author, April 29, 2014, Lilongwe, Malawi.

[22] For an extended discussion of "covering" practices among sexual minorities, see Kenji Yoshino, *Covering: The Hidden Assault on Our Civil Rights* (New York: Random House, 2007).

[23] Deborah, interview with the author, April 27, 2014, Lilongwe, Malawi.

[24] Ibid.

socialization. Ndlovu, a bisexual man in his late twenties, explained
that when he met gay men, he advised them,

Being a gay here in Malawi is difficult. So there is need for one to be
disciplined everywhere you are. Don't show that you are gay because people
have known us and they can attack us because our laws do not accept [us].[25]

His gay and bisexual male friends "conduct [them]selves like the way
normal people do when they are chatting" to ensure that no one paid
undue attention to them or suspected that they were queer.[26] Ndlovu's
counsel implicitly recommended to gay and bisexual men that they
avoid dressing or behaving in a gender-nonconforming way that could
identify them to strangers as gender and/or sexual minorities and
render them vulnerable to violence.[27] Like Ndlovu, Mark, a twenty-
two-year-old gay man, disapproved of gay men who did little to
camouflage their sexual identities. When gay men who "start touching
each other or kissing ... on the minibus [public transportation], they
show [a] bad image [of gay men] to people."[28] Mark also objected to
gay men who "go and maybe fuck straight guys" because, for him,
such men perpetuated the homophobic myth that gay men converted
heterosexual people into sexual minorities.[29]

To some observers, LGB Malawians' advice that sexual minorities
disguise their gender and sexual nonconformity might seem socially
conservative. On its face, this advice does little to upend or transform
asphyxiating gender norms that confine women and men to limiting
roles and behaviors. Some critics might interpret the guidance that men
eschew feminine gender presentations and behaviors as reinforcing
social and politicized homophobias that depend on the "repudiation

[25] Ndlovu, interview with Malawian research assistant, April 29, 2014, Lilongwe,
     Malawi.
[26] Ibid.
[27] LGB Malawians were not the only queer Africans to recommend and even
     enforce such gendered strictures in their social networks. For instance, in South
     Africa, black lesbian activists instructed other black lesbians to avoid expressing
     their affection for their women partners in public and mingling with
     heterosexual men at taverns as safety strategies intended to protect them from
     becoming the victims of homophobic assault, sexual violence, or even murder.
     Currier, *Out in Africa.*
[28] Mark, interview with Malawian research assistant, May 10, 2014, Mzuzu,
     Malawi.
[29] Ibid.

of the feminine."[30] Deborah described conventional gender roles that subordinated women: "men always want to be on top of everything ... They want a woman to be the second one all the time."[31] Conversely, the fact that queer people socialized with one another publicly in groups was an important step in creating community that could nurture oppositional consciousness. By recommending that queer people monitor their own public presentations and behaviors, some LGB people were trying to create safe spaces ensconced within public spaces, such as bars. These safe spaces could enable LGB people to find one another in cities or towns that lacked known queer-friendly establishments.

Some LGB people either avoided socializing with gender and sexual minorities or interacted with more heterosexuals than with other queer people. Rebecca, a thirty-two-year-old woman, tried "to interact much with men so that [other people wouldn't] know that I am a bisexual. So I try as much as possible to have more male friends and interact much [more] with them than [with] women."[32] She developed this strategy on her own after realizing that "the more I come close to a woman, the more my feelings are magnified."[33] In other words, Rebecca believed that others would notice her attraction to other women, necessitating that she stop associating with women. She maintained a "limited" number of "female friends because" she feared that a female friend might reveal her bisexual identity to others; she felt safer about having men as friends, as she did not share "secret stuff" with them.[34] Rebecca also admitted that she avoided socializing with other queer people, especially "tomboys" whose gender nonconformity was visible.[35] She thought that if others saw her with tomboys, she would "not have that opportunity to deny" that she was bisexual "because they have the evidence that I like moving out with tomboys."[36] Peter, a gay man living in Lilongwe, exercised caution about associating with other gay men. Like some bisexual and gay men, he carefully chose the gay men

---

[30] Barbara Boswell, "On Miniskirts and Hegemonic Masculinity: The Ideology of Deviant Feminine Sexuality in Anti-Homosexuality and Decency Laws," in *Contested Intimacies: Sexuality, Gender, and the Law in Africa*, edited by Derrick Higginbotham and Victoria Collis Buthelezi (Cape Town, South Africa: Siber Ink, 2015), 52.

[31] Deborah, interview with the author, April 27, 2014, Lilongwe, Malawi.

[32] Rebecca, interview with the author, April 29, 2014, Lilongwe, Malawi.

[33] Ibid.   [34] Ibid.   [35] Ibid.   [36] Ibid.

with whom he was seen, selecting only those who "look straight."[37] Thus, he preferred to be seen with other gender-normative men. He worried that socializing with feminine gay men might lead others to surmise that he is also gay.[38]

Sexual minorities' visibility strategies also involved managing their interactions with journalists who became more interested in stories about same-sex sexualities, as I discuss in Chapter 1. Even before Chimbalanga and Monjeza's trial, journalists occasionally published stories about lesbians and gay men that perpetuated the myth that sexual minorities were gendered oddities.[39] A 2007 exposé about "homosexuals" portrayed Joseph, a feminine gay man, as "the woman" in a committed relationship: "Joseph speaks about what a girlfriend he is. His catwalk gait, tiny voice, and verbal articulation and facial and hand gesturing artistry perfectly pitch him in the woman's image."[40] This portrayal cast Joseph as a feminized man who approximated a woman's position and gender role in a heteronormative relationship. During and after Chimbalanga and Monjeza's trial, Malawian newspapers included coverage about homosexuality regularly, such as human-interest stories about LGBT people or articles speculating on celebrities' sexual minority identities.[41]

Coming out as lesbian, gay, or bisexual in news coverage mostly produced negative consequences for people, exacerbating some people's personal insecurity. Mercy Kumwenda experienced multiple

---

[37] Peter, interview with the author, July 11, 2012, Lilongwe, Malawi.   [38] Ibid.

[39] Mapondera, "Any Malawians Who Are Gays?," 24.

[40] Mpaka, "Waiting in a Homosexual Closet," 14.

[41] James Chavula, "An Hour with a Confessed Lesbian," *Nation*, March 31, 2014, http://mwnation.com/an-hour-with-a-confessed-lesbian/; Josephine Chinele, "Facing Sexual Orientation Realities," *Nation*, January 17, 2014, http://mwnation.com/facing-sexual-orientation-realities/; "Malawi Man Says 'I Do' in Brussels Gay Marriage," *Nyasa Times*, July 21, 2013, www.nyasatimes.com/malawi-man-says-i-do-in-brussels-gay-marriage/; Bright Mhango, "Are Gays Born or Made?," *Weekend Nation*, August 18, 2012, 22–23; Bright Mhango, "Please Accept Us" *Weekend Nation*, August 11, 2012, 20–21; Agnes Mizere, "Encounter with a Malawian Drag Queen," *Sunday Times*, January 3, 2010, 10; Ephraim Munthali, "40 Gays Take on Clergy," *Nation*, September 9, 2013, 1–3; Jacob Nankhonya, "Lesbian Comes Out in the Open," *Daily Times*, February 7, 2013, article on file with author; Rogers Siula, "I'm Not Gay – Theo Thomson," *Nation*, December 7, 2012, 4; Arkangel Tembo-Panos, "Same-Sex Relationship Denies 2 Girls Education in Malawi," *Nyasa Times*, June 30, 2014, www.nyasatimes.com/same-sex-relationship-denies-2-girls-education-in-malawi/.

homophobic threats after disclosing that she was a lesbian in a 2013 newspaper interview. Repudiating the homophobic trope that people sought out same-sex relationships to become wealthy, she stated, "I am a lesbian and trust me I don't do this because I want to make money... I know many others who choose not to come out because they are afraid of the society's reaction."[42] She also dismissed the misconception that same-sex sexualities were un-African. Kumwenda explained, "Lesbianism is not something people copied from the western countries. It has been amidst us for a long time."[43] After coming out in public, Kumwenda received death and rape threats over the phone and through social media. In a follow-up interview, she stated, "I have been receiving anonymous calls telling me that I should stop being lesbian or else I will be harmed. One of the callers said ... We will hunt you down and rape you if you don't stop being lesbian."[44] CEDEP and CHRR leaders condemned the harassment Kumwenda suffered.

Although Malawian journalists were not known to out people forcibly,[45] some LGB people were leery of sharing sensitive information that could generate unwanted visibility for them, even if they consented to an "anonymous" interview. Deborah became suspicious when she learned that a "guy who said he was a reporter" was seeking information about her specifically.[46] According to Deborah,

he went to this other girl I used to chat with. He started asking something about me from that girl, but I was strong enough. I called the guy. I asked who he is. He says, "I'm a reporter. I'm taking information about lesbians in Malawi." I said, "No, you're not supposed to go to this person. If you knew I was the one, why don't you just come to me and ask me instead of asking

---

[42] Nankhonya, "Lesbian Comes Out in the Open."

[43] Ibid. Kabwila supported Kumwenda's assertion, pointing out that many Malawian sexual minorities "have never been outside the country and one wonders how they copied homosexuality from foreigners ... [I]t has been here all along, only that the country is in denial." Edwin Nyirongo, "Homosexuality Not Foreign – Kabwila-Kapasula," *Nation*, November 7, 2012, 3.

[44] "Lesbian Claims Death, Rape Threats," *Daily Times*, February 10, 2013, article on file with author.

[45] It is important to distinguish Malawian newspapers from tabloid newspapers in other African countries, such as Uganda, that published lists of people the newspaper labeled as lesbian or gay; in some cases, tabloid publications forcibly outed gender and sexual minorities.

[46] Deborah, interview with the author, April 27, 2014, Lilongwe, Malawi.

these things from someone else?" I just told him, "I don't know nothing about it [lesbian issues]."[47]

Deborah practiced a cautious strategy of denying that she knew anything about lesbians. She encountered the same "reporter" later at a drinking establishment where she was eating with friends. She admitted that she was "drunk" when she noticed the reporter's presence.[48] Then, she started "talking shit about" his attempt to elicit information from her about lesbians in Malawi.[49] He came over to the table she was sharing with her friends. Deborah stated, "He wanted to tell the police to arrest us because we are lesbians. Because I was drunk, we started arguing. It was nasty; it was not good. So he pushed me" and promised to beat Deborah up.[50] Another bar patron asked the "reporter," "Why are you doing this? They're just ladies. They just sit here."[51] After the patron's intervention, the scuffle ended. In this instance, Deborah's attempt to guard her sexual identity backfired when she crossed paths with the so-called reporter again. Deborah deliberately kept her lesbian identity from strangers and her own family, fearing social ostracism and potential violence that could result from sudden public visibility within her community as a sexual minority woman.

Anti-Queer Prejudice in Families and Communities

Due to entrenched social heteronormativity, many Malawians experienced difficulty accepting and grasping that their loved ones wanted to share their lives and start families with a person of the same sex. Deborah shared that many Malawians believe that same-sex-loving people are "possessed with evil" and viewed as "outcasts."[52] She explained the impossibility of telling her family that she wants to marry her girlfriend. She imagined them asking, "'To which boy?' All they will ask is 'to which boy?'"[53] Deborah implied that her family was incapable of envisioning her with a loving woman life partner because they could only reference heteronormative social arrangements, such as heterosexual marriage. Anticipating such responses from family members, Deborah kept silent about her relationships.

[47] Ibid.   [48] Ibid.   [49] Ibid.   [50] Ibid.   [51] Ibid.   [52] Ibid.   [53] Ibid.

Anti-queer prejudice often emerged when acquaintances or family members confronted LGB people with their suspicions about their sexual identities. Rebecca, a bisexual woman, explained how acquaintances from school acted on a rumor about her sexuality. She narrated that young men approached her and

said, "I understand you are a lesbian." I was like, "What? Me? No, no, no." I tried to back myself up; then the other guys started murmuring, saying that "they [women] can't do such a thing [have sex with other women]. It's a taboo. It's not human."[54]

On another occasion, a man who lived near her condemned her sexuality. Rebecca stated that he cast his accusation in terms of young women's risks for becoming pregnant. Explaining the context of this man's denunciation, she asserted, "When a child, more especially a girl child, becomes thirteen or fourteen, the possibility of the girl to proceed in school [is] very low. They end up being pregnant."[55] When criticizing Rebecca's sexuality, her neighbor contended, "It's better to have a child than [be] a lesbian."[56] The neighbor deployed a form of issue ranking when he declared that an adolescent girl's pregnancy was preferable to being lesbian. Rebecca remembered being taken aback by her neighbor's logic: "I was like, 'What?' I didn't continue. I just stopped there. Then I just walked out of the place because I felt [I was] being humiliated. I was with my friend [who did not] know that I am a bisexual."[57] Opting to leave this unwanted social interaction, Rebecca sought to protect herself and social reputation from this neighbor's smear attempt.

A number of LGB Malawians attributed strain in familial relationships to the rise of politicized homophobia in the country. For instance, Ibrahim, a bisexual man in his twenties, shared how his family

heard the rumors that I was [gay]. They have been asking me; I have been refusing, denying [it]. You know, I can't come clean about these because I know how they will react. So I think my family have been hearing about rumors from friends, family or some neighbors. You know how it is.[58]

---

[54] Rebecca, interview with the author, April 29, 2014, Lilongwe, Malawi.
[55] Ibid.   [56] Ibid.   [57] Ibid.
[58] Ibrahim, interview with the author, May 22, 2014, Blantyre, Malawi. I originally met Ibrahim in 2012.

Ibrahim believed that his sister's discovery of "lubricating jellies and condoms in my bedroom" confirmed the rumors that he was "gay."[59] His sister showed these items to their mother. When Ibrahim's parents learned that police had questioned him, his relationship with his parents became tenuous. After they learned that Ibrahim had been arrested, Ibrahim stated, "I brought shame to them."[60] Because his parents were "elders" in their mosque, his mother and stepfather "disowned" him, prompting him to flee to South Africa.[61] Soon after he arrived there, Ibrahim contacted me through email to see if I knew "anyone in South Africa who [could] help me. But [luckily] enough, Amnesty [International] came in and helped me ... While I was there, you know, [my gay] character is like pregnancy, you can't hide it; I was still going on with my behavior [with other men]."[62] Despite Amnesty International's assistance, Ibrahim could not secure "refugee status" with the South African Ministry of Home Affairs. Because Ibrahim lacked legal standing to work in South Africa, Ibrahim "decided to come back to Malawi," believing that he could weather social and politicized homophobia as long as he could obtain paid employment. Finding work in Malawi was preferable to experiencing financial insecurity indefinitely in South Africa and being at risk for xenophobic violence.[63]

Homophobia in faith-based communities emerged in many LGB people's narratives. Religious homophobia is a feature of the lives of many LGBT people, not only in sub-Saharan African countries[64] but

[59] Ibid.   [60] Ibid.   [61] Ibid.   [62] Ibid.

[63] Since 2008, African migrants, including Malawians, have been victims of sporadic xenophobic violence. See Nicole Johnston and Riaan Wolmarans, "Xenophobic Violence Grips Johannesburg," *Mail & Guardian*, May 18, 2008, https://mg.co.za/article/2008-05-18-xenophobic-violence-grips-johannesburg/. In 2015, xenophobic violence in South Africa claimed the lives of Malawian migrants and resulted in the injuries of many more, prompting the Malawian government to assist in repatriating migrants who wanted to return to Malawi. Alfred Chauwa, "2 Malawians Confirmed Killed in Xenophobic Violence," *Nyasa Times*, April 20, 2015, http://mwnation.com/malawi-xenophobia-victims-reach-3-200-two-dead/; Jacob Nankhonya, "Malawi Xenophobia Victims Reach 3,200, Two Dead," *Nation*, April 21, 2015, http://mwnation.com/malawi-xenophobia-victims-reach-3–200-two-dead/.

[64] Ezra Chitando and Adriaan van Klinken, eds. *Christianity and Controversies over Homosexuality in Contemporary Africa* (New York: Routledge, 2016); Adriaan van Klinken and Ezra Chitando, eds. *Public Religion and the Politics of Homosexuality in Africa* (New York: Routledge, 2016).

also in Western nations.[65] Adam, a twenty-seven-year-old bisexual man who was a Seventh-Day Adventist, contended that church leaders spoke about sexual diversity "in an insulting way."[66] Pretending to be his church's minister, Adam offered an example of the antigay vitriol that peppered the minister's sermons: "These people who sleep with their fellow men, . . . they are Satanic people. So we don't want them here. Let us pray hard for God to forgive them, for God to punish them."[67] Adam tried not to internalize these antigay statements because, for him, "time wasted [is] never regained."[68] Justin affirmed that some religious leaders reproduced and fused together different antigay tropes, such as claiming that sexual minorities "want to be rich" and are "Satanic" in one sermon.[69] Richard, a twenty-seven-year-old, Christian gay man, wished that church leaders would abandon homophobia and embrace a truly Christian way of loving sexual minorities. He explained, "What we need is for the church [to] come openly and . . . love the people not hate the people."[70]

When David, a twenty-nine-year-old bisexual man who was a Jehovah's Witness, was on his way to a worship service, he encountered strangers presumably on their way to church who began hurling homophobic epithets at him. Although David did not know them, they began speculating that he was a sexual minority. He heard these people asking, "Does this one pray also? Is he not a *mathanyula* guy? What is he going to pray for?"[71] They expressed incredulity about David's faith and the fact he was a sexual minority. Some LGB people, like Augustine, a twenty-one-year-old Christian bisexual man, left their faith communities because religious homophobia overwhelmed them; he had not attended church for nine years, although he "prayed on [his] own."[72] For others, leaving was not an option. For Grace, going

[65] Barton, *Pray the Gay Away*; Marian Duggan, *Queering Conflict: Examining Lesbian and Gay Experiences of Homophobia in Northern Ireland* (New York: Routledge, 2011).

[66] Adam, interview with the author, April 28, 2014, Lilongwe, Malawi.

[67] Ibid.   [68] Ibid.

[69] Justin, interview with the author, May 11, 2014, Mzuzu, Malawi.

[70] Richard, interview with the author, May 10, 2014, Mzuzu, Malawi.

[71] David, interview with research assistant, April 28, 2014, Lilongwe, Malawi. *Mathanyula* refers to anal sex between men. Alan Msosa, "Why Malawi Is Not (Currently) Repealing Anti-Gay Laws," University of Essex, Human Rights Centre Blog, April 26, 2017, https://hrcessex.wordpress.com/2017/04/26/why-malawi-is-not-currently-repealing-anti-gay-laws/.

[72] Augustine, interview with the author, May 10, 2014, Mzuzu, Malawi.

to church was crucial to passing as a heterosexual woman. She stated, "If I stop going to church, that means my parents and other people will also wonder what is happening to me," leading them to probe into her life, which could yield the discovery that she was a lesbian.[73] People revealed to be sexual minorities risked being expelled from their churches or mosques, as Chimbalanga and Monjeza experienced first-hand after the trial.[74]

The Specter of Criminalization

Criminalization affected how many LGB people arranged their lives and interacted with others who did not know about their sexual minority identities. Although the law criminalized both sex between men and sex between women, the majority of people who feared being or had been arrested were cisgender gay and bisexual men. As a specter, criminalization haunted sexual minorities' moves and decisions as they considered their options when faced with certain dilemmas. The conflation of same-sex sexualities and criminality produced a status of "homocriminality" that entrapped sexual minorities.[75] If LGB people were arrested on suspicion of violating the antisodomy law, their arrest would publicly confirm for onlookers that they were sexual minorities. Much in the way that criminalization hurt African sex workers, as Chi Adanna Mgbako persuasively demonstrates,[76] criminalization also harmed African sexual minorities. The criminalization of same-sex sex forced sexual minorities "underground and into the shadows with little to no access to . . . health care services and other social and economic safety nets."[77] Criminalization also rendered LGB people vulnerable to abuse from police who regarded them as "criminals" and failed to protect them "when they are the victims of crime."[78] When sexual minorities withdrew from social networks, withheld information about their sexual identities from friends and relatives, or censored their behavior to avoid arousing suspicion about their sexual identities, they engaged in gender and sexual strategies intended to protect their invisibility as sexual minorities. However, these strategies also put them at risk for negative

---

[73] Grace, interview with the author, April 29, 2014, Lilongwe, Malawi.
[74] I discuss their expulsion from their church in Chapter 2.
[75] Wahab, "Homophobia as the State of Reason," 488.
[76] Mgbako, *To Live Freely in This World*, 19–66.   [77] Ibid., 52.   [78] Ibid.

mental and physical health outcomes or for being victimized by acquaintances or strangers who discovered their sexual identities.

As I explain in Chapter 2, the trial and sentencing of Chimbalanga and Monjeza negatively affected a number of Malawian gender and sexual minorities, prompting some to change how they performed their gender. The trial served as an important reference point for LGB people. Silas recalled that when he was in primary and secondary school, he "used to love girls' stuff, like the girlish shoes. I used to put [on] my sister's shoes ... I used to play with girls."[79] When Silas realized that he was bisexual, he believed that if he

continue[d] doing these kind of things, people will suspect something. When they do, it's not gonna be okay for me. So I need to stop doing this kind of things. You see? That was the time that the Tiwonge Chimbalanga issue came in the open. That's when I made a concrete decision that I will never ever do anything in the open that will make people suspect that that person might be [gay].[80]

The trial served as a wake-up call for many LGB people who, like Silas, realized that homophobia was saturating their families and social networks. In response to growing homophobic sentiments after the trial, Silas and other LGB people opted to suppress their gender and/or sexual nonconformity.[81] Like Silas, Yasmin, a bisexual woman in her early twenties, feared being arrested. Yasmin stated, "I was also afraid because I was like [Chimbalanga and Monjeza, a sexual minority]. People were saying bad things about it ... 'All the lesbians must be killed or something' ... I was scared ... So how would I tell people about me [being bisexual]" when faced with intense opposition to homosexuality?[82] Yasmin would have been an adolescent during Chimbalanga and Monjeza's trial; the specter of criminalization may have hit her particularly hard at a time when she was exploring different aspects of her sexual subjectivity.

Social interactions could escalate into altercations that jeopardized sexual minorities' freedom. In such cases, some sexual minorities faced

---

[79] Silas, interview with Malawian research assistant, April 29, 2014, Lilongwe, Malawi.

[80] Ibid.

[81] Thomas McNamara, "Not the Malawi of Our Parents: Attitudes toward Homosexuality and Perceived Westernisation in Northern Malawi," *African Studies*, 73, no. 1 (2014): 84–106.

[82] Yasmin, interview with the author, May 15, 2014, Mangochi, Malawi.

the prospect of being arrested on suspicion of violating the antisodomy law. For Ibrahim, the threat of arrest materialized on New Year's Eve a couple of years before our interview. He related how his two brothers became the targets of antigay harassment at a party. Party-goers asked his brothers, "Where is your brother? Your brother is gay, and I don't know how you people are entertaining him. And your mother is a coward in your house [for letting Ibrahim stay]."[83] His brothers expressed incredulity and replied, "We don't know what you are talking about."[84] Ibrahim explained, "You know how drunk people react, and my brothers couldn't take the shame; they started fighting."[85] Those involved in this altercation "went to the police, and they reported the matter," which resulted in Ibrahim "being called by the police, and I had to make my own statement."[86] Although Ibrahim did not attend the party, police believed that other people's accusations that Ibrahim was gay constituted enough evidence to require his presence at the local police station. Eventually, police lost interest in Ibrahim.

Sometimes, when sexual minorities reported their harassment or abuse to the police, perpetrators turned the table and claimed that sexual minorities had raped them. When Gilbert, who was a CEDEP officer and a gay man in his thirties, lived in a town a few hours from Blantyre in 2010, some men he identified as "friends" stole his mobile phone and some shoes from his residence. He called his phone, and when they answered, one man stated that they were taking his belongings and threatened that if Gilbert reported the theft to the police, the men would "report me as a gay person."[87] Undeterred by their threat, Gilbert filed a report with local police.

When the police apprehended them, they said, "No, he was trying to have sex with us." They created a story that I raped one of the guys. So they were taken for the medical test at the hospital. Fortunately, the medical people did not see any sign that one of them has been raped. The guys were arrested.[88]

---

[83] Ibrahim, interview with the author, May 22, 2014, Blantyre, Malawi.
[84] Ibid.   [85] Ibid.   [86] Ibid.
[87] Gilbert, interview with the author, May 15, 2014, Mangochi, Malawi.
[88] Ibid. The "medical test" Gilbert mentioned is a mandatory anal examination to which men suspected of sodomy are sometimes subjected.

However, Gilbert was also "arrested for being gay because the guys told the police that I was gay."[89] As a result of the thieves' allegation, Gilbert had to spend "24 hours in a police cell."[90] Gilbert's humiliation did not end with his detention. Police officers taunted that they were going to invite reporters to the police station because he had been arrested when the Chimbalanga and Monjeza trial gripped the country. Exploiting the fact that same-sex sexualities had saturated social and political discourses, police officers threatened, "We are going to invite TV [reporters] ... so that people should see you as one of those guys who were gay."[91] Although Gilbert knew "they were just teasing me," he was still overcome with shame because groups of police officers came into the holding cell and gawped at him "as if I [were] an animal in a zoo."[92] A day after his arrest, police released Gilbert. In this example, police exploited the threat of the political spectacle associated with Chimbalanga and Monjeza's arrest and trial to intimidate Gilbert into submission, a ploy that did not work. Fear of forced outing and shaming for being sexual minorities led many LGB people to monitor and censor their behavior so that they evaded police and public scrutiny.

Exposure: Threats, Blackmail, and Extortion

Forced outing concerned many LGB Malawians who had not disclosed their sexual identities to family, friends, or coworkers. Forced outing refers to the unwanted disclosure of one's sexual identity to strangers, relatives, neighbors, coworkers, or community members. In some cases, LGB people experienced threats from others that they would reveal their sexual identities to other people; in almost all cases of blackmail or extortion[93] mentioned by Malawian research

---

[89] Ibid.   [90] Ibid.   [91] Ibid.   [92] Ibid.

[93] Ryan Richard Thoreson offers a useful distinction between blackmail and extortion: "[t]he crime of extortion involves obtaining money, property or services from another person through, for example, intimidation or threats of physical harm. The crime of blackmail is similar, but involves threats to disclose information that a person believes to be potentially damaging to their reputation or safety. Typically, extortion involves the threat of acts (if there is failure to comply with demands) that would be criminal in and of themselves – for example, threatening to vandalize a person's property or harm their person. By contrast, the threat to disclose information is, for the most part, not criminal per se. For example, speculating about another person's sexual orientation publicly is likely not a crime – except when the person threatening to make such a disclosure is doing so to manipulate another person to comply with their

participants, those targeted for blackmail were men.[94] Although some purveyors of these threats expected payoffs in the form of cash or material goods, such as computers or other electronic equipment, not everyone expected such bribes in exchange for their silence.[95] Instead, hatred seemed to motivate such individuals' threats to out LGB people. Myths about gay men's affluence also fueled perceptions that people could get much-needed cash by blackmailing gay men. A 2009 study of the HIV-prevalence rate among Malawian MSM showed that 18 percent of the 200 MSM research participants had been blackmailed or extorted.[96]

Many bisexual and gay men interviewed for this study attributed the rise of blackmail and extortion threats in large part to the fact that politicized homophobia saturated Malawian society, beginning in 2010 with Chimbalanga and Monjeza's trial. Roger, a gay man and CEDEP officer, confidently asserted that "almost" all LGB Malawians were

being blackmailed . . . because of the political tension . . . It was very common because then the political terrain was not easy. You remember that was the reign of Bingu [wa Mutharika] who used to bash tables and say, "I can never accept homosexuality in Malawi." It wasn't that easy [for LGBT people] . . . It wasn't welcoming.[97]

In 2011, for a study commissioned by IGLHRC, CEDEP discovered that thirty Malawian gay and bisexual men were blackmail victims.

demands." Ryan Richard Thoreson, "Blackmail and Extortion of LGBT People in Sub-Saharan Africa," in *Nowhere to Turn: Blackmail and Extortion of LGBT People in Sub-Saharan Africa*, edited by Ryan Thoreson and Sam Cook (New York: International Gay and Lesbian Human Rights Commission, 2011), 7–8.

[94] Although most Malawian research participants targeted for blackmail were men, in other African countries, lesbian and bisexual women were targeted for extortion and blackmail. Unoma Azuah, "Extortion and Blackmail of Nigerian Lesbians and Bisexual Women," in *Nowhere to Turn: Blackmail and Extortion of LGBT People in Sub-Saharan Africa*, edited by Ryan Thoreson and Sam Cook (New York: International Gay and Lesbian Human Rights Commission, 2011), 46–59.

[95] Thoreson asserts that African LGBT blackmail and extortion victims "have purchased homes, cars, or other expensive goods for their blackmailer, been coerced into unwanted sexual activity and virtual servitude, and have quit their jobs, dropped out of school, or fled their town, region, or country and changed their name to escape blackmail and extortion." Thoreson, "Blackmail and Extortion of LGBT People in Sub-Saharan Africa," 5.

[96] Baral, et al., "HIV Prevalence," 4–5.

[97] Roger, interview with the author, May 23, 2014, Blantyre, Malawi.

The study's author Wiseman Chibwezo explains how easy it is "to take advantage of gay people for one's own benefit."[98] The criminalization of same-sex sex and politicized, social, and religious homophobias combined to lay "the groundwork" for cornering LGB people. According to Chibwezo, would-be blackmailers "just need to set up a compromising scenario to get their rewards. The victim not only loses their money or their property, but is also subject to a form of entrapment that is psychologically and emotionally taxing" because victims never know when or if the blackmail will end.[99]

Clever, a thirty-two-year-old gay man, related how a former schoolmate threatened him with forced outing when he was dancing with his former boyfriend at a club. The schoolmate approached him and asked why two men were dancing together when there "are a lot of girls here. Why are you not dancing with the girls? You are just dancing with this guy; what is happening? I am going to tell this to your family" and employer.[100] The schoolmate followed through on his threat and told Clever's colleague about his sexuality, but Clever's colleague dismissed the information because he already knew Clever was gay. Clever explained that other blackmail attempts failed with him because he tended to "challenge them and say, 'Go and report me. I don't care. Even if I have to be jailed, let them jail me for what I am.'"[101] Would-be blackmailers might back down to such responses to report men because they knew that police might arrest them.

Due to social homophobia and the risks of being blackmailed, some gay and bisexual men opted not to enter into committed relationships with other men. For instance, Machipisa, a Catholic feminine-identified gay man, explained that he was not "in a relationship. I do hit and run because people blackmail each other."[102] As a self-identified "top," Machipisa expressed concerns that a "bottom" partner, who "depends on the top for everything," would be more likely to

---

[98] Wiseman Chibwezo, "Blackmail among Gay People in Malawi," in *Nowhere to Turn: Blackmail and Extortion of LGBT People in Sub-Saharan Africa*, edited by Ryan Thoreson and Sam Cook (New York: International Gay and Lesbian Human Rights Commission, 2011), 74.

[99] Ibid.

[100] Clever, interview with the author, May 22, 2014, Blantyre, Malawi.

[101] Ibid.

[102] Machipisa, interview with research assistant, April 28, 2014, Lilongwe, Malawi.

blackmail him because of income inequalities in their relationship.[103] He opted for "hit-and-run" liaisons, one-off sexual encounters in which he formed no lasting attachment with sexual partners.[104] If men knew little about him, he could insulate himself from the risks of blackmail. Of course, this meant that he might form no enduring intimate bond with a sexual partner. As with other strategic dilemmas, avoiding blackmail entailed choosing between two risky options: form a lasting erotic attachment to a man who might betray and blackmail him, or seek out one-off sexual encounters with strangers, which came with other risks, such as being victimized.

Sometimes, bisexual and gay men were blackmailed for what were large sums of money to ordinary Malawians, such as MWK 50,000 or 80,000 (US$73–116), according to Clever. Ndlovu shared the story of a male friend in a relationship with another man who "wasn't in the relationship for love. He was in it for money. Every time they had sex, he would demand money."[105] Although the lover asking for money was not blackmailing Ndlovu's friend per se, his demands for money confirmed that some Malawians associated gay and bisexual men with wealth. When Ndlovu's friend realized his lover's plan, his friend ended the relationship. According to Ndlovu, the spurned lover "connived with soldiers" to blackmail Ndlovu's friend.[106] Ndlovu explained how the blackmail unfolded.

The soldiers would follow him at his workplace ... and take all the money he made at that particular time. Maybe they would find him at beer-drinking joints or maybe find him at his house because they knew it since [the ex-lover] guided them there. They would get to his house before he wakes up. They have been doing a lot of bad things to him like snatching his cell phones and all the money.[107]

His friend turned to Ndlovu for help. Ndlovu "reported this matter at the CEDEP office so that they [could] offer some help."[108] Although Ndlovu did not share the outcome of CEDEP's involvement, it is significant that he identified the NGO as able to render assistance to blackmail victims. Ndlovu's friend was fortunate that he could access CEDEP's services locally, but rural queer Malawians are not so lucky.

---

[103] Ibid.   [104] Ibid.
[105] Ndlovu, interview with Malawian research assistant, April 29, 2014, Lilongwe, Malawi.
[106] Ibid.   [107] Ibid.   [108] Ibid.

According to Fortune Banduka, a pseudonym for a gay man inter-viewed for a 2012 news article, "[t]hose of us living in cities can at least get treatment [for STIs], but what about a gay person in Ntaja [a rural area east of Liwonde National Park in the Southern Region], for example? We also do not have access to legal services in case of blackmail and other forms of victimisation."[109]

When blackmailers and extortionists followed through on their threats to out bisexual and gay men, the repercussions could upend these men's lives. Ibrahim became trapped by blackmail. Although he feared being outed, he stated that he "was still going on about my behavior with people" because he was not going to suppress his sexual desire for other men.[110] While he dated different men, he became involved with "another guy who was straight at that time" and "wanted some money."[111] This man "kind of blackmailed" Ibrahim, but the would-be blackmailer's plan failed because Ibrahim had no money.[112] Unhappy with the outcome of his foiled blackmail plot, the man "went to [the] police and reported" that Ibrahim had coerced him into a sexual relationship. Ibrahim explained that he went to the police station for questioning, but the police did not arrest him immediately. Like Clever, Ibrahim adopted a confident demeanor in his interaction with the police.

Since I know my rights as a gay person in Malawi, it wasn't hard for me because I am civilized. I know all those sorts of things. So I was like, "Okay, if this happened, do you have any proof that I did to him or he did to me?" So there was no proof; so the matter was adjourned.[113]

As a well-educated, "civilized" Malawian, Ibrahim distinguished him-self from undereducated LGB Malawians who might not have resisted the police.[114] Because of his education, Ibrahim was able to inquire what proof the police had to confirm the blackmailer's allegation that Ibrahim had forced him to have sex. Ibrahim fared better than other bisexual and gay men who were jailed under similar circumstances.

The police were often unhelpful in cases of blackmail or extortion. Solomon, a gay man who had worked at CEDEP in the past, related that bisexual or gay men who sought police assistance, in the rare

---

[109] Bright Mhango, "Please Accept Us," *Nation*, August 11, 2012, 21.
[110] Ibrahim, interview with the author, May 22, 2014, Blantyre, Malawi.
[111] Ibid.   [112] Ibid.   [113] Ibid.   [114] Ibid.

instances that they did so, faced serious obstacles or threats from the police. Solomon explained,

What the police do [is] they capitalize on the homosexual story and may even call the person who is blackmailing you or who's accused of blackmailing. And if he says, "Oh, yes, this one is gay" ... The police will come to you and say, "Are you gay?"[115]

Because the police might express interest in the blackmail victim's sexuality, this development deterred bisexual and gay men from reporting blackmail to the police, who were unlikely to pursue the case and might even arrest the blackmail victim. Solomon observed, "That is why most LGBT people are afraid to go to police even to report physical violence."[116] Many sexual minorities not only feared being arrested and sent to prison but also contended with the potential problem of being blackmailed or extorted.

Ill Treatment: Anti-Queer Interactions with Healthcare Providers

Criminalization constrained how and when Malawian sexual minorities procured healthcare.[117] Some MSM fail to seek or delay procuring medical attention for HIV/AIDS-related conditions or sexually transmitted infections (STIs). Timothy Mtambo, CHRR's executive director, enumerated some indignities that LGB people could face when seeking medical treatment. He stated, "[I]nstead of just treating them like any other patient, some medical personnel make fun of homosexuals; some refuse to treat them or ask them so many irrelevant questions."[118] One study shows that less than 10 percent of Malawian MSM revealed their sexual identity to healthcare workers, and almost 18 percent of MSM research participants were reluctant to seek healthcare because of their sexuality.[119] In an anecdote related to me by an LGBT rights activist in 2012, a young gay man was unable to obtain treatment for an anal STI after medical personnel congregated to gawk at his condition; he feared that a nurse had surmised that his

---

[115] Solomon, interview with the author, June 28, 2012, Blantyre, Malawi.
[116] Ibid.   [117] Wirtz, et al., "A Qualitative Assessment."
[118] Precious Kumbani, "Gays Claim Abuse in Hospitals," *Nation*, February 8, 2016, http://mwnation.com/gays-claim-abuse-in-hospitals/.
[119] Baral et al., "HIV Prevalence," 4.

anal STI stemmed from having sex with a male partner and called the police to arrest him for having same-sex sex. He fled the clinic without receiving treatment.

When seeking medical treatment, many LGB people tried to prevent the disclosure of their sexual identities so that they received complete, unbiased medical attention. When Silas sought treatment for malaria, he recalled that healthcare professionals treated him "normally because there was no [reason] to mention my sexual orientation. So I am a normal person to them."[120] Silas speculated that if he had shared his bisexual identity or "had gone there as a bisexual man ... it would have been a different thing altogether. Maybe, for instance, having an STI like at the anus, they would ask me a lot of questions, 'How did you get this?' And [if] I would tell them I am bisexual, it would have been a totally different thing altogether."[121] Silas feared the judgment, scrutiny, and possible arrest that might stem from revealing his sexual identity. Silas' fears were well founded. Tina, a twenty-one-year-old lesbian, shared how a gay friend of hers was refused medical treatment because the doctor, who was from the same area, "knew he was gay."[122] Tina's friend complained of abdominal pain, but the doctor ordered medical staff not to treat him because he claimed his abdominal pain stemmed from "something [sexual] he has agreed [to do] with his fellow boys. It has to be sperms or whatever."[123] Tina believed that the doctor's antigay prejudice led to her friend's death. In addition, a healthcare provider interviewed for a study about Malawian MSM experiences with homophobia in healthcare settings admitted that other healthcare providers exhibited "resistance ... talking about men who have sex with men" and their vulnerability to HIV/AIDS.[124]

Benjamin, a bisexual man and former CEDEP officer, related the experience of another gay man who was arrested after he sought treatment for an STI. According to Benjamin, a "gay man walked into a clinic, and he had an STI, an unknown STI, and when the doctor, or the nurse, or clinician discovered that this person has been sleeping with another man, he actually called the police. And the police walked

---

[120] Silas, interview with Malawian research assistant, April 29, 2014, Lilongwe, Malawi.
[121] Ibid.   [122] Tina, interview with the author, May 22, 2014, Blantyre, Malawi.
[123] Ibid.   [124] Wirtz et al., "A Qualitative Assessment," 5.

into the clinic and arrested this guy."[125] This episode incensed Benjamin, who asserted, "Somebody should be able to walk into a clinic and get the services without being intimidated or not being denied of any services, because that's their ... right. Everybody's got a right to health."[126] Benjamin was not alone in relating stories from friends or rumors about an LGB person's mistreatment at a clinic; circulating rumors and stories shaped how individuals viewed and interacted with healthcare providers and whether they would seek medical care.

Humiliation characterized Ndlovu's encounters with healthcare providers. Ndlovu frequented health clinics primarily to undergo screenings for HIV and STIs. When healthcare workers treated Ndlovu,

it was the first visit [in which] I received mockery when I explained how I was feeling because they suspected that I was gay; they never helped me. I never explained that I was bisexual, but the [illness] that I suffered from one time ... made them notice that I was bisexual ... They were asking mocking questions. Because I was not in the mood of responding to their mocking questions and the way I was responding to them, ... I left without being helped.[127]

Rejecting healthcare providers' ridicule of his sexual identity, Ndlovu opted to protect his dignity and leave without obtaining treatment; instead, he decided to procure treatment at another clinic. Friends of Roger, a CEDEP officer, have sought treatment at a clinic or hospital and divulged, "'I had sex with my fellow man.' And doctors are like, 'What?'"[128] He interpreted medical personnel's response as viewing homosexuality as "alien in nature."[129] Roger understood why sexual minorities opted not to disclose their identities to healthcare providers because they worried about "los[ing their] personal dignity ... It's a killer instinct that you still have to preserve your own [safety]."[130] This "killer instinct" kept some sexual minorities safe.

Researching and safeguarding the health of gender and sexual minorities continues to be a priority for CEDEP. The NGO has partnered with healthcare providers and researchers to identify and offer

---

[125] Benjamin, interview with the author, June 27, 2012, Blantyre, Malawi.
[126] Ibid.
[127] Ndlovu, interview with Malawian research assistant, April 29, 2014, Lilongwe, Malawi.
[128] Roger, interview with the author, May 23, 2014, Blantyre, Malawi.
[129] Ibid.   [130] Ibid.

sexual minorities access to healthcare facilities where they can safely disclose their sexual identities and practices to trusted healthcare providers. For Noah, a twenty-three-year-old bisexual man, such partnerships identified trusted, "gay-friendly doctors" who treat sexual minorities "well."[131] In addition, some sexual minorities like Alan, a twenty-five-year-old gay man, were able to tell trusted doctors that they were LGB.[132] Yet the safety concerns identified by LGB research participants continued to interfere with their ability to procure reliable, confidential healthcare. During a 2012 study cosponsored by CEDEP and intended to "target and mitigate the structural-, social-, and individual-level barriers to HIV prevention found to be associated with higher HIV risks among MSM in Malawi," unnamed "security threats affecting gay men and other MSM" prompted researchers to suspend the study temporarily, although they resumed the study five months later.[133] Unfortunately, these security threats were not isolated experiences. Other research demonstrates that "[i]nterventions such as specialised clinics can be dangerous for clients and healthcare providers alike—attacks on such clinics have been reported."[134]

Rape and Unwanted Sex

With the rise of politicized homophobia, some Malawians began assuming that lesbian and bisexual women and gay and bisexual men were sexually available. In some cases, heterosexuals presumed that LGB people would willingly have sex with anyone who propositioned them. The hypersexualization of LGB people rendered them vulnerable to sexual violence, especially when this form of violence was coupled with other forms of homophobic oppression, such as the threat of forced outing. Silas explained that "there were particular situations whereby . . . people know that the person is like this [LGB], they always

---

[131] Noah, interview with research assistant, May 10, 2014, Mzuzu, Malawi.

[132] Alan, interview with research assistant, May 11, 2014, Mzuzu, Malawi.

[133] Andrea L. Wirtz, Gift Trapence, Vincent Jumbe, Eric Umar, Sosthenes Ketende, Dunker Kamba, Mark Berry, Susanne Strömdahl, Chris Beyrer, Adamson S. Muula, and Stefan Baral, "Feasibility of a Combination HIV Prevention Program for Men Who Have Sex with Men in Blantyre, Malawi," *Journal of Acquired Immune Deficiency Syndromes*, 70, no. 2 (2016): 156, 157.

[134] Paul Semugoma, Steave Nemande, and Stefan D. Baral, "The Irony of Homophobia," *The Lancet*, 380, no. 9839 (2012): 313.

want to sleep with you."[135] According to Silas, when heterosexual people gossiped about LGB people's sexual identities, they exchanged information about LGB people's sexual availability, even reviewing LGB people's sexual prowess. Silas mimicked a heterosexual man recommending a gay or bisexual man to another friend:

> They can sleep with somebody today, and that person will tell a friend, "You know what? I slept with him. My! It's so good. I want you to go and try him" ... So he will take that friend and introduce him to you with an aim that you should sleep with him.[136]

For Silas, the social saturation of homosexuality produced assumptions and interactions in which other Malawians treated LGB people first and foremost as always interested in sex. Such assumptions created social exchanges in which those who sexually propositioned LGB people ignored and took for granted LGB people's sexual consent.

Some lesbians reported being accosted by male acquaintances or friends who believed that they could initiate sexual relationships with them. Such men acted on male, heterosexual privilege when they imagined they could freely approach all women with requests for sex. In such instances, lesbians' status as isolated sexual minority women might have rendered them eligible targets for sexual assault or harassment in attackers' eyes. Martha, a twenty-two-year-old lesbian, recalled a time when a man "was proposing [to] me," which involved him asking her to date him.[137] When she "denied" his request for a date, he accused her of being a "lesbian" and attacked her.[138] Lesbian baiting was a typical response from some men who refused to accept women's rebuffs to their sexual advances; thus, calling women "lesbians" or "bitches" was a common homophobic, misogynistic response.[139] Refusing to remain silent about the attack, Martha told her father what had happened. Martha's father "wanted to go to the

---

[135] Silas, interview with Malawian research assistant, April 29, 2014, Lilongwe, Malawi.

[136] Ibid.

[137] Martha, interview with Malawian research assistant, May 15, 2014, Mangochi, Malawi.

[138] Ibid.

[139] Ann Pellegrini, "S(h)ifting the Terms of Hetero/Sexism: Gender, Power, Homophobias," in *Homophobia: How We All Pay the Price*, edited by Warren J. Blumenfeld (Boston, MA: Beacon, 1992), 49–50.

police to report" the physical assault so that the attacker "should get arrested," but ultimately, Martha decided not to report it.[140] When she crossed paths with the attacker after the assault, she explained, "I just sit and am quiet" as a way not to engage him in conversation; her refusal to speak with him insulated her from the possibility of harm in her mind.[141] Monica, a nineteen-year-old lesbian, narrowly escaped a violent attack when a male friend who knew that she was a lesbian tried to force her into marriage. One night, she encountered him, and Monica recalled that he "touched my breast" and declared, "From today, you will be my wife."[142] When she declined his marriage proposal, the man "was threatening to kill me with a knife, and then other young men who were coming from the video show ... rescued me."[143] Monica informed a teacher about the attack, and the teacher counseled her not to report the incident to the police, likely because she feared that police might arrest Monica on suspicion of having sex with women. Men's confidence that they should have unfettered sexual access to women's bodies, a hallmark of heteropatriarchy, motivated these attacks.

Silas was particularly concerned that the sexual exploitation of LGB individuals was happening at a time when an estimated 21 percent of Malawian bisexual and gay men were HIV positive.[144] Reflecting on how HIV/AIDS peer educators with CEDEP advised men who have sex with men about "multiple concurrent partners – the dangers of having a lot of sexual partners," Silas worried that heterosexuals propositioning LGB people was confusing.[145] Silas stated, "And then right there, you find that person telling you, 'I want to sleep with you.'"[146] He especially disliked the sexual objectification of LGB people who were "being used" sexually by heterosexual partners with whom they have "totally no connection."[147] Recalling a time when a heterosexual man approached him with a request to have sex with him, Silas spurned him: "You know what? What you are doing is not good. I can't just

---

[140] Martha, interview with Malawian research assistant, May 15, 2014, Mangochi, Malawi.
[141] Ibid.
[142] Monica, interview with Malawian research assistant, May 15, 2014, Mangochi, Malawi.
[143] Ibid.   [144] Fay, et al., "Stigma, Health Care Access."
[145] Silas, interview with Malawian research assistant, April 29, 2014, Lilongwe, Malawi.
[146] Ibid.   [147] Ibid.

have sex or you can't just have sex with me just because I am bisexual, just because you have heard that I am bisexual."[148] Concerned about his health and preferring an emotional connection with sexual partners, Silas repudiated the proposition, but the man would not accept his denial and offered Silas money if he agreed to sex. The offer of money for sex offended Silas, who remembered replying, "I am not in need [of] money. If I wanted that, I would have approached you."[149] Distinguishing himself from other LGB people who might engage in paid sex work, Silas thought that transactional sex work "is like selling your dignity, which is not supposed to be like that."[150] Silas' views toward transactional sex work was an example of some sexual minorities' attempts to manage anti-queer stigma by blaming sex workers, particularly queer sex workers, as exacerbating politicized and social homophobias that enveloped their lives.[151]

For some LGB Malawians, politicized homophobia required that they seek sexual liaisons under a cloak of secrecy, which could result in sexual coercion. Richard, a twenty-seven-year-old gay man, contended, "When we are talking about sex, it's something which is secret; you cannot do it openly. It's something you do secretly."[152] Because of economic precarity, many gender and sexual minorities were underemployed, lived at home with their family, and depended on family for economic support. Richard portrayed the neediness of sexual minorities in a very particular way. He asserted,

Most of the Malawian gays are depending on parents. We are depending on family members. We are depending on friends. We are staying with our relatives. [There are] other ways we can say [gays are] parasites. You know the meaning of parasite? It is an animal [that] feeds on another animal. That's a parasite; this is what Malawian gays are like. Most Malawian gays are parasites.[153]

Although Richard's parasite metaphor unfortunately depicted sexual minorities as siphoning resources, financial and otherwise, from others, it illustrated that sexual minorities' material dependency on

---

[148] Ibid.   [149] Ibid.   [150] Ibid.

[151] For a discussion about similar dynamics among exotic dancers in the United States, see Bernadette Barton, *Stripped: Inside the Lives of Exotic Dancers* (New York: New York University Press, 2006), 73–88.

[152] Richard, interview with the author, May 10, 2014, Mzuzu, Malawi.

[153] Ibid.

family members left them with little physical space for same-sex intimacy. Often, LGB people have to share rooms with others at home, necessitating that they seek alternative spaces for same-sex intimacy, sometimes on the fly. Richard described this situation as bisexual and gay men having "sex at a wrong place and at the wrong time. You know once you go home, 'I am safe with my parents; I will not [have sex at home].'"[154] Hooking up with other men happened away from home, such as at a bar or "bottle store" where men consumed alcohol together. Richard explained that men desiring sex would signal one another that they should "go to the toilet and have sex."[155] For Richard, public toilets and other similar semipublic venues "are not good places," but "places [for sex] are not there."[156] Richard portrayed sex between men shrouded in secrecy as resulting in coercive sex.

Just as sexual minorities' economic precarity often made them reliant on family members, their unmet needs also rendered them vulnerable to sexual abuse and rape. Kondwani, a twenty-five-year-old gay man, experienced sexual victimization after his parents evicted him from their house because they suspected he was gay. Kondwani stated, "After being chased away from my parents, I was in need of a place to sleep." A mutual friend escorted Kondwani to another friend able to provide him housing for two days. When the man offering housing asked Kondwani why he was not living at home, Kondwani shared that his parents forced him out of the house because they believed he was gay. The man immediately became hostile and stated, "'We do not want gays here," but then asked Kondwani if he was gay. Kondwani stated he was not gay. According to Kondwani, the man stated, "Okay, if you are gay, I will fuck you, and if you deny that you are gay, then I will tell people that you are gay." The man sought to exploit Kondwani's vulnerability for sex, threatening him with forced outing. Defending himself and trying to protect his sexual identity, Kondwani "told him that 'I have not come here to be fucked; I am not gay.'" Unrelenting in his pursuit of Kondwani, the man stated, "You are gay. Let's have fun. I will fuck you." Under duress and fearful of people's responses upon learning that he was gay, Kondwani submitted to the man's sexual demands but acknowledged the experience "was like raping. I didn't want to do it, but I just allowed it because I was afraid

[154] Ibid.   [155] Ibid.   [156] Ibid.

that he will tell people that I am gay." The next morning, Kondwani packed his belongings and slept in the shop that a friend owned, until he could find safe housing for himself. Kondwani filed a report with a human rights NGO, but he said that nothing happened.[157] Kondwani's urgent need for safe housing and fear of the negative consequences that could accompany forced outing eroded his limited agency, rendering him vulnerable to rape.

Social, politicized, and religious homophobias heightened the punitive dimension of rape threats, according to some sexual minorities. When Tina was in secondary school, boys threatened her with rape because of her perceived gender and sexual nonconformity. Tina played on boys' sports teams and recalled that as "a girl, I would be a star of the game. Girls [would] become crazy for me."[158] According to Tina, her athletic prowess generated other girls' sexual interest in her, but the "boys became angry," particularly when they realized that Tina had rebuffed boys' attempts to court her.[159] She recalled boys gathering around her one day, threatening, "You refuse when we propose you, but you are making our girls crazy. What do you do? We will rape you."[160] Boys interpreted Tina's rejection of them and ability to attract girls' sexual interest as threatening their masculinity and heterosexuality. Boys threatened to rape Tina to punish her not only for transgressing gender and sexual norms but also for taking presumably heterosexual girls away from them. Standing her ground, Tina asked them, "Why are you going to rape me? Your girls [seek] me [out]. I don't know why they [seek] me [out]."[161] The assembled boys tried to confirm Tina's sexual identity by asking if she was a lesbian, but she pleaded ignorance, exploiting the common misconception that sex between women did not count as "sex." She remembered replying, "'How can a girl have sex with a fellow girl?' I just lied to them, but deep down in my heart, I knew the truth [that I was a lesbian]."[162] The boys did not follow through with their threat to rape Tina, but it made her cautious about showing women affection in public.

At the same time that the social saturation of homosexuality familiarized Malawians with sexual diversity, it also produced unfortunate discourses that exoticized same-sex sexualities and LGB people. In this

---

[157] Kondwani, interview with research assistant, April 29, 2014, Lilongwe, Malawi. All quotations in this paragraph come from this source.
[158] Tina, interview with the author, May 22, 2014, Blantyre, Malawi.   [159] Ibid.
[160] Ibid.   [161] Ibid.   [162] Ibid.

case, the social saturation of homosexuality generated conditions that sexually objectified LGB people. When these conditions were coupled with economic precarity, sexual minorities could become particularly vulnerable to rape, sexual abuse, and unwanted sex.

Antigay Harassment and Violence

Just as some sexual minorities continually worked to protect themselves from sexual violence, they also had to navigate public encounters that could erupt into a gauntlet of antigay harassment and potential violence. In such circumstances, "publicly performed acts of violence communicate a force, whose violence they endlessly threaten to repeat."[163] Rumors about the violence experienced by sexual minorities also had a disciplining function, as some LGB internalized these stories and developed routines and strategies to insulate them from violence. As publicly visible defenders of gender and sexual diversity in the country, CEDEP officers and volunteers were particularly susceptible to antigay harassment and violence. Not only were CEDEP's offices targeted for burglaries and police raids,[164] but CEDEP staff and volunteers also encountered harassment and violence when educating others about safer-sex practices, HIV/AIDS, and sexual diversity. In 2012, men involved with a CEDEP research project were arrested when students at a secondary school in Zomba believed that they were trying to rape another student. CEDEP canvassers approached a male student who became worried when he learned that they were documenting the number of "homosexuals" in the country and educating MSM about safer-sex practices. A group of students began fighting with the CEDEP canvassers and called the police who arrested them "for being connected to the alleged sexual practices with a boy."[165] Activists sought the men's release from jail and stated that they were trying to "sensitise people about freedom of homosexuality

---

[163] Rosalind C. Morris, "The Mute and the Unspeakable: Political Subjectivity, Violent Crime, and 'the Sexual Thing' in a South African Mining Community," in *Law and Disorder in the Postcolony*, edited by Jean Comaroff and John L. Comaroff (Chicago: University of Chicago Press, 2006), 79.

[164] I discuss burglaries and raids of CEDEP's offices in Chapter 2. Jacob Nankhonya, "Centre for the Development of People (CEDEP) Offices Ransacked," *Daily Times*, October 14, 2013, article on file with author.

[165] Howard Milozi, "Sodomy Haunts Zomba Students," *Daily Times*, March 9, 2012, article on file with author.

in the country," not trying to entice young men into same-sex sex.[166] Misunderstandings about CEDEP officers and volunteers' work put them at risk for harassment, arrest, and even violence.

CEDEP officers and volunteers were not the only ones who dealt with homophobic harassment and violence. With the rise of politicized homophobia, some LGB people asserted that instances of homophobic street harassment and violence had become more common in their communities and in the businesses they frequented. Ndlovu recalled a time when he experienced antigay harassment while drinking with some friends at a local bar. A drunk man with whom Ndlovu had had sex some time ago began telling strangers at the bar, "We do this and that together," pointing to Ndlovu when making the admission. Bar patrons approached and asked Ndlovu, "'Is it true that you do this and that?' I told them, 'Who was telling you that? You can't come and ask me if I did it [unless I had sex] with you.'" Ndlovu tried to use social norms of respect, privacy, and decency to repel the aggressive tactics bar patrons employed to pry information from him. Instead of backing down, bar patrons began insulting him. According to Ndlovu, "they said, 'You are an idiot. Can you have sex through the anus? [You only have sex with men because of] witchcraft or else you want money.'" The bar patrons who hurled slurs at Ndlovu exploited common homophobic tropes, insinuating that men only had sex with men if they had been bewitched or sought money. As antigay animus spread among bar patrons, Ndlovu described how they dropped all pretenses of social respect and began directing epithets at him, "saying ... 'That's a *gay*. He does have sex through the anus. That's a *mathanyula*.'" Disgusted with his treatment by strangers, Ndlovu opted to leave and visit another bar; he did not want to be harassed while he was trying to relax with friends. A number of LGB people who reported being subjected to violence because of their sexual identities tried to retreat from violent encounters as quickly as they could; most LGB people did not fight back or retaliate.[167]

---

[166] Ibid. News coverage of these arrests in the *Nation* omitted reference to students' suspicions that the "homosexuality researchers" were trying to entice a student into same-sex sex. Grace Ndau, "Police Arrest 5 Suspected 'Homosexuality Researchers,'" *Nation*, March 8, 2012, 4.

[167] Ndlovu, interview with Malawian research assistant, April 29, 2014, Lilongwe, Malawi. All quotations in this paragraph come from this interview.

Like Ndlovu, Gilbert, a gay man and CEDEP officer, experienced antigay verbal harassment when he and a gender-nonconforming male friend visited a bar. Gilbert recalled that his "friend was obvious … He was used to cross-dressing, dressing like a woman." Bar patrons responded negatively to his friend's gender-nonconforming presentation and began insulting both of them, calling them, "You ugly people. You are such people that we do not want." Gilbert remembered that bar patrons threatened to kill them, taunting them with the belief they could kill gay men without facing repercussions. This frightening episode coincided with Chimbalanga and Monjeza's trial, which made social conditions

very hard for the [sexual] minority people … The issue was hot because we were debating it, and everyone was talking about it. So, if they see you associating with MSM or if they realize that you are an MSM, then they will attack you with their verbal accusations, yeah. They would say a lot of things, you know? And the people running this country, [they say], "We don't want you. You should be dead."

Politicized homophobia animated antigay sentiments among ordinary Malawians who believed that they could verbally harass, intimidate, and even physically assault gender and sexual minorities with impunity.[168]

On another occasion, when Gilbert was visiting Mangochi on CEDEP business, he was attacked after he had been drinking at a local bar. As Gilbert walked through a parking lot, a man stopped him and asked, "What do you do in Mangochi? We understand that gays from Blantyre are here; they have a project here."[169] The man was referring to CEDEP's presence in town. Suddenly, "seven men" surrounded Gilbert and "started beating" him.[170] Gilbert explained,

I tried to run away, but I couldn't because the crowd overpowered me. I fell down on the floor. Then somebody picked me up … They came to rescue me, and they said, "My friend, you have to run away for your life. Otherwise, these people are serious; they can kill you."[171]

After the attack, Gilbert "reported the matter to the police," but because the police had not updated him about the case, he was unsure

[168] Gilbert, interview with the author, May 15, 2014, Mangochi, Malawi. All quotations in this paragraph come from this interview.
[169] Ibid.   [170] Ibid.   [171] Ibid.

if they arrested anyone.[172] Recalling the attack, he stated, "I don't know how people realized that I was gay."[173] Gilbert had developed a masculine gender presentation to indicate his compliance with hegemonic forms of masculinity and kept his sexual identity a secret. After the assault, Gilbert sought medical treatment for a facial wound. Reflecting on why he did not disclose his sexual identity to others, Gilbert explained,

It is just difficult telling people about my sexual orientation . . . People do not tell me their sexual orientation; so why should I tell them mine? Nobody has come up and said, "I am a straight person." So why should I keep going? Yeah, I don't go telling people that I am gay. My sexuality is private.[174]

Whereas Gilbert and other sexual minorities retreated from harassment or violence as quickly as possible, some LGB people fought their attackers, even if they were outnumbered. For example, Justin was unwilling to back down from a fight if he found himself the target of homophobic violence. Justin stated, "We cannot let them [beat us]. We can also be doing [this] against them in retaliation for their attacks."[175] He was one of the few LGB people I met unafraid to defend himself.

Some LGB people were targeted in a string of antigay attacks. In 2012, Jacob, a nineteen-year-old gay man, experienced a series of violent assaults when people learned he was gay, which he characterized as "real violence." While walking in his community, he encountered and spoke with "two guys [who] were gays, too." Several men began following Jacob and asked him what he was saying to his friends. Jacob replied, "'Nothing, what have I done to [cause you to] speak to [me]?' Then, [the men] started beating me up, and it was very bad. People came watching, and they beat me up to the fullest." After learning of the beating, Jacob's mother encouraged him to report the assault to the police, but Jacob refused to go to the police, fearing arrest and imprisonment; at this time, Jacob's mother did not know he was gay. Jacob's brushes with violence did not stop. Three months after the first assault, Jacob was attacked again, and he did not report the matter to the police. Six months after the second assault, he became the victim of a third assault when he and some friends walked to a store

---

[172] Ibid.   [173] Ibid.   [174] Ibid.
[175] Justin, interview with the author, May 11, 2014, Mzuzu, Malawi.

in the evening to buy mobile phone airtime. Jacob described himself as having a feminine gender presentation, and on this day, he was wearing "skinny jeans," clothing that these men interpreted as confirmation that he was gay.[176] Eight men followed them from the store and began taunting them. They asked Jacob and his friends, "What do you mean by this? What is it? ... Don't you know that [you] people are wearing skinny jeans?" The men mocked Jacob and his friends' clothing and gender presentations, referring to Jacob as "it" when they saw his skinny jeans; dehumanization was a common feature of anti-queer violence. Jacob recalled that the men "started beating us ... When I say beaten, I was beaten indeed. [The attack lasted] 10 to 15 minutes. I had some money; they took it. I had a hat; they took it and my shoes, too. I was swollen" from the attack.[177] One of Jacob's friends reported the assault to a CEDEP employee who advised him to report it to the police. Jacob reported the violent assault to the police and received medical treatment at the local hospital where they "treated [him] well," unlike some sexual minorities' experiences with clinic or hospital staff.

News of Jacob's gay identity circulated quickly in the local community and in his home village. Threats poured in. Jacob heard that local "Muslims were angry" and "planned to burn my friend's house. They were saying that we are [men] married [to each other]." When Jacob learned of this threatened hostility, he took steps to protect himself from further attacks. When he was on his way to a relative's house, Jacob encountered "some of the Muslims, and they held my hair and beat me on the cheek. They questioned me, [but] I didn't answer anything." The attackers threatened again to burn down Jacob's house, a threat that he interpreted as "too heavy." Although Jacob and his friend reported the threat to LGBT and human rights NGOs, Jacob stated, "They didn't do anything." At this time, Jacob's relatives "were also accusing me, and it was very hard." Jacob opted to go into "hiding." He stated, "If I try to walk, people were just mocking me. Even to church, I was not going."[178]

---

[176] Mark explained, "People think that if you are gay, you [wear] tight clothes" to accentuate one's body. Mark, interview with research assistant, May 10, 2014, Mzuzu, Malawi.

[177] Jacob, interview with research assistant, May 15, 2014, Mangochi, Malawi. All quotations in this paragraph come from this interview.

[178] Ibid. All quotations in this paragraph come from this interview.

Jacob came out of "hiding" for a relative's funeral; a friend accompanied him on the trip to his home village. On a minibus on the way to the funeral, "the church people and some relations ... mock[ed] and insult[ed] us." During the funeral service, "the preacher was also preaching against homosexuals, and I knew that they were targeting us." After the funeral, people on the minibus "started insulting [and calling us], 'You sinners, dogs, you will be burned. You deserve punishment.'" After bearing the brunt of this public antigay harassment, Jacob recalled being "ashamed that even the villagers know that I am gay. I was so ashamed for myself." Even Jacob's family began denouncing him because he was gay. The pastor at Jacob's church threatened to excommunicate him if he did not "preach against this homosexuality in the church." Jacob refused to comply with the pastor's demand because "even if [I] start preaching against [homosexuality], ... people will still know [me] as gay. So dismiss [me] from the church." A few months later, the pastor carried out his threat and barred Jacob from the church, prompting Jacob to distance himself from Christianity. Violence enveloped Jacob's life. Men punished his perceived gender and sexual nonconformity with violence. Much in the way that negative discourses about same-sex sexualities saturated the public sphere as homophobia became politicized, rumors about Jacob's gay sexuality and identity circulated throughout his community and home village, further endangering him and his friends. Going into "hiding" did not completely shield him from violence.[179]

Antigay Vigilantism

I share the experiences of Godfrey, a bisexual man and LGBT rights advocate in a town near Lake Malawi, because his account of surviving antigay violence demonstrates the intersection of politicized, social, and religious homophobias.[180] Godfrey's experience illustrates what Biruk and Trapence refer to as the "economy of harms" that can befall LGBT rights advocates and peer educators in Malawi, as "they subject themselves to risks through affiliation with 'gay'

---

[179] Ibid. All quotations in this paragraph come from this interview.
[180] Godfrey, interview with the author, May 15, 2014. With the exception of secondary quotations, all quotations in this section come from this interview.

projects."[181] According to Godfrey, local Muslim residents outed him as part of a larger mobilization against perceived social transgressions. I am careful not to perpetuate the racist and Islamophobic stereotype of all Muslims as homophobes.[182] In Godfrey's narrative, local men used and rescripted Islam to label same-sex sexualities along with beer and pork as going against Islam; politicized homophobia fostered and nurtured local religious homophobia in this community. Local residents wielded homophobia to defend Islam from what they perceived as dangers. To be clear, Godfrey did not intend his narrative to claim that Islam was innately homophobic.

Late in 2013, some Muslims in the district mobilized "against all that is evil according to them," according to Godfrey. Friends told Godfrey that Muslim residents had "announced" that he was "one of the guys who are promoting homosexuality in the district. And then [Muslim] people are planning to destroy [different] places," including beer manufacturers and distributors and butcher shops selling pork. Godfrey recalled how a group of people he assumed were Muslim "went to Chibuku Products where they make beer, and they destroyed the place. They went to … pork shops and destroyed the places." Godfrey feared for his family's safety when a family member received a tip that the crowd intended to "destroy his house." He immediately contacted senior CEDEP officers who advised him to flee his home. After he escorted family members to safety, Godfrey booked a room at a local

rest house. And then I left a person whom I employed as a houseboy for that night, and then the houseboy called me to say people are singing Muslim songs outside your house. They are stoning the glasses [windows]. And then I talked to my organization [CEDEP]. They said, "No, don't go there." But then I felt like they are going to destroy my things. I said [to the houseboy], "What did they say they want?" He said, "They want you. If you come, they will talk to you, and they will leave." I had no choice; I had to go back. When I went there, I talked to the people: "No, don't destroy the house. I just rent the house. You don't have to destroy the house. What do you want?" They said, "We want you."

[181] Biruk and Trapence, "Community Engagement in an Economy of Harms," 343.

[182] For a critique of racist mischaracterizations of Muslims as homophobes, see Puar, *Terrorist Assemblages*.

When Godfrey characterized this frightening episode, he portrayed the homophobic crowd as using words associated with sexual intimacy – wanting – to convey their intentions to cause him bodily injury. Homophobia, in Godfrey's experience, translated into intense "political feelings" that sutured the group of residents together.[183]

Next, Godfrey described how about a dozen men kidnapped him and a friend, a fellow LGBT rights activist, and took them to the "local airport" where these men "beat" and "whipped us." Explaining why the men were "whipping" Godfrey and his friend, Godfrey recalled that these men accused them of being

"people [who] are teaching people homosexuality in the district," which is against their Muslim beliefs. And they said it is written in the holy Muslim book [that] whenever the Muslim sees that a friend is bringing something that is evil, they need to take it out with their hand. So they were trying to whip us so that we should be intimidated, I think, and then we would stop teaching people homosexuality.

In Godfrey's narrative, the climate of politicized homophobia ignited a punitive religious homophobia that imperiled men whom residents identified as LGBT rights activists. Like antigay vigilante groups in other African countries who used collective violence to discipline those perceived to be social deviants, such as thieves, witches, and gender and sexual minorities, this group of men turned to violence to deter these men from continuing their LGBT rights activism.[184] In this particular case, the crowd labeled "pork sellers, homosexuals, and the people who were selling beer" as those promoting social deviance.

---

[183] Deborah Gould, "On Affect and Protest," in *Political Emotions*, edited by Janet Staiger, Ann Cvetkovich, and Ann Reynolds (New York: Routledge, 2010), 24; Paul Hoggett and Simon Thompson, "Introduction," in *Politics and the Emotions: The Affective Turn in Contemporary Political Studies*, edited by Simon Thompson and Paul Hoggett (New York: Continuum, 2012), 7–12.

[184] Steffen Jensen and Lars Buur, "Everyday Policing and the Occult: Notions of Witchcraft, Crime, and 'the People,'" *African Studies*, 63, no. 2 (2004): 193–211; Hassan J. Ndzovu, "'Un-Natural,' 'Un-African,' and 'Un-Islamic': The Three Pronged Onslaught Undermining Homosexual Freedom in Kenya," in *Public Religion and the Politics of Homosexuality in Africa*, edited by Adriaan van Klinken and Ezra Chitando (New York: Palgrave Macmillan, 2016), 84; Adam Nossiter, "Mob Attacks More Than a Dozen Gay Men in Nigeria's Capital," *New York Times*, February 16, 2014, A8; David Pratten, "'The Thief Eats His Shame': Practice and Power in Nigerian Vigilantism," *Africa*, 78, no. 1 (2008): 64–83.

To be clear, these local residents were not the only Malawians who resorted to violent vigilantism, as evidenced in news coverage of vigilantes who in 2016 stormed a Dedza police station and killed a man being held on suspicion of murder.[185]

Police intervention spared Godfrey and his friend from further harm. When a friend heard that they were "being whipped at the airport," the friend called the police "who came and rescued us," Godfrey gratefully related. "If the police [hadn't come], maybe we could have been killed. But when the police came, people ran away." Godfrey's narrow escape from serious injury and even possible death viscerally unnerved him. Although Godfrey had few injuries, apart from bruises on his face and leg, his friend suffered more severe leg injuries. In response to my question about what further action the police took in response to his kidnapping and violent assault, Godfrey explained that police took only his statement and recommended that he leave town "for some time before coming back." This advice resembled the actions that some human rights activists took in the aftermath of the July 20 protests, as they fled their homes for safe houses to evade vigilantes and state repression. Police then gave Godfrey and his friend their official statements so that they could receive medical attention at the local hospital.[186]

Local police arrested no one who participated in the group kidnapping of and assaults on Godfrey and his friend. According to Godfrey, police "were afraid of the community reaction. They just told us to leave the town. They said that if they had arrested the people, the whole Muslim community could have reacted against us [the LGBT community]. So it could have been more violent than it was before." When I asked Godfrey to reflect on the police's decision not to arrest anyone, he worried that if the police had arrested the men who attacked him,

maybe they could have done more than they did. Even now, the LGBT [people] are passing through more challenges in the district, but nobody is arrested because they are afraid of the community's reaction, which keeps a

[185] Precious Kumbani, "Angry Mob Kills Suspect in Dedza," *Nation*, March 30, 2016, http://mwnation.com/angry-mob-kills-suspect-in-dedza/.

[186] Interviewees explained that when Malawians were the victims of violent assault and needed to visit a public, government-funded hospital or health clinic, they had to present a police statement to medical staff so that they could receive medical treatment.

lot of LGBT people under to say, "We can't even have access to our rights like everyone else because if we are being beaten, the police will do nothing." They will arrest nobody. Because what they do, they just give us letters and say, "Go to the hospital." That's what they do. They are afraid of the community's reaction.

Recognizing that police could not curb local political and religious violence and that a strong police response could have further aggravated antigay vigilantism, Godfrey ultimately agreed with their decision not to arrest anyone involved with the homophobic attack he and his friend suffered.

The violence Godfrey experienced is an example of nonstate repression initiated by actors who may have felt that state-sponsored homophobia authorized antigay violence.[187] Godfrey's experience serves as a cautionary, yet exceptional, tale of how politicized homophobia could inflame religious and social homophobias, producing a violent intersection that could trap sexual minorities. Although this antigay episode of violence subsided and has not reemerged, the violence experienced by Godfrey and another activist left an imprint on their lives and activist work.

Strategies of Coping and Resistance

Sexual minorities did not suffer indefinitely from familial, social, or politicized homophobia. Some LGB people developed intentional gender and sexual strategies to insulate themselves from the effects of homophobia. Diana, a gay man whose narrative appears in *Queer Malawi*, developed the capacity to shrug off antigay taunts. Diana states, "Now that I'm mature I really do not care what people say behind my back. I know how to control myself, I go places with my gay friends even though people stare at us and call us bad names."[188] In the brave narrative offered by Diana, the inevitability of homophobic insults did not deter Diana from socializing with LGBT friends. Diana's narrative suggests that some gender and sexual dissidents could transcend or age out of some harmful effects of homophobia, such as

---

[187] Anti-queer vigilantism is not widespread in Malawi, although it has been a sporadic feature of anti-queer mobilization in Liberia and Nigeria, for instance. See Currier and Cruz, "The Politics of Pre-Emption"; Rudolf Pell Gaudio, "Dire Straights in Nigeria," *Transition*, 114 (2014): 60–68.

[188] CEDEP, *Queer Malawi*, 18.

internalizing the negative emotions that homophobic gibes can induce. Both Joseph and Thomas, two gay men profiled in a 2007 human-interest story, expressed no shame in being gay. Despite being "suscep-tible to emotional injury just like every other human being," Thomas stated that he "did not feel sorry for myself. People will say whatever they please because they are not me, because they are not gay."[189] Joseph and Thomas couched their positive interpretations of being gay in terms of a "born-this-way" argument. Thomas explained, "You don't choose to be born male or female. Being gay is not a matter of choice. It's the way you were born. It's the way you are. Nothing can change that and I am proud of who I am."[190] Joseph asserted that being gay was "normal ... [W]hen you love something, nothing can stop you from going for it. It's only God who can undo it because I believe he's the one who made me the way I am."[191]

Despite a prevailing homophobic sociopolitical environment, some LGB people characterized their same-sex sexualities and/or gender diversity strictly in affirmative terms. For instance, Ellen, a masculine-presenting lesbian in her twenties, clearly stated, "To be a lesbian is good."[192] In particular, she took comfort believing that having sex exclusively with women protected her from HIV/AIDS and pregnancy. Ellen explained that lesbians "can't take ... in the HIV/AIDS ... You can't get pregnant." She also contrasted being in a relationship with a woman to being involved with a man. "Some-times when you love a guy, it's hard. A guy can break your heart" because he might be sexually involved with multiple women simultan-eously. For Ellen, being with a woman was "better ... because I'm here"; she did not believe that a lesbian would have sexual dalliances outside of a same-sex relationship because "she can't do that if she really loves me; she can't do that to another girl. A girl loves a lot. A girl loves [more] than a guy." Although Ellen deployed a gender-normative logic emphasizing how women experienced love more intensely than men, she understood sexual relationships between women as both physically and emotionally safer than being involved with men.

---

[189] Mpaka, "Waiting in a Homosexual Closet," 14.   [190] Ibid.   [191] Ibid.
[192] Ellen, interview with the author, July 7, 2012, Lilongwe, Malawi. All quotations in this paragraph come from this interview.

Anti-queer discrimination, harassment, and violence surrounded many Malawian sexual minorities, constraining the decisions they could make and actions they could take. However, sexual minorities are not reducible to their experiences with anti-queer prejudice and discrimination. It is important to document sexual minorities' experiences with homophobic and transphobic harassment and violence not only to combat ethical loneliness but also to allow them to speak for themselves. Their narratives illustrate how overlapping politicized, religious, and social homophobias coupled with poverty and heteropatriarchy cornered sexual minorities, constraining how they could live their lives.

Conclusion

The Reach and Limits of Politicized Homophobia

Documenting the reach, limits, and failures of politicized homophobia as a strategy is an important scholarly act at a time when international outcry about homophobia relies on and reproduces erroneous assumptions. Understanding how elites wield politicized homophobia requires outlining the contours and limits of this strategy. In the first part of this chapter, I map the reach and limits of politicized homophobia as a weapon, in the interest of contesting an Afro-pessimism that fuels harmful stereotypes of Africans as homophobes. After all, efforts to contain gender and sexual dissidence can and do fade away.

In the second part of the chapter, I show how politicized homophobia continues to constrain LGBT people's lives in Malawi. I share ethnographic episodes from my fieldwork in Malawi that demonstrate how politicized homophobia and the criminalization of same-sex sex imperil sexual minorities, specifically gay and bisexual men. Although politicized homophobia has damaging effects on LGBT Malawians and different social movements, this form of repression has clear limits.

Discovering "Homophobic Africa"

When the Malawian government prosecuted Tiwonge Chimbalanga and Steven Monjeza for violating the antisodomy law in 2010, the "international community 'discovered' Queer Africa," according to Keguro Macharia.[1] He refers to the growing international (and Northern) obsession with monitoring LGBT rights in different African countries, another form of international surveillance of the continent. In this way, international observers created "homophobic Africa" in news reports and lists of the world's "most homophobic" countries. For

---

[1] Keguro Macharia, "Yes, There Are Gays in Africa!," *New Black Magazine*, January 3, 2011, www.thenewblackmagazine.com/view.aspx?index=2527.

example, a 2014 *Guardian* editorial definitively declared Africa as the "most homophobic continent" and exploited the trope of war-torn, authoritarian African nations to buttress the claim that the continent is mired in conflict, fanning the flames of Afro-pessimism.[2] Five African countries – Nigeria, Senegal, Sudan, Uganda, and Zimbabwe – appear in *Newsweek*'s 2014 list of the "top twelve most homophobic nations."[3] Two out of the five "most homophobic" countries named by the *International Business Times* in 2014 were on the African continent: Cameroon and Uganda.[4] Northern interest in LGBT rights and antihomosexuality campaigns and bills in several African countries produced simplistic, monolithic portrayals of an "African homophobia" that persists today.[5] Such depictions contribute to the unfortunate image of homophobia circulating on the African continent like a virus and conflate Africans with antigay hatred.[6]

Contemporary transnational imaginaries treat Africans as homophobes and Northern countries as beacons of social and political progress. Ranking nations based on how progressive or retrogressive their policies on gender and sexual diversity are bolsters homonationalism.[7] In addition, this ranking system "implicitly valorize[s], as points of comparison, the supposedly humane countries" that are presumably located in the global North.[8] The conflation of the African continent with homophobia enacts and reinforces a form of "population racism" that may not only result in negative economic

---

[2] David Smith, "Why Africa Is the Most Homophobic Continent," *Guardian*, February 22, 2014, www.theguardian.com/world/2014/feb/23/africa-homophobia-uganda-anti-gay-law.

[3] Max Strasser, "Top Twelve Most Homophobic Nations," *Newsweek*, February 27, 2014, www.newsweek.com/top-twelve-most-homophobic-nations-230348.

[4] Lydia Smith, "Which Countries Are the Most Homophobic in the World?," *International Business Times*, February 13, 2014, www.ibtimes.co.uk/which-countries-are-most-homophobic-world-1436308.

[5] Keguro Macharia, "Homophobia in Africa Is Not a Single Story," *Guardian*, May 26, 2010, www.guardian.co.uk/commentisfree/2010/may/26/homophobia-africa-not-single-story; Sibongile Ndashe, "The Single Story of 'African Homophobia' Is Dangerous for LGBTI Activism," in *Queer African Reader*, edited by Sokari Ekine and Hakima Abbas (Dakar, Senegal: Pambazuka, 2013), 155.

[6] Scholars continue to work against racist constructions of African countries as hopelessly homophobic. See Marc Epprecht, "Is Africa the Most Homophobic Continent?," CNN, February 28, 2014, www.cnn.com/2014/02/28/opinion/uganda-anti-gay-law-marc-epprecht/.

[7] Puar, *Terrorist Assemblages*, 39.   [8] Patton, "Stealth Bombers of Desire," 200.

sanctions for "unruly" African nations but also exacerbate antigay backlash against local queer activists perceived to be impugning their nation's global reputation.[9] I mean my criticism not to endorse politicized homophobia in some African nations, but rather to point out what is at stake in transnational feminist and queer politics when labeling an entire continent as "homophobic."

The designation "African homophobia" reduces ethnic and cultural complexity on the continent to the singular assignation of "African" and consigns citizens of African nations to the category of "homophobes," leaving little room for considering how age cohorts, ethnic groups, and religious groups vary in their attitudes toward sexual diversity. In addition, the construction of "African homophobia" equates "Africa" with hopeless homophobia and imagines queer Africans as living in an "African gay-deathtrap."[10] These portrayals imbue "African homophobia" with an ahistorical timelessness and singularity that forget the roles that colonial and apartheid racism, predatory capitalism, and Christian proselytizing played in installing racial sexual hierarchies in colonial and postcolonial African societies.[11]

Against Virality: Why Politicized Homophobia Is Not Infecting Africa

Multiple news stories convey the same message: "Africa" is "homophobic," a form of Afro-pessimism taken to an extreme. As Afro-pessimism "foregrounds only the negative things that happen on the [African] continent," the image of an intractable "homophobic Africa" generates an outpouring of emotions – sympathy for African gender and sexual dissidents and anger directed toward African political, religious, and traditional leaders.[12] Implicit in this viral construction of "homophobic Africa" is concern that homophobia is rampant in all African societies, spilling over from one country to another.

---

[9] Patricia Ticineto Clough and Craig Willse, "Gendered Security/National Security: Political Branding and Population Racism," *Social Text*, 105 (2010): 50.

[10] Coly, "Introduction," 22.

[11] Epprecht, *Heterosexual Africa?*; Hoad, *African Intimacies*; Tavia Nyong'o, "Queer Africa and the Fantasy of Virtual Participation," *Women's Studies Quarterly*, 40, no. 1–2 (2012): 41.

[12] Evan Maina Mwangi, *Africa Writes Back to Self: Metafiction, Gender, Sexuality* (Albany: State University of New York Press, 2009), 58.

A viral explanation for "African homophobia" is present when journalists, commentators, scholars, and activists claim or intimate that unbridled antihomosexual animus is crossing African national borders. Viral explanations may use sweeping generalizations to assert that "[h]omophobia is the norm throughout Africa," a phrase used without qualification by *New York Times* journalists in a story about Zimbabwean state leaders' antihomosexuality positions in 2010.[13] Viral explanations depend on the simultaneity and similitude of forms of antihomosexual prejudice to suggest that homophobia on the African continent acts like a virus, poisoning Africans with homophobic hatred. Viral explanations rely on the "generative metaphor" of the virus.[14] Generative metaphors typically "simplify complex social situations, often reducing such complexities to normative dualisms, such as health/disease."[15] The viral metaphor is powerful and stubborn in large part because it is "non-falsifiable" and exaggerates "Africa's" cultural and ethnic differences to the point that non-Africans do not challenge the constructed difference of "Africa" from "Europe" and "North America."[16] Virality is similar to other metaphors, including

---

[13] Barry Bearak and Alan Cowell, "Zimbabwe Shrugs Off Gay Rights," *New York Times*, March 27, 2010, A4. Mainstream media are not alone in offering sensationalist accounts of "African homophobia." Tavia Nyong'o is critical of *The Advocate*'s misleading cover headline, "Get Out of Africa," in September 2010. *The Advocate* is a leading US LGBT magazine. He queries, "Who exactly is in Africa here and what position are they in to get out? . . . Is it a warning to the potential gay Western tourist to a homophobic African country? Advice to imperiled African queers? Or even an imperative to interfering US Christian evangelicals?" Nyong'o, "Queer Africa," 44–46.

[14] Eileen Stillwaggon, "Racial Metaphors: Interpreting Sex and AIDS in Africa," *Development and Change*, 34, no. 5 (2003): 815.

[15] Ibid.

[16] Ibid. I do not unilaterally oppose viral explanations for characterizing mutating forms of social movements and political collectives. See Jasbir K. Puar, "Homonationalism as Assemblage: Viral Travels, Affective Sexualities," *Jindal Global Law Review*, 4, no. 2 (2013): 23–43. Viral accounts have their place in studies of gender and sexuality movements. Research suggests that the US AIDS Coalition to Unleash Power's (ACT UP) modular protest tactics in the 1980s and 1990s evoked the unpredictability of the human immunodeficiency virus (HIV), while prodding the federal government to overturn its obstructionist abdication of responsibility and act on the HIV/AIDS epidemic. This line of scholarship fittingly projects the metaphor of contagion on to the performative politics of AIDS activism that necessarily had to mutate to elicit swift responses from government and scientific bureaucracies. See Julian Gill-Peterson, "Haunting the Queer Spaces of AIDS: Remembering ACT UP/New York and an Ethics for an Endemic," *GLQ*, 19, no. 3 (2012): 279–300. The viral metaphor lends itself to

wave and wildfire tropes, which portray homophobia as inundating or threatening African countries. Recent political-science research suggests that although Africans' attitudes toward same-sex sexualities remain largely negative, approximately 6 percent of Africans polled "somewhat" or "strongly liked" homosexuals, and 15 percent were indifferent to them, suggesting some favorable change, albeit slow, in Africans' perceptions of sexual diversity.[17] These findings dispute viral explanations of politicized homophobia on the African continent.

Viral explanations conceal the intentionality behind political elites' deployment of politicized homophobia as a strategy or weapon. Specifically, they decontextualize and distort the origins, dissemination, and consequences of homophobia. Such obfuscation prevents identifying the agents and situatedness of homophobia.[18] To understand who is involved in the activation and dispersion of homophobia and the conceptual limits of viral explanations of politicized forms of homophobia, I turn to theorizing about diffusion. Diffusion theory explains how and why diffusion items, which can include ideologies, social phenomena, cultural artifacts, and political processes, travel from one place and time to others. Diffusion theory emphasizes the agency of actors involved in distributing movement tactics or ideas as either "transmitters" or "adopters," which is compatible with my understanding of politicized homophobia as a strategy that political elites intentionally deploy.[19] Social movement theorists have identified four modes of diffusion: "reciprocation," "adaptation," "accommodation," and "contagion."[20] First, "reciprocation"

describing changeable, emotional protest tactics tied to the politics of life and death, which ACT-UP movingly rendered in urban protests. However, viral accounts are not universally suitable for use in diagnosing the emergence of organized hostility to gender and sexual variance in different national contexts, such as that of Malawi.

[17] Dulani, Sambo, and Dionne, "Good Neighbours?," 3.

[18] For a discussion of "situated knowledges," see Donna Haraway, "Situated Knowledges: The Science Question in Feminism and the Privilege of Partial Perspective," *Feminist Studies*, 14, no. 3 (1988): 575–599.

[19] Currier, "Political Homophobia"; Sarah A. Soule, "Diffusion Processes within and across Movements," in *The Blackwell Companion to Social Movements*, edited by David A. Snow, Sarah A. Soule, and Hanspeter Kriesi (Malden, MA: Blackwell, 2004), 300.

[20] Doug McAdam and Dieter Rucht differentiate between "relational diffusion" and "nonrelational diffusion" more broadly to distinguish between the "direct" relationships between transmitters and adopters and possible lack of contact between adopters and transmitters, as the former borrows the latter's practices

involves a motivated transmitter and adopter who work together in diffusing an item from one place to another. When the transmitter and adopter are mutually interested in diffusion, this process may occur quickly. Second, "adaptation" involves an "active adopter and a passive transmitter" such that the adopter imports a diffusion item with little or no input from the transmitter.[21] Third, "accommodation" involves a motivated transmitter who retrofits diffusion items for a "fairly passive adopter" who, in turn, deploys the frame, identity, or tactic with relative ease.[22]

Unlike some sociologists,[23] social movement scholars tend to discount "contagion" as a fourth mode of diffusion of collective-action processes.[24] As a diffusion mode, contagion prevents serious contemplation of source and recipient contexts because "neither the adopter nor the transmitter have any interest in the item being diffused; both are passive and/or uninterested in the item and its diffusion."[25] Thus, the contagion mode occludes consideration of actors' strategic interests, conjuring a "nonrational and nonagentic process" for scholars.[26] As a viral explanation, contagion preempts the possibility of identifying agents who devise, deploy, and weaponize homophobia. For this reason, viral explanations are inadequate for the task of understanding the emergence, transmission, and denouement of politicized homophobia.

in the "nonrelational" mode. Doug McAdam and Dieter Rucht, "The Cross-National Diffusion of Movement Ideas," *Annals of the American Academy of Political and Social Science*, 528 (1993): 59–60.

[21] Adaptation resembles the "nonrelational" mode of diffusion that McAdam and Rucht describe. McAdam and Rucht, "The Cross-National Diffusion of Movement Ideas," 59–60.

[22] Soule, "Diffusion Processes," 300–301. All quotations in this paragraph come from this source.

[23] Jeannette A. Colyvas and Stefan Jonsson, "Ubiquity and Legitimacy: Disentangling Diffusion and Institutionalization," *Sociological Theory*, 29, no. 1 (2011): 27–53.

[24] James E. Stobaugh and David A. Snow, "Temporality and Frame Diffusion: The Case of the Creationist/Intelligent Design and Evolutionist Movements from 1925 to 2005," in *The Diffusion of Social Movements: Actors, Mechanisms, and Political Effects*, edited by Rebecca Kolins Givan, Kenneth M. Roberts, and Sarah A. Soule (New York: Cambridge University Press, 2010), 34–55.

[25] Soule, "Diffusion Processes," 301.

[26] Stobaugh and Snow, "Temporality and Frame Diffusion," 35.

Population Racism and "African Homophobia"

Viral accounts of "African homophobia" perpetuate population racism, which disparages and punishes African countries associated with politicized homophobia and rewards countries in the global North viewed as shining examples of recognizing and respecting LGBT rights.[27] In this way, viral accounts of "African homophobia" and population racism are subsets of Afro-pessimism. In times of crisis,[28] population racism can "flood" certain "populations with attention and affective responses but also shaming, even damning responses that can all but criminalize populations," according to Patricia Ticineto Clough.[29] In the case of politicized homophobia in African countries, such responses range from pity for gender and sexual minorities perceived to be trapped in homophobic danger, to anger at African political elites viewed as acting on irrational hatred and sex negativity, and calls for economic sanctions intended to compel politicians to treat LGBT rights as human rights.[30]

In a racialized hierarchy that ranks nations based on their stances on LGBT rights, "good" countries, which are located mostly in the global North, have pro-LGBT rights and policies and practice democratic governance, and "bad" countries, which are mostly in the global South, are characterized by authoritarian governance, the lack of pro-LGBT rights and policies, and draconian antihomosexuality laws.[31] "Good" and "bad" countries can experience material and symbolic

---

[27] According to Patricia Clough, "[p]opulation racism ... measure[s] populations in terms of life capacities ... Population racism is plastic, defined in application; it is often deadly when populations are marked for massacre and extinction and perhaps less so when deployed to affectively brand policy, program, and legislation." Patricia Ticineto Clough, "The Case of Sociology: Governmentality and Methodology," *Critical Inquiry*, 36, no. 4 (2010): 636.

[28] Following Jocelyn Viterna, I understand "crisis as an urgent, life-threatening event that requires immediate action on behalf of ... [possible victims] to avoid being severely traumatized, abused, or killed." Jocelyn Viterna, *Women in War: The Micro-Processes of Mobilization in El Salvador* (New York: Oxford University Press, 2013), 95.

[29] Ibid., 637.   [30] Nyong'o, "Queer Africa," 41.

[31] See Cynthia Weber's research connecting queer theorizing and international relations scholarship to understand the treatment of nations based on their LGBT rights positions in a global context. Cynthia Weber, *Queer International Relations: Sovereignty, Sexuality, and the Will to Knowledge* (New York: Oxford University Press, 2016).

consequences for their official policies and positions on gender and sexual minority rights. "Bad" homophobic countries populated by "ethnicized others" are more likely to face threats from Northern donors about the possible suspension of development aid.[32] "Good," homoprotectionist countries sit in judgment of "bad" countries, positioned as possible "saviors" ready to rescue LGBT Africans mired in life-threatening hostilities.[33] "Homoprotectionism" involves political elites using the state apparatus "to protect LGBTQ people from persecution and domination," thereby guaranteeing the nationalist loyalty of newly protected queer citizens.[34] Distinctions between "good" and "bad" countries vis-à-vis the absence or presence of politicized homophobia regard such homophobia as an "aspect of 'tradition' inevitably to be overcome," if "bad" countries hope to be taken seriously in modern, transnational, and supranational political spaces.[35]

Population racism in cases involving politicized homophobia in African countries unfolds according to a racialized hierarchy of sexual modernity with colonialist origins. Anti-blackness exists at the heart of this hierarchy. African countries' constructed racial otherness serves as the epistemological and political surface on which a racialized hierarchy of nations' progressive positions on gender and sexual minority rights is erected.[36] The urge to rank nations, such as Gambia, Kenya, Malawi, Namibia, Nigeria, Uganda, and Zimbabwe, based on the virulence of politicized homophobia motivates the ill-conceived

---

[32] Fatima El-Tayeb, *European Others: Queering Ethnicity in Postnational Europe* (Minneapolis: University of Minnesota Press, 2011), 13.

[33] Momin Rahman develops the concept of "homocolonialism" to reflect how the circulation of LGBT rights "renders resistant populations inferior in relation to superior Western values, rather than simply being populations that are 'lagging behind' Western development." Momin Rahman, "Queer Rights and the Triangulation of Western Exceptionalism," *Journal of Human Rights*, 13, no. 3 (2014): 275.

[34] Christine (Cricket) Keating, "Conclusion: On the Interplay of State Homophobia and Homoprotectionism," in *Global Homophobia: States, Movements, and the Politics of Oppression*, edited by Meredith L. Weiss and Michael J. Bosia (Urbana: University of Illinois Press, 2013), 247. See also, Lind and Keating, "Navigating the Left Turn."

[35] Michael J. Bosia, "To Love or to Loathe: Modernity, Homophobia, and LGBT Rights," in *Sexualities in World Politics: How LGBTQ Claims Shape International Relations*, edited by Manuela Lavinas Picq and Markus Thiel (New York: Routledge, 2015), 39. For similar arguments, see Rao, "The Locations of Homophobia," and Rahman, "Queer Rights."

[36] Agathangelou, "Neoliberal Geopolitical Order and Value," 470.

ranking of nations as the "worst" places in the world to be queer.[37] The population racism accompanying viral anxieties about politicized homophobia in the global South has contributed to several problematic dilemmas.

First, some academic research works to validate perceptions that African nations are homophobic. Western scholars have attempted to predict whether politicized homophobia in Uganda will yield an anti-queer genocide.[38] Tavia Nyong'o warns against yielding to the temptation to view the AHB as "protogenocidal" because it "extends stereotypes of a violent Africa."[39] Yet, using Uganda as an example, one group of scholars proposes creating a "barometer of gay rights (BGR)."[40] Describing the impetus for this barometer, Susan Dicklitch, Berwood Yost, and Bryan M. Dougan rely on emotional appeals to encourage other scholars to join their efforts to identify potential human rights violations and to protect vulnerable gender and sexual minorities. They argue, "The proposed law was also a wake-up call to the rest of the world to the shocking level of hatred towards gays in what was thought to be one of the more progressive countries in Africa."[41] Amar Wahab depicts the BGR as a "global check-box formula for assessing homophobia and rationalizing human rights intervention based on evaluative categories such as de jure and de facto (civil/political) state protection of homosexuals, gay rights advocacy, socioeconomic rights, and societal persecution."[42]

Second, population racism affects not only distinctions among and hierarchies ranking homophobic and homoprotectionist countries but also the constructions of migrants and refugees from homophobic

---

[37] Rao, "The Locations of Homophobia."

[38] Sue E. Spivey and Christine M. Robinson, "Genocidal Intentions: Social Death and the Ex-Gay Movement," *Genocide Studies and Prevention*, 5, no. 1 (2010): 68–88; Christina DeJong and Eric Long, "The Death Penalty as Genocide: The Persecution of 'Homosexuals' in Uganda," in *Handbook of LGBT Communities, Crime, and Justice*, edited by Dana Peterson and Vanessa R. Panfil (New York: Springer, 2014), 339–362.

[39] Nyong'o, "Queer Africa," 41.

[40] Susan Dicklitch, Berwood Yost, and Bryan M. Dougan, "Building a Barometer of Gay Rights (BGR): A Case Study of Uganda and the Persecution of Homosexuals," *Human Rights Quarterly*, 34, no. 2 (2012): 448–471.

[41] Ibid., 450.

[42] Amar Wahab, "'Homosexuality/Homophobia Is Un-African'? Un-Mapping Transnational Discourses in the Context of Uganda's Anti-Homosexuality Bill/Act," *Journal of Homosexuality*, 63, no. 5 (2016): 701.

countries seeking homes in homoprotectionist nations.[43] Migrants from "homophobic" countries face worrisome assumptions in receiving countries that they carry homophobia with them, a form of racist exclusion. Some citizens of Northern receiving countries express concerns that new migrants will inflame homophobia in immigrant communities that could spill over into dominant (white) society. Often, Islamophobia accompanies racist assumptions in homoprotectionist countries about migrants' homophobia, if migrants hail from Muslim-majority nations.[44] Paul Mepschen and Jan Willem Duyvendak argue, "In order to criticize Muslims as backward and as enemies of European culture, gay rights are now heralded as if they have been the foundation of European culture for centuries."[45] Much in the way that historical amnesia is a staple of politicized homophobia as some African political elites allege that there is no history of homosexuality in their societies,[46] historical amnesia also appears in homoprotectionist discourse in Northern countries, as citizens conveniently forget the legacy of anti-LGBT hatred in their societies.

Third, population racism can offer perverse advantages to African gender and sexual minorities seeking asylum or trying to resettle in Northern countries. As images of "homophobic" Southern countries circulate in national and transnational imaginaries, sympathy for gender and sexual minorities "stuck" in these countries swells in Northern countries. For instance, when African gender and sexual minorities seek asylum in European or North American countries, their legal counsel, if they have access to lawyers, may exploit the homophobic reputations of their countries of origin to argue that their lives will be in danger if they are repatriated.[47] In this way, asylum cases

---

[43] Paul Mepschen and Jan Willem Duyvendak, "European Sexual Nationalisms: The Culturalization of Citizenship and the Sexual Politics of Belonging and Exclusion," *Perspectives on Europe*, 42, no. 1 (2012): 74.

[44] El-Tayeb, *European Others*, 119–120; Puar, *Terrorist Assemblages*.

[45] Mepschen and Duyvendak, "European Sexual Nationalisms," 71.

[46] Currier, "Political Homophobia in Postcolonial Namibia."

[47] Connie G. Oxford, "Protectors and Victims in the Gender Regime of Asylum," *NWSA Journal*, 17, no. 3 (2005): 18–38; Connie Oxford, "Queer Asylum: US Policies and Responses to Sexual Orientation and Transgendered Persecution," in *Gender, Migration, and Categorisation: Making Distinctions between Migrants in Western Countries, 1945–2010*, edited by Marlou Schrover and Deirdre M. Moloney (Amsterdam: Amsterdam University Press, 2013), 128–148; Charlotte Walker-Said, "Sexual Minorities among African Asylum Claimants: Human Rights Regimes, Bureaucratic Knowledge, and the Era of

depend on and reproduce hierarchies that rank nations according to state positions on LGBT rights.

Finally, urgent calls to contain "African homophobia" complicate indigenous resistance to politicized homophobia. According to some scholars, Northern activists who advocate for African gender and sexual minorities may exaggerate politicized homophobia to justify their interventions.[48] In other words, the "eagerness of white gays to save brown [and black] gays from brown [and black] homophobes" may spur some Northern activists to portray contemporary African societies as inherently dangerous for gender and sexual dissidents.[49] Emboldened by a sense of cultural and political superiority that accompanies homonationalism, some Northern gay activists seek to liberate African gender and sexual minorities from antihomosexual discourses and practices. Such interventions may ignore and trample on local antihomophobic mobilization.

Well-meaning Northern activists can thwart "African agency and dignity" and expose African LGBT activists to "heightened risk," if antigay groups associate non-African LGBT organizing with grassroots resistance.[50] For instance, during Chimbalanga and Monjeza's 2010 trial, Malawian news media investigated claims made by Voice of America (VOA)[51] that three human rights activists advocating for the couple's release were arrested and subsequently freed on bail. The VOA story quoted Peter Tatchell, a British LGBT rights activist who frequently comments on LGBT rights issues in different countries and

Sexual Rights Diplomacy," in *African Asylum at a Crossroads: Activism, Expert Testimony, and Refugee Rights*, edited by Iris Berger, Tricia Redeker Hepner, Benjamin N. Lawrance, Joanna T. Tague, and Meredith Terretta (Athens: Ohio University Press, 2015), 203–224.

[48] Epprecht, *Heterosexual Africa?*; Gaudio, *Allah Made Us*; Joseph Massad, "Re-Orienting Desire: The Gay International and the Arab World," *Public Culture*, 14, no. 2 (2002): 361–385.

[49] Rahul Rao, *Third World Protest: Between Home and the World* (New York: Oxford University Press, 2010), 182. In this quotation, Rahul Rao modifies Gayatri Chakravorty Spivak's well-known formulation that "[w]hite men are saving brown women from brown men." Gayatri Chakravorty Spivak, "Can the Subaltern Speak?," in *Marxism and the Interpretation of Culture*, edited by Cary Nelson and Lawrence Grossberg (Urbana: University of Illinois Press, 1988), 296.

[50] Epprecht, *Heterosexual Africa?*, 22.

[51] "Malawi Intensifies Prosecution of Gay Minorities and Their Defenders," *Voice of America*, January 6, 2010, www.voanews.com/content/malawi-gay-trial-1-7-2010-80880227/152738.html.

claimed that police had charged one of the three human rights activists with possession of pornography, which were, in fact, HIV/AIDS safer-sex educational materials. Tatchell interpreted these alleged arrests as Malawi "slipping backwards into the bad old ways during the era of the Hastings Banda dictatorship."[52] In response to the allegation about activists' arrests, police spokesperson Davie Chingwalu asked why Tatchell did not supply the arrested activists' names and speculated that Northern gay rights activists like Tatchell "just want to create a bad image of Malawi so that we should be seen as if we're violating people's rights for nothing. From the way they comment on this issue, one can conclude ... they want to win international attention."[53] Additionally, Undule Mwakasungula, CHRR's executive director, knew nothing about the supposed arrests and stated, "[I]t would be unfair for the international media to create stories where there is [sic] none. That is irresponsible journalism."[54] Although Chingwalu and Mwakasungula were on opposite sides of the LGBT rights issue, they agreed that Northern intrusion into Malawian sexual-rights debates could be problematic.

Although transnational pleas for solidarity for persecuted gender and sexual minorities across Africa are laudable, they often ignore the organic efforts of gender and sexual diversity defenders and sympathetic allies throughout the continent.[55] African activists continue to contest antihomosexuality and transphobic campaigns and increasingly stand up to Northern activist encroachment in their efforts. In 2013, the United States-based Human Rights Campaign announced that it was expanding its work into international LGBT rights advocacy. This development unnerved Wanja Muguongo, who leads UHAI, the East African Sexual Health and Rights Initiative, because she believed this initiative could jeopardize African LGBT activists' work. Muguongo stated, "We are not sitting down somewhere waiting for salvation to come from the North ... There are organizations that are

---

[52] Ibid.

[53] Watipaso Mzungo, Jr., "Foreign Media Lies on Activists' Arrests," *Daily Times*, January 11, 2010, 4.

[54] Ibid.

[55] Tamale, "Confronting the Politics of Nonconforming Sexualities in Africa."

working locally and they have their own ideas about what the struggle means."[56] Muguongo's statement repudiates the notion that African gender and sexual minorities are waiting for foreigners to rescue them. In many different African countries, activists have formulated campaigns to address the specific forms and perpetrators of homophobias and transphobias. In Malawi, NGOs like CEDEP and CHRR continue to fight multiple homophobias and to challenge the antisodomy law, which entrapped some gender and sexual dissidents like Jonah, whose story I share shortly.

The Looming Threat of Arrest

Documenting the emergence and consequences of politicized homophobia in one country demystifies the origin and trajectory of this form of homophobia, rendering it more finite and knowable. However, tracking politicized homophobia does not mitigate its negative, life-altering consequences for some African sexual minorities. In April and May 2014, I traveled to several Malawian towns and cities, including Blantyre, Lilongwe, Mangochi, Mzuzu, and Nkhata Bay, to interview sexual minorities about their perceptions of politicized homophobia and experiences with violence. This round of fieldwork allowed me to become reacquainted with the brilliant, hard-working staff at CEDEP offices in Blantyre and Lilongwe and to meet scores of CEDEP staff, volunteers, and LGBT constituents. Although I gathered most evidence of how Malawian sexual minorities perceived how politicized homophobia adversely affected their lives from retrospective interviews, during my fieldwork, I witnessed firsthand how the antisodomy law could ensnare gender and sexual minorities. In 2012, news stories reported that the government had suspended the antisodomy law,[57] meaning that police were not supposed to arrest people for consensual same-sex sex, but the arrest of a key gatekeeper during my fieldwork confirmed that police still enforced the law. As

---

[56] J. Lester Feder, "Human Rights Campaign's Move into International Work Puts Global LGBT Advocates on Edge," *BuzzFeed*, November 5, 2013, www.buzzfeed.com/lesterfeder/human-rights-campaigns-move-into-international-work-puts-glo#1pt01xk.

[57] "Malawi Suspends Anti-Homosexuality Laws."

Chapter 5 demonstrates, the specter of arrest structured the daily routines and sexual relationships that sexual minorities sought to protect from prying eyes.

While traveling to a town in northern Malawi in mid-May 2012, my hired car broke down. Kind strangers helped us push the car up the hill to a primary school, a safe place out of the way of long-haul trucks that descended the steep hill at high speeds. Since I had no friends in the nearby town, I reached out to Jonah, a gay man, CEDEP employee, and gatekeeper in the local LGBT community who was helping arrange interviews for my research team. It had been two years since I had seen Jonah. Local LGBT community members were fond of Jonah, who had an extensive network of friends; his family lived several hours away. I explained our situation and location to Jonah over the phone, and he graciously agreed to see if he could convince someone with a truck to tow us to town. Within an hour, Jonah arrived with two men who towed us the rest of the way. After I thanked and paid the men who escorted us, I invited Jonah to have dinner with me at a restaurant within close walking distance so that we could catch up.

Over dinner, Jonah confided that he feared he was going to be arrested soon. After returning from an international trip, he received a phone message from police in Lilongwe asking him to report for an interview. Although the message did not indicate the nature of the requested interview, Jonah surmised that his partner, a man several years younger, had filed a complaint with the police alleging that Jonah had coerced the younger man into a sexual relationship, a violation of the antisodomy law. While he was out of the country, Jonah learned that his partner had been having sex with other men; Jonah explained that they were monogamous. As an HIV/AIDS peer educator, Jonah preached monogamy to the MSM he counseled, and he practiced it himself as a way to protect himself from HIV. Fearing that his partner's sexual liaisons with other men could imperil his health, Jonah ended the relationship. The relationship's demise meant the end of his partner's financial dependence on Jonah; his partner could no longer rely on Jonah to pay for his school fees, food, and housing. Jonah believed that his partner filed a police complaint against him in retaliation for terminating the relationship. I counseled Jonah to consult with a lawyer and CEDEP leaders before submitting to a police interview and mentioned that the police may want to speak to him about a completely unrelated matter.

A few days after meeting with Jonah, I traveled to Lilongwe to attend the International Day Against Homophobia and Transphobia (IDAHOT) event sponsored by CEDEP and CHRR at the Crossroads Hotel, a three-star hotel, where I hoped to see Jonah again. A sign advertising the event greeted hotel visitors. Before the meeting, Gift Trapence, CEDEP's executive director, told me that this event could not have occurred in 2005, a year in which MHRRC proposed decriminalizing same-sex sex and amending the constitution to include a sexual-orientation nondiscrimination clause, suggestions that Malawian politicians and NGOs decried at the time. He shared his delight in seeing two hotel workers hanging two rainbow flags on the walls, a request that the hotel might have denied in the past. The fact that CEDEP and CHRR were able to rent such an exclusive hotel meeting space for this event signaled the significant donor funding they received for their projects. That hotel management did not object to the IDAHOT event being held at Crossroads also suggested that some local elites were slowly becoming more receptive to LGBT rights.

People from all over the country gathered for the IDAHOT event in a large meeting room equipped with a data projector and screen. Participants included Malawian LGBT people, journalists, Muslim imams, Christian ministers, traditional authorities, representatives from different NGOs, and CEDEP employees and volunteers. CEDEP officers from around the country traveled to Lilongwe for the event. I looked for Jonah in the audience but did not find him. A CEDEP officer who served as the event's master of ceremonies apologized for the delayed start and explained the event's purpose.[58] He stated that LGBT people were "different from the rest of the majority. We're ... people" whose sexual orientations and gender expressions differ from the majority. According to the CEDEP officer, IDAHOT events give LGBT advocacy groups a "voice" and ability to articulate opposition to homophobia and transphobia. Although this event was not the first time Malawi had commemorated IDAHOT, the day was "special." The moderator stressed that the event was not about promoting "special rights" but about extending equal rights to all people, including gender and sexual minorities.

---

[58] The event started late because the national elections scheduled for May 20, 2014, were siphoning attendees' time and attention.

The IDAHOT event educated the audience about the current state of gender and sexual minority rights in Malawi and gave LGBT people the chance to voice how homophobia and transphobia influenced their lives. Trapence delivered keynote remarks on "Freedom of Expression for Sexual and Gender Minorities." This IDAHOT event coincided with the national elections, a heady time for the country's democracy. He asked, "What kind of leaders are we going to elect?"[59] He went on to explain, "Homophobia and transphobia are prevalent in our society." He defined homophobia as the "irrational fear" of lesbians and gay people and "transphobia" as the "fear" of gender minorities because people "do not conform" to "heteronormative" expectations of society. According to Trapence, people express such fears through "hateful speech," violence, and "castigation." He referred to the recent call by a Muslim imam for the death penalty for sexual minorities and cautioned that these demands could exacerbate and authorize violence against LGBT people.[60] He promoted the right to privacy and warned against people who claim that decriminalization disguised Western attempts to "recolonize" African societies because such claims weakened human rights campaigns. Trapence claimed that the penal code created obstacles for LGBT people to access healthcare, harmed

[59] CEDEP and CHRR representatives publicly lamented how political parties were not taking gender and sexual minority rights seriously during the national election or were adopting cryptic positions on LGBT rights. See Wisdom Chimgwede, "Running Mates Offer No Hope for Gays," *Nation*, March 10, 2014, http://mwnation.com/running-mates-offer-hope-gays/; Dyson Mthawanji, "CHRR Slams Politicians on Gay Rights," *Nation*, March 19, 2014, https://mwnation.com/chrr-slams-politicians-on-gay-rights/.

[60] Sheikh Salmim Idruss Omar, the general secretary of the Muslim Association of Malawi (MAM), claimed that the Muslim stance "on homosexuals is that they must face the death penalty," but he never solicited government officials to take action on this viewpoint. Frank Namangale, "MAM Calls for Death Penalty for Gays," *Nation*, February 2, 2014, http://mwnation.com/mam-calls-for-death-penalty-for-gays/. Certainly, not all Muslim imams shared MAM's position on sexual diversity. Speaking at an event organized by CEDEP in 2013, Sheikh Mdala Ali Tambuli publicly endorsed LGBT rights in the country. Ephraim Munthali, "Sheikh Backs Gay Rights," *Nation*, October 20, 2013, http://mwnation.com/sheikh-backs-gay-rights/. After Tambuli's support for gay rights became public, MAM rebuked his position on same-sex sexualities and reminded imams to "respect the hierarchy" of Muslim clerics in Malawi by refraining from commenting on matters of public interest. "Malawi Muslim Group Condemn Sheikh Tambuli, Gay Campaigners," *Nyasa Times*, October 24, 2013, www.nyasatimes.com/malawi-muslim-group-condemn-sheikh-tambuli-gay-campaigners/.

their self-esteem, and reproduced homophobia; such laws bolstered corrupt governance and enabled the government to take advantage of citizens' low literacy rates in the campaign against homosexuality. He also mentioned other pressing issues like poverty and maternal mortality, which the government had done little to redress. The government claimed that they had sovereignty, but "what have they done with it" after leading a sovereign state for fifty years? Trapence stated, "They [government officials] make a mockery of our struggle[s]." The Western world has "done away with" antisodomy laws, but the Malawian government ignores the Western origin of antisodomy laws. Trapence viewed the anticolonial defense of politicized homophobia as a red herring. CEDEP called on the president to repeal the antisodomy law and continued to pressure the new government to respect gender and sexual minority rights.[61]

I witnessed the harmful effects of homophobia after the uplifting IDAHOT event. A CEDEP officer informed me that police had arrested Jonah for violating the antisodomy law. Jonah had traveled to Lilongwe specifically for CEDEP's IDAHOT event but apparently visited a police precinct in Lilongwe when he arrived in town. A CEDEP officer told me that Jonah did not consult with staff in the Lilongwe office before he went to the police station; if Jonah had alerted them in advance, they would have advised him to go to the station with a trusted lawyer. Jonah thought he was submitting to a police interview, but police arrested him instead. Since Jonah was arrested on a Friday, May 16, 2014, he faced spending the rest of the weekend in the holding cell; in fact, he risked being held in jail well into the following week because lawyers and police were gearing up for the national election on Tuesday, May 20, 2014.

Before heading to the police station, I ventured to a grocery store to buy food and drinks for Jonah because he had not eaten since lunch the day before, information that CEDEP staff shared with me. I purchased juice and food to last Jonah for the next two days, as his friends were several hours away. Malawian prisons and jails often provide prisoners with one meal a day, but family and friends frequently had to supplement these meals with additional food and drinks to combat

---

[61] Malawians elected Bingu wa Mutharika's brother, Peter, as president in May 2014, handing defeat to Joyce Banda. Peter Mutharika's win ushered the DPP back into power.

malnutrition.[62] At the police station, I asked for directions to the holding cells where I met up again with CEDEP officers who arrived before me. They had concluded their visit with Jonah and were trying to locate a lawyer who could represent him, but many lawyers had already traveled out of town, either to their hometown to vote in the election or to serve as an election monitor elsewhere in the country. CEDEP officers offered social support and legal assistance to staff members under arrest. I informed the duty officer in the holding-cell area that I was there to see Jonah.

After waiting for a few minutes, I saw another officer lead about fifteen men from one set of holding cells to a large cell behind the duty officer's desk; the officer announced to visitors that they could go into the cell. I embraced Jonah whose usually upbeat demeanor had been replaced by an understandably worried mindset. I gave the bags of juice and food to Jonah who eagerly reached for some food to eat, as police had not fed him since arresting him. Although the holding cell smelled of urine, it was a far cry from the overcrowded holding cells in which Malawians had asphyxiated in the past.[63] Jonah confirmed that he was being detained because his ex-partner filed charges alleging that Jonah had raped him. What Jonah's ex-partner failed to realize before filing a complaint was that police viewed his complaint as confessing to letting Jonah have sex with him; they subsequently arrested Jonah's ex-partner for also violating the antisodomy law. Jonah did not blame his ex-partner for going to the police. In fact, he was able to speak with his former partner because they were both detained in the same holding cell; Jonah pointed his ex-partner out to me. He stated that his ex-partner's family pressured him to report Jonah to the police because they were unhappy that he had been in a same-sex relationship. It was an ironic visit because I had just finished participating in the

---

[62] Food shortages in Malawian jails and prisons have been recurring problems. In another sodomy case in 2012 in which CEDEP and CHRR came to the defense of the accused, the lawyer pleaded with the court to grant the jailed suspect bail because he "has no relation or close acquaintance in Zomba who can provide him with food and other basic necessities of life," which confirms that jail and prison authorities expect suspects' friends and relatives to provide food and drinks for them. Anthony Kasunda, "State Holds on to Sodomy Suspect," *Nation*, January 12, 2012, 3.

[63] Overcrowding contributed to the deaths of seventeen men by asphyxiation in a Lilongwe police station holding cell in March 1996. Chinyeke Tembo, "Report on 17 Cell Deaths Out," *Daily Times*, April 3, 1996, 1.

invigorating IDAHOT event in which Malawian religious and traditional leaders and LGBT people committed themselves to combatting homophobia and transphobia.

When I visited Jonah the next day and brought him more food and drinks, I briefly spoke with Jonah's lawyer who was working on securing his bail. A few hours after my visit with Jonah, his lawyer called and asked if I could assist with paying Jonah's bail, which was about US$100. I immediately said that I would and traveled to the police station. After handing the lawyer the money for Jonah's bail, I waited for Jonah in the parking lot. Police released both Jonah and his ex-partner on bail.[64] A weary Jonah greeted me, grateful to be out of jail. We stopped for a meal before I escorted him to a friend's home in Lilongwe, and we spoke about his future. He feared that his legal troubles would continue and result in his inevitable conviction and incarceration, rendering him vulnerable to contracting HIV/AIDS in prison.[65] When we parted, I gave him enough money to pay for his meals and transportation back home. I wish I could say that Jonah's legal tribulations ended and that police did not pursue his case. He was subsequently rearrested on the same charges.

Other Malawian men who were convicted of sodomy remain incarcerated. Many of them were in same-sex relationships or sought sexual pleasure with other men. CEDEP and CHRR leaders have been working to secure the release of these men and to persuade lawmakers and judges to support decriminalizing same-sex sex. The case contested the convictions of three men convicted of sodomy who received prison sentences ranging between ten and fourteen years, the maximum prison term for sodomy.[66] Other groups supporting the legal challenge included CHRR, MANERELA+, MLS, UNAIDS, and University of

---

[64] I also paid Jonah's bail so that he would not have to ask his family for this money. Jonah had a warm relationship with family members, but given his emotional fragility after being arrested, I did not ask him questions about his contact with family.

[65] Based on Jonah's fears, I inferred that he worried that as a known gay man in prison, he would be coerced into having unprotected sex with other men, possibly exposing him to HIV and other STIs. Prison officials do not distribute condoms in Malawian jails and prisons to incarcerated men.

[66] Josephine Chinele, "Battle on Malawi Sodomy Case Continues," *Daily Times*, June 12, 2014, article on file with author. Frank Namangale, "Supreme Court Stops Proceedings on Gay Case," *Nation*, February 3, 2014, https://mwnation.com/supreme-court-stops-proceedings-on-gay-case/.

Malawi law faculty.[67] The Malawi Human Rights Commission (MHRC) declined to join the group of NGOs challenging the antisodomy law, and CEDEP and CHRR threatened to sue if MHRC did not join the legal challenge as a friend of the court.[68] Zione Mtaba, a High Court judge who supported CEDEP's application, was promoted to the Supreme Court, a tactic that Trapence characterized as trying to block the case from moving forward in remarks he gave at the IDAHOT event.[69] The government succeeded in obtaining a stay from the court, which stalled the case. Trapence promised that CEDEP would keep advocating for the decriminalization of same-sex sex. As long as the antisodomy law's future is uncertain, it will continue to instill fear in many queer Malawians.

The experiences of Jonah, LGBT people, and different activists with politicized homophobia in Malawi demonstrate how homophobic discourses and practices constrain gender and sexually diverse people's lives and social movements' actions. In *Politicizing Sex in Contemporary Africa: Homophobia in Malawi*, I have charted the rise, contours, and effects of politicized homophobia in Malawi to prevent misleading portrayals of this phenomenon as freely coursing throughout the African continent. I emphasize the limits of politicized homophobia so that analysts and observers do not inaccurately assume that all African countries are mired in unbridled antigay aggression.

Throughout the book, I have stressed how important it is for activists and scholars to approach politicized homophobia in terms of particularity and contingency. Injecting specificity and contingency into analyses of politicized homophobia in African countries and in nations elsewhere in the global South preempts the temptation to make generalizations about how pervasive politicized homophobia is. I have treated politicized homophobia as a strategy that political elites have used to strengthen their positions in Malawi, a country undergoing

---

[67] Frank Namangale, "Court Throws Out AG's Application on Gays," *Nation*, January 21, 2014, https://mwnation.com/court-throws-out-ag's-application-on-gays/; Namangale, "Supreme Court Stops"; Ngwira, "Malawi's Controversial Gay Law."

[68] Anthony Kasunda, "MHRC Under Fire over Gay Rights," *Nation*, January 25, 2014, https://mwnation.com/mhrc-underfire-over-gay-rights/; Frank Namangale, "Join Gay Case or Face Lawsuit, MHRC Told," *Nation*, February 26, 2014, http://mwnation.com/join-gay-case-or-face-lawsuit-mhrc-told/.

[69] "Judge Speaks on Gay Rights," *Nation*, January 20, 2014, https://mwnation.com/judge-speaks-on-gay-rights/.

rapid social change. Although the effects of politicized homophobia have harmed some NGOs and sexual minorities, documenting the rise and consequences of politicized homophobia is a means to curb this political strategy. Part of the impetus for this project stemmed from my belief that if politicized homophobia has a beginning, then it also can and should have an end. Yet what undermines African efforts to challenge and extirpate politicized homophobia is the reproduction of the image of "homophobic Africa," a construction that produces the illusion of a timeless homophobia and an African continent out of step with Northern sexual modernity.[70] To work against this problematic construction of "homophobic Africa," I have identified sources of pro-LGBT rights solidarity and resistance to prevent assumptions that the situation created by politicized homophobia in Malawi is hopeless. LGBT rights defenders, such as CEDEP and CHRR, constitute important voices in human rights mobilization and ongoing democratization efforts in the country.

---

[70] Awondo, Geschiere, and Reid, "Homophobic Africa?," 149.

References

Aarmo, Margrete. 1999. "How Homosexuality Became 'Un-African': The Case of Zimbabwe." In *Female Desires: Same-Sex Relations and Transgender Practices across Cultures*, edited by Evelyn Blackwood and Saskia E. Wieringa, 255–280. New York: Columbia University Press.

Adam, Barry D. 2008. "Theorizing Homophobia." *Sexualities* 1(4): 387–404.

"African Bishops Break from West Seminaries." 2004. *Weekend Nation*, November 6–7, 5.

"African Statement in Response to British Government on Aid Conditionality." 2013. In *Queer African Reader*, edited by Sokari Ekine and Hakima Abbas, 209–210. Dakar, Senegal: Pambazuka.

Agathangelou, Anna M. 2013. "Neoliberal Geopolitical Order and Value: Queerness as a Speculative Economy and Anti-Blackness as Terror." *International Feminist Journal of Politics* 15(4): 453–476.

Alexander, M. Jacqui. 1994. "Not Just (Any) Body Can Be a Citizen: The Politics of Law, Sexuality, and Postcoloniality in Trinidad and Tobago and the Bahamas." *Feminist Review* 48: 5–23.

——— 2005. *Pedagogies of Crossing: Meditations on Feminism, Sexual Politics, Memory, and the Sacred*. Durham, NC: Duke University Press.

Aloisi, Silvia. 1999. "Gay-Bashing Continues in Africa." *Daily Times*, October 6, 9.

Altman, Dennis. 1983. *The Homosexualization of America*. Boston: Beacon.

Amar, Paul. 2013. *The Security Archipelago: Human-Security States, Sexuality Politics, and the End of Neoliberalism*. Durham, NC: Duke University Press.

Amnesty International. 2012. "Suspension of Anti-Homosexuality Laws in Malawi a Historic Step Forward." November 5. www.amnesty.org/en/news/suspension-anti-homosexuality-laws-malawi-historic-step-forward-2012-11-05.

ANP/AFP. 2012. "No Regrets for Malawian Jailed for Gay Wedding." *Radio Netherlands Worldwide*, December 9. https://sg.news.yahoo.com/no-regrets-malawian-jailed-gay-wedding-045851350.html/.

"Anti-Gay Bishops May Say No to US Funds." 2004. *Nation*, April 14, 7.

Awondo, Patrick. 2010. "The Politicisation of Sexuality and Rise of Homosexual Movements in Post-Colonial Cameroon." *Review of African Political Economy* 37(125): 315–328.

Awondo, Patrick, Peter Geschiere, and Graeme Reid. 2012. "Homophobic Africa? Toward a More Nuanced View." *African Studies Review* 55(3): 145–168.

Ayoub, Phillip M. and David Paternotte, eds. 2014. *LGBT Activism and the Making of Europe: A Rainbow Europe?* New York: Palgrave Macmillan.

Azuah, Unoma. 2011. "Extortion and Blackmail of Nigerian Lesbians and Bisexual Women." In *Nowhere to Turn: Blackmail and Extortion of LGBT People in Sub-Saharan Africa*, edited by Ryan Thoreson and Sam Cook, 46–59. New York: International Gay and Lesbian Human Rights Commission.

Bacchetta, Paola. 1999. "When the (Hindu) Nation Exiles Its Queers." *Social Text* 61: 141–166.

Badgett, M. V. Lee. 2009. *When Gay People Get Married: What Happens When Societies Legalize Same-Sex Marriage.* New York: New York University Press.

"Bad Laws Should Be Repealed." 2012. *Daily Times*, February 3, 4.

Bamusi, McDonald. 2005. "Increase in Rape Cases Blamed on Traditions." *Daily Times*, December 18, 2.

Banda, Francis Makanda. 2005. "On Legalising Homosexuality." *Daily Times*, February 23, 8.

Banda, Mabvuto. 1999. "NGOs Condemn Muluzi's Statement." *Daily Times*, October 6, 3.

    2011. "Malawi Report Says 19 Killed, 58 Shot in Protests." *Reuters*, August 15. www.reuters.com/article/2011/08/15/ozatp-malawi-protests-idAFJOE77E0N920110815.

Banda, Jr., Sam. 2007. "NGOs Told to Act, Not Workshop." *Daily Times*, November 5, 2.

Banda, Unandi. 2007. "Rights in Malawi." *Nation*, January 27, 20.

Baral, Stefan, Gift Trapence, Felistus Motimedi, Eric Umar, Scholastika Iipinge, Friedel Dausab, and Chris Beyrer. 2009. "HIV Prevalence, Risks for HIV Infection, and Human Rights among Men Who Have Sex with Men (MSM) in Malawi, Namibia, and Botswana." *PLoS ONE* 4(3): doi:10.1371/journal.pone.0004997.

Barton, Bernadette. 2006. *Stripped: Inside the Lives of Exotic Dancers*. New York: New York University Press.

    2012. *Pray the Gay Away: The Extraordinary Lives of Bible Belt Gays.* New York: New York University Press.

Batolo, Taonga. 2005. "Clergy Say Big 'No' to Homosexuality." *Daily Times*, December 11, 5.

————. 2012. "Kamlepo Calls for Anti-Gay Protests: 'Malawi Should Not Allow Homosexuality.'" *Nyasa Times*, November 6. www.nyasatimes.com/kam lepo-calls-for-anti-gay-protests-malawi-should-not-allow-homosexuality/.

Bearak, Barry and Alan Cowell. 2010. "Zimbabwe Shrugs Off Gay Rights." *New York Times*, March 27, A4.

Berlant, Lauren and Michael Warner. 1998. "Sex in Public." *Critical Inquiry* 24(2): 547–566.

Bernstein, Mary, Constance Kostelac, and Emily Gaarder. 2003. "Understanding 'Heterosexism': Applying Theories of Racial Prejudice to Homophobia Using Data from a Southwestern Police Department." *Race, Gender, & Class* 10(4): 54–74.

Betha, Edyth. 2006. "Gay Clergy: What the Local Church Says." *Weekend Nation*, July 8–9, 12.

"Be Vigilant against Abuse of Children." 2002. *Nation*, January 23, 10.

Biruk, Crystal. 2014. "'Aid for Gays': The Moral and the Material in 'African Homophobia' in Post-2009 Malawi." *Journal of Modern African Studies* 52(3): 447–473.

————. 2016. "Life Stories in Context: Being Lesbian, Bisexual, and Gender-Nonconforming in Malawi." In *Proudly Malawian: Life Stories from Lesbian and Gender-Nonconforming Individuals*, edited by Makhosazana Xaba and Crystal Biruk, 14–27. Braamfontein, South Africa: MaThoko's Books.

————. 2016. "Studying Up in Critical NGO Studies Today: Reflections on Critique and the Distribution of Distributive Labour." *Critical African Studies* 8(3): 291–305.

Biruk, Crystal and Gift Trapence. 2017. "Community Engagement in an Economy of Harms: Reflections from an LGBTI-Rights NGO in Malawi." *Critical Public Health* 28(3): 340–351.

Blasius, Mark. 1994. *Gay and Lesbian Politics: Sexuality and the Emergence of a New Ethic*. Philadelphia: Temple University Press.

Blee, Kathleen M. 2012. *Democracy in the Making: How Activist Groups Form*. New York: Oxford University Press.

Blumenfeld, Warren J., ed. 1992. *Homophobia: How We All Pay the Price*. Boston: Beacon.

Blumer, Herbert. 1971. "Social Problems as Collective Behavior." *Social Problems* 18(3): 298–306.

Boellstorff, Tom. 2004. "The Emergence of Political Homophobia in Indonesia: Masculinity and National Belonging." *Ethnos* 69(4): 465–486.

Bompani, Barbara and Caroline Valois. 2016. "Sexualizing Politics: The Anti-Homosexuality Bill, Party-Politics, and the New Political Dispensation in Uganda." *Critical African Studies* 8(2): 1–19.

Bond, Patrick. 2003. *Against Global Apartheid: South African Meets the World Bank, IMF, and International Finance.* Second edition. New York: Zed.

Bosia, Michael J. 2013. "Why States Act: Homophobia and Crisis." In *Global Homophobia: States, Movements, and the Politics of Oppression,* edited by Meredith L. Weiss and Michael J. Bosia, 30–54. Urbana: University of Illinois Press.

2014. "Strange Fruit: Homophobia, the State, and the Politics of LGBT Rights and Capabilities." *Journal of Human Rights* 13(3): 256–273.

2015. "To Love or to Loathe: Modernity, Homophobia, and LGBT Rights." In *Sexualities in World Politics: How LGBTQ Claims Shape International Relations,* edited by Manuela Lavinas Picq and Markus Thiel, 38–53. New York: Routledge.

Bosia, Michael J. and Meredith L. Weiss. 2013. "Political Homophobia in Comparative Perspective." In *Global Homophobia: States, Movements, and the Politics of Oppression,* edited by Meredith L. Weiss and Michael J. Bosia, 1–29. Urbana: University of Illinois Press.

Boswell, Barbara. 2015. "On Miniskirts and Hegemonic Masculinity: The Ideology of Deviant Feminine Sexuality in Anti-Homosexuality and Decency Laws." In *Contested Intimacies: Sexuality, Gender, and the Law in Africa,* edited by Derrick Higginbotham and Victoria Collis Buthelezi, 46–65. Cape Town, South Africa: Siber Ink.

Bottoman, Lucas. 2011. "Bingu Warns Demo Organizers." *Malawi News,* July 23–29, 3, 7.

Branch, Adam and Zachariah Mampilly. 2015. *Africa Uprising: Popular Protest and Political Change.* New York: Zed.

Bromwich, Jonah Engel. 2017. "How US Military Policy on Transgender Personnel Changed under Obama." *New York Times,* July 26. www.nytimes.com/2017/07/26/us/politics/trans-military-trump-timeline.html.

Butler, Judith. 1990. *Gender Trouble: Feminism and the Subversion of Identity.* New York: Routledge.

Brickell, Chris. 2006. "The Sociological Construction of Gender and Sexuality." *The Sociological Review* 54(1): 87–113.

Brooks, Ethel C. 2007. *Unraveling the Garment Industry: Transnational Organizing and Women's Work.* Minneapolis: University of Minnesota Press.

Bryant, Karl and Salvador Vidal-Ortiz. 2008. "Introduction to Retheorizing Homophobias." *Sexualities* 11(4): 387–396.

Bystydzienski, Jill M. 2001. "The Feminist Movement in Poland: Why So Slow?" *Women's Studies International Forum* 24(5): 501–511.

Cammack, Diana. 2012. "Malawi in Crisis, 2011–12." *Review of African Political Economy* 39(132): 375–388.

Cammack, Diana and Tim Kelsall. 2011. "Neo-Patrimonialism, Institutions, and Economic Growth: The Case of Malawi, 1964–2009." *IDS Bulletin* 42(2): 88–96.

"CEDEP Wants Homosexuality Referendum." 2010. *Daily Times*, January 7, 4.

Centre for the Development of People. 2010. *Queer Malawi: Untold Stories.* Johannesburg, South Africa: Gay and Lesbian Memory in Action.

Chabot, Sean and Jan Willem Duyvendak. 2002. "Globalization and Transnational Diffusion between Social Movements: Reconceptualizing the Dissemination of the Gandhian Repertoire and the 'Coming Out' Routine." *Theory & Society* 31(6): 697–740.

Chakwera, Nick. 2012. "Vote: No!" *Malawi News*, May 26–June 1, 11.

Chalera, James. 2010. "Gay Ruling Too Harsh." *Nation*, May 23.

Chalira, Luntha. 2010. "Mixed Views on 14-Year Sentence." *Nation*, May 25, 4.

Chanika, Emmie, John L. Lwanda, and Adamson S. Muula. 2013. "Gender, Gays, and Gain: The Sexualised Politics of Donor Aid in Malawi." *Africa Spectrum* 48(1): 89–105.

Chapalapata, McDonald. 2000. "Tourist Arrested for Abuse." *Daily Times*, July 20, 1, 4.

Chauwa, Alfred. 2015. "2 Malawians Confirmed Killed in Xenophobic Violence." *Nyasa Times*, April 20. www.nyasatimes.com/2-malawians-confirmed-killed-in-xenophobic-violence-evacuation-budget-revised/.

Chapulapula, Theresa. 2010. "Gays Remain Silent." *Daily Times*, April 7, 1, 3.

———. 2012. "Govt Acts on Bad Laws." *Malawi News*, May 5–11, 3.

Chapulapula, Theresa and Simeon Maganga. 2012. "No Money for Bad Laws' Review." *Daily Times*, February 3, 1, 3.

Chapulapula, Theresa and Wezzie Nkhoma-Somba. 2010. "Gays Guilty." *Daily Times*, May 19, 1, 3.

———. 2010. "Ruling Excites Clergy." *Daily Times*, May 21, 3.

Chavula, James. 2010. "Embracing the Gay Phenomenon." *Nation*, January 11, 21.

———. 2014. "An Hour with a Confessed Lesbian." *Nation*, March 31. http://mwnation.com/an-hour-with-a-confessed-lesbian/.

Chenjezi, Thokozani. 2011. "People Impound CHRR, CEDEP Cloth." *Daily Times*, May 20, 4.

Chibaya, Samuel. 2010. "Chiefs Hail Usiwa Usiwa." *Nation*, May 23, 4.

Chibwezo, Wiseman. 2011. "Blackmail among Gay People in Malawi." In *Nowhere to Turn: Blackmail and Extortion of LGBT People in Sub-Saharan Africa*, edited by Ryan Thoreson and Sam Cook, 74–88. New York: International Gay and Lesbian Human Rights Commission.

Chikoko, Rex. 2013. "Peter, Atupele for Vote on Gays." *Nation*, October 7, 1, 2.

Chikoto-Schulz, Grace and Kelechi Uzochukwu. 2016. "Governing Civil Society in Nigeria and Zimbabwe: A Question of Policy Process and Non-State Actors' Involvement." *Nonprofit Policy Forum* 7(2): 137–170.

Chilanga, Yokoniya. 2012. "Malawi Becoming a Donor Fearing Nation." *Daily Times*, June 11, 9.

Chimbuto, Joseph. 2003. "Homosexuality Hits Hard at Chichiri Prison." *Daily Times*, June 3, 5.

Chimgwede, Wisdom. 2011. "The Only July 20, 2011." *Zodiak Online*, July 18. Article on file with author.

——— 2014. "Running Mates Offer No Hope for Gays." *Nation*, March 10. http://mwnation.com/running-mates-offer-hope-gays/.

Chimpweya, James and Caroline Somanje. 2010. "Kaliati Slams Court for Acquitting Lesbian Suspect." *Nation*, January 21, 2.

Chimwaza, Edward. 1998. "Relation Connotation Main Cause of Incest, Child Abuse." *Malawi News*, June 13–19, 9.

Chinele, Josephine. 2014. "Battle on Malawi Sodomy Case Continues." *Daily Times*, June 12. Article on file with author.

——— 2014. "Facing Sexual Orientation Realities." *Nation*, January 17. http://mwnation.com/facing-sexual-orientation-realities/.

Chinoko, Clement. 2012. "Lesbians Engage." *Sunday Times*, May 20, 1, 3.

Chinsinga, Blessings. 2012. "Of Gay Rights and Section 65." *Sunday Times*, June 10, 7.

Chinyama, Portia. 1996. "I Should Have Been a Boy." *Nation*, September 20, 15.

Chipalasa, Mike. 2010. "Norway Comments on Gay Arrest." *Daily Times*, March 8, 3.

Chipiri, Chipiri wa. 2012. "Criticism of JB's Stance on Gay Rights Unfair." *Malawi News*, May 26–June 1, 7.

Chisambo, Edward. 2010. "Gay Issues Refusing to Die." *Malawi News*, May 15–21, 14.

Chitando, Ezra and Adriaan van Klinken, eds. 2016. *Christianity and Controversies over Homosexuality in Contemporary Africa*. New York: Routledge.

Chiumia, Thom. 2015. "Malawi Marriage Bill Spurns Same-Sex Liaisons." *Nyasa Times*, February 17. www.nyasatimes.com/malawi-marriage-bill-spurn-same-sex-liasons/.

Chua, Lynette J. 2012. "Pragmatic Resistance, Law, and Social Movements in Authoritarian States: The Case of Gay Collective Action in Singapore." *Law & Society Review* 46(4): 713–748.

"Church Disowns Gay Couple." 2012. *Nation*, January 14. http://mwnation.com/church-disowns-gay-couple/.

Clough, Patricia Ticineto. 2010. "The Case of Sociology: Governmentality and Methodology." *Critical Inquiry* 36(4): 627–641.

Clough, Patricia Ticineto and Craig Willse. 2010. "Gendered Security/National Security: Political Branding and Population Racism." *Social Text* 105: 45–63.

Cohen, Cathy J. 1997. "Punks, Bulldaggers, and Welfare Queens: The Radical Potential of Queer Politics?" *GLQ* 3(4): 437–465.

Coly, Ayo A. 2013. "Introduction." *African Studies Review* 56(2): 21–30.

Colyvas, Jeannette A. and Stefan Jonsson. 2011. "Ubiquity and Legitimacy: Disentangling Diffusion and Institutionalization." *Sociological Theory* 29(1): 27–53.

Comaroff, Jean and John L. Comaroff. 2006. "Preface." In *Law and Disorder in the Postcolony*, edited by Jean Comaroff and John L. Comaroff, vii–x. Chicago: University of Chicago Press.

"Constitution Clear on Gay Rights, Politicians Aren't." 2013. *Daily Times*, November 19. Article on file with author.

Cooper, Helene and Thomas Gibbons-Neff. 2018. "New Policy Lets Transgender Troops Stay in Service, but with Restrictions." *New York Times*, March 24, A13.

Currier, Ashley. 2010. "Political Homophobia in Postcolonial Namibia." *Gender & Society* 24(1): 110–129.

2011. "Decolonizing the Law: LGBT Organizing in Namibia and South Africa." *Studies in Law, Politics, and Society* 54: 17–44.

2012. "The Aftermath of Decolonization: Gender and Sexual Dissidence in Postindependence Namibia." *Signs: Journal of Women in Culture and Society* 37(2): 441–467.

2012. *Out in Africa: LGBT Organizing in Namibia and South Africa*. Minneapolis: University of Minnesota Press.

2015. "Transgender Invisibility in Namibian and South African LGBT Organizing." *Feminist Formations* 27(1): 91–117.

Currier, Ashley and Joëlle M. Cruz. 2014. "Civil Society and Sexual Struggles in Africa." In *The Handbook of Civil Society in Africa*, edited by Ebenezer Obadare, 337–360. New York: Springer.

2016. "Religious Inspiration: Indigenous Mobilisation against LGBTI Rights in Postconflict Liberia." In *Public Religion and the Politics of Homosexuality in Africa*, edited by Adriaan van Klinken and Ezra Chitando, 146–162. New York: Routledge.

2018. "The Politics of Pre-Emption: Mobilisation against LGBT Rights in Liberia." *Social Movement Studies*. www.tandfonline.com/doi/abs/10.1080/14742837.2017.1319265.

Currier, Ashley and Matthew Thomann. 2016. "Gender and Sexual Diversity Organizing in Africa." In *Understanding Southern Social Movements: A Quest to Bypass Northern Social Movement Theory*, edited by Simin Fadaee, 87–103. New York: Routledge.

Currier, Ashley and Tara McKay. 2017. "Pursuing Social Justice through Public Health: Gender and Sexual Diversity Activism in Malawi." *Critical African Studies* 9(1): 71–90.

Damala, Cydric. 2010. "Government's Threats to Ban Some NGOs Are a Timely Disciplinary Measure." *Sunday Times*, March 28, 8–9.

Dean, Jodi. 1996. *Solidarity of Strangers: Feminism after Identity Politics*. Berkeley: University of California Press.

Dearham, Kaitlin. 2013. "NGOs and Queer Women's Activism in Nairobi." In *Queer African Reader*, edited by Sokari Ekine and Hakima Abbas, 186–202. Dakar, Senegal: Pambazuka.

Decoteau, Claire Laurier. 2013. "The Crisis of Liberation: Masculinity, Neoliberalism, and HIV/AIDS in Postapartheid South Africa." *Men and Masculinities* 16(2): 139–159.

DeJong, Christina and Eric Long. 2014. "The Death Penalty as Genocide: The Persecution of 'Homosexuals' in Uganda." In *Handbook of LGBT Communities, Crime, and Justice*, edited by Dana Peterson and Vanessa R. Panfil, 339–362. New York: Springer.

Desai, Gaurav. 2001. "Out in Africa." In *Postcolonial, Queer: Theoretical Intersections*, edited by John C. Hawley, 139–164. Albany: State University of New York Press.

Dicklitch, Susan, Berwood Yost, and Bryan M. Dougan. 2012. "Building a Barometer of Gay Rights (BGR): A Case Study of Uganda and the Persecution of Homosexuals." *Human Rights Quarterly* 34(2): 448–471.

Dionne, Kim Yi and Boniface Dulani. 2012. "Constitutional Provisions and Executive Succession: Malawi's 2012 Transition in Comparative Perspective." *African Affairs* 112(446): 111–137.

"Don't Impose Projects on People – ADRA." 2010. *Daily Times*, April 27, 4.

Douglas, Mary. 1966. *Purity and Danger: An Analysis of Concepts of Pollution and Taboo*. New York: Praeger.

Downey, Dennis J. and Deana A. Rohlinger. 2008. "Linking Strategic Choice with Macro-Organizational Dynamics: Strategy and Social Movement Articulation." *Research in Social Movements, Conflicts, and Change* 28: 3–38.

Duggan, Lisa. 2003. *The Twilight of Equality? Neoliberalism, Cultural Politics, and the Attack on Democracy*. Boston: Beacon Press.

Duggan, Marian. 2011. *Queering Conflict: Examining Lesbian and Gay Experiences of Homophobia in Northern Ireland*. New York: Routledge.

Dulani, Boniface. 2009. "Nurtured from the Pulpit: The Emergence and Growth of Malawi's Democracy Movement." In *Movers and Shakers: Social Movements in Africa*, edited by Stephen Ellis and Ineke van Kessel, 138–155. Boston: Brill.

Dulani, Boniface, Gift Sambo, and Kim Yi Dionne. 2016. "Good Neighbours? Africans Express High Levels of Tolerance for Many, but Not for All." *Afrobarometer Dispatch* 74: 1–27. http://afrobarometer.org/publications/tolerance-in-africa/.

Dwyer, Peter and Leo Zeilig. 2012. *African Struggles Today: Social Movements since Independence*. Chicago: Haymarket Books.

Dzinyemba, Heinrich H. 2005. "Homosexuality Is Unnecessary and Undesirable." *Malawi News*, February 19–25, 6.

Earl, Jennifer. 2003. "Tanks, Tear Gas, and Taxes: Toward a Theory of Movement Repression." *Sociological Theory* 21(1): 44–68.

2011. "Political Repression: Iron Fists, Velvet Gloves, and Diffuse Control." *Annual Review of Sociology* 37: 261–284.

Edelman, Murray. 1988. *Constructing the Political Spectacle*. Chicago: University of Chicago Press.

Edwards, Bob and Sam Marullo. 1995. "Organizational Mortality in a Declining Social Movement: The Demise of Peace Movement Organizations in the End of the Cold War Era." *American Sociological Review* 60(6): 908–927.

Effler, Erika Summers. 2010. *Laughing Saints and Righteous Heroes: Emotional Rhythms in Social Movement Groups*. Chicago: University of Chicago Press.

El-Tayeb, Fatima. 2011. *European Others: Queering Ethnicity in Postnational Europe*. Minneapolis: University of Minnesota Press.

Engelke, Matthew. 1999. "'We Wondered What Human Rights He Was Talking About': Human Rights, Homosexuality, and the Zimbabwe International Book Fair." *Critique of Anthropology* 19(3): 289–314.

Englund, Harri. 2006. *Prisoners of Freedom: Human Rights and the African Poor*. Berkeley: University of California Press.

Enloe, Cynthia. 2016. *Globalization and Militarism: Feminists Make the Link*. Second edition. Lanham, MD: Rowman and Littlefield.

Epprecht, Marc. 2008. *Heterosexual Africa? The History of an Idea from the Age of Exploration to the Age of AIDS*. Athens: Ohio University Press.

2012. "Sexual Minorities, Human Rights, and Public Health Strategies in Africa." *African Affairs* 111(443): 223–243.

2013. *Hungochani: The History of a Dissident Sexuality in Southern Africa*. Second edition. Montréal, Canada: McGill-Queen's University Press.

2013. *Sexuality and Social Justice in Africa: Rethinking Homophobia and Forging Resistance*. New York: Zed.

2014. "Is Africa the Most Homophobic Continent?" CNN, February 28. www.cnn.com/2014/02/28/opinion/uganda-anti-gay-law-marc-epprecht/.

Esacove, Anne. 2016. *Modernizing Sexuality: US HIV Prevention in Sub-Saharan Africa*. New York: Oxford University Press.

Essig, Laurie. 2014. "'Bury Their Hearts': Some Thoughts on the Specter of Homosexuality Haunting Russia." *QED: A Journal of GLBTQ World-making* 1(3): 39–58.

Fay, Heather, Stefan D. Baral, Gift Trapence, Felistus Motimedi, Eric Umar, Scholastika Iipinge, Friedel Dausab, Andrea Wirtz, and Chis Beyrer. 2011. "Stigma, Health Care Access, and HIV Knowledge among Men Who Have Sex with Men in Malawi, Namibia, and Botswana." *AIDS and Behavior* 15(6): 1088–1097.

Feder, J. Lester. 2013. "Human Rights Campaign's Move into International Work Puts Global LGBT Advocates on Edge." *BuzzFeed*, November 5. www.buzzfeed.com/lesterfeder/human-rights-campaigns-move-into-international-work-puts-glo#1pt01xk.

Ferree, Myra Marx. 2004. "Soft Repression: Ridicule, Stigma, and Silencing in Gender-Based Movements." *Research in Social Movements, Conflict, and Change* 25: 85–101.

Fetner, Tina. 2008. *How the Religious Right Shaped Lesbian and Gay Activism*. Minneapolis: University of Minnesota Press.

"First Lesbian Priest Comes Out." 1995. *Nation*, March 21, 5.

Foucault, Michel. 1978. *The History of Sexuality, Volume 1: An Introduction*. New York: Vintage.

Frank, David John and Dana Moss. 2017. "Cross-National and Longitudinal Variations in the Criminal Regulation of Sex, 1965–2005." *Social Forces* 95(3): 941–969.

"From Victim to Father of Street Kids." 2013. *Nation*, January 27. http://mwnation.com/from-victim-to-father-of-street-kids/.

Gabay, Clive. 2014. "Two 'Transitions': The Political Economy of Joyce Banda's Rise to Power and the Related Role of Civil Society Organisations in Malawi." *Review of African Political Economy* 41(141): 374–388.

2015. *Exploring an African Civil Society: Development and Democracy in Malawi, 1994–2014*. Lanham, MD: Lexington Books.

Gallo, Pia Grassivaro, Debora Moro, and Miriam Manganoni. 2009. "Female Genital Modifications in Malawi: Culture, Health, and Sexuality." In *Circumcision and Human Rights*, edited by George C.

Denniston, Frederick Mansfield Hodges, and Marilyn Fayre Milos, 83–95. New York: Springer.

Gaudio, Rudolf Pell. 2009. *Allah Made Us: Sexual Outlaws in an Islamic African City*. Malden, MA: Blackwell.

——— 2014. "Dire Straights in Nigeria." *Transition* 114: 60–68.

"Gays in Botswana Are Upset." 1995. *Daily Times*, December 19, 9.

Gevisser, Mark. 2014. "Love in Exile." *Guardian*, November 27. www.the guardian.com/news/2014/nov/27/-sp-transgender-relationship-jail-exile-tiwonge-chimbalanga.

Gill-Peterson, Julian. 2012. "Haunting the Queer Spaces of AIDS: Remembering ACT UP/New York and an Ethics for an Endemic." *GLQ* 19(3): 279–300.

Gilman, Lisa. 2009. *The Dance of Politics: Gender, Performance, and Democratization in Malawi*. Philadelphia: Temple University Press.

"Give Gays a Break." 2010. *Sunday Times*, May 23, 6.

Goddard, Keith. 2004. "A Fair Representation: GALZ and the History of the Gay Movement in Zimbabwe." *Journal of Gay and Lesbian Social Services* 16(1): 75–98.

Gould, Deborah B. 2009. *Moving Politics: Emotion and ACT UP's Fight against AIDS*. Chicago: University of Chicago Press.

——— 2010. "On Affect and Protest." In *Political Emotions*, edited by Janet Staiger, Ann Cvetkovich, and Ann Reynolds, 18–44. New York: Routledge.

"Government Asked to Finance Civil Society." 2002. *Daily Times*, March 6, 2.

"Government Condemns NGOs." 2001. *Daily Times*, December 21, 1.

Graff, Agnieska. 2010. "Looking at Pictures of Gay Men: Political Uses of Homophobia in Contemporary Poland." *Public Culture* 22(3): 583–603.

de Gruchy, John W. 1997. "Christian Witness at a Time of African Renaissance." *The Ecumenical Review* 49(4): 476–482.

Gruszczynska, Anna. 2009. "Sowing the Seeds of Solidarity in Public Space: Case Study of the Poznan March of Equality." *Sexualities* 12(3): 312–333.

Gunya, Fatsani. 2010. "Donors, Rights Groups Wrong to Condemn Gays Sentence." *Nation*, May 27, 6.

——— 2010. "More Speak on Presidential Pardon." *Nation*, June 1, 4.

Gwayazani, Peter. 2006. "Anglican Bishop Denies Being Gay." *Daily Times*, February 13, 3.

Gwede, Wanga. 2011. "Malawi Refuses 'Homosexuality' Aid Condition." *Nyasa Times*, February 9. Article on file with author.

——— 2012. "Malawi Lesbian Couple Won't Be Prosecuted." *Nyasa Times*, May 21. www.nyasatimes.com/malawi-lesbian-couple-wont-be-prosecuted-justice-minister/.

Haines, Herbert H. 1984. "Black Radicalization and the Funding of Civil Rights: 1957–1970." *Social Problems* 32(1): 31–43.

Halperin, David M. 1995. *Saint Foucault: Towards a Gay Hagiography.* New York: Oxford University Press.

Haraway, Donna. 1988. "Situated Knowledges: The Science Question in Feminism and the Privilege of Partial Perspective." *Feminist Studies* 14(3): 575–599.

Hassett, Miranda K. 2007. *Anglican Communion in Crisis: How Episcopal Dissidents and Their African Allies Are Reshaping Anglicanism.* Princeton, NJ: Princeton University Press.

Heng, Geraldine. 1997. "'A Great Way to Fly': Nationalism, the State, and the Varieties of Third-World Feminism." In *Feminist Genealogies, Colonial Legacies, Democratic Futures*, edited by M. Jacqui Alexander and Chandra Talpade Mohanty, 30–45. New York: Routledge.

Heng, Geraldine and Janadas Devan. 1992. "State Fatherhood: The Politics of Nationalism, Sexuality, and Race in Singapore." In *Nationalisms and Sexualities*, edited by Andrew Parker, Mary Russo, Doris Sommer, and Patricia Yaeger, 343–364. New York: Routledge.

Herdt, Gilbert. 2009. "Introduction." In *Moral Panics, Sex Panics: Fear and the Fight Over Sexual Rights*, edited by Gilbert Herdt, 1–46. New York: New York University Press.

Herek, Gregory M. 2004. "Beyond 'Homophobia': Thinking about Sexual Prejudice." *Sexuality Research & Social Policy* 1(2): 6–24.

Hildebrandt, Timothy. 2012. "Development and Division: The Effect of Transnational Linkages and Local Politics on LGBT Activism in China." *Journal of Contemporary China* 21(77): 845–862.

Hoad, Neville. 2007. *African Intimacies: Race, Homosexuality, and Globalization.* Minneapolis: University of Minnesota Press.

   2016. "Queer Customs against the Law." *Research in African Literatures* 47(2): 9–11.

Hoggett, Paul and Simon Thompson. 2012. "Introduction." In *Politics and the Emotions: The Affective Turn in Contemporary Political Studies*, edited by Simon Thompson and Paul Hoggett, 1–19. New York: Continuum.

Holzhacker, Ronald. 2013. "State-Sponsored Homophobia and the Denial of the Right of Assembly in Central and Eastern Europe: The 'Boomerang' and the 'Ricochet' between European Organizations and Civil Society to Uphold Human Rights." *Law & Policy* 35(1–2): 1–28.

"Homosexual Jailed." 1998. *Daily Times*, July 30, 2.

Hooper, Charlotte. 2001. *Manly States: Masculinities, International Relations, and Gender Politics.* New York: Columbia University Press.

Howe, Cymene. 2013. *Intimate Activism: The Struggle for Sexual Rights in Postrevolutionary Nicaragua.* Durham, NC: Duke University Press.

Htun, Mala. 2003. *Sex and the State: Abortion, Divorce, and the Family under Latin American Dictatorships and Democracies.* New York: Cambridge University Press.

Human Rights Watch. 2014. "Uganda: Anti-Homosexuality Act's Heavy Toll." May 14. www.hrw.org/news/2014/05/14/uganda-anti-homosexuality-acts-heavy-toll.

———. 2015. *The Issue Is Violence: Attacks on LGBT People on Kenya's Coast.* New York: Human Rights Watch. www.hrw.org/sites/default/files/report_pdf/kenya0915_4upr.pdf.

———. 2016. "Dignity Debased: Forced Anal Examinations in Homosexuality Prosecutions." July 12. www.hrw.org/report/2016/07/12/dignity-debased/forced-anal-examinations-homosexuality-prosecutions.

———. 2016. "'Tell Me Where I Can Be Safe': The Impact of Nigeria's Same Sex Marriage (Prohibition) Act." www.hrw.org/sites/default/files/report_pdf/nigeria1016_web.pdf.

Human Rights Watch and the International Gay and Lesbian Rights Commission (IGLHRC). 2003. *More Than a Name: State-Sponsored Homophobia and Its Consequences in Southern Africa.* New York: HRW and IGLHRC. www.iglhrc.org/binary-data/ATTACHMENT/file/000/000/160-1.pdf.

Incite! Women of Color against Violence, ed. 2009. *The Revolution Will Not Be Funded: Beyond the Non-Profit Industrial Complex.* Boston: South End Press.

Iob, Emilie. 2013. "Challenges Remain for LGBT in South Africa." *Voice of America*, May 1. www.voanews.com/content/challenges-remain-for-lgbt-in-south-africa/1652570.html.

Ireland, Patrick R. 2013. "A Macro-Level Analysis of the Scope, Causes, and Consequences of Homophobia in Africa." *African Studies Review* 56(2): 47–66.

Irvine, Janice. 2008. "Transient Feelings: Sex Panics and the Politics of Emotions." *GLQ* 14(1): 1–40.

Izugbara, Chimaroke O. and Jerry Okal. 2011. "Performing Heterosexuality: Male Youth, Vulnerability, and HIV in Malawi." In *Men and Development: Politicising Masculinities*, edited by Andrea Cornwall, Jerker Edström, and Alan Greig, 21–32. New York: Zed.

Janoff, Douglas Victor. 2005. *Pink Blood: Homophobic Violence in Canada.* Toronto: University of Toronto Press.

Jensen, Steffen and Lars Buur. 2004. "Everyday Policing and the Occult: Notions of Witchcraft, Crime, and 'the People.'" *African Studies* 63(2): 193–211.

Jere, Peter Qeko. 2006. "Homosexuality and the Bible." *Daily Times*, July 9, 7.

Jimu, Jacob. 2005. "Homosexuality under Scrutiny." *Weekend Nation*, April 9–10, 24–25.

Johnson, Janet Elise and Aino Saarinen. 2013. "Twenty-First Century Feminisms under Repression: Gender Regime Change and the Women's Crisis Center Movement in Russia." *Signs* 38(3): 543–567.

Johnston, Nicole and Riaan Wolmarans. 2008. "Xenophobic Violence Grips Johannesburg." *Mail & Guardian*, May 18. https://mg.co.za/article/2008-05-18-xenophobic-violence-grips-johannesburg/.

Jolofani, Dorothy and Joseph DeGabriele. 1999. *HIV/AIDS in Malawi Prisons: A Study of HIV Transmission and the Care of Prisoners with HIV/AIDS in Zomba, Blantyre, and Lilongwe Prisons*. Paris: Penal Reform International.

Judge, Melanie. 2018. *Blackwashing Homophobia: Violence and the Politics of Sexuality, Gender, and Race*. New York: Routledge.

Judge, Melanie, Anthony Manion, and Shaun de Waal, eds. 2008. *To Have and to Hold: The Making of Same-Sex Marriage in South Africa*. Johannesburg: Fanele.

"Judge Speaks on Gay Rights." 2014. *Nation*, January 20. https://mwnation.com/judge-speaks-on-gay-rights/.

Juma, Chikondi. 2012. "DPP Wants Kasambara Fired." *Daily Times*, November 12, 1, 3.

——— 2012. "JB Will Not Take a Stand on Homosexuality—State House." *Daily Times*, November 16, 2.

Justice, Daniel Heath. 2010. "Notes toward a Theory of Anomaly." *GLQ* 16(1–2): 207–242.

Kabwila, Jessie. 2013. "Seeing beyond Colonial Binaries: Unpacking Malawi's Homosexuality Discourse." In *Queer African Reader*, edited by Sokari Ekine and Hakima Abbas, 377–392. Dakar, Senegal: Pambazuka.

Kabwila Kapasula, Jessie. 2006. "Challenging Sexual Stereotypes: Is Cross-Dressing 'Un-African?'" *Feminist Africa* 6: 69–72.

Kachere, Reen. 2005. "No to Homosexuality." *Nation*, February 14, 19.

Kaingana, Akimu. 1997. "NGOs to Adopt Strict Code." *Daily Times*, March 27, 2.

Kainja, Jimmy. 2013. "Giving Hypocrisy Its Meaning: Child Abuse in a 'God-Fearing' Malawi." *Nyasa Times*, July 31. www.nyasatimes.com/giving-hypocrisy-its-meaning-child-abuse-in-a-god-fearing-malawi/.

Kakande, Austin. 2012. "CSOs on JB's Neck over Homosexual Laws: She Should Be Last Person to Promote Homophobia – Undule." *Malawi Voice*, October 1. Article on file with author.

Kaler, Amy. 2003. *Running after Pills: Politics, Gender, and Contraception in Colonial Zimbabwe*. Portsmouth, NH: Heinemann.

2004. "The Moral Lens of Population Control: Condoms and Controversies in Southern Malawi." *Studies in Family Planning* 35(2): 105–115.

"Kaliati's Sex Assault Claims on Kasambara Rubbished." 2012. *Nyasa Times*, February 14. www.nyasatimes.com/kaliatis-sex-assault-claims-on-kasambara-rubbished/.

Kalizang'oma, Paul. 2004. "Consider Prisoners with Condoms." *Nation*, May 24, 15.

Kalua, Taweni. 2007. "Vera against Gay Marriages." *Nation*, August 27, 4.

"Kambalazaza Denounces Gay Marriages." 2007. *Weekend Nation*, February 10–11, 12.

Kamlomo, Gabriel. 1998. "Prisoners' Plight: Who Will Listen?" *Nation*, June 3, 15.

2000. "Gays, Lesbians Surface in Malawi." *Daily Times*, August 24, 2.

2012. "CSOs Demand All Inclusive Govt." *Daily Times*, April 11, 4.

2012. "NGOs Decry Homophobia in Malawi." *Daily Times*, May 21, 4.

Kampondeni, Tiwonge. 2005. "Rastas against Homosexuality." *Daily Times*, March 11, 4.

Kana, Clement. 2010. "Thumbs Up for Usiwa Usiwa!" *Nation*, May 28, 15.

Kandiero, Caroline. 2011. "Bingu Makes War Threats." *Daily Times*, August 26, 1, 3.

Kanyinji, Jeffrey. 2006. "Big No to Homosexuality." *Daily Times*, January 1, 15.

Kaoma, Kapya J. 2013. "The Marriage of Convenience: The US Christian Right, African Christianity, and Postcolonial Politics of Sexual Identity." In *Global Homophobia: States, Movements, and the Politics of Oppression*, edited by Meredith L. Weiss and Michael J. Bosia, 75–102. Urbana: University of Illinois Press.

Kasakula, George. 2012. "Can JB Govt Decide on Gays?" *Weekend Nation*, November 10, 31.

Kasakura, Archibald. 2012. "Contact Group/NGOs Set on Showdown over Timeframe." *Malawi News*, January 28–February 3, 2–3.

2012. "German Govt for Minority Rights." *Daily Times*, November 27, 4.

2012. "JB Won't Push MPs on Same Sex Law." *Malawi News*, May 26–June 1, 1–2.

Kashoti, Dickson. 2010. "UK, US Condemn Gays' 14-Year Sentence." *Daily Times*, May 21, 3.

2011. "Expelled Malawi Envoy Jets In." *Daily Times*, May 4, 1, 3.

2011. "Expulsion of British Envoy Unfortunate – EU." *Daily Times*, May 9, 2.

Kashoti, Dickson and Simeon Maganga. 2011. "No Demos, Bingu Warns." *Daily Times*, August 12, 1, 3.

Kassé, Mouhamadou Tidiane. 2013. "Mounting Homophobic Violence in Senegal." In *Queer African Reader*, edited by Sokari Ekine and Hakima Abbas, 262–272. Dakar, Senegal: Pambazuka.

Kasunda, Anthony. 2005. "High Court Throws Out Anglican Case." *Daily Times*, May 26, 1, 3.

———. 2006. "Anglican Bishop's Offices Still Closed." *Daily Times*, March 7, 2.

———. 2011. "Mwakasungula Gets Death Threats." *Nation*, March 25, 1–2.

———. 2012. "Accept Sexual Minorities, Malawians Urged." *Nation*, May 17, 4.

———. 2012. "Govt's Gay Hypocrisy." *Nation*, February 24, 1–3.

———. 2012. "Donors Caution on Gay Rights." *Nation*, October 8, 1–2.

———. 2012. "State Holds on to Sodomy Suspect." *Nation*, January 12, 3.

———. 2013. "Referendum on Same Sex Wrong." *Nation*, October 25, 3.

———. 2014. "MHRC Under Fire over Gay Rights." *Nation*, January 25. https://mwnation.com/mhrc-underfire-over-gay-rights/.

Kasunda, Anthony and George Singini. 2012. "Satan Using Bingu—NGOs." *Nation*, January 2, 2.

Kasunda, Grey. 2010. "Homosexuality Is Alien to Malawi." *Nation*, January 8, 4.

———. 2010. "Malawians Want Kids Off Streets." *Nation*, January 12, 4.

———. 2010. "Referendum, Solution to Homosexuality." *Nation*, January 5, 4.

Kawina, Bartholomew. 2010. "Balaka Differs on Gays Pardon." *Nation*, June 3, 6.

———. 2010. "More Support 14-Year Gays Sentence." *Nation*, May 26, 6.

Keating, Christine (Cricket). 2013. "Conclusion: On the Interplay of State Homophobia and Homoprotectionism." In *Global Homophobia: States, Movements, and the Politics of Oppression*, edited by Meredith L. Weiss and Michael J. Bosia, 246–254. Urbana: University of Illinois Press.

Keck, Margaret E. and Kathryn Sikkink. 1998. *Activists beyond Borders: Advocacy Networks in International Politics*. Ithaca, NY: Cornell University Press.

Kenani, Stanley Onjezani. 2005. "Away with Homosexuality." *Nation*, February 4, 15.

———. 2012. "Love on Trial." In *The Caine Prize for African Writing 2012*, edited by Caine Prize, 49–66. Oxford: New Internationalist.

Khanje, Thom. 2010. "Donors Speak on Gay Rights." *Daily Times*, March 17, 1, 3.

Khunga, Suzgo. 2005. "Legalise Homosexuality, Parliament Asked." *Sunday Times*, November 20, 3.

———. 2010. "Anti-Gay Movement Formed." *Daily Times*, March 30, 3.

———. 2010. "Bingu Stops Comments on Gays." *Daily Times*, June 3, 1, 3.

———. 2010. "Gay Couple Pardoned." *Sunday Times*, May 30, 1, 3.

2010. "Ministry Warns Defiant Children." *Sunday Times*, April 4, 2.

2010. "UNAIDS, Global Fund Bosses Discuss Gays with Bingu." *Daily Times*, May 26, 4.

2011. "Malawi Expels British Envoy." *Daily Times*, April 28, 3–4.

2012. "'For Sale' Posters Pasted at Undule's Home, Office." *Daily Times*, March 6, 3.

2013. "Thugs Target CEDEP, Steal Office Equipment." *Nation*, October 14, 3.

Khunga, Suzgo and Macdonald Thom. 2011. "Bishop Bvumbwe Warns on UK Ties." *Daily Times*, April 29, 3.

Kiama, Wanjira. 1998. "Where Are Kenya's Homosexuals?" *Nation*, November 18, 5.

Klausen, Susanne M. 2015. *Abortion under Apartheid: Nationalism, Sexuality, and Women's Reproductive Rights in South Africa*. New York: Oxford University Press.

Kluchin, Rebecca M. 2011. *Fit to Be Tied: Sterilization and Reproductive Rights in America, 1950–1980*. New Brunswick, NJ: Rutgers University Press.

Korycki, Katarzyna and Abouzar Nasirzadeh. 2013. "Homophobia as a Tool of Statecraft: Iran and Its Queers." In *Global Homophobia: States, Movements, and the Politics of Oppression*, edited by Meredith L. Weiss and Michael J. Bosia, 174–195. Urbana: University of Illinois Press.

Kulick, Don. 2009. "Can There Be an Anthropology of Homophobia?" In *Homophobias: Lust and Loathing across Time and Space*, edited by David A. B. Murray, 19–33. Durham, NC: Duke University Press.

Kumbani, Precious. 2016. "Angry Mob Kills Suspect in Dedza." *Nation*, March 30. http://mwnation.com/angry-mob-kills-suspect-in-dedza/.

2016. "Gays Claim Abuse in Hospitals." *Nation*, February 8. http://mwnation.com/gays-claim-abuse-in-hospitals/.

Kumwenda, Olivia. 2005. "Clergy Warns on Gaiety." *Nation*, April 8, 1–2.

LaFont, Suzanne. 2009. "Not Quite Redemption Song: LGBT-Hate in Jamaica." In *Homophobias: Lust and Loathing across Time and Space*, edited by David A. B. Murray, 105–122. Durham, NC: Duke University Press.

Lancaster, Roger N. 2011. *Sex Panic and the Punitive State*. Berkeley: University of California Press.

Langa, Joseph. 2000. "Prison Illtreatment Irks Prison Reform Committee." *Daily Times*, February 7, 4.

"Lawyers Urged to Promote Rights." 2012. *Daily Times*, June 26, 2.

Leonard, Ajussa. 2015. "After Being Gay: Monjeza Cries Out!" *Nation*, March 16. http://mwnation.com/after-being-gay-monjeza-cries-out/.

"Lesbian Claims Death, Rape Threats." 2013. *Daily Times*, February 10. Article on file with author.

"Lesbian Story Scheme by DPP, Court Grants Reporter Bail." 2012. *Nyasa Times*, May 20. www.nyasatimes.com/lesbian-story-scheme-by-dpp-court-grants-reporter-bail/.

Levitsky, Sandra. 2007. "Niche Activism: Constructing a Unified Movement Identity in a Heterogeneous Organizational Field." *Mobilization* 12(3): 271–286.

Ligomeka, Brian. 2001. "British National Arrested for Sodomy." African Eye News Service, November 21. http://allafrica.com/stories/20011121 0116.html.

Likongwe, Giles. 1997. "Government Should Inspect NGOs." *Daily Times*, February 19, 9.

Lind, Amy and Christine Keating. 2013. "Navigating the Left Turn: Sexual Justice and the Citizen Revolution in Ecuador." *International Feminist Journal of Politics* 15(4): 515–533.

Linden, Annette and Bert Klandermans. 2006. "Stigmatization and Repression of Extreme-Right Activism in the Netherlands." *Mobilization* 11(2): 213–228.

Lindsay, Jennie. 1986. "The Politics of Population Control in Namibia." *Review of African Political Economy* 13(36): 58–62.

López, Iris. 2008. *Matters of Choice: Puerto Rican Women's Struggle for Reproductive Freedom*. New Brunswick, NJ: Rutgers University Press.

Lorway, Robert. 2014. *Namibia's Rainbow Project: Gay Rights in an African Nation*. Bloomington: Indiana University Press.

Luibhéid, Eithne. 2002. *Entry Denied: Controlling Sexuality at the Border*. Minneapolis: University of Minnesota Press.

Luibhéid, Eithne and Sasha Khokha. 2001. "Building Alliances between Immigrant Rights and Queer Movements." In *Forging Radical Alliances across Difference: Coalition Politics for the New Millennium*, edited by Jill M. Bystydzienski and Steven P. Schacht, 77–90. Lanham, MD: Rowman & Littlefield.

Luirink, Bart and Madeleine Maurick. 2016. *Homosexuality in Africa: A Disturbing Love*. Soesterberg, Netherlands: Uitgeverij Aspekt.

Machado, Francis. 2005. "5 Years in Jail for Sodomy." *Daily Times*, February 25, 4.

Macharia, Keguro. 2010. "Homophobia in Africa Is Not a Single Story." *Guardian*, May 26. www.guardian.co.uk/commentisfree/2010/may/26/ homophobia-africa-not-single-story.

2011. "Yes, There Are Gays in Africa!" *New Black Magazine*, January 3. www.thenewblackmagazine.com/view.aspx?index=2527.

Maganga, Simeon. 2011. "Government Must Apologise to Britain." *Daily Times*, April 22, 1, 3.

———. 2012. "Kasambara Denies Suspending Gay Law." *Daily Times*, November 7, 3.

———. 2012. "Let Malawians Vote on Homosexuality." *Daily Times*, June 13, 2.

———. 2012. "Petra Queries Homosexuality Legalisation Hastened," *Daily Times*, May 21. Article on file with author.

———. 2012. "UK Engages JB on Human Rights." *Daily Times*, May 31, 1, 3.

Majono. 2010. "14 Years of 'Hell on Earth.'" *Sunday Times*, May 23, 10.

Makhumula, Emma. 2010. "Stop Associating Me with Monjeza." *Daily Times*, December 6, 2.

Makossah, Peter. 2003. "Jails Fertile Ground for Homosexuality." *Nation*, October 22, 3.

———. 2003. "Man Rapes Fellow Man." *Weekend Nation*, January 18–19, 3.

Makossah, Peter and Denis Mzembe. 2003. "Man Rapes Boy, 15." *Nation*, October 3, 3.

Malamula, Felix. 2005. "Anglicans Say No to Bishop-Elect." *Nation*, December 2, 3.

"Malawi Activists 'in Hiding after Mutharika Threat.'" 2011. BBC, July 25. www.bbc.co.uk/news/world-africa-14276599.

Malawi Human Rights and Resource Centre. 2004. "Draft Proposals for Constitutional Amendments: Submission to the Law Commission." September, Word document.

"Malawi Intensifies Prosecution of Gay Minorities and Their Defenders." 2010. *Voice of America*, January 6. www.voanews.com/content/malawi-gay-trial-1-7-2010-80880227/152738.html.

Malawi Law Commission. 2007. Report of the Law Commission on the Review of the Constitution. Law Commission Report No. 18.

"Malawi 'Lesbian Couple' Sue for K50, 'It Was Movie Shoot' – Lawyer." 2012. *Nyasa Times*, May 23. www.nyasatimes.com/malawi-lesbian-couple-sue-for-k50m-it-was-movie-shoot-lawyer/.

"Malawi Man Says 'I Do' in Brussels Gay Marriage." 2013. *Nyasa Times*, July 21. www.nyasatimes.com/malawi-man-says-i-do-in-brussels-gay-marriage/.

"Malawi Muslim Group Condemn Sheikh Tambuli, Gay Campaigners." 2013. *Nyasa Times*, October 24. www.nyasatimes.com/malawi-muslim-group-condemn-sheikh-tambuli-gay-campaigners/.

Malawi News Agency. 2000. "4 Prisoners Rape Fellow Inmate." *Daily Times*, January 7, 2.

———. 2000. "Man Gets 9 Months for Sodomy." *Daily Times*, October 10, 4.

———. 2003. "Malawi Anglicans Denounce Gay Bishop Appointment." *Daily Times*, August 11, 1, 3.

2009. "Woman in Court for Sexually Assaulting Maids." *Nation*, December 10, 6.

Malawi News Agency and Times Reporters. 2010. "Linking Aid to Gay Rights Is Absurd." *Daily Times*, May 24, 1, 3.

"Malawi Suspends Anti-Homosexuality Laws: 'Police Cannot Arrest Gays for Now.'" 2012. *Nyasa Times*, November 5. www.nyasatimes.com/malawi-suspends-anti-homosexuality-laws-police-cannot-arrest-gays-for-now/.

"Malawi to End Ban on Homosexual Acts, Says President Banda." 2012. *Nyasa Times*, May 18. www.nyasatimes.com/malawi-to-end-ban-0n-homosexual-acts-says-president-banda/.

Mama, Amina. 1998. "Khaki in the Family: Gender Discourses and Militarism in Nigeria." *African Studies Review* 41(2): 1–17.

Manyonganise, Molly. 2016. "'We Will Chop Their Heads Off': Homosexuality versus Religio-Political Grandstanding in Zimbabwe." In *Public Religion and the Politics of Homosexuality in Africa*, edited by Adriaan van Klinken and Ezra Chitando, 63–77. New York: Routledge.

Mapondera, Godfrey. 2005. "Any Malawians Who Are Gays?" *Sunday Times*, November 27, 24.

Mason, Gail and Stephen Tomsen. 1997. *Homophobic Violence*. Sydney, Australia: Hawkins Press.

Massad, Joseph. 2002. "Re-Orienting Desire: The Gay International and the Arab World." *Public Culture* 14(2): 361–385.

Mataka, Aubrey. 2004. "Sex and the Bible." *Weekend Nation*, July 10–11, 6.

Matebeni, Zethu. 2009. "Feminizing Lesbians, Degendering Transgender Men: A Model for Building Lesbian Feminist Thinkers and Leaders in Africa?" *Souls* 11 (3): 347–354.

Matebule, Tamanda. 2001. "CONGOMA Accuses NGOs of Misusing Donor Aid." *Daily Times*, September 11, 2.

Matonga, Golden. 2012. "DPP Presses Govt on Gays, Abortion." *Daily Times*, November 28, 1, 3.

2012. "Malawians See Hope in JB Speech." *Daily Times*, May 21. Article on file with author.

2015. "UN Summons NGO Board Chair over Squabble." *Nation*, October 18. http://mwnation.com/un-summons-ngo-board-chair-over-squabble/.

Mbembe, Achille. 2006. "On Politics as a Form of Expenditure." In *Law and Disorder in the Postcolony*, edited by Jean Comaroff and John L. Comaroff, 299–336. Chicago: University of Chicago Press.

McAdam, Doug and Dieter Rucht. 1993. "The Cross-National Diffusion of Movement Ideas." *Annals of the American Academy of Political and Social Science* 528: 56–74.

McCabe, Janice. 2009. "Racial and Gender Microaggressions on a Predominantly-White Campus: Experiences of Black, Latina/o, and White Undergraduates." *Race, Gender, & Class* 16(1–2): 133–151.

McClintock, Anne. 1995. *Imperial Leather: Race, Gender, and Sexuality in the Colonial Contest.* New York: Routledge.

McCormack, Mark. 2012. *The Declining Significance of Homophobia: How Teenage Boys Are Redefining Masculinity and Heterosexuality.* New York: Oxford University Press.

McCracken, John. 2012. *A History of Malawi, 1859–1966.* Rochester, NY: Boydell & Brewer.

Mchazime, Henry. 2010. "Government Slams NGOs." *Daily Times*, October 11, 3.

Mchila, Vales. 2010. "Malawi Has Rights, Too." *Daily Times*, May 24, 9.

Mchulu, Aubrey. 1996. "Law for NGOs Credibility, Integrity." *Nation*, June 4, 1.

1997. "NGOs Launch Code of Conduct." *Daily Times*, May 27, 2.

1999. "Muluzi Warns NGOs." *Nation*, October 6, 1, 3.

McKay, Tara. 2013. "Invisible Men: Constructing Men Who Have Sex with Men as a Priority at UNAIDS and Beyond." PhD dissertation. Los Angeles: University of California, Los Angeles, Department of Sociology.

McKay, Tara and Nicole Angotti. 2016. "Ready Rhetorics: Political Homophobia and Activist Discourses in Malawi, Nigeria, and Uganda." *Qualitative Sociology* 39(4): 397–420.

McNamara, Thomas. 2014. "Not the Malawi of Our Parents: Attitudes toward Homosexuality and Perceived Westernisation in Northern Malawi." *African Studies* 73(1): 84–106.

Mepschen, Paul and Jan Willem Duyvendak. 2012. "European Sexual Nationalisms: The Culturalization of Citizenship and the Sexual Politics of Belonging and Exclusion." *Perspectives on Europe* 42(1): 70–76.

Meyer, Doug. 2015. *Violence against Queer People: Race, Class, Gender, and the Persistence of Anti-LGBT Discrimination.* New Brunswick, NJ: Rutgers University Press.

Meylakhs, Peter. 2009. "Drugs and Symbolic Pollution: The Work of Cultural Logic in the Russian Press." *Cultural Sociology* 3(3): 377–395.

Mfune, Saustin Kazgeba. 2003. "On Homosexuality." *Weekend Nation*, August 16–17, 6.

2003. "On Homosexuality." *Weekend Nation*, August 23–24, 6.

Mgbako, Chi Adanna. 2016. *To Live Freely in This World: Sex Worker Activism in Africa.* New York: New York University Press.

Mgunda, Temwani. 2006. "NGOs: Achievers or Deceivers?" *Daily Times*, April 7, 27.

Mhango, Bright. 2012. "Are Gays Born or Made?" *Weekend Nation*, August 18, 22–23.

2012. "Please Accept Us." *Nation*, August 11, 20–21.

Mhango, George. 2012. "Government Has Taken Good Direction on Minority Rights." *Nation*, May 23, 1, 8.

2012. "Govt Should Take a Stand on Gays – Dausi." *Nation*, December 5, 1.

Milozi, Howard. 2012. "Sodomy Haunts Zomba Students." *Daily Times*, March 9. Article on file with author.

Mita, Cheu. 1999. "283 Sexual Offences Last Year." *Nation*, February 18, 3.

Mitchell, Timothy. 2006. "Society, Economy, and the State Effect." In *The Anthropology of the State: A Reader*, edited by Aradhana Sharma and Akhil Gupta, 169–186. Malden, MA: Blackwell.

Mizere, Agnes. 2010. "Churches Challenge Donors on Gays." *Daily Times*, March 19, 3.

2010. "Clinton Praises Local Gay Activists." *Sunday Times*, June 27, 3.

2010. "Encounter with a Malawian Drag Queen." *Sunday Times*, January 3, 10.

2010. "Sodomised Orphan Appeals for Justice." *Sunday Times*, April 4, 2.

2011. "Malawi Violating Human Rights Obligations – ICJ." *Daily Times*, February 11, 3.

2012. "Review Anti-Gay Laws." *Daily Times*, September 5, 2.

2012. "Where Are the Gays? – Chief Asks." *Sunday Times*, October 14, 4.

Mizere, Agnes and Suzgo Khunga. 2011. "Envoy Was Not Deported." *Sunday Times*, May 1, 1, 3.

Mizere, Agnes and Temwani Mgunda. 2011. "Don't Bring Foreign Cultures to MW: Bingu." *Daily Times*, May 11.

Mkandawire, Lucky. 2016. "MLS Wants PP's Msonda Probed for Gay Remarks." *Nation*, January 5. http://mwnation.com/mls-wants-pps-msonda-probed-for-gay-remarks/.

Mkhize, Nonhlanhla, Jane Bennett, Vasu Reddy, and Relebohile Moletsane. 2010. *The Country We Want to Live In: Hate Crimes and Homophobia in the Lives of Black Lesbian South Africans*. Cape Town, South Africa: HSRC Press.

Mkula, Charles. 2009. "Gays: Malawi's Dangerous Society." *Sunday Times*, October 11, 11.

Mlenga, Joe. 2012. "How Sociology Enriches Human Rights: The Case Study of Malawi's First Openly-Gay Couple." In *Beyond the Law: Multi-Disciplinary Perspectives on Human Rights*, edited by Frans Viljoen, 95–115. Pretoria, South Africa: Pretoria University Law Press.

Mmana, Deogratias. 2010. "Children's Court to Join Govt in Relocating Street Children." *Weekend Nation*, January 30, 6.

2010. "Exposed: Street Children Homosexually Abused." *Nation*, January 9, 1–4.

2011. "Homosexuals Deserve to Die – Apostle." *Weekend Nation*, April 30, 3.

Mmana, Deogratias and George Singini. 2012. "Clerics Query Same Sex Laws." *Nation*, May 22, 1–3.

Mohanty, Chandra Talpade. 2003. *Feminism without Borders: Decolonizing Theory, Practicing Solidarity*. Durham, NC: Duke University Press.

"Monjeza Dumps Aunt Tiwo for a Woman." 2010. *Nation*, June 8, 1–2.

Moreau, Julie and Ashley Currier. 2018. "Queer Dilemmas: LGBT Activism and International Funding." In *Queer Development Studies: A Reader*, edited by Corinne Mason, 223–238. New York: Routledge.

Morris, Rosalind C. 2006. "The Mute and the Unspeakable: Political Subjectivity, Violent Crime, and 'the Sexual Thing' in a South African Mining Community." In *Law and Disorder in the Postcolony*, edited by Jean Comaroff and John L. Comaroff, 57–101. Chicago: University of Chicago Press.

Mosse, George L. 1995. "Racism and Nationalism." *Nations and Nationalism* 1(2): 163–173.

Moya, Limbani. 1998. "Sickness and Death in Jail." *Malawi News*, June 6–12, 9.

Moyo, Judith. 2011. "Malawi Leader Says Homosexuals 'Worse than Dogs.'" May 16. www.southernafricalitigationcentre.org/2011/05/16/malawi-malawi-leader-says-homosexuals-worse-than-dogs/.

Mpaka, Charles. 2007. "Homosexuality in Malawi Real – Research." *Daily Times*, July 7, 2.

2007. "Q & A Saturday: Gift Trapence." *Malawi News*, April 14–20, 5.

2007. "Waiting in a Homosexual Closet." *Daily Times*, April 15, 14.

Mpaso, Paida. 2010. "Religious Leaders Support 'Gay' Ruling." *Nation*, May 23, 1.

Mponda, Felix. 2009. "Malawi Has 10,000 Gays – Expert." *Malawi News*, September 26–October 2, 3–4.

2012. "Blues Will Eat Humble Pie." *Daily Times*, May 20. Article on file with author.

Mpotazingwe, Max. 2010. "Gay Case Ruling March 22." *Daily Times*, February 19, 3.

Msibi, Thabo. 2011. "The Lies We Have Been Told: On (Homo)Sexuality in Africa." *Africa Today* 58(1): 56–67.

Msika, Burnet, Chrispine Ngwena, and Baxter Chimlambe. 2005. "MHRRC under Fire." *Nation*, February 9, 15.

Msiska, Karen. 2005. "Wanna Do Takes NGO Ills to Stage." *Nation*, March 16, 25.

2010. "Kandodo Upbeat on Donor Funding." *Daily Times*, April 2, 3.

Msiska, Karen and Suzgo Khunga. 2011. "Synod Condemns Government on UK Envoy Expulsion." *Daily Times*, May 2, 3.

Msosa, Alan. 2017. "Why Malawi Is Not (Currently) Repealing Anti-Gay Laws." University of Essex, Human Rights Centre Blog, April 26. https://hrcessex.wordpress.com/2017/04/26/why-malawi-is-not-currently-repealing-anti-gay-laws/.

Msowoya, Victoria. 1998. "Non Governmental Organisations Cry Out." *Daily Times*, April 1, 11.

1998. "Our Fellow Women Disappoint Us." *Malawi News*, August 22–28, 14.

Mtambo, Timothy and Gift Trapence. 2013. "On UDF, DPP Referendum Proposal." *Weekend Nation*, October 12, 7.

Mthawanji, Dyson. 2014. "CHRR Slams Politicians on Gay Rights." *Nation*, March 19. https://mwnation.com/chrr-slams-politicians-on-gay-rights/.

Mtumodzi, Chikumbutso. 1998. "Asian Arrested for Oral Sex." *Daily Times*, April 28, 2.

Mucciaroni, Gary. 2009. *Same Sex, Different Politics: Success and Failure in the Struggle over Gay Rights*. Chicago: University of Chicago Press.

"Mugabe Lashes Out at Gays, US Leaders." 1995. *Malawi News*, August 19–25, 3.

Muhariwa, Marcus. 2006. "Parliamentary Committee Rejects Homosexuality." *Sunday Times*, December 17, 2.

Muheya, Green. 2012. "Malawi Lesbian Couple Fake, Lawyer Says No Case." *Nyasa Times*, May 21. www.nyasatimes.com/malawi-lesbian-couple-fake-lawyer-says-no-case/.

Muholi, Zanele. 2004. "Thinking through Lesbian Rape." *Agenda* 61: 116–125.

Munthali, Ephraim. 2013. "40 Gays Take on Clergy." *Nation*, September 9, 1–3.

2013. "Sheikh Backs Gay Rights." *Nation*, October 20. http://mwnation.com/sheikh-backs-gay-rights/.

Munthali, Kondwani. 2010. "Leave Us Alone – Aunt Tiwo." *Nation*, June 3, 2.

2010. "Mulanje MP Blasts Gay Advocates." *Weekend Nation*, January 30, 4.

2011. "Accept Prostitutes, Gays, Urges Bishop." *Nation*, February 28, 1–2.

2011. "Gays Worse Than Dogs – Bingu." *Nation*, May 16, 2.

2011. "Police Used Lethal Force – Report." *Nation*, August 16, 2.

2011. "Slow Down Mr. President – NGOs." *Nation*, May 6, 1–2.

2011. "There's Plan to Attack Demos, Arrest Leaders – NGOs." *Nation*, July 19, 1–2.

Munthali, Kondwani and Anthony Kasunda. 2011. "PAC, MHRC Caution Government on Violence." *Nation*, July 19, 1–3.

Murray, David A. B., ed. 2009. *Homophobias: Lust and Loathing across Time and Space*. Durham, NC: Duke University Press.

Musa, Madalitso. 2011. "Bingu Okays Demonstrations: DPP Cadets Terror on the Loose." *Daily Times*, July 20, 1, 3.

2011. "Group Urges Bingu against Hate Speech." *Daily Times*, August 15, 4.

2011. "Malawians, EU Fault Government on UK Envoy." *Daily Times*, April 29, 3.

2011. "Rev. Sembereka's House Torched." *Daily Times*, September 12, 1, 3.

2012. "Repeal All Bad Laws – JB Told." *Daily Times*, April 25, 3.

2012. "UK Aid Not Tied to Gay Rights." *Daily Times*, June 1, 1, 3.

Muwamba, Emmanuel. 2010. "African NGOs Want Gay Suspects Released." *Nation*, February 1, 2.

2012. "JB Says Malawi Unlikely to Repeal Anti-Gay Laws." *Nation*, October 1, 3.

2012. "Nkhoma CCAP Synod Warns MPs on Gay Laws." *Nation*, June 3, 3.

2012. "UN Hopes Malawi Will Review Same Sex Laws." *Nation*, December 13, 2.

Mwafulirwa, Sangwani. 2005. "I Am Not Gay, Says Anglican Bishop." *Sunday Times*, September 18, 13.

Mwakasungula, Undule. 2013. "The LGBT Situation in Malawi: An Activist Perspective." In *Human Rights, Sexual Orientation, and Gender Identity in the Commonwealth: Struggles for Decriminalisation and Change*, edited by Corinne Lennox and Matthew Waites, 359–379. London: Institute of Commonwealth Studies. http://sas-space.sas.ac.uk/4824/9/13Mwakasungula_LGBTMalawiActivist.pdf.

Mwakasungula, Undule and Gift Trapence. 2012. "Anti-Gay Laws Must Be Reviewed!" *Weekend Nation*, December 15, 7.

2012. "Church Hypocrisy." *Weekend Nation*, November 17, 7.

2012. "Constitutional Rights and Public Opinion on Homosexuality in Malawi, Part I." *Weekend Nation*, October 13, 7.

2012. "Homosexuality, Constitutional Rights, and Public Opinion in Malawi, Part II." *Weekend Nation*, October 20, 7.

2012. "Homosexuality, Constitutional Rights, and Public Opinion in Malawi, Part III." *Weekend Nation*, October 27, 7.

2012. "Is the Church Ignorant of Gay Issues? (Part 1)." *Weekend Nation*, November 24, 7.

2012. "Letter from a Gay Man 'in Hiding.'" *Weekend Nation*, November 10, 7.

2012. "Living Together in Sexual Diversity." *Weekend Nation*, September 22, 7.

2012. "Malawi's Homophobic Culture." *Weekend Nation*, November 3, 7.

2012. "MIAA's Statement Is Total Misleading and Fabrication of Facts." *Weekend Nation*, December 29, 7.

2012. "Overcoming Homophobia May Save Lives." *Weekend Nation*, September 29, 7.

2012. "Politicisation of Gay Issue." *Weekend Nation*, December 8, 7.

2012. "Would Jesus Embrace Homosexuals?" *Weekend Nation*, December 22, 7.

Mwangi, Evan Maina. 2009. *Africa Writes Back to Self: Metafiction, Gender, Sexuality*. Albany: State University of New York Press.

Mwikya, Kenne. 2013. "The Media, the Tabloid, and the Uganda Homophobia Spectacle." In *Queer African Reader*, edited by Sokari Ekine and Hakima Abbas, 141–154. Dakar, Senegal: Pambazuka.

2014. "Unnatural and Un-African: Contesting Queer-Phobia by Africa's Political Leadership." *Feminist Africa* 19: 98–105.

Myers, Daniel J. 2008. "Ally Identity: The Politically Gay." In *Identity Work in Social Movements*, edited by Jo Reger, Daniel J. Myers, and Rachel L. Einwohner, 167–187. Minneapolis: University of Minnesota Press.

"My Take on Whether It Is Good for Malawi to Support Minority Rights." 2012. *Nation*, May 30, 8.

"My Take on Whether Malawians Are Justified to Deny Gay Relationships as a Right." 2012. *Nation*, July 11, 8.

"My Take on Whether Same Sex Relationships Should Be Decriminalised." 2012. *Nation*, June 20, 8.

Mzale, Dumbani. 2010. "Norway Tells Malawi to Respect Vulnerable Group." *Nation*, May 20, 1, 3.

Mzembe, Dennis. 2003. "Homosexuality Still a Scourge in Prisons." *Nation*, August 9–10, 3.

Mzunga, Bob. 2006. "Anglican Bishops Should Stand Firm." *Daily Times*, March 8, 8.

Mzungo, Jr., Watipaso. 2010. "Foreign Media Lies on Activists' Arrests." *Daily Times*, January 11, 4.

Namangale, Frank. 2002. "Briton Gets 12 Years for Sodomy." *Daily Times*, January 23, 1, 3.

2003. "Homosexuality Worsens HIV/AIDS Cases in Prison." *Daily Times*, May 28, 11.

2003. "Muluzi Pardons British Sodomite." *Daily Times*, May 20, 1.

2005. "Churches, NGO Slum Homosexuality Proposal." *Daily Times*, February 3, 4.

2010. "Aunt Tiwo Is a Man – Doctor." *Nation*, January 28, 3.

2010. "Aunt Tiwo's Fate March 22." *Nation*, February 19, 2.

2011. "Police Seize Gay Campaign Cloth." *Nation*, May 18, 3.

2011. "Rights Activists Raise Death Threats Alarm." *Nation*, March 2, 1–2.

2012. "It Is Cruel to Jail People for Being Unnatural – PP." *Weekend Nation*, May 26, 3–4.

2012. "Kasambara Sues IG, 10 Others." *Nation*, February 23, 1–2.

2012. "Petra against Repeal of Same Sex Law." *Nation*, May 21, 3.

2014. "Aunt Tiwo Finds New Love." *Nation*, October 26. http://mwnation.com/aunt-tiwo-finds-new-love/.

2014. "Court Throws Out AG's Application on Gays." *Nation*, January 21. https://mwnation.com/court-throws-out-ag's-application-on-gays/.

2014. "Join Gay Case or Face Lawsuit, MHRC Told." *Nation*, February 26. http://mwnation.com/join-gay-case-or-face-lawsuit-mhrc-told/.

2014. "MAM Calls for Death Penalty for Gays." *Nation*, February 2. http://mwnation.com/mam-calls-for-death-penalty-for-gays/.

2014. "Supreme Court Stops Proceedings on Gay Case." *Nation*, February 3. https://mwnation.com/supreme-court-stops-proceedings-on-gay-case/.

Nankhonya, Jacob. 2012. "NGOs 'Bark Like Dogs.'" *Sunday Times*, February 26, 3.

2013. "Centre for the Development of People (CEDEP) Offices Ransacked." *Daily Times*, October 14. Article on file with author.

2013. "Lesbian Comes Out in the Open." *Daily Times*, February 7. Article on file with author.

2015. "Malawi Xenophobia Victims Reach 3,200, Two Dead." *Nation*, April 21. http://mwnation.com/malawi-xenophobia-victims-reach-3-200-two-dead/.

2016. "Government Says Won't Change Policy on Gays." *Nation*, January 21. http://mwnation.com/government-says-wont-change-policy-on-gays/.

Nassah, Idriss Ali. 2005. "Things Stranger Than Fiction." *Sunday Times*, November 20, 4.

Ndashe, Sibongile. 2013. "The Single Story of 'African Homophobia' Is Dangerous for LGBTI Activism." In *Queer African Reader*, edited by Sokari Ekine and Hakima Abbas, 155–164. Dakar, Senegal: Pambazuka.

Ndau, Grace. 2012. "Police Arrests 5 Suspected 'Homosexuality Researchers.'" *Nation*, March 8, 4.

Ndzovu, Hassan J. 2016. "'Un-Natural,' 'Un-African,' and 'Un-Islamic': The Three Pronged Onslaught Undermining Homosexual Freedom in Kenya." In *Public Religion and the Politics of Homosexuality in Africa*, edited by Adriaan van Klinken and Ezra Chitando, 78–91. New York: Palgrave Macmillan.

Nel, Juan A. and Melanie Judge. 2008. "Exploring Homophobic Victimisation in Gauteng, South Africa: Issues, Impacts, and Responses." *Acta Criminologica* 21(3): 19–36.

Ngalawa, Harold. 1997. "NGOs Are Dictators." *Daily Times*, July 1, 3.

Ng'ambi, Maxwell. 2005. "Pro-Gay Bishop Rejected." *Daily Times*, December 2, 1, 3.

Ng'ombe, Sr., Maxwell. 1998. "Church Leaders Decision Was Wrong." *Daily Times*, May 27, 8.

"NGOs a Nightmare to Government." 2001. *Daily Times*, March 16, 15.

"NGOs Set New Rules." 1995. *Daily Times*, May 22, 1.

"NGOs Worried with Govt. Move." 1996. *Nation*, December 20, 3.

"NGO That Covers Nefarious Activities." 1997. *Malawi News*, January 11–17, 8.

Ngwira, Kandani. 2009. "Nkando Homophile Arrested." *Sunday Times*, December 6, 4.

———. 2014. "Malawi's Controversial Gay Law Case Gains High Level Support." *Daily Times*, January 21. Article on file with author.

Nhlane, Steven. 2010. "Chileka 'Lovebirds' Are Sick." *Malawi News*, January 2–8, 15.

Niebuhr, Gustav. 1998. "Anglican Conference Takes Tough Line on Homosexuals." *New York Times*, August 6, A12.

Njiragoma, Wycliffe. 2011. "Bingu Blasts Donors." *Daily Times*, March 21, 1.

———. 2011. "Bingu Responds to July 20 Petition." *Daily Times*, August 15, 1.

———. 2011. "Britain Warns Malawi Govt." *Daily Times*, April 20, 1, 3.

Nkamanga, Emily L. 1995. "Keep an Eye on NGOs." *Nation*, May 19, 9.

Nkhata, Mwiza J. and Mandala Mambulasa. 2007. "Should the Law Legalize Homosexuality?" *Daily Times*, February 4, 12–13.

Nkhoma-Somba, Wezzie. 2010. "Gays Get 14 Years." *Daily Times*, May 21, 1, 3.

———. 2010. "Gays to Appeal." *Daily Times*, May 27, 1, 3.

———. 2010. "Lawyer's Licence Affects Gays Case." *Daily Times*, February 4, 3.

———. 2012. "CHRR, CEDEP against Injunction Bill." *Sunday Times*, June 19, 3.

Nkolokosa, Jika. 2005. "We'll Talk Gay on the Right Day." *Daily Times*, February 2, 8.

Nossiter, Adam. 2013. "Senegal Cheers Its President for Standing Up to Obama on Same-Sex Marriage." *New York Times*, June 29, A6.

———. 2014. "Mob Attacks More Than a Dozen Gay Men in Nigeria's Capital." *New York Times*, February 16, A8.

Ntata, P. R. T., A. S. Muula, and S. Siziya. 2008. "Socio-Demographic Characteristics and Sexual Health Related Attitudes and Practices of Men Having Sex with Men in Central and Southern Malawi." *Tanzania Journal of Health Research* 10(3): 124–130.

Nthara, Eliah. 2010. "Address Plight of Street Children." *Nation*, January 11, 4.

——. 2010. "Court Right to Impose 14 Years on Gays." *Nation*, May 24, 4.

——. 2010. "Mixed Views on Legalising Homosexuality." *Nation*, January 4, 4.

Ntonya, George. 2000. "Good Prison Conditions a Far Cry." *Nation*, December 19, 11.

Nussbaum, Martha C. 2010. *From Disgust to Humanity: Sexual Orientation and Constitutional Law*. New York: Oxford University Press.

Nyadani, Daveson. 2009. "Same-Sex Sexuality and HIV/AIDS: A Perspective from Malawi." In *From Social Silence to Social Science: Same-Sex Sexuality, HIV and AIDS, and Gender in South Africa*, edited by Vasu Reddy, Theo Sandfort, and Laetitia Rispel, 137–142. Cape Town, South Africa: HSRC Press.

Nyangulu, Deborah. 2006. "Hooligans Attack Anglican Church." *Daily Times*, July 3, 2.

Nyangulu-Chipofya, Deborah. 2010. "No to Gays in Malawi – Movement." *Daily Times*, April 9, 1, 3.

Nyanzi, Stella. 2013. "Rhetorical Analysis of President Jammeh's Threats to Behead Homosexuals in the Gambia." In *Sexual Diversity in Africa: Politics, Theory, Citizenship*, edited by S. N. Nyeck and Marc Epprecht, 67–87. Montreal: McGill-Queen's University Press.

Nyeck, S. N. 2013. "Mobilizing against the Invisible: Erotic Nationalism, Mass Media, and the 'Paranoid Style' in Cameroon." In *Sexual Diversity in Africa: Politics, Theory, Citizenship*, edited by S. N. Nyeck and Marc Epprecht, 151–169. Montreal: McGill-Queen's University Press.

Nyirenda, Lizzie. 1998. "Churches Condemn FOCCESA Inclusion of Homosexuals." *Daily Times*, May 6, 3.

Nyirongo, Edwin. 2009. "Court Throws Out Anglican Church Case." *Nation*, May 13, 3.

——. 2011. "NGOs Selling Malawi for Money – Bingu." *Nation*, June 8, 4.

——. 2012. "Homosexuality Not Foreign – Kabwila-Kapasula." *Nation*, November 7, 3.

——. 2015. "Changing Police Perception towards Homosexuality." *Nation*, January 5. http://mwnation.com/changing-police-perception-towards-homosexuality/.

——. 2015. "Gay Men Claim Ill-Treatment." *Nation*, December 14. http://mwnation.com/gay-men-claim-ill-treatment/.

Nyong'o, Tavia. 2012. "Queer Africa and the Fantasy of Virtual Participation." *Women's Studies Quarterly* 40(1–2): 40–63.

Nyoni, Silvester. 2000. "30 Months IHL for Indecent Assault." *Daily Times*, August 25, 3.

Nyoni, Yolamu. 2006. "Legalise Homosexuality." *Daily Times*, January 1, 15.

Onaliyera. 2010. "Why Being Lenient on Defilers?" *Sunday Nation*, May 23.

Open-Minded Observer. 2002. "Homosexuality Is Happening." *Nation*, September 18, 13.

The Other Foundation. 2016. *Progressive Prudes: A Survey of Attitudes towards Homosexuality and Gender Non-Conformity in South Africa*. Johannesburg, South Africa: The Other Foundation. http://repository .hsrc.ac.za/bitstream/handle/20.500.11910/10161/9400.pdf?sequence= 1&isAllowed=y.

Otomani, Wadza. 2003. "Primates to Commission Anti-Gay Anglican Bishop." *Daily Times*, September 4, 5.

"Our Laws Need Harmonisation." 2010. *Sunday Times*, May 30, 4.

Oxford, Connie G. 2005. "Protectors and Victims in the Gender Regime of Asylum." *NWSA Journal* 17(3): 18–38.

———. 2013. "Queer Asylum: US Policies and Responses to Sexual Orientation and Transgendered Persecution." In *Gender, Migration, and Categorisation: Making Distinctions between Migrants in Western Countries, 1945–2010*, edited by Marlou Schrover and Deirdre M. Moloney, 128–148. Amsterdam: Amsterdam University Press.

Paliani, Penelope. 2001. "Amnesty International Petitions Government over Prison Sodomy." *Daily Times*, January 8, 2.

———. 2001. "Incredible Tales of Juvenile Prisoners." *Daily Times*, August 2, 13.

Pascoe, C. J. 2007. *Dude, You're a Fag: Masculinity and Sexuality in High School*. Berkeley: University of California Press.

Patton, Cindy. 2002. "Stealth Bombers of Desire: The Globalization of 'Alterity' in Emerging Democracies." In *Queer Globalizations: Citizenship and the Afterlife of Colonialism*, edited by Arnaldo Cruz- Malavé and Martin F. Manalansan IV, 195–218. New York: New York University Press.

———. 2007. "Inventing 'African AIDS.'" In *Culture, Society, and Sexuality: A Reader*, edited by Richard G. Parker and Peter Aggleton, 387–404. New York: Routledge.

Payton, Naith. 2015. "Malawi's New Anti-LGBT Law Comes into Effect." *Pink News*, April 17. www.pinknews.co.uk/2015/04/17/malawi-anti-lgbt-law-signed-in/.

Pellegrini, Ann. 1992. "S(h)ifting the Terms of Hetero/Sexism: Gender, Power, Homophobias." In *Homophobia: How We All Pay the Price*, edited by Warren J. Blumenfeld, 39–56. Boston: Beacon.

Peterson, Abby and Mattias Wahlström. 2015. "Repression: The Governance of Domestic Dissent." In *The Oxford Handbook of Social Movements*, edited by Donatella della Porta and Mario Diani, 634–652. New York: Oxford University Press.

Peterson, V. Spike. 1999. "Sexing Political Identities/Nationalism as Hetero-sexism." *International Feminist Journal of Politics* 1(1): 34–65.

Phelan, Shane. 2001. *Sexual Strangers: Gays, Lesbians, and the Dilemmas of Citizenship*. Philadelphia: Temple University Press.

Phiri, D. D. 2004. "Human Rights and Morality." *Nation*, March 30, 8.
    2004. "Marriage and Divorce." *Nation*, September 14, 7.
    2006. "Moral Decline." *Nation*, November 21, 10.

Piludzu. 2012. "Gay Issue." *Sunday Times*, November 25, 5.

Plummer, Ken. 2004. "The Sexual Spectacle: Making a Public Culture of Sexual Problems." In *Handbook of Social Problems: A Comparative International Perspective*, edited by George Ritzer, 521–541. Thousand Oaks, CA: Sage.

Pommerolle, Marie-Emmanuelle. 2010. "The Extraversion of Protest: Conditions, History, and Use of the 'International' in Africa." *Review of African Political Economy* 37(125): 263–279.

Posel, Deborah. 2005. "Sex, Death, and the Fate of the Nation: Reflections on the Politicization of Sexuality in Post-Apartheid South Africa." *Africa* 75(2): 125–153.

Pratten, David. 2008. "'The Thief Eats His Shame': Practice and Power in Nigerian Vigilantism." *Africa* 78(1): 64–83.

Puar, Jasbir K. 2007. *Terrorist Assemblages: Homonationalism in Queer Times*. Durham: Duke University Press.
    2013. "Homonationalism as Assemblage: Viral Travels, Affective Sexualities." *Jindal Global Law Review* 4(2): 23–43.

Puri, Jyoti. 2002. "Nationalism Has a Lot to Do with It! Unraveling Questions of Nationalism and Transnationalism in Lesbian/Gay Studies." In *Handbook of Lesbian and Gay Studies*, edited by Steven Seidman and Diane Richardson, 427–442. Thousand Oaks, CA: Sage.
    2016. *Sexual States: Governance and the Struggle over the Antisodomy Law in India*. Durham, NC: Duke University Press.

Rahman, Momin. 2014. *Homosexualities, Muslim Cultures, and Modernity*. New York: Palgrave Macmillan.
    2014. "Queer Rights and the Triangulation of Western Exceptionalism." *Journal of Human Rights* 13(3): 274–289.

Rai, Shirin M. 2009. "Feminizing Global Governance." In *Gender and Global Politics in the Asia-Pacific*, edited by Bina D'Costa and Katrina Lee-Koo, 95–111. New York: Palgrave Macmillan.

Rao, Rahul. 2010. *Third World Protest: Between Home and the World*. New York: Oxford University Press.
    2012. "On 'Gay Conditionality,' Imperial Power, and Queer Liberation." January 1. https://kafila.online/2012/01/01/on-gay-conditionality-imperial-power-and-queer-liberation-rahul-rao/.

2014. "The Locations of Homophobia." *London Review of International Law* 2(2): 169–199.

Reddy, Vasu. 2001. "Homophobia, Human Rights, and Gay and Lesbian Equality in Africa." *Agenda* 50: 83–87.

2002. "Perverts and Sodomites: Homophobia as Hate Speech in Africa." *Southern African Linguistics and Applied Language Studies* 20: 163–175.

Reid, Graeme and Teresa Dirsuweit. 2002. "Understanding Systemic Violence: Homophobic Attacks in Johannesburg and Its Surrounds." *Urban Forum* 13(3): 99–126.

Resnick, Danielle. 2013. "Two Steps Forward, One Step Back: The Limits of Foreign Aid on Malawi's Democratic Consolidation." In *Democratic Trajectories in Africa: Unravelling the Impact of Foreign Aid*, edited by Danielle Resnick and Nicholas van de Walle, 110–138. New York: Oxford University Press.

"Respect Gay Rights, UN's Ban Tells African Leaders." 2012. *Nyasa Times*, January 29. www.nyasatimes.com/respect-gay-rights-uns-ban-tells-afri can-leaders/.

Reuters. 2009. "Gay Rights Way to Fight AIDS in Malawi – Official." *Nation*, September 15. Article on file with author.

Richardson, Matt. 2013. *The Queer Limit of Black Memory: Black Lesbian Literature and Irresolution*. Columbus: Ohio State University Press.

"Rights Groups, Lawyer Welcome Gays' Pardon." 2010. *Sunday Times*, May 30, 3.

Rocke, Michael. 1998. *Forbidden Friendships: Homosexuality and Male Culture in Renaissance Florence*. New York: Oxford University Press.

Rotberg, Robert I. 2004. "The Failure and Collapse of Nation-States: Breakdown, Prevention, and Repair." In *When States Fail: Causes and Consequences*, edited by Robert I. Rotberg, 1–48. Princeton, NJ: Princeton University Press.

Rothschild, Cynthia. 2005. *Written Out: How Sexuality Is Used to Attack Women's Organizing*. New York: IGLHRC and Center for Women's Global Leadership.

Rubin, Gayle S. 2011. "Thinking Sex: Notes for a Radical Theory of the Politics of Sexuality." In *Deviations: A Gayle Rubin Reader*, 137–181. Durham, NC: Duke University Press.

Rukunuwa, Phillip. 2011. "Hold Your Breath, Mr. President." *Daily Times*, May 11, 8.

Sabola, Taonga. 2010. "All Eyes on Malawi as Court Sentences Gay Couple." *Nation*, May 20, 6.

2010. "Righting Human Wrongs." *Nation*, May 27, 15.

Sadgrove, Joanna, Robert M. Vanderbeck, Johan Andersson, Gill Valentine, and Kevin Ward. 2012. "Morality Plays and Money Matters: Towards a Situated Understanding of the Politics of Homosexuality in Uganda." *Journal of Modern African Studies* 50(1): 103–129.

Schilt, Kristen and Laurel Westbrook. 2009. "Doing Gender, Doing Heteronormativity: 'Gender Normals,' Transgender People, and the Social Maintenance of Heterosexuality." *Gender & Society* 23(4): 440–464.

"Sebokolo—Man or Woman." 1995. *Daily Times*, December 6, 14.

Semu, Pilirani. 2001. "Future for NGOs Bleak – CONGOMA." *Nation*, August 17, 2.

2001. "NGOs Gang Up against Law." *Nation*, September 25, 1–2.

2001. "NGOs to Fight for New Law." *Nation*, February 9, 1–2.

Semugoma, Paul, Steave Nemande, and Stefan D. Baral. 2012. "The Irony of Homophobia." *The Lancet* 380(9839): 312–314.

Serrano-Amaya, José Fernando. 2018. *Homophobic Violence in Armed Conflict and Political Transition.* New York: Palgrave Macmillan.

Sharra, Albert. 2012. "We Have Not Yet Started Talking Same-Sex Marriages." *Weekend Nation*, June 2, 4.

Showden, Carisa. 2011. *Choices Women Make: Agency in Domestic Violence, Assisted Reproduction, and Sex Work.* Minneapolis: University of Minnesota Press.

Simeza, Kennedy. 1996. "Foleni." *Malawi News*, February 24–March 1, 10.

Simwaka, Fletcher. 2010. "Reasoning beyond 14." *Daily Times*, May 28, 5.

Simwaka, Joseph Claude. 2010. "Govt to Rid City Streets of Children." *Nation*, March 12, 3.

Sithole, Emelia. 1996. "Angry Crowd Trashes Gay Stand at ZIBF." *Daily Times*, August 5, 4.

Siula, Rogers. 2012. "I'm Not Gay – Theo Thomson." *Nation*, December 7, 4.

Slootmaeckers, Koen, Heleen Touquet, and Peter Vermeersch, eds. 2016. *The EU Enlargement and Gay Politics: The Impact of Eastern Enlargement on Rights, Activism, and Prejudice.* New York: Palgrave Macmillan.

Smith, Adrian D., Placide Tapsoba, Norbert Peshu, Eduard J. Sanders, and Harold W. Jaffe. 2009. "Men Who Have Sex with Men and HIV/AIDS in Sub-Saharan Africa." *The Lancet* 374(9687): 416–422.

Smith, Anne Marie. 1994. *New Rights Discourse on Race and Sexuality: Britain, 1968–1990.* New York: Cambridge University Press.

Smith, David. 2014. "Why Africa Is the Most Homophobic Continent." *Guardian*, February 22. www.theguardian.com/world/2014/feb/23/africa-homophobia-uganda-anti-gay-law.

Smith, Lydia. 2014. "Which Countries Are the Most Homophobic in the World?" *International Business Times*, February 13. www.ibtimes.co.uk/which-countries-are-most-homophobic-world-1436308.

Somanje, Caroline. 2006. "Malawi NGOs Are Gold Diggers, Says Diplomat." *Malawi News*, August 12–18, 3.

2009. "Blantyre Gay Couple Arrested." *Nation*, December 29, 2.

2009. "Gay Couple Charged with Three Counts." *Nation*, December 31, 2.

2009. "Gay Couple in Court Today." *Nation*, December 30, 2.

2009. "Gays Engage." *Nation*, December 28, 2.

2010. "14 Years IHL!" *Nation*, May 21, 1–2.

2010. "Amnesty Wants Gays Released." *Nation*, January 8, 1–2.

2010. "'Aunt Tiwo' Concealed Status for Money – Witness." *Nation*, January 12, 2.

2010. "'Aunt Tiwo,' Monjeza Denied Bail for Safety." *Nation*, January 5, 2–3.

2010. "Bingu Blasts Donors on Gays." *Nation*, June 3, 1, 3.

2010. "Chimbalanga Says Not Bitter with Monjeza." *Nation*, June 9, 2.

2010. "Gay Posters Campaigner Given Community Service." *Nation*, February 8, 3.

2010. "Govt's HIV Prevention Strategy Recognises Gay Relationships." *Nation*, March 9, 3.

2010. "I Still Love Aunt Tiwo – Monjeza." *Nation*, May 31, 1–2.

2010. "Law Society Faults Bingu on Gays Information Directive." *Nation*, June 4, 2.

2010. "Pardoned Monjeza, Chimbalanga Offered Asylum." *Nation*, June 1, 3.

2010. "Police Arrest Man for Pasting Gay Rights Posters." *Nation*, February 2, 3.

2010. "There Are Many Gays in Malawi." *Nation*, January 1, 3.

2012. "Police Detain Kasambara." *Nation*, February 14, 1–2.

2013. "Monjeza Released from Jail." *Nation*, November 22. http://mwnation.com/monjeza-released-from-jail/.

2015. "Ed's Note: Monjeza Needs 'Help.'" *Nation*, March 8. Article on file with author.

Sonani, Bright. 1999. "NGOs Not for Politics." *Daily Times*, July 20, 3.

2006. "I'm Not Gay – Rejected Bishop." *Nation*, February 13, 1, 3.

2006. "Malango Okays Pro-Gay Bishop Visit." *Nation*, February 10, 2.

2009. "Recognise Gays in AIDS Fight – Shawa." *Nation*, September 16, 2.

2010. "Churches Condemn Donors on Gay Rights." *Nation*, March 19, 2.

2011. "Court Reverses Injunction, LL Marches in Afternoon." *Nation*, July 21, 3.

2011. "Gays Vital in HIV Fight." *Nation*, April 27, 3.

2011. "Govt Says NGOs Staged Attack on Undule." *Nation*, March 10, 2.

2011. "Govt Using Gay Issues to Distract Malawians – HRCC." *Nation*, July 14, 3.

2011. "NGOs Attack Church on Gays." *Nation*, February 26, 3.

2011. "Police Invade Undule's Karonga Home." *Nation*, March 14, 3.

2011. "Thugs Attack Undule's Offices." *Nation*, March 4, 1–2.

2012. "Activists Trash DPP Stand on Gay Laws." *Nation*, August 7, 3.

2012. "Activists Want Kalinde to Withdraw Remarks." *Nation*, August 13, 3.

2012. "DPP Cautions Govt on Gay Laws." *Nation*, August 1, 2.

2012. "Law Society Faults Govt." *Nation*, November 7, 1–2.

Soule, Sarah A. 2001. "Situational Effects on Political Altruism: The Student Divestment Movement in the United States." In *Political Altruism? Solidarity Movements in International Perspective*, edited by Marco Giugni and Florence Passy, 161–176. Lanham, MD: Rowman & Littlefield.

2004. "Diffusion Processes within and across Movements." In *The Blackwell Companion to Social Movements*, edited by David A. Snow, Sarah A. Soule, and Hanspeter Kriesi, 294–310. Malden, MA: Blackwell.

Sperling, Valerie. 2015. *Sex, Politics, and Putin: Political Legitimacy in Russia*. New York: Oxford University Press.

Spivak, Gayatri Chakravorty. 1988. "Can the Subaltern Speak?" In *Marxism and the Interpretation of Culture*, edited by Cary Nelson and Lawrence Grossberg, 271–313. Urbana: University of Illinois Press.

Spivey, Sue E. and Christine M. Robinson. 2010. "Genocidal Intentions: Social Death and the Ex-Gay Movement." *Genocide Studies and Prevention* 5(1): 68–88.

Ssebaggala, Richard. 2011. "Straight Talk on the Gay Question in Uganda." *Transition* 106: B-44–B-57.

Stauffer, Jill. 2015. *Ethical Loneliness: The Injustice of Not Being Heard*. New York: Columbia University Press.

Stein, Arlene. 2002. *The Stranger Next Door: The Story of a Small Community's Battle over Sex, Faith, and Civil Rights*. Boston: Beacon.

Stetson, Dorothy McBride, ed. 2002. *Abortion Politics, Women's Movements, and the Democratic State: A Comparative Study of State Feminism*. New York: Oxford University Press.

Stillwaggon, Eileen. 2003. "Racial Metaphors: Interpreting Sex and AIDS in Africa." *Development and Change* 34(5): 809–832.

Stobaugh, James E. and David A. Snow. 2010. "Temporality and Frame Diffusion: The Case of the Creationist/Intelligent Design and Evolutionist Movements from 1925 to 2005." In *The Diffusion of Social Movements: Actors, Mechanisms, and Political Effects*, edited by Rebecca Kolins Givan, Kenneth M. Roberts, and Sarah A. Soule, 34–55. New York: Cambridge University Press.

Stone, Amy L. and Jane Ward. 2011. "From 'Black People Are Not a Homosexual Act' to 'Gay Is the New Black': Mapping White Uses of

Blackness in Modern Gay Rights Campaigns in the United States." *Social Identities* 17(5): 605–624.

"Stop the Blame Game." 2011. *Malawi News,* July 23–29, 4.

Strand, Cecilia. 2012. "Homophobia as a Barrier to Comprehensive Media Coverage of the Ugandan Anti-Homosexual Bill." *Journal of Homosexuality* 59(4): 564–579.

Strasser, Max. 2014. "Top Twelve Most Homophobic Nations." *Newsweek,* February 27. www.newsweek.com/top-twelve-most-homophobic-nations-230348.

Sue, Derald Wing. 2010. *Microaggressions in Everyday Life: Race, Gender, and Sexual Orientation.* Hoboken, NJ: Wiley.

Sullivan, Nikki. 2003. *A Critical Introduction to Queer Theory.* New York: New York University Press.

Sundu, Yvonne. 2012. "Minority Rights Misconception Encouraging AIDS Spread." *Nation,* August 24, 7.

Sutton, Barbara. 2010. *Bodies in Crisis: Culture, Violence, and Women's Resistance in Neoliberal Argentina.* New Brunswick, NJ: Rutgers University Press.

Swarr, Amanda Lock. 2012. "Paradoxes of Butchness: Lesbian Masculinities and Sexual Violence in Contemporary South Africa." *Signs* 37(4): 961–986.

Sweetman, Caroline. 2013. "Introduction, Feminist Solidarity, and Collective Action." *Gender & Development* 21(2): 217–229.

Swidler, Ann. 2006. "Syncretism and Subversion in AIDS Governance: How Locals Cope with Global Demands." *International Affairs* 82(2): 269–284.

Tamale, Sylvia. 2013. "Confronting the Politics of Nonconforming Sexualities in Africa." *African Studies Review* 56(1): 31–45.

Tembo, Chinyeke. 1996. "Report on 17 Cell Deaths Out." *Daily Times,* April 3, 1.

Tembo-Panos, Arkangel. 2014. "Same-Sex Relationship Denies 2 Girls Education in Malawi." *Nyasa Times,* June 30. www.nyasatimes.com/same-sex-relationship-denies-2-girls-education-in-malawi/.

Tenthani, Raphael. 2012. "Flip-Floppers." *Sunday Times,* November 11, 2.
2012. "Let's Take a Stand on Gays." *Sunday Times,* November 25, 2.

Thomann, Matthew. 2014. "The Price of Inclusion: Sexual Subjectivity, Violence, and the Nonprofit Industrial Complex in Abidjan, Côte d'Ivoire." PhD dissertation. Washington, DC: Department of Anthropology, American University.

Thomas, Greg. 2007. *The Sexual Demon of Colonial Power: Pan-African Embodiment and Erotic Schemes of Empire.* Bloomington: Indiana University Press.

Thomas, Lynn M. 2003. *Politics of the Womb: Women, Reproduction, and the State in Kenya*. Berkeley: University of California Press.

Thoreson, Ryan Richard. 2011. "Blackmail and Extortion of LGBT People in Sub-Saharan Africa." In *Nowhere to Turn: Blackmail and Extortion of LGBT People in Sub-Saharan Africa*, edited by Ryan Thoreson and Sam Cook, 4–18. New York: International Gay and Lesbian Human Rights Commission.

——— 2014. *Transnational LGBT Activism: Working for Sexual Rights*. Minneapolis: University of Minnesota Press.

——— 2014. "Troubling the Waters of a 'Wave of Homophobia': Political Economies of Anti-Queer Animus in Sub-Saharan Africa." *Sexualities* 17(1–2): 23–42.

Trappolin, Luca, Alessandro Gasparini, and Robert Wintemute, eds. 2012. *Confronting Homophobia in Europe: Social and Legal Perspectives*. Oxford: Hart Publishing.

"Trouser Attacks: How It All Began." 2012. *Nation*, January 22. http://mwnation.com/trouser-attacks-how-it-all-began/.

"Undule Mwakasungula Welcomes Government's Move to Suspend Anti-Gay Laws." 2012. *Malawi Voice*, November 6. Article on file with author.

Ungar, Mark. 2000. "State Violence and Lesbian, Gay, Bisexual, and Transgender (lgbt) Rights." *New Political Science* 22(1): 61–75.

United States Government. 2010. "10LILONGWE37, Malawi: Donors to Rare Tour D'Horizon with President Mutharika." WikiLeaks, January 19, http://wikileaks.org/cable/2010/01/10LILONGWE37.html.

"US Commends Joyce Banda's 'Bold Actions.'" 2012. *Nyasa Times*, May 22. www.nyasatimes.com/us-commends-joyce-bandas-bold-actions/.

Van Dyke, Nella and Holly J. McCammon, eds. 2010. *Strategic Alliances: Coalition Building and Social Movements*. Minneapolis: University of Minnesota Press.

van Klinken, Adriaan. 2014. "Homosexuality, Politics and Pentecostal Nationalism in Zambia." *Studies in World Christianity* 20(3): 259–281.

van Klinken, Adriaan and Ezra Chitando, eds. 2016. *Public Religion and the Politics of Homosexuality in Africa*. New York: Routledge.

Viterna, Jocelyn. 2013. *Women in War: The Micro-Processes of Mobilization in El Salvador*. New York: Oxford University Press.

Wahab, Amar. 2012. "Homophobia as the State of Reason: The Case of Postcolonial Trinidad and Tobago." *GLQ* 18(4): 481–505.

——— 2016. "Calling 'Homophobia' into Place (Jamaica): Homo/Trans/Nationalism in the Stop Murder Music (Canada) Campaign." *Interventions: International Journal of Postcolonial Studies* 18(6): 908–928.

2016. "'Homosexuality/Homophobia Is Un-African'? Un-Mapping Transnational Discourses in the Context of Uganda's Anti-Homosexuality Bill/Act." *Journal of Homosexuality* 63(5): 685–718.

Waidzunas, Tom. 2015. *The Straight Line: How the Fringe Science of Ex-Gay Therapy Reoriented Sexuality*. Minneapolis: University of Minnesota Press.

Walker-Said, Charlotte. 2015. "Sexual Minorities among African Asylum Claimants: Human Rights Regimes, Bureaucratic Knowledge, and the Era of Sexual Rights Diplomacy." In *African Asylum at a Crossroads: Activism, Expert Testimony, and Refugee Rights*, edited by Iris Berger, Tricia Redeker Hepner, Benjamin N. Lawrance, Joanna T. Tague, and Meredith Terretta, 203–224. Athens: Ohio University Press.

Walters, Suzanna Danuta. 2014. *The Tolerance Trap: How God, Genes, and Good Intentions Are Sabotaging Gay Equality*. New York: New York University Press.

Ward, Jane. 2008. *Respectably Queer: Diversity Culture in LGBT Activist Organizations*. Nashville, TN: Vanderbilt University Press.

Watkins, Susan Cotts and Ann Swidler. 2013. "Working Misunderstandings: Donors, Brokers, and Villagers in Africa's AIDS Industry." *Population and Development Review* 38(S1): 197–218.

2017. *A Fraught Embrace: The Romance and Reality of AIDS Altruism in Africa*. Princeton, NJ: Princeton University Press.

Watkins, Susan Cotts, Ann Swidler, and Thomas Hannan. 2012. "Outsourcing Social Transformation: Development NGOs as Organizations." *Annual Review of Sociology* 38: 285–315.

Weber, Cynthia. 2016. *Queer International Relations: Sovereignty, Sexuality, and the Will to Knowledge*. New York: Oxford University Press.

Weiss, Meredith L. 2013. "Prejudice before Pride: Rise of an Anticipatory Countermovement." In *Global Homophobia: States, Movements, and the Politics of Oppression*, edited by Meredith L. Weiss and Michael J. Bosia, 149–173. Urbana: University of Illinois Press.

Whittier, Nancy. 2009. *The Politics of Child Sexual Abuse: Emotion, Social Movements, and the State*. New York: Oxford University Press.

Wieringa, Saskia Eleonora. 2009. "Postcolonial Amnesia: Sexual Moral Panics, Memory, and Imperial Power." In *Moral Panics, Sex Panics: Fear and the Fight over Sexual Rights*, edited by Gilbert Herdt, 205–233. New York: New York University Press.

Winskell, Kate and Gaëlle Sabben. 2016. "Sexual Stigma and Symbolic Violence Experienced, Enacted, and Counteracted in Young Africans' Writing about Same-Sex Attraction." *Social Science & Medicine* 161: 143–150.

Wirtz, Andrea L., Dunker Kamba, Vincent Jumbe, Gift Trapence, Rehana Gubin, Eric Umar, Susanne K. Strömdahl, Chris Beyrer, and Stefan D. Baral. 2014. "A Qualitative Assessment of Health Seeking Practices among and Provision Practices for Men Who Have Sex with Men in Malawi." *BioMed Central International Health and Human Rights* 14(20): www.biomedcentral.com/1472-698X/14/20.

Wirtz, Andrea L., Gift Trapence, Vincent Jumbe, Eric Umar, Sosthenes Ketende, Dunker Kamba, Mark Berry, Susanne Strömdahl, Chris Beyrer, Adamson S. Muula, and Stefan Baral. 2016. "Feasibility of a Combination HIV Prevention Program for Men Who Have Sex with Men in Blantyre, Malawi." *Journal of Acquired Immune Deficiency Syndromes* 70(2): 155–162.

"Woman Gives Birth to Hermaphrodite." 2000. *Daily Times*, June 1, 3.

"Woman Transfigures." 2000. *Daily Times*, November 9, 4.

Wroe, Daniel. 2012. "Donors, Dependency, and Political Crisis in Malawi." *African Affairs* 111(442): 135–144.

Xaba, Makhosazana and Crystal Biruk, eds. 2016. *Proudly Malawian: Life Stories from Lesbian and Gender-Nonconforming Individuals.* Braamfontein, South Africa: MaThoko's Books.

Yoshino, Kenji. 2007. *Covering: The Hidden Assault on Our Civil Rights.* New York: Random House.

Youde, Jeremy. 2017. "Patriotic History and Anti-LGBT Rhetoric in Zimbabwean Politics." *Canadian Journal of African Studies* 51(1): 61–79.

Zagwazatha, Tione P. 2005. "Homosexuality Madness." *Daily Times*, February 4, 8.

Zürn, Michael. 2014. "The Politicization of World Politics and Its Effects: Eight Propositions." *European Political Science Review* 6(1): 41–71.

Index